The Meaning of Poetry:

 A Guide to Explication

Walton Beacham

Virginia Commonwealth University

ALLYN AND BACON, INC., BOSTON

And if my private universe scans right,
So does the verse of galaxies divine
Which I suspect is an iambic line.

John Shade

Library of Congress Catalog Number: 73-22874

PRINTED IN THE UNITED STATES OF AMERICA

ACKNOWLEDGEMENTS

Jack A. Butler, "The Crooked Lover." Excerpt reprinted by permission of the author.

E. E. Cummings, "in Just —," "a man who had fallen among thieves," "my father moved through dooms of love" (excerpt). Copyright 1923, 1954 by E. E. Cummings. Copyright 1926 by Horace Liveright; copyright, 1954, by E. E. Cummings. Copyright 1940 by E. E. Cummings; renewed in 1968 by Marion Morehouse Cummings. All reprinted from *Poems 1923-1954*, by permission of Harcourt Brace Jovanovich, Inc.

Walter de la Mare, "The Listeners." From *Collected Poems*. Excerpt granted by permission of The Literary Trustees of Walter de la Mare and The Society of Authors as their representative.

James Dickey, "In the Mountain Tent." Copyright © 1961 by James Dickey. Reprinted from *Poems 1957-1967*, by James Dickey, by permission of Wesleyan University Press. This poem was first published in *The New Yorker*.

Emily Dickinson, "It was not Death." Excerpt reprinted by permission of the publishers and Trustees of Amherst College from Thomas H. Johnson, Editor, *The Poems of Emily Dickinson*, Cambridge, Mass.: The Belknap Press of Harvard University Press, 1951, 1955, by the President and Fellows of Harvard College.

T. S. Eliot, "Journey of the Magi," and excerpts from "Sweeney Among the Nightingales," "Burnt Norton," "The Waste Land," and "The Love Song of J. Alfred Prufrock." From *Collected Poems 1909-1962* by T. S. Eliot, copyright 1936, by Harcourt Brace Jovanovich, Inc.; copyright © 1963, 1964 by T. S. Eliot. Reprinted by permission of the publisher, and Faber and Faber Ltd., London.

Robert Frost, "After Apple-Picking," "Desert Places," "Stopping by Woods on a Snowy Evening," "Tree At My Window," and excerpts from "West-Running Brook" and "Mending Wall" from *The Poetry of Robert Frost*, edited by Edward Connery Lathem. Copyright 1923, 1928, 1930, 1939, © 1969 by Holt, Rinehart and Winston, Inc. Copyright 1936, 1942, 1951, © 1956, 1958 by Robert Frost. Copyright © 1964, 1967, 1970 by Lesley Frost Ballantine. Reprinted by permission of Holt, Rinehart and Winston, Inc.

John Hollander, "For a Thirtieth Birthday with a Bottle of Burgundy," from *Movie-Going* by John Hollander. Copyright © 1958, 1962 by John Hollander. Reprinted by permission of Atheneum Publishers.

Gerard Manley Hopkins, "The Windhover." Excerpt from *Poems of Gerard Manley Hopkins*, 4th Edition, edited by W. H. Gardner and N. M. MacKenzie. Copyright © The Society of Jesus 1967. Reprinted by permission of Oxford University Press.

A. E. Housman, "Epitaph on an Army of Mercenaries," from *The Collected Poems of A. E. Housman*. Copyright 1922 by Barclays Bank Ltd. Reprinted by permission of Holt, Rinehart and Winston, Inc., The Society of Authors as the literary representative of the estate of A. E. Housman, and Jonathan Cape Ltd.

Holly Anna Jones, "Cemetary." Reprinted by permission of the author.

Joyce Kilmer, "Trees." Copyright 1913 and renewed 1941. Copyright assigned to Jerry Vogel Music Co., Inc., 121 West 45th Street, New York, N. Y. 10036. Used by permission of copyright owner; reproduction prohibited.

Philip Larkin, "Church Going," and "Home Is So Sad." Reprinted from *The Less Deceived*, © The Marvell Press, Yorkshire, England; from *The Whitsun Wedding*, © 1964 by Philip Larkin, used by permission of Random House, Inc., and Faber and Faber Ltd.

Robert Lowell, "The Holy Innocents." Excerpt reprinted from *Lord Weary's Castle* by permission of Harcourt Brace Jovanovich, Inc.

Contents

The graphic ornament indicates the units that cover the fundamental aspects of poetry in their most basic form. The symbol is repeated within the text as a reference guide for the reader.

Preface

The Meaning of Poetry is a programmed guide which can be used as a primary text for a course in poetry, a supplementary text for a survey course, or as an aid for any reader who wants to understand poetry. The reader is free to absorb the text from start to finish like any other book, read selectively to pick up the fundamental aspects of poetry, or use the book as a reference to any number of general and technical poetic concepts. Because of the self-teaching design of *The Meaning of Poetry,* readers can learn the essential tools for explication with little outside assistance and come to see the poem as a composite of emotion, intellect, and craft.

The Meaning of Poetry has been organized for use primarily as a guide and then as a reference book. As a guide, the book permits the reader to approach poetry on whatever level he wishes. The graphic ornament in the table of contents indicates the units that cover the fundamental aspects of poetry in their most basic form. The symbol is repeated in the text alongside the section number reference keys. As a reference, *The Meaning of Poetry* contains all of the information an alert reader needs for understanding difficult poetry. At certain points in the text, key examples and applications of a particular poetic concept have been used in a "self-teaching" question-and-answer sequence. Here the answers on one side of the page can be masked by the reader and the questions read as a self-testing method to check understanding of the main concepts.

The study of poetry can, of course, be as simple or complex as the reader wants it to be. This book invites the reader to look at poetry on whatever level his interest requires, although he constantly faces the potential challenge of responding at a more demanding level when sharing his feelings about a poem with another demanding reader. The response can be a simple "I like it," a search for a compact summary of theme, or the pursuit of a particular interpretation to be shared with another interested reader.

The organization of *The Meaning of Poetry* does not represent a simplified scheme, but one which gives a complete and careful view of how the parts of a poem relate to the impact of the whole. A full range of material is offered not to discourage the reader from finding pleasure in poetry, but to help make him or her aware that a full response to poetry requires more than mere intuition. The reader who can take a complex poem through many steps will achieve a higher level of shared experience than the intuitive reader will get at a glance.

The Meaning of Poetry is not intended to be a definitive work on the theory of prosody, but is designed as a thorough guide to explication. It approaches poetry from the poet's point of view; by understanding how the poet thinks during the time when he is crafting his work into the most suitable form, readers can see clearly what makes up the poem. This insight establishes a foundation for explication which is more systematic than intuitive because it demands that the reader examine his own responses to the poem by explaining how the poet achieved control for the emotions and ideas he wanted to shape.

I am indebted, gratefully, to Professor James Whitehead, whose system of prosody and approach to literature formed the premise for my work, and whose careful guidance established an intellectual frame of reference for understanding poetry; to my wife, Erin, who originally proposed the usefulness of a programmed guide to explication; and to Professor Ben Kimpel, George Newtown, and the University of Richmond for assistance in editing and preparing the manuscript.

W. B.

The Sum—What Makes a Poem?

At one time or another, almost all of us have had a "favorite poem" (or perhaps a song), whether or not it seemed sophisticated or fashionable to like it. Several factors probably contributed to the our enjoyment of the poem, but one of the most important was the emotional qualities which it imparted. It became our favorite poem because we were able to respond emotionally to one or more of its parts — either to what was being said, or how it was being said, or both. Nonsense verse may have appealed to us because of its sound or images, while ballads may have appealed to us because of the story they told.

Take, for example, "The Eagle," a poem which has been a favorite for a long time.

> He clasps the crag with crooked hands;
> Close to the sun in lonely lands,
> Ringed with the azure world, he stands.
>
> The wrinkled sea beneath him crawls;
> He watches from his mountain walls,
> And like a thunderbolt he falls.

ALFRED, LORD TENNYSON

We might respond emotionally to this poem because of its sound (notice the *c-* and *s-* sounds and the rhyme scheme), because of the image of the eagle and nature, or because the sound and sense of the last line contrast with that in the first five lines. All of these are valid reasons for liking "The Eagle," but the person to whom the poem is most meaningful is one who is responsive to the differences between earth and sky, fascinated with flight, or curious about the azure world. "The Eagle" is important to this person because the poet has taken him to the eagle's world and let him fall, giving him an imaginative thrill of identification with that which he can never experience as the eagle experiences it.

For the person whose favorite poem is "The Eagle," there are many external factors which make the poem important. The poet has been able to shape words which appeal to that reader, but it is because of the reader's receptiveness that the poem succeeds. Because of this, we can say that poetry is, in part, an emotional unity between poet and reader; how the poet controls his readers' emotions is the artistic process, and the most difficult aspect of poetry since every reader will bring different emotions to the poem. Poetry, then, is the union between poet and reader, and what each gives or brings to the poem will determine how successfully communication is achieved.

The emotion that every reader brings to poetry will largely be determined by events external to the poem. It matters how happy the reader is, what mood he is in while reading the poem, what he thinks generally about poetry, what opinions he has about the subject which the poet is treating; all this contributes to his emotional reaction to the poem. For example, Joyce Kilmer's poem "Trees" fosters many different reactions.

> *I think that I shall never see*
> *A poem lovely as a tree.*
>
> *A tree whose hungry mouth is pressed*
> *Against the earth's sweet flowing breast;*   4
>
> *A tree that looks to God all day,*
> *And lifts her leafy arms to pray;*
>
> *A tree that may in summer wear*
> *A nest of robins in her hair;*   8
>
> *Upon whose bosom snow has lain;*
> *Who intimately lives with rain.*
>
> *Poems are made by fools like me,*
> *But only God can make a tree.*   12
>
> JOYCE KILMER

A reader coming to this poem after a hard day's work may find many appealing qualities in it. First, there is a humility attached to the poem — perhaps poems are not as lovely as trees, and the poet is merely a fool doing the best he can with what he has, which may be exactly what the reader feels about his own life. Second, there is a reverence for nature, and the language makes the reader recall the pleasant images which he might have had during the spring of the year he was first in love. Third, the tree loves God, and is noble in its forebearance against winter. And finally, there is a syllogism which even the tiredest, dullest reader can make:

> *Trees, which are beautiful, are made by God;*
> *I can appreciate and love the beauty of trees;*
> *therefore, I love and appreciate God.*

and with this syllogism comes the satisfaction of worshipping.

On the other hand, the emotional response of a reader who is more concerned with artistic development than basking in sentiment may be entirely different from that of the first reader. To the technical eye, the poem is very bad. There is only one metrical variation in the whole poem (line 11); the poem jogs along in tetrameter couplets, a form most frequently associated with doggerel verse; the metaphors are inconsistent (e.g., the image in stanza two is that of a suckling babe, while stanza three depicts a full-grown tree) and vague (how is a tree like a man?); and the progression of thought from stanza to stanza is absurd. (Stanza one compares poetry to trees; stanza two concentrates on the tree as a babe, with no transition linking babes to poems; stanza three shows the adult tree in prayer; stanza four imagines the adult tree being dressed; stanza five gives the image of the tree as suffering mother; finally, stanza six attempts to return to the initial metaphor comparing trees to poems, but gets mixed up about who makes what so that the poem loses all continuity and possibilities for theme. By way of contrast, compare the images and metaphors in "Trees" with those in "Arrival," Frame B-25.)

The second objection which the critical reader would have to "Trees" is the poem's logic. Kilmer never really faces his subject of showing the relationship between writing poems and making trees; that is to say, since poets don't try to make trees, or God poems, there is no logic inherent in the last stanza. Had Kilmer compared God's imagination in making trees to the poet's imagination in composing poems, there might have been some logic involved, but Kilmer doesn't do that, and the critical reader is disturbed by it because metaphors are based on the logical process.

We can see from the two entirely different readings which two people might give to "Trees" that Kilmer is unable to control his readers' emotional responses. Those readers who share Kilmer's attitudes toward God and trees may like the poem, while others may be appalled at the sentimental level to which Kilmer stoops. There is, of course, nothing wrong, or shameful, or unintelligent about liking "Trees," but if art is to be a medium between readers, then the poet must be able to hold up his end of the communication with reasonable control of the readers' emotions through his poetical tools, the language, and the common elements which all men share. In other words, the poet should endeavor to reduce the possibility of distracting from his message through external emotions or purely subjective (hence uncommunicated) emotions which might extensively influence the poem; he should try to rely on the emotions which the poem itself generates.

Indeed, if readers had to agree with poets' moral, religious, and political attitudes in order to enjoy poetry, there would be very few poems which any of us could tolerate. We do, of course, look for pieces of literature which reinforce our own beliefs about life, but intelligent readers can enjoy poetry for many reasons other than finding themes which agree with their philosophy. Look at the following poem, for example:

> These, in the day when heaven was falling,
>> The hour when earth's foundations fled,
> Followed their mercenary calling
>> And took their wages and are dead.   4
>
> Their shoulders held the sky suspended;
>> They stood, and earth's foundations stay;
> What God abandoned, these defended,
>> And saved the sum of things for pay.   8

EPITAPH ON AN ARMY OF MERCENARIES
A. E. HOUSMAN

On the first reading, "Epitaph on an Army of Mercenaries" may seem quite offensive to some people, since Housman accuses God of abandoning man in his time of need, and praises the mercenaries for filling in for God. The tone of the poem is also flippant, poking at religion with phrases such as "heaven was falling," "followed their mercenary calling," and "saved the sum of things for pay." It is, indeed, a harsh poem, leaving no room for sentimentality, but in spite of whatever personal resentment the reader may have toward poems which challenge his beliefs, "Epitaph" is still an artistically excellent work, and, unlike "Trees," can be enjoyed as much for its treatment of the nobility of man as it can be detested for its blasphemy. Readers who are willing to accept Housman on his own terms find him rewarding, and can take fresh emotions from his poetry.

* * * * *

The emotions which we as readers bring to the poem will in part determine the emotions we take away from it, but if the poet is good, the poem will not depend completely on the reader's external emotional state. Certainly, much of the pleasure derived from poetry occurs because of our emotional reaction to it, but those emotions will have been "crafted" by the artist who has taken into account the external factors, as Housman has when he writes a blasphemous poem which can still be pleasurable, even to God-fearing men, because of its irony.

Every serious reader hopes to find poems which can affect his emotions in such a way that for a moment or a lifetime, his relationship to life and the cosmos becomes more meaningful. This is the ultimate goal of poetry, and when it happens — when meaning, rhythm, and sound fuse with the reader's intellect and emotions to create a unified experience — it can only be called the magic of poetry, for something has happened between reader and poet which is unexplainable in rational terms.

Unfortunately, the magic of poetry may happen infrequently, and what we initially think to be a great poem may later disappoint us because the magic has disappeared, but this should not destroy the poem for us. Most good poems are not completely magical, although they are still good and give much pleasure; and of course, a poem which is magical to one reader may not be magical to the next. But there *is* a potential magic about poetry which is undeniable, and we should look for it in every poem. Poems which work their spell on us — or fail to work their spell on us — succeed or fail for technical as well as emotional reasons, and analyzing our responses to the poem is an important part of our explication. Let us look at one example.

President Theodore Roosevelt said of E. A. Robinson's poem, "Luke Havergal," that he had no idea what it meant, but that it was his favorite poem. Obviously "Luke Havergal" worked its magic on the President, and the magic is worth analyzing because it may help us discover how the emotional qualities of the poem are achieved.

> *Go to the western gate, Luke Havergal,*
> *There where the vines cling crimson on the wall,*
> *And in the twilight wait for what will come.*
> *The leaves will whisper there of her, and some,*
> *Like flying words, will strike you as they fall;*
> *But go, and if you listen, she will call.*   6
> *Go to the western gate, Luke Havergal —*
> *Luke Havergal.*
>
> *No, there is not a dawn in eastern skies*
> *To rift the fiery night that's in your eyes;*
> *But there, where western glooms are gathering,*
> *The dark will end the dark, if anything:*   12
> *God slays Himself with every leaf that flies,*

And hell is more than half of paradise.
No, there is not a dawn in eastern skies —
In eastern skies.

Out of a grave I come to tell you this,
Out of a grave I come to quench the kiss   18
That flames upon your forehead with a glow
That binds you to the way that you must go.
Yes, there is yet one way to where she is,
Bitter, but one that faith may never miss.
Out of a grave I come to tell you this —
To tell you this.   24

There is the western gate, Luke Havergal,
There are the crimson leaves upon the wall.
Go, for the winds are tearing them away, —
Nor think to riddle the dead words they say,
Nor any more to feel them as they fall;
But go, and if you trust her she will call.   30
There is the western gate, Luke Havergal —
Luke Havergal.

LUKE HAVERGAL
E. A. ROBINSON

Although "Luke Havergal" is one of the most difficult poems in English, as Teddy Roosevelt knew, we will come closer to understanding what Robinson was trying to communicate by asking the right questions of its emotional qualities.

1. One of the magical aspects of the poem is that we become interested in the characters. What is it about Luke and the narrator that is so interesting? What is their relationship? Who is the "she" for whom Luke is waiting?

2. One of Robinson's techniques in "Luke Havergal" is repetition. Where does it occur? What is its effect?

3. The verbs in the poem are particularly emotional and powerful. Which verbs affect the mood and tone most?

4. There is a great deal of ambiguity in the poem which leaves us confused. Where are some of the places which are particularly vague? What is our reaction to being left in the dark? (Refer to frames 0-1 ff for a discussion of "Luke Havergal")

As we can infer from "Luke Havergal," the emotional qualities of poetry are directly influenced through sound, word choice, meter, and tone, but if poetry is ultimately an emotional experience, it is the intellectual properties which shape the emotional response, and while the poet has little control over the external emotions which readers bring to the poem, he can use poetry's intellectual qualities to decide the internal emotional effects. The poet has at his disposal certain tools with which he can carve the lines; he has a bulk of scholarship and criticism to which he can allude and demand that his reader study; and he has the force of his age — the political and sociological events which give his times their character — which he can play against while developing theme and emotion. Poets use these intellectual properties in varying proportions, and the reader should analyze what effect each has on the poem and how each is achieved. As we take an overview of these poetic resources and the terms that describe them in examples that follow, we will italicize the key terms that will be more carefully examined in later sections of the book.

In the following poem for example, we can talk about each of the intellectual elements in great detail, and show how they help the poem to achieve its emotional qualities.

> *I wander through each chartered street,*
> *Near where the chartered Thames does flow*
> *And mark in every face I meet*
> *Marks of weakness, marks of woe.*   4
>
> *In every cry of every man,*
> *In every infant's cry of fear,*
> *In every voice; in every ban,*
> *The mind-forged manacles I hear:*   8
>
> *How the chimney-sweeper's cry*
> *Every blackening church appalls,*
> *And the hapless soldier's sigh*
> *Runs in blood down palace-walls.*   12
>
> *But most, through midnight streets I hear*
> *How the youthful harlot's curse*
> *Blasts the new-born infant's tear,*
> *And blights with plagues the marriage-hearse.* 16

LONDON
WILLIAM BLAKE

In the first two lines, Blake chooses his words and meter carefully in order to give the reader three important aspects of the poem: the *dramatic situation*, the *mood*, and a *point of view*, and these devices are skillfully worked to set the tone and theme.

The bard of the first two lines (and the narrating "I" whose *point of view* carries throughout the poem) is able to "wander" at free will through London, and his wandering confrontations constitute the *dramatic situation*. But everything else is "chartered" by nature or society. The "chartered streets" are plotted in the mapping of the city, but they are also chartered in the sense that they are confined by the stacks of dwellings which line the curbs of the streets. Like the streets which are confined within the rows of houses (connoting slum conditions), the Thames is confined within its banks, a natural barrier; and the banks of the Thames are also chartered — i.e., rented out as real estate. When "chartered" is repeated in the second line, it becomes clear that Blake is using the term in a pejorative manner. The repeated sense of confinement establishes a consistent *mood* for the poem.

Here Blake calls on whatever *historical sense* his readers might have of the English democratic system to push the irony; the nation whose system of government was founded by charters from the King, charters which freed the people, is being threatened by those very charters. And the people's representative, William Pitt, was daily issuing charters — bans — which perpetuated the chartered conditions under which the people suffered. But the Thames can still flow, and the bard can still wander, even if everything else is trapped.

We can see that through word repetition and historical ironies Blake quickly sets up emotional expectations, but in addition to this, Blake relies on another of his tools, *meter,* for emotional emphasis. The *rhythm* in the first two lines establishes the *iambic tetrameter base* from which Blake can deviate for emphasis, but the striking aspect of the first two lines when compared to lines 3-7 is that there is very little rise and fall within the iambic structure. The evenness of the *rhythm*, the *repetition* of "chartered," and the *internal rhyme* "Near where" (line 2), all give an impression of an unemotional monotone, which is however counterpointed by short, emotional statements in lines 3-7, while line 8 climaxes the stanza, returning to the even meter of lines 1-2.

By the time Blake gets to line 3, he is ready to introduce the reader to the degree and severity of the lives of the "chartered" Londoners, which he achieves, in addition to his meter, with word choice. When the bard says that he "marks in every face" marks of weakness and woe, it is clear that "every" can be taken literally. The two-syllable words stand out among the one-syllable words, and the short, quick-moving iambs (in contrast to the preceding lines) convey a feeling of regimentation, an impression that every Londoner along the "chartered streets" has been affected by Pitt's bans.

If lines 3 and 4 anticipate the description of severity which is to come in the second stanza, lines 5, 6, and 7 are written both in imagery and prosody to focus on line 8. The "Marks of weakness, marks of woe," which the bard saw in the first stanza, now become sounds which the suffering utter, and the bard emphasizes the thoroughness of the suffering by the repetition of the words "in" and "every." The "cry" of the men who understand the source of the conditions, and their outrage against injustice, contrast with the actual crying of the "infants" who intuitively and physically feel that result in their society. The voices of the men in line 5 (which seem to be unattached to their owners; voices crying out in the wilderness like Dante's souls in hell) and the voices which pass on to the illiterate who cannot read Pitt's "charters" the meaning of the new "bans," join with the crying in line 6, so that by the end of line 7 the reader is hearing cacophonous shouting amid the strict and quick-moving meter.

Lines 3-7 are very effective in preparing the reader for the emphasis which the poet wishes to place on line 8. The bard has clearly stated the conditions which exist in London, and the *tone* makes it clear that he abhors the situation. As the bard lists the conditions beginning with line 3, the reader begins to pick up momentum (after the long *duration* of the stresses in lines 1-2), and by the middle of line 6 he is racing toward the end of the stanza. The reader's expectation is that the bard will either continue with the brutal description, or condemn the social source of the conditions, and when Blake introduces "ban" at the end of line 7, it seems certain that he is about to attack William Pitt. Instead, Blake relates what he hears in the sounds, and he achieves the force of his wisdom with a line which clangs louder than the wails and moans of the suffering in the preceeding lines. The three *consecutive stresses* in "mind-forged manacles," and the difficulty with which "mind-forged manacles" is read contrast with the *established meter* and *expectations*. The bard is most bitter at this point in the poem (as emphasized by the rhythmic *substitution*); it is not merely the physical atrocities that appall the bard, but also the bonds which enslave the mind. Men enslave other men, but they also enslave themselves, and the manacles of their minds will not allow them to perceive beyond what is immediately clear.

By reinforcing his manacles of the mind with an enslaving meter, Blake has caused his reader to become emotionally involved by the end of stanza 2, and the ironies he portrays become more forceful.

"Hear" at the end of line 8 looks forwards and backwards; we have heard the sounds of the suffering in stanza two, and the colon at the end of line 8 anticipates more sounds of the iron-forged manacles; we are now prepared to identify with the poem because it is the mind that creates the bondage. Like the hammer and the anvil which molded the "Tyger's brain" (in another Blake poem), the mind-forged manacles are blasted in the brain's furnace which the bard proceeds to describe in stanzas three and four, and it is here that Blake turns his readers' feelings for the times onto his poem.

Blake recognized two social forces which controlled Londoners: the Church and the government, and he placed equal blame on them for social evil. One of the most cruel conditions that existed in Pitt's England was the practice of selling children into slavery. The small boys sold as chimney sweepers almost before they could scarcely cry " 'weep! 'weep! 'weep!" died from lung diseases (usually cancer) after a few years of servitude. Two acts had been passed by Parliament which were designed to protect children who might be sold as chimney sweepers, but the acts were ineffective partly because the Church would not speak out against the injustice. The Church was content to save the children's souls but not their bodies.

The image of the chimney sweeper in stanza three is a fusion of both sound and sight, especially when an *allusion* is made to Blake's "Chimney Sweeper" (*Songs of Innocence*). The cry is transformed into a blanket of soot which palls (drapes) the Church which to Blake is nothing more than a coffin where the chimney sweeper and everyone else who accepts its authority must suffer and die. The unusual use of "blackening" as an adjective emphasizes the *irony* which Blake is working. The Church which "blackens" — cries out against evil — is the very instrument which perpetrates it, not only in a theological and philosophical sense, but also in a physical sense, when it contributes to the destruction of the poor. The most bitter irony toward the Establishment comes in line 10. Were the chimney sweeper quietly suffering his plight, as good Christians must do, the Church would not have been appalled, but the child's cry — the fact that the child dares to cry out — shocks the Church, and surely the Establishment will condemn the chimney sweeper for his outburst.

Like the image of the chimney sweeper's cry, the soldier's sigh is a fusion of both sound and sight. Perhaps some of the success of the image comes because of a change in rhythm in stanza three. After "mind-forged manacles" in line 8 which requires a sigh-like *release of breath* when read aloud, the *falling rhythm* in lines 9 and 10 creates a feeling of relief and exhaustion similar to the feeling created by a sigh. And because the prosody has done its job so well, when the sigh is mentioned, the image is felt, and becomes heavy (massive) as it begins to diffuse. The sigh now has life of its own as it spreads out, running down the palace walls.

If the reader again turns to history and what he knows about Blake's life, he will discover that the image of the soldier's sigh alludes to both the seriousness of the discontent in England and to the revolution in France. Blake at age 23 had, himself, been caught up in a mob which was massacred by the King's soldiers, and he recognized the horror for both the rioters and the soldiers. Just as he had been caught in the mob, the soldiers had been trapped by their duty and forced to kill their countrymen. The French Revolution, to which the English poets were sympathetic, resulted in brutal massacres for both sides, but in spite of the death which accompanied the revolt against the "palace," the general feeling was that the Revolution would free men from the Establishment, and the French Revolution was held to be a divine revelation.

For Blake, though, the Revolution was only an impossible dream which would eventually result in no progress toward freeing men. The soldier whose lot it is to guard the palace is indeed "hapless," as is the lot of those who attempt to overthrow the Establishment. The soldier may be sighing from regret, or from boredom, or from frustration at his plight, but in any case, the result of his chartered life will be that the palace will run with both the people's blood and his own, but to no successful end. The motive which leads the people to revolt — Pitt's oppression — is merely an outward manifestation of a deeper motive which is controlled and contained by the mind-forged manacles. It is clear that it is not merely the mind of Pitt but the mind of all men which enslaves the Londoners.

The last stanza moves from the specific social enslavement to more general type of bondage, presumably that which nature places on us. More than the chimney sweeper's cry and the soldier's sigh, the bard sees the limitations both in physical nature, in which the plague of venereal disease has blinded the harlot's child, and also in psychological nature, which creates in man the jealousy and distrust that necessitates the institutional practice of marriage to stabilize his psychological disorders. Nature, symbolically represented by the harlot, becomes the furnace in which these restraining manacles were blasted, and for Blake, nature is the mind's enemy. Marriage becomes a hearse, much like the Church in line 10, and also the devil's disciple because it has become a restraint on man's potential relationship to the world of "experience."

At this point, readers who have become interested in the poem and wish to clarify its *philosophy* will want to see "London" in relation to other Blake poems published as part of the same series, *Songs of Innocence* and *Songs of Experience*. After looking at the entire series, we would find it significant in this poem that the restraints which men place on themselves (line 8) are mentioned and emphasized above the restraints which men place on each other (lines 9-12). "Experience" to Blake is not the world of Pitt's London; it is not the liberation of man from social turmoil; it is not even the relief from nature's catastrophes. Experience is in the mind, not the city, and the energy of the Tyger is the force which can break the manacles. The bans (line 7) may be Pitt's charters, or the curse of the harlot, or even the marriage proclamation, but these are only the result of the restrained mind. The bard can see these things and can prophesy what social conditions should come with an English revolution because he is not restrained.

Thus while we can see that the basic motif is a *theme* of social criticism and political protest, we should also investigate how "London" may fit into the philosophy underlying the other songs. If we can assume that "London" is as subtle and complex as Blake's other poems, then it will be more than social commentary. It is in fact a decisive statement to those who might attack Blake's philosophy of innocence and experience by asking if it is necessary for man to suffer the social conditions of Pitt's London in order to become "experienced." "London" asserts that the city is not true "experience" at all, but represents the end to a *lack* of experience by the men (both the rulers and the ruled) who have created the social conditions. Were men truly experienced, they would know the answers to the social dilemmas, and they would conquer the jealousies which support marriage as a hearse. Certainly, Blake condemns the Establishment in Pitt's England, and he condemns establishments in general, but the poem is not only about social disorders, and until the environment of London is seen as the antithesis of experience and a ridicule of those who cannot understand the basis of liberation, it is not possible to place the poem in context with the other *Songs of Innocence* and *Songs of Experience.*

We can see, then, that Blake has relied on his poetical tools and the conditions of the times to create the emotional responses he desired, but he has also counted on his reader to know something of the French Revolution and Pitt's government in order to establish the distance necessary for understanding the ironies of the poem. Finally, Blake has drawn upon a literary tradition in picking his verse form and in expecting his reader to see the poem as part of a larger body, *Songs of Innocence* and *Songs of Experience,* which contains companion poems that reflect on each other. Everything Blake has done in "London" is a part of his attempt to influence the reader's emotions; beyond this point, the reader is out of the poet's grip. It is clear that Blake in this poem is outraged, and that he spits out his social criticism as Housman spits out his religious criticism. Poets who are attacking some element in their society often create poems which have a strongly emotional character, but of course not all poems are written with that particular attitude. That is not to say that other sorts of poems are less emotional; only that the emotion is portrayed more quietly, even when using intellectual tools similar to those Blake used so effectively in "London." The image of the eagle in Tennyson's poem, for example, stirs the reader's sense of falling, and flight from the azure world, and so in another way it is as emotional as "London," but the emotion is turned inward rather than outward in social wrath.

The following poem, "Year's End," is quiet and reflective, and its emotional qualities result from Wilbur's skill in making the reader feel the images which are gradually transformed into an awareness of man's frailty. Thus we come to realize a theme with which we are all concerned: that we are destroyed in the present, not in the future, and that the units of time which man has established (as a year) and those which he recognizes in nature (as a season) are not the same as those moments of time in which we perish. Let us look at "Year's End" in greater detail, and establish how Wilbur has used the intellectual devices to create emotional responses.

> *Now winter downs the dying of the year,*
> *And night is all a settlement of snow;*
> *From the soft street the rooms of houses show*
> *A gathered light, a shapen atmosphere,*
> *Like frozen-over lakes whose ice is thin*
> *And still allows some stirring down within.*   **6**

I've known the wind by water banks to shake
The late leaves down, which frozen where they fell
And held in ice as dancers in a spell
Fluttered all winter long into a lake;
Graved on the dark in gestures of descent,
They seemed their own most perfect monument.   12

There was perfection in the deaths of ferns
Which laid their fragile cheeks against the stone
A million years. Great mammoths overthrown
Composedly have made their long sojourns,
Like palaces of patience, in the gray
And changeless lands of ice. And at Pompeii   18

The little dog lay curled and did not rise
But slept the deeper as the ashes rose
And found the people incomplete, and froze
The random hands, the loose unready eyes
Of men expecting yet another sun
To do the shapely thing they had not done.   24

These sudden ends of time must give us pause.
We fray into the future, rarely wrought
Save in the tapestries of afterthought.
More time, more time. Barrages of applause
Come muffled from a buried radio.
The New-year bells are wrangling with the snow.   30

YEAR'S END
RICHARD WILBUR

Throughout the poem Wilbur considers time units, both man-made and natural, and sets up a dicotomy between time and timelessness. Consider the example questions about Wilbur's use of time in the following "self-checking" sequence (for best results, use a paper mask to block the "answer" column, and see how completely you can follow and fill in the sentence blanks):

Example/self-check

1 The first mention of a time unit after the title comes in line 1 with the season _____. The calendar time unit which man uses, a _____, comes in the middle of the seasonal unit, which is our first indication that the poem will treat the conflict of units.

	winter
	year

2 While line 1 suggests seasons and years as time units, line 2 adds another one, _____. "A settlement of snow" is not a unit per se, but suggests both the natural

night

units of cold and hot, and the timeless mood of new snow. Similarly, the _____ in line 5 suggests cold and hot, and the knowledge that this will melt.

ice

3 In stanza 1 the terms indicating sequence units — winter, years, night, snow, and ice — establish for the reader the security of recurring _____; that is, the reader knows that another year, night and season will come again.

time

4 In stanza 2, we move from the recurring units to the "late leaves," which is the first mention of something organic (i.e., alive, or once alive). But these are late leaves, and are somehow out of _____.

season

5 Because these leaves defied their seasonal time barriers and fell throughout the _____ and in the dark, their defiance is captured and preserved by winter's ice, which forms a monument to them, but we know that in the spring that monument will disappear too.

winter

6 Although we know that the leaves' _____ to themselves will deteriorate too, the urgency of time is lessened, and a feeling of timelessness begins to seep into the poem.

monument

7 Stanza 3 expands the relatively short periods of time into periods which we usually think of as timeless. The ferns (organic material) have become fossils through a million years, and the prehistoric mammoths have disappeared because of the _____ Age.

Ice

8 The ice monuments in stanza 2, which encased the leaves, are now stone monuments in stanza 3 which encase another type of leaf, and they seem much more permanent. Likewise, the seasonal ice in stanza 2 has now become ice which remained on earth for millions of years and formed a tomb for the _____.

mammoths

9 The time span has been extended through each of the stanzas, then, but in each case — with the leaves, ferns, and mammoths — only remains exist to remind us of the life. There are, however, some important levels of difference between the leaves of stanza 2 which perished because their season was ended, the ferns which

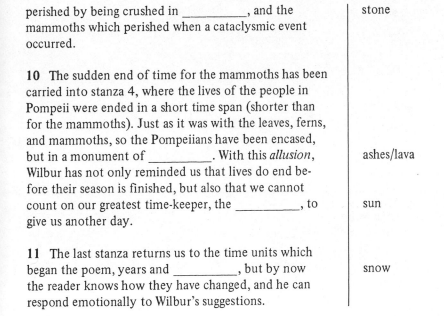

perished by being crushed in _____, and the
mammoths which perished when a cataclysmic event
occurred.

stone

10 The sudden end of time for the mammoths has been
carried into stanza 4, where the lives of the people in
Pompeii were ended in a short time span (shorter than
for the mammoths). Just as it was with the leaves, ferns,
and mammoths, so the Pompeiians have been encased,
but in a monument of _____. With this *allusion*,
Wilbur has not only reminded us that lives do end before their season is finished, but also that we cannot
count on our greatest time-keeper, the _____, to
give us another day.

ashes/lava

sun

11 The last stanza returns us to the time units which
began the poem, years and _____, but by now
the reader knows how they have changed, and he can
respond emotionally to Wilbur's suggestions.

snow

Just as Blake in "London" counted on the reader's knowing certain historical things
about social conditions in England and France, Wilbur expects the reader to know (or
learn about) and apply to the poem some historical facts. In stanza 3 the reader must
know how fossils are formed and realize the *irony* in becoming perfected through
death; he must know about the ice age and what happened to the prehistoric animals if
he is to understand the progression of time and catch the irony of "composedly" (organic matter decomposes normally); he must know how Pompeii was covered with lava ash,
and that the people had very little warning that a catastrophe was about to befall them,
(and even then apparently ignored what warning they had); he should know the children's
story of the little dog which tried to save his blind master from the danger; and if he is
very astute, the reader will recognize that "sun" (line 23) takes on several connotations.
First, there is the scientific fact that the sun is cooling, and that someday there will not
be enough solar heat to sustain life on earth. When this occurs, man, and the solar system,
will be encased in a tomb of coldness just like the leaves and mammoths. Second, readers
bringing knowledge of a literary tradition to the poem may choose to read "sun" as a
pun for "son," inferring that the men of Pompeii may seem to be awaiting another gener-
ation (which is a new unit of time brought to the poem) to complete their lives. And
while it is not precisely in the poem, the reader of puns and literary traditions might
want to see "sun/son" as Christ, and perhaps some hoped-for Second Coming, which
would set up still another unit of time.

"Year's End" is absolutely dependent on its *images, metaphors,* and word usage
(*connotation* and *denotation*). A reader need not be able to see every image to understand
the poem, but he should absorb the total effect toward which the images are working.
Examine each stanza closely enough to be able to articulate the images and metaphors,
and tie them in with the theme of the poem.

Example/self-check (continued)

12 The unusual use of "downs" and "dying" in line 1
creates emphasis, but the *image* isn't clear until line 2,
when we realize that the settlement of snow may be to
the new season as down is to a newborn _____.   duck
We don't see "dying of the year" as an image; i.e.,
nothing is dying which we can visualize; "dying of the
year" is another way of saying the "_____ of   ending
the year."

13 From the "soft street," i.e., a street covered with
_____, we see into the lighted houses, and the   snow
light from within reveals a gathering, presumably of
people come to celebrate the New Year. From without,
where there seems to be endless darkness, the atmosphere inside seems shaped by the light, and people,
moving like the waters beneath a frozen lake (lines
5-6).

14 The lights and people, "shapen" in the room, are
projected *metaphorically* into a lake, where they are
stirring under an ice film, like whatever life may be
below. From this we might begin to sense that the
people in the room live in a mutable atmosphere, and
that some change could come over their "shapen world"
just as the ice has come on the _____.   lake

15 Stanza 2 is as imagistic as stanza 1, and the images
are quite clear through line 10. It is easy for us to imagine leaves by water being shaken off trees, and then
frozen as dancers who don't move, but line 11 may be
a bit harder to visualize because of the word "graved"
(used primarily to mean "engraved" but also as a pun
on burial) and the reverse syntax. However, if the reader
has seen leaves frozen in a thin film over a dark pond,
he can visualize the fallen leaf, partly melting the
frozen surface (from heat absorption) as it starts to en-
grave or carve its own monument out of the _____.   dark ice
The main importance of the line, however, is in the ironic observation that while the leaf is engraving its grave
and monument with gestures of descent, it has not yet
quite descended to a final resting place, but is suspended
until the ice melts.

16 Stanza 3 is much less imagistic than stanzas 1 and 2,
and rather than setting up *fixed images*, as in "laid their

fragile cheeks against the stone," Wilbur simply suggests
that both the frail fern and great mammoths were killed
and preserved in a similar manner. Similarly, if the
mammoths made their sojourns patiently in the changeless lands of ice, the men of Pompeii were content in
their assuredness of another day, and the grey and
changeless lands of ice in stanza 3 are like the deep
_____ of stanza 4.

ashes

17 By comparison (*metaphorically*), then, the methods
of entombment for the late leaves, ferns, mammoths,
and _____ are similar, and this becomes significant
because each was taken out of season. We know that
Wilbur expects us to see these as metaphors, and to
recognize that the random hands and unready eyes
weren't literally "_____"; indeed, the lava ash
burned before it preserved.

men/Pompeiians

frozen

18 "Shapely" in line 24 is not an image, but counts on
the imagery for its effectiveness. "Shapely thing" means
"important thing," but ironically, the frozen men themselves become shapes in the frozen lava which, like the
late leaves, form their own most perfect _____
of unreadiness for death.

monument

19 Stanza 5 does not form images for us, but depends
on our noticing the subtle use of words which lead us
to form our own images (*free imagery*). By seeing time
as having "ends," we are not only prepared for the
theme of our last moments, but we are also ready for
the unusual use of "fray" in line 26 and can somehow
see time as a rope with frayed _____; our lives,
then, are like an unraveled rope or thread, and we are as
unready to die as the Pompeiians.

ends

20 Wilbur tells us that we fray into the future, and that
the only shape ("wrought") we give ourselves is by reflecting on the ends of time. Somehow, we must take
the frayed ends and weave them into "_____"
which may save us from our untimely death. It is only
then that we are given to pause (Wilbur does not say
that the ends of time "make" us pause), and can plead
for more time to do our shapely things we have not
done.

tapestries

21 Wilbur now returns us to the poem's beginning as we are reminded of the New Year's party taking place in the "shapen atmosphere," and the people there who are like those of Pompeii. This *controlling metaphor* leads us to both the theme and end of the poem, and we know that the barrages of applause welcoming in the _____   New Year are also artificial barriers set against time. The New Year bells are wrangling with the snow — fighting with nature's unit of time — to give men more time; if only we could hear the Pompeiians' voices muffled on the radio, we might not fray as quickly.

Just as Blake skillfully employed his metrical tools in "London," Wilbur uses *metrics, form, alliteration,* and *sound* as contributors to theme.

The most impressive aspect of the form is that Wilbur manages so much flexibility within it. The *iambic pentameter base* and the *abbacc rhyme scheme* to which Wilbur rigidly adheres suggest the boundaries which men place on themselves. The inner *couplets* in lines 2-3 of each stanza are bound within rhyming lines (1 and 4), while the end couplet serves as a rigid climax to a tight stanza. Given the subject — that at the end of the year this meditation must take place (or at the "sudden ends of time" which are described) — this type of stanza works well because it tends to emphasize the couplet at the end. And except for the third stanza, each end couplet gives the feeling that an era of time or thought has terminated at this point; so that when the poet does refer to the sudden ends of time in the last stanza, the reader is ready to accept Wilbur's divisions as "ends."

Another device, which Wilbur uses to bind together the stanzas themselves and the lines within stanzas, is alliteration (consonants or vowels occurring at the beginning of different syllables which have similar sounds). Stanza 1 sets up the *s* and *d* alliteration which is carried throughout the poem, and stanza two adds *w* and *l* alliteration. In addition to these, there is an *f, t,* and *r* alliteration which acts as a lesser binding force throughout the poem. The barrage of *s* sounds (some 63 in all) creates another effect: to slow down the poem, and to give it the desired momentum. Whenever Wilbur wants to step up the tempo, he cuts down on the *s* sounds; when he wants the reader to simmer in slow motion (as in "And still allows some stirring down within") he strings out the *s*.

What gives "Year's End" its tremendous flexibility, however, is Wilbur's use of *substitutions* (replacing one type of foot with another). He is able to give variety to the meter, build tension, and create individual sounds within the given mood and form. For example, the tension between the first and second parts of line 5 creates an effect which may suggest through its rhythm that the ice is thin. Wilbur also uses his *regular* lines (no substitutions) most effectively, as in line 12. Coming after two lines which have two substitutions each, the regular meter draws attention to itself, and brings the end of the stanza to a rigid close (the last line of each stanza is regular and serves this same function).

In addition to the substitutions, Wilbur uses *punctuation* as an important control over rhythm, particularly in the last stanza where five periods occur. In stanza 4 Wilbur has permitted most of the lines to run into the next line (called *enjambment*), with pauses (*caesuras*) coming internally in the line, and the reader is prepared for enjambment to continue in stanza 5, especially since the meter is similar. What happens, however, is that Wilbur is using this stanza to inflect the meaning of the observations on time, and as he is telling the reader that we must pause, he is making us pause at a time when we are unprepared for it. In line 26 we are given a little time with the caesura and enjamb-ment, but the time we get with the meter is like the time we buy with our civilization, when in the end we can only plead for "more time" "to do the shapely thing" we have not done. We are not, however, given more time; as with Pompeii and the mammoths, time stops abruptly for us, and the full stop in the middle of line 28 drives this point to the reader. Here he must stop and listen to "These sudden ends of time." The enjamb-ment in line 28 and the *full stop* at the end of line 29 act almost as a warning to us, telling us that the divisions which we make in time — the years and centuries — are not the divisions of time by which we die, and by which civilizations perish. Line 30 comes so abruptly, and is so brutally isolated, that Wilbur seems to be ringing the last bells of this culture. That the important phrase "Must give us pause" comes from Hamlet's famous "To be, or not to be," soliloquy reinforces Wilbur's theme that man measures life and death with false psychological yardsticks.

There are, of course, other techniques which Wilbur uses to his advantage in order to create the poem's emotional qualities, but these few demonstrate the poet's skill. The sound of words and the metrics make "Year's End" as formal as the histories which tell us of great mammoths and Pompeii; consequently the tone of the poem is quiet, reflect-ing a narrator who probes for an emotional response which makes the reader feel his own frailty. However, without the intellectual tools available to him, Wilbur could not have achieved the emotional forcefulness which comes through unobtrusively in "Year's End," and it is easy to see why this poem is artistically more complex than nursery rhymes, which depend on sound to arouse the reader's emotions, or "Trees," which appeals only to the intellectual bias readers might bring to the poem. This is not to say that Wilbur ignores the reader's external feelings; quite the contrary is true. It is to say that Wilbur is artistically able to control responses, which, like Blake, he achieves because he under-stands that the poem's parts are technical means which make possible a greater sum, and the magic of poetry.

The Parts

INTRODUCTION

Once we have begun to feel that a poem is an entity which interacts with readers to become greater than itself, then we are prepared to examine the parts in order to see how the poet has achieved unity. Unless the reader understands how each part contributes to the whole, he is not likely to make valid judgments about the poem's consistency, and without insights into consistency, it isn't possible for the reader to discover the poem's themes or ambitions.

This section of the book treats each of the parts in detail, dissecting poems unmercifully as it attempts to demonstrate how the parts make the poem possible. Once we have mastered the parts and absorbed how they function, we can put them in the back of our minds, but not until they are fused into our subconscious response to the poem as another tool for perceiving.

THE READER'S KNOWLEDGE
AND DISTANCE

◄‖►**Dramatic Situation**

Dramatic situation and *point of view* (A-19ff) are so closely related that each must be determined before the other can be understood. Since it is impossible to fully understand dramatic situation without point of view, and vice-versa, they should be considered simultaneously, although each has different functions and characteristics.

GENERAL

A-1   The first step in explicating poetry is to establish what is happening in the poem on a literal basis. Who is doing what to whom at what time constitutes the poem's action, and just as we speak of a drama as representing a piece of action, we speak of the action in the poem as the dramatic situation.

A-2   Dramatic situation in poetry may be generally defined as the action or situation in which the *persona speaker* must function. Since dramatic situation is the means which allows the action to be located and placed into perspective, it must consist of a concrete set of circumstances which we can describe in a prose statement.

A-3   Dramatic situation, then, does not concern itself with anything other than the physical circumstances which create the *setting,* and when the reader/explicator attempts to describe the dramatic situation, it will necessarily sound simplistic and unexciting, unlike the dramatic situation in much fiction and drama.

A-4   The dramatic situation in poetry creates the setting, and while it is not the central device, it is important because the poet uses it to establish a frame for the other devices, to give unity to the structure, and to raise questions about the *persona* (speaker) or *narrator.*

A-5   Dramatic situation, then, is not merely a means for adding interest to the poem, but is an essential element for creating a structural frame and for raising questions about the narrator.

USE FOR EMPHASIS

A-6   Because dramatic situation does deal with the basic question of "what's happening," whatever the poet chooses to leave unanswered may be an essential question whose answer may give the reader a foothold for understanding the relationship between narrator and theme. In "Stopping by Woods on a Snowy Evening," for example, it is the combination of what we know about the dramatic situation and what the poet deliberately omits that becomes essential to the theme.

> *Whose woods these are I think I know.*
> *His house is in the village though;*
> *He will not see me stopping here*
> *To watch his woods fill up with snow.*   4
>
> *My little horse must think it queer*
> *To stop without a farmhouse near*
> *Between the woods and frozen lake*
> *The darkest evening of the year.*   8
>
> *He gives his harness bells a shake*
> *To ask if there is some mistake.*
> *The only other sound's the sweep*
> *Of easy wind and downy flake.*   12
>
> *The woods are lovely, dark and deep,*
> *But I have promises to keep,*
> *And miles to go before I sleep,*
> *And miles to go before I sleep.*   16

ROBERT FROST

A-7 If we were asked to reduce the dramatic situation in Frost's poem to a prose statement, we could say that:

A man in a carriage drawn by a horse has stopped by woods to watch the snow fall. There is no one around, and there is no farmhouse between the woods and lake. It has been cold enough for the lake to freeze, and because the snow is now falling it must be about 32 degrees F.. The only noises are the sound of the horse shaking his harness bells, the wind blowing easily, and the snow falling. The man seems to be thinking or talking to someone whose presence is not felt in the poem. (This last sentence describes *point of view* [B-1] as well.)

This objective description of the dramatic situation, however, leaves a number of questions unanswered, and because the poet has avoided telling us what we want to know, the questions are emphasized. Questions such as: where has the persona come from? where is he going? why did he stop? what time of day is it? why is he in a horse-drawn vehicle? These are just as much a part of the dramatic situation as what is given us, and if we can understand the implications which surround the unanswered questions, we will have a fuller understanding of the poem.

SHIFTING THE DRAMATIC SITUATION

A-8 Dramatic situation will not, of course, always be as simple as it is in "Stopping by Woods," and it may change during the course of the poem. However, even though dramatic situation may change during the poem, it is not to be confused with a change in scene, mood, or idea.

For example, in "The Rime of the Ancient Mariner," the dramatic situation centers on an old sailor who has stopped one of three men and has proceeded to tell him a story. Within that basic dramatic situation though, there are many scenes in which various actions take place, but the scenes do not constitute a shift in dramatic situation, since they are all included within the Mariner's story.

A-9 We can say, then, that scenes, moods, and ideas may change *within* the dramatic situation without actually changing it, and unless the scene is changed so that it affects the persona at the present time, and changed radically enough as not to be identifiable with the first situation, then we do not consider that a shift in dramatic situation has occurred.

A-10 Likewise, almost every long poem contains a general narrative action which gives purpose or motivation to the deeds of the persona. In Lord Byron's "Don Juan," for example, the general narrative action is Juan's journey from innocence to hell, but this general *structure* does not constitute dramatic situation. Thus while the general situation in many narrative poems does create an important structural element, giving credence to the persona's deeds, narrative action is not necessarily dramatic situation.

A-11 The dramatic situation in a narrative poem must be connected with the person who is telling the story; i.e., the dramatic situation might be set in a tavern where one sailor tells his mates the story, and whatever happens in the tavern at the present time is the dramatic situation.

A-12 While it is possible to talk about the dramatic situation *within* a scene (i.e., the "play within a play" has its own dramatic situation), the dramatic situation of the poem as a whole must deal with the present time; all other occurrences are part of a scene within the narrator's story in which there will certainly be another situation.

A-13 Dramatic situation, then, must involve a specific place and time from which the poem is being told. When reading carefully and explicating, it is important to determine dramatic situation and to consider all possible questions raised by it. Not every poem, however, will have a clearly defined dramatic situation, and others may leave some unanswerable problems. Every poem will have a speaker, but in some his identity is less important.

A-14 Because dramatic situation is important, and because some poems do not have clearly defined dramatic situations, the reader must use good judgement in deciding how far dramatic situation is applicable to meaning and tone. However, defining the dramatic situation is the first important step to understanding the poem.

EFFECT ON STRUCTURE

Example/self-check

A-15 While the form of the poem constitutes one of the most important elements of structure, _____ | dramatic

situation also contributes to the final unity. Notice how
dramatic situation contributes to unity in the following
poem:

> *Snow falling and night falling fast, oh, fast*
> *In a field I looked into going past,*
> *And the ground almost covered smooth in snow,*
> *But a few weeds and stubble showing last.*   4
>
> *The woods around it have it — it is theirs.*
> *All animals are smothered in their lairs.*
> *I am too absent-spirited to count;*
> *The loneliness includes me unawares.*   8
>
> *And lonely as it is that loneliness*
> *Will be more lonely ere it will be less —*
> *A blanker whiteness of benighted snow*
> *With no expression, nothing to express.*   12
>
> *They cannot scare me with their empty spaces*
> *Between stars — on stars where no human race is.*
> *I have it in me so much nearer home*
> *To scare myself with my own desert places.*   16

DESERT PLACES
ROBERT FROST

A-16   Stanza 1 describes a general scene: _____
falling into a field. In stanza 2 the woods are described
as belonging to the field, and the animals to the woods,
which gives the scene a more specific situation.

> snow

A-17   The poet has moved the scene from very general
(the field) to less general (the field with woods) to
_____ (the field with woods with animals).

> more specific/(least general)

A-18   In lines 7 and 8 the poet compares himself with
the _____, and because the poem is structured
so that we are moving from the general to the specific,
we can expect that the poet will move to himself.
We have proceeded, then, as follows: From very general
(lines 1-4) to less general (line 5) to more specific (lines
6-8) to very specific (lines 9-12).

> animals

A-19   With this dramatic structure, Frost has given
unity to the poem, and while the most important function of dramatic situation in "Desert Places" is not to
strengthen the poem's _____, it does contribute
to structure because the pattern of development sets
up expectations.

> unity

Point of View

Point of view and *dramatic situation* (A-1ff) are so closely related that each must be determined before the other can be understood. Since it is impossible to understand point of view fully in many poems without knowing the dramatic situation, they should be considered simultaneously, although each has different functions and characteristics. Point of view also becomes an essential element for understanding *tone* (F-1ff).

GENERAL

A-19 *Point of view* may be simply defined as the eyes through which we see the dramatic situation. As implied by its name, point of view consists only of what which the narrator can see, and it will therefore be restricted by the dramatic situation.

A-20 Point of view is often essential in helping the reader understand the *tone* and *theme* of the poem, but point of view itself is restricted to what the reader or narrator can see. Any interpretation which *results* from a particular point of view should be considered a point of *interpretation*.

A-21 Point of view consists only of those elements which can be determined through the narrator's senses; those which come through his *mind* are points of "interpretation," even though they may *result* from a particular vantage point. For example, in "Stopping by Woods on a Snowy Evening" (A-6), we are looking at the dramatic situation through the narrator's eyes, and we see the snow, woods, farmhouse, horse, etc. as he sees them, and that is point of view. When we begin to wonder about what is left out (A-7), or when the narrator comments on the dramatic situation, we have a point of "interpretation." The differences between the poem's point of view, the narrator's point of interpretation, and the *reader's* point of interpretation will often reveal the meaning of the poem (also see *irony*, G-13 ff).

A-22 As in fiction, the poem may be told from first, second, or third person, singular or plural, limited or omniscient. *Limited* point of view means that the persona can see only what the poet wants him to see, while *omniscient* point of view means that the narrator can see everything, including the thoughts and motives of others.

FIRST PERSON SINGULAR

A-23 Although poems have been successfully told from all points of view, a great many poems are told from *first person singular,* especially the shorter lyrical poems.

A-24 Because much poetry during the Renaissance and since the beginning of the Romantic period has been lyrical in nature, many poems are told in first person singular. First person poems seem to be especially adaptable to lyrical poetry since the lyric tends to be highly subjective, taking the reader to the depths of the narrator's thoughts. The reader should not, however, consider the narrator's voice (A-31) as that of the poet himself. Many readers make this mistake, and it leads to frustration and misunderstanding when explicating several poems by the same poet. If we consider the narrator's voice the poet's, we have trouble accepting any different voice from one poem to the next.

USES FOR FIRST PERSON

A-25   Poets write in first person for one of two reasons: to allow the reader to get into the persona's (narrator's) mind, thereby coming to know what the persona knows; or to provide a character who can convey a personal reaction to an event. When we encounter a poem written in first person, we know that the poet wants us either to understand and identify with the persona, or to understand an event because we understand the persona's reaction to it.

A-26   In other words, the poet can give pleasure and instruct in a first person poem by showing us a character in a situation, and by taking us into his mind, telling us what the persona thinks of that situation.

A-27   In addition to showing us what a character thinks about his situation, the poet can, through first person, show us how a character reacts to a situation without taking us into the exposed mind, and by showing us the reaction, he can imply what the persona has been thinking. In either case the reader is expected to identify with and/or react to the narrator more than to the situation.

THE NARRATOR'S PERSPECTIVE AND VOICE

A-28   First person poems often strive toward making the narrator the central point of the poem, more than the situation, and the reader's reaction is formed as he identifies with the narrator. The meaning of the poem may lie in the differences between the narrator's thoughts, emotions, and reactions to his situation, and the reader's. If there are differences, the reader will eventually realize them, and become aware of elements in the poem which he did not understand before. Notice how first person point of view creates differences between what the narrator and reader can see in the following sonnet.

> *I met a traveller from an antique land*
> *Who said: Two vast and trunkless legs of stone*
> *Stand in the desert . . . Near them, on the sand,*
> *Half sunk, a shattered visage lies, whose frown,*
> *And wrinkled lip, and sneer of cold command,*   5
> *Tell that its sculptor well those passions read*
> *Which yet survive, stamped on these lifeless things,*
> *The hand that mocked them, and the heart that fed;*
> *And on the pedestal these words appear;*
> *"My name is Ozymandias, king of kings:*   10
> *Look on my works, ye Mighty, and despair! "*

> *Nothing beside remains. Round the decay*
> *Of that colossal wreck, boundless and bare*
> *The lone and level sands stretch far away.*

OZYMANDIAS
PERCY BYSSHE SHELLEY

A-29   The narrator in "Ozymandias" says that he met a traveller who told him a story, which indicates that the traveller is no longer present and that the narrator is remembering the episode. Since the traveller is not present, the narrator is simply addressing the reader, and there is no interchange of reactions between the characters within the poem.

Interior Monologue

A-30   When the narrator is speaking only to the reader, or to someone who has no function in the poem, we say that the narrator is engaged in interior monologue. *Interior monologues* may reveal the narrator's thoughts, reactions, or both; whatever the narrator thinks is part of that monologue, whether it be a description of the surroundings, what someone else has said or an interpretation of events.

A-31   Whenever the narrator combines point of view and *point of interpretation,* as in interior monologue, we sometimes talk about the voice of the poem. *Voice* generally connotes the narrator as a personality rather than a sensory device, and since most first person poems are lyrical, most first person poems have a voice. However, the word "voice" sometimes is used to describe a speaker who lacks emotion, which is sometimes the case when a first person narrator looks at the situation as a third person narrator might (see Frames A-57 ff for "poetical voice").

Points of View in "Ozymandias"

A-32   The principal point of view in "Ozymandias," then, is first person singular told in interior monologue, but there are also two other points of view within the controlling point of view. Beginning with line 2 and running throughout the poem, the narrator tells us the traveller's story, which indicates that the poet is using the narrator's reaction to what he has heard, and not the event itself, to convey mood and meaning. Notice that there is no specified dramatic situation within the controlling point of view; i.e., the narrator is not in a definable situation, so we must imagine what the dramatic situation was at the time when the narrator first heard the story from the travellers. Projecting the meeting of the two, it appears that the narrator and traveller are strangers since the narrator gives the traveller no identity at all. In addition to this fact, the narrator's careful use of the language permits us to assume another probability. Since the narrator says, "I met a traveller" and not "I met one who travelled," it is reasonable to say that the traveller was still travelling when he met the narrator.

Example/self-check

A-33   If the traveller was still _____ when the narrator met him, then one of two situations is likely:

travelling (A-32)

(1) that both were in a foreign land, or (2) that the narrator is in his own country which the traveller is visiting.

A-34 In either case it is clear that the _____ has not visited the "antique land," or at least was not in that land at the same time the traveller was.

narrator (A-33)

A-35 This means, in terms of the traveller's point of view, that he has had time to think about the colossal wreck before telling the _____ about it.

narrator

A-36 Thus there has been a lapse of time between the moment the traveller saw the wreck and the moment he told the narrator about it; likewise there has been a _____ of time between the moment the narrator heard the story and the present when he is telling it to us. So we must question whether the narrator is reacting to the story or to the traveller's reaction to the wreck, and whether the narrator is relating the traveller's story in the same language it was related to him, or whether he has reinterpreted the story in his own words.

lapse

A-37 Two questions posed by the point of view of the poem which will help the explicator to understand the meaning if answered are these: (1) Is the narrator reacting to the story or to the reaction of the _____ to the wreck; and (2) has the narrator _____ the story or is he telling it as it was told to him?

traveller
reinterpreted

A-38 Just as there is the traveller's point of view which comes through the narrator's point of view, there is a third point of view in lines 10 and 11: Ozymandias'. His quotation, combined with the poem's imagery, almost takes us back to another dramatic situation within a scene: _____ standing over his empire.

Ozymandias

A-39 We can say, then, that there are three points of view which influence the theme of the poem: the _____, the _____, and _____.

narrator's; traveller's; Ozymandias'

A-40 The difference between what Ozymandias saw and what the traveller saw forms the basis for the reaction of the _____, who has taken the traveller's story, reworked it in his own imagination so that it has become his own story, and in his sense of amazement − in his reaction to the story − he learns about

narrator

the mutability of immutable things, and we can say that
mutability becomes the theme of the poem.

Dramatic Monologue

A-41   Most first person poems are presented as interior monologues, but there are two
other important first person points of view: *dramatic monologue* and *dramatic dialogue.*
(A-49.)

A-42   As the names imply, dramatic monologue is distinguished from dramatic dialogue
by the number of persons speaking in the poem. There are at least two persons present in
dramatic monologue; the speaking persona addresses the silent listener(s) who never
speaks throughout the poem.

A-43   The principal reason for writing in dramatic monologue is to control the speech
of the major persona by the implied reaction of the silent one, and to show how one or
both react to what is being said. Because there are two persons present, the reader feels
or infers that the speaking persona is adapting his speech to the reaction of the silent
listener.

A-44   In other words, the poem attempts to avoid being static or fixed, or to give the
feeling of predestination by allowing the speaker's voice to be altered as the silent person
hears and reacts to what is being said. Just as in conversation, the way the listener reacts
will determine what the speaker says. In dramatic monologue the focus is on only one of
the characters — the speaker. The other character(s), however, must affect the development of the poem; otherwise the poem functions as an *interior monologue* (A-30).

A-45   Notice how dramatic monologue functions in the first two stanzas of the following excerpt:

> For God's sake hold your tongue, and let me love,
>   Or chide my palsy, or my gout,
> My five gray hairs, or ruined fortune flout;
>   With wealth your state, your mind with arts improve,
>   Take you a course, get you a place;   5
>   Observe his honor, or his grace;
>   Or the king's real, or his stamped face
>   Contemplate; what you will, approve,
>   So you will let me love.
>
> Alas, alas, who's injured by my love?   10
>   What merchant's ships have my sighs drowned?
> Who says my tears have overflowed his ground?
>   When did my coals a forward spring remove?
>   When did the heats which my veins fill

Add one more to the plaguey bill?   15
Soldiers find wars, and lawyers find out still
Litigious men, which quarrels move,
Though she and I do love.

THE CANONIZATION
JOHN DONNE

The first indication that there are two persons present in the poem comes in line 1 when the speaker tells the silent listener to "hold your tongue." Apparently, the silent listener has reprimanded the speaker before the poem opened, and the speaking persona is angry. He lashes back at the listener, demanding to be left alone because his love affair is not hypocritical.

A-46 By the end of stanza 1, however, the speaker realizes that he is getting nowhere with his argument; so beginning with stanza 2 he changes his approach, and we can feel the other's presence because of the way the speaker changes his arguments in stanza 2.

A-47 What the poet has done, then, is to show us in stanza 1 an argument which the listener will not accept, and in stanza 2 and the rest of the poem show us what does work; the difference between the arguments gives us a clear idea what the listener is like. Not only do we know what the speaker is like, but we also know what the listener is like because we have seen the difference between what the silent persona accepts and rejects.

A-48 The effect of showing us the difference is to satirize people like the listener. However, had we not felt the presence of the listener and seen how this person reacted to the first argument, we would not have known what the poet was trying to do.

A-49 *Dramatic dialogue* has been most successfully used in verse plays, but there are some poems which use it quite well. There can be any number of persons in dramatic dialogue, and there can be intrusions on the part of the poet or the voice which monitors the poem, but there must be at least two persons who speak.

A-50 In dramatic dialogue there must be at least two speakers; usually the personae speak to each other, and technically they must if there is to be dialogue, but occasionally two monologues can function as dialogue if there is some monitoring force which correlates the two. Ideally, dramatic dialogue is used to show the step-by-step building toward a final resolution of the conversation.

A-51 The focus, then, is on both persons, and we should be able to see how both react. In some *poems*, however, one of the persona may be used only as a launching pad for the other. For example, the lesser persona might ask questions which the major persona answers. In some plays, a minor character (usually a servant, sometimes called a "confidant") will ask the right questions to make a major character reveal inner feelings which would seem ridiculous if verbalized without the presence of an on-stage listener. The best dramatic dialogues, however, occur when both personae react, and it is for this reason that the poet can justify using this form.

A-52   Although the principal reason for using dramatic dialogue is to show how both persons react, there is a second advantage to this point of view: to give the poem a less formal feeling; to remove slightly (but only slightly) from the reader's subconscious the preconceived notions of poetry as a rigid form. (Which is also one of the functions of free verse, K-153 ff.) Because dialogue tends to be relaxed and natural, we can assume that a poem which uses it is attempting to achieve its aims in an unobtrusive way.

A-53   Frequently the impression or conclusion left on one of the personae at the end of the poem will formulate the impression which the poet wants the reader to have but sometimes the reader will be expected to fuse the two presentations to form a third.

A-54   At the end of a dramatic dialogue the reader should be able to form an impression, either through the impression of one of the personae or by fusing the impressions of all the personae. Notice how the dramatic dialogue is working in the following excerpt:

> "Fred, where is north?"
> > "North? North is there, my love.
> The brook runs west."
> > West-running Brook then call it."
> (West-running Brook men call it to this day.)
> "What does it think it's doing running west
> When all the other country brooks flow east
> To reach the ocean? It must be the brook
> Can trust itself to go by contraries
> The way I can with you — and you with me —
> Because we're — we're — I don't know what we are.
> What are we?"
> > "Young or new?"
> > > "We must be something.
> We've said we two. Let's change that to we three.
> As you and I are married to each other,
> We'll both be married to the brook. We'll build
> Our bridge across it, and the bridge shall be
> Our arm thrown over it asleep beside it.
> Look, look, it's waving to us with a wave
> To let us know it hears me."
> > > "Why, my dear,
> That wave's been standing off this jut of shore — "
> (The black stream, catching on a sunken rock,
> Flung backward on itself in one white wave,
> And the white water rode the black forever,
> Not gaining but not losing, like a bird
> While feathers from the struggle of whose breast
> Flecked the dark stream and flecked the darker pool

Below the point, and were at least driven wrinkled
In a white scarf against the far shore alders.)
"That wave's been standing off this jut of shore
Ever since rivers, I was going to say,
Were made in heaven. It wasn't waved to us."

"It wasn't yet it was. If not to you
It was to me — in an annunciation."

"Oh, if you take it off to lady-land,
As 'twere the country of the Amazons
We men must see you to the confines of
And leave you there, ourselves forbid to enter, —
It's your brook! I have no more to say."

"Yes, you have, too. Go on. You thought of something."
                    * * * *
                    FROM: WEST-RUNNING BROOK
                    ROBERT FROST

A-55 "West-running Brook" is a poem about contraries, and the poet reinforces this concept with his personae (Fred and the woman) who are in a sense contraries, but who, by running contrary to each other, find motion which leads them toward their source. Without two personae in the poem, it would have been more difficult for Frost to reinforce his theme about contraries. The people run contrary to each other, but they, like the brook, find motion toward their source.

Poetical Intrusion

A-56 The *poetical intrusion* in line 3 is used to give perspective to the poem; with any first-person poem the reader cannot really trust the personae, but with two persons looking at each other and a third *omniscient* person (A-22) looking at the whole situation, the reader gets a perspective which he can trust.

Poetical Voice

A-57 Sometimes the speaker in a first person poem seems so far removed from the poem that it is difficult for the reader to imagine that he is describing his own thoughts or reactions. When the voice in a first person poem seems removed from the events of the poem, it is helpful to distinguish it from dramatic monologue (A-41) and voice (A-31), and call it *"poetical voice."*

A-58 When the poet wants to convey as little emotion as possible on the part of the character — when a lack of emotion is more forceful than portraying it — then poetical voice is a suitable point of view.

A-59   With poetical voice the lack of emotion is more forceful than emotion, and reveals more of what the character is thinking than an emotional response.

A-60   Sometimes there is very little information in a poetical voice poem that we can associate with the persona to give him identity; thus the point of view seems more closely associated with *third person* (A-63) than with first person. The distinction, however, can finally be made by determining how closely the persona is related to the events in the poem. If the narrator has in some way affected the outcome of the event, or been a part of it, then it is a first person poem if he has responded to it at all.

A-61   However, since the real value of first person is to take the reader into the narrator's mind in an effort to interpret the event and the emotions surrounding it, the poet, except in special instances, loses the assets of first person by denying the natural characteristics of it.

A-62   By denying the natural characteristics of first person, the poet hopes to call attention to them; so when explicating poetical voice, it is worthwhile to determine why the poet is emphasizing lack of personal emotion (see A-67 for further discussion).

◄▐▌► THIRD PERSON

A-63   When the narrator has not been a part of the event or affected it, and if he is not probing for his own relationship to it but is only describing what has happened and further, has not allowed intrusion of the word "I," then he is using *third person* (second person is almost never used for an entire poem, although it is sometimes interspersed within first and third person.)

A-64   One important distinction between *poetical voice* (A-57) and third person is that in third person the narrator has no direct relationship to the event, but is describing what has happened. Third person narrators who can see the emotions and thoughts of the *participants* as well as describing the event are said to be omniscient (A-22).

USES FOR THIRD PERSON

A-65   There are three principal reasons why a poet uses a third person narrator, either limited or omniscient: (1) to establish a distance between the reader and the subject; (2) to give credibility to the telling of a large expanse of narration which would be impossible for one person to experience; and (3) to allow the poem to include a number of characters who can comment on each other as well as be commented on by the non-participating narrator.

A-66   Thus, in order to prevent the reader from identifying too closely with the poem, or becoming too emotional about the narrator's association with the event, the poet uses third person, which creates a distance between the reader and the subject. If the event is too large for one character to experience or interpret in first person, third person is used to give credibility to the story. Third person narration is also able to include a large number of characters who can comment on and complement and interact with each other much as do characters observed on a stage by a detached observer.

DIFFERENCES BETWEEN POETICAL VOICE AND THIRD PERSON

A-67 The principal difference between third person and poetical voice is that the third person narrator does not feel that the events in the poem affect him, and he can therefore take an objective look at what has happened, while the poetical voice does feel related to the poem, even though that feeling may be very slight (A-57).

A-68 Although the third person narrator does not feel directly affected by the events, his response to the events can be a crucial element for explicating the poem. The poet will sometimes use the narrator's response to an event in the poem to call attention to it, and the narrator's attitudes will help determine what the reader is supposed to think. When explicating a third person poem, it is a good idea to characterize the narrator and his attitudes to see how he fits into the poem.

SECOND PERSON

A-69 It is obvious that a poem cannot easily be told at length from second person; by saying "you" we imply that there is an "I" who is looking on and narrating the point of view — a somewhat tense situation that is difficult to sustain at length. However, poets do attempt to project the reader into the poem by shifting the point of view toward the reader. We do the same thing in conversation when in telling a story we casually interject "you know."

A-70 The usual purpose in temporarily shifting toward a second person point of view is to project the reader into the poem, thereby making him identify more closely with it. Notice how the poet momentarily shifts to second person in order to involve the reader:

> *Then we came to a tavern with vine-leaves over the lintel,*   26
> *Six hands at an open door dicing for pieces of silver,*
> *And feet kicking the empty wine-skins.*
> *But there was no information, and so we continued*
> *And arrived at evening, not a moment too soon*
> *Finding the place; it was (you may say) satisfactory.*   31

> FROM: JOURNEY OF THE MAGI
> T. S. ELIOT

In "Journey of the Magi" Eliot switches from first person to a type of second person in order to involve the reader.

A-71 The use of "you" in a poem has a tendency to make the reader identify himself with the person so addressed. However, the poet may not be pointing at the reader, but be talking to another persona in dramatic monologue or dialogue. Thus, in Donne's "Canonization," for example, the "you" is obviously another person in the poem. Yet while the point of view is first person there, and not second, the mention of "you" makes the reader shift uncomfortably, even though he can tell that the listener is being addressed.

A-72   Because almost every reader is self-conscious, it often happens that when second person is suggested, even if there is no shift to it, the reader may become uncomfortable. Frequently the poet intends to do this in order to make the reader realize his own responsibility to the poem. So we can say that while there is technically no real "second person" point of view, whenever the focus is shifted so that the responsibility falls on the reader rather than on the poet or narrator, the poet has achieved a "second person" perspective.

A-73   Once the poet has reminded the reader of his responsibility, there is no need for second person to be continued; if it is the reader will become irritated by it, and it will lose its effectiveness.

◀▐▌▶ SUMMARIZING DRAMATIC SITUATION AND POINT OF VIEW

A-74   In summary, then, we can say that point of view can be an important and revealing element in the poem. The difference between what the persona knows and what the reader knows, or the personality of the persona or narrator, or the persona's (narrator's) reaction within the dramatic situation are crucial to the understanding of some poems. Usually it is necessary to place the persona in time and space in order to understand his point of view, and for this reason dramatic situation (A-1) and point of view are inseparable, although one may be more important to the poem than the other.

Example/self-check

A-75   Let us discuss dramatic situation and point of view in the following poem:

> *Once I am sure there's nothing going on*
> *I step inside, letting the door thud shut.*
> *Another church: matting, seats, and stone,*
> *And little books; sprawlings of flowers, cut*   4
> *For Sunday, brownish now; some brass and stuff*
> *Up at the holy end; the small neat organ;*
> *And a tense, musty, unignorable silence,*
> *Brewed God knows how long. Hatless, I take off*   8
> *My cycle-clips in awkward reverence,*
>
> *Move forward, run my hand around the font.*
> *From where I stand, the roof looks almost new —*
> *Cleaned or restored? Someone would know: I don't.*   12
> *Mounting the lectern, I peruse a few*
> *Hectoring large-scale verses, and pronounce*
> *"Here endeth" much more loudly than I'd meant.*
> *The echoes snigger briefly. Back at the door*   16

I sign the book, donate an Irish sixpence,
Reflect the place was not worth stopping for.

Yet stop I did: in fact I often do,
And always end much at a loss like this,   20
Wondering what to look for; wondering, too,
When churches fall completely out of use
What we shall turn them into, if we shall keep
A few cathedrals chronically on show,   24
Their parchment, plate, and pyx in locked cases,
And let the rest rent-free to rain and sheep.
Shall we avoid them as unlucky places?

Or, after dark, will dubious women come   28
To make their children touch a particular stone;
Pick simples for a cancer; or in some
Advised night see walking a dead one?
Power of some sort or other will go on   32
In games, in riddles, seemingly at random;
But superstition, like belief, must die,
And what remains when disbelief has gone?
Grass, weedy pavement, brambles, buttress, sky.   36

A shape less recognizable each week,
A purpose more obscure, I wonder who
Will be the last, the very last, to seek
This place for what it was; one of the crew   40
That tap and jot and know what rood-lofts were?
Some ruin-bibber, randy for antique,
Or Christmas-addict, counting on a whiff
Of gown-and-bands and organ-pipes and myrrh?   44
Or will he be my representative,

Bored, uninformed, knowing the ghostly silt
Dispersed, yet tending to this cross of ground
Through suburb scrub because it held unspilt   48
So long and equably what since is found
Only in separation — marriage, and birth,
And deaths, and thoughts of these — for whom was built
This special shell? For, though I've no idea   52
What this accoutred frowsty barn is worth,
It pleases me to stand in silence here;

A serious house on serious earth it is,
In whose blent air all our compulsions meet,   56
Are recognized, and robed as destinies.
And that much never can be obsolete,
Since someone will forever be surprising

A hunger in himself to be more serious,   60
And gravitating with it to this ground,
Which, he once heard, was proper to grow wise in,
If only that so many dead lie round.

CHURCH GOING
PHILIP LARKIN

Going through the poem stanza by stanza, we discover
the following about the dramatic situation:

Stanza 1

A-75 (1)   The point of view is _____ _____
_____. Thus, since the listener (if there is one) has
little effect on the speaker, the poem is told in _____
monologue.

first person
singular (A-23)
interior (A-30)

A-75 (2)   There (is, is not) a ceremony in progress. Had
there been, the narrator (would, would not) have entered
the church. How does the tone (F-1) reveal this?

is not
would not

A-75 (3)   From his hesitancy we can infer that the narrator (does, does not) feel he belongs.

does not

A-75 (4)   It is a (Sunday, weekday) now.

weekday (line 5)

A-75 (5)   Someone (has, has not) removed the flowers
from Sunday, although someone bothered to place them
there.

has not

A-75 (6)   Since the narrator refers to "brass and stuff"
at "the holy end," it (is, is not) probable that he accepts
the sacredness of the altar.

is not

A-75 (7)   The church is silent; so the speaker's noise
must be the only sound present; yet for him the silence
has about it an _____ quality (line 7); silence
which reverberates with sounds from the distant past.

unignorable

A-75 (8)   The narrator (can, cannot) tell how long this
silence has been brewed.

cannot (line 8)

A-75 (9)   Lines 8 and 9 reveal two things about the
situation: that the narrator feels the necessity to take
something off in _____, and that he has come to
the church by cycle.

reverence

Stanza 2

A-75 (10)   After taking a look at things from the
_____ of the church (where the massive doors   rear
have closed him in), the narrator moves forward and
runs his hand around the _____, the basin used for   font (line 10)
the baptismal service.

A-75 (11)   He looks at the _____ and wonders   roof (line 11)
about its good state of repair. It has been cleaned or
_____; he doesn't know which, but thinks that   restored (line 12)
some expert would know.

A-75 (12)   He climbs to the _____ (which is   lectern (line 13)
called a pulpit in church terms), and recites some verses
which may or may not be part of the church liturgy.

A-75 (13)   The narrator closes his large scale lectur-
ings with _____ _____, which he somehow   "here endeth" (line 15)
knows is the proper phrase.

A-75 (14)   The loud _____ sounds like a snig-   echo (line 15)
ger reflecting on his attempt at preaching and the fact
that the church is empty.

A-75 (15)   With this he returns to the back of the
church, the entrance, signs the _____ (guest regis-   book (line 17)
ter), and leaves a donation.

A-75 (16)   The Irish sixpence confirms our suspicion
that the scene takes place in _____.   Europe

A-75 (17)   Lines 18 and 19 indicate that he has
stopped at other places of interest; so he probably
(is, is not) touring the country on cycle.   is

A-75 (18)   He seems to consider his money a _____   donation (line 17)
rather than an offering, which makes us wonder what
he is donating to: the religion, the country, the priest,
the building.

A-75 (19)   He (does, does not) think the place worth   does not (line 18)
a tour stop.

Stanza 3

A-75 (20)   Line 19 tells us that he stops for cathedrals
_____, which gives us the impression that he is a   often

a wanderer of sorts, roaming about in search for places
which might be meaningful to him (we already know that
he is not an authority on churches); yet they always end
at a _____.

loss (line 20)

A-75 (21)   In line 19, the present tense of the first two
ʿstanzas is suddenly made _____, and the rest of the
poem will be the narrator's reflection on the preceding
action. The dramatic situation hence ceases to carry the
poem further, and point of view takes over as the controlling element.

past

A-75 (22)   What the narrator says about the downfall
of churches — the _____ of churches as opposed
to going to church — tells us about his character as well
as revealing his attitude toward church going, but it is
not part of the dramatic situation.

going

A-75 (23)   Even though only 2/7 of the poem deals
with dramatic situation, it is quite important because
it familiarizes us with the narrator before he begins his
discourse on church going. Had the narrator been the
priest, or had we not known who the narrator was, then
what he had to say, and the *tone* (F-1) of his saying it
would not have worked nearly so well.

For a more complete discussion of the dramatic situation in "Church Going" refer to the
explication on page 292.

⫴▸Imagery

Imagery is one of the most frequently used and complex devices in poetry. It should be studied carefully, along with *metaphor* (B-26 ff) and *symbol* (C-1 ff).

HOW IMAGES WORK

B-1   Critics are quick to define imagery as the representation of an experience of the senses, but it is difficult — almost impossible in many instances — to separate imagery from an idea *about* a sense experience; so it is dangerous to look at imagery as if it were only a pure sense response.

B-2   In other words, an image is traditionally thought of as a sensory response which is aroused by words that are somehow related to the experience; if a word recalls a warm, lazy, summer afternoon with breezes blowing grass beside the lake where fish are jumping, then we can safely say that the word which triggered this scene had the power of forming an image. But in most poems, images are not used to make pictures vivid; they are used to develop an idea or emotion, so that the word recalls the image, which in turn recalls responses surrounding the experience.

B-3   What a poetically complex image does is to first recall the sensory experience; i.e., a sense "picture" of the scene; but it does not stop at this. The image also recalls the emotional and intellectual responses which surround the experience. So the image works in two ways, first recalling the sensory experience, then the emotions which surrounded it.

B-4   Because images do demand a particular response from the reader, they must be unique enough for the reader to be able to distinguish their properties and remember them; the more memorable the image the more vivid the response that can accompany it as long as the image is within the reader's experience.

B-5   The word "tree," for example, does not form a vivid image because the reader's mind cannot focus on any particular type or aspect of tree, while the thud of the door in "Church Going" is more vivid. Readers must be able to focus on a particular sensory experience in order to evoke any emotions accompanying it, and because the abstractness and generality of the word *tree* lets everyone have a different notion of "treeness," there can be no sharing of any unique response to the word.

B-6   Vivid imagery is essential if the poet is to control the reader's emotions, but even a vivid image does not make a poem; the image must be a part of a central them or idea.

39

Images usually do not exist for their own sake (an exception of this is a body of imagistic poetry written for the purpose of exploring the possibilities of images without ideas, only emotions); they become a part of a central theme, and when a reader is explicating, it is essential in most poems to find how the image supports the theme or idea.

B-7   Some poems result from taking an idea and reinforcing it with several images; others result from taking images set within a central focus. But in either case the image and idea must be consistent with each other. Thus, knowing that image and idea must be consistent with each other gives the explicator two directions from which he can approach the poem. Either the idea or the image can suggest a means of understanding the other element.

B-8   In the following fragment the poet is building images which function as a contribution to the central idea.

> *The sea is calm tonight.*
> *The tide is full, the moon lies fair*
> *Upon the straits; on the French coast the light*
> *Gleams and is gone; the cliffs of England stand,*
> *Glimmering and vast, out in the tranquil bay.*
> *Come to the window, sweet is the night air!*   6
>
> *Only, from the long line of spray*
> *Where the sea meets the moon-blanched land,*
> *Listen! you hear the grating roar*
> *Of pebbles which the waves draw back, and fling,*
> *At their return, up the high strand,*
> *Begin, and cease, and then again begin,*   12
> *With tremulous cadence slow, and bring*
> *The eternal note of sadness in.*

FROM: DOVER BEACH
MATTHEW ARNOLD

Example/self-check

B-8 (1)   The dramatic situation is that the persona is standing at a _____ from which he can see both the Cliffs of Dover (on the English side of the channel) and the lights along the French coast, and he is describing what he perceives to someone who is in the room with him.

window (line 6)

B-8 (2)   Before we can fully appreciate and understand the imagery in a poem, it is necessary to establish the _____ _____; in "Dover Beach," the poem is being told in dramatic _____.

dramatic situation
monologue (A-41)

B-8 (3)   The speaker can see the coasts of two countries, France and England. On the English side are _____, objects formed through nature, and on the French side are _____, man-made objects.

cliffs (line 4)
lights (line 3)

B-8 (4)   Each of the lines in these first two stanzas forms an _____ which contributes toward the larger controlling image of the poem: the eternal quality associated with the sea (as opposed to the ephemeralness of man which is treated in the last stanza).

image

B-8 (5)   Each of the smaller images contributes to a _____ image, i.e., one that runs throughout the poem and is central to the theme. (See B-58)

controlling

B-8 (6)   Looking at the poem carefully, we can visualize or feel the following elements in the scene:

(a)   Because the sea is calm, there is nothing to frighten us, and no strong winds to impair hearing the sea sounds.

(b)   It is high tide and the water is against the sheer banks of the cliffs.

(c)   The moon illuminates the calm sea and cliffs.

(d)   The lights on the French coast glimmer; because of the distance across the channel, the lights are not constant.

(e)   In contrast to the distant shores, the cliffs loom in front of the window, surrounded by a tranquil bay.

(f)   The atmosphere and physical qualities of cool night air are refreshing.

B-8 (7)   The mood of the first stanza, then, as depicted by its images, is one of _____. From the elements described there is no need for us to be _____ as the night refreshes us.

calm or peacefulness
frightened

B-8 (8)   In Stanza 2, however, the images turn from those of sight and feel to sound. We can hear above the calm sounds of the lapping waves in the bay the sound of waves thundering against the shore. The waves take the rocks out, then fling them hard against the cliffs. Because the sea is calm, the thundering comes periodically, establishing a slow cadence which saddens the ____.

narrator (line 14)

B-8 (9)   The images in Stanza 2 are primarily aimed at the sense of _____, while those in Stanza 1 stemmed from sight and feeling.

sound – B-8 (8)

B-8 (10)   Set against the calm in the first stanza, the slow _____ in Stanza 2 moves the imagery toward a more violent state.

cadence – B-8 (8)

B-8 (11)   The images working together have evoked a response from the narrator which is leading him into an idea which goes beyond the image, and the poet will concern himself with what "the eternal note of sadness" is and how the sea image reinforces it. We can say, then, that the images in "Dover Beach" are used to evoke a response which leads to an idea which the imagery reinforces.

FREE AND FIXED IMAGES

B-9   In "Dover Beach" the images are fairly constant for most readers; i.e., the scene will be about the same for everyone though it may vary slightly if the ocean or pictures of oceans which the reader has seen differ from the English Channel.

B-10   Images evoke a response because the experience lies within the reader's power to recall something similar to it; in "Dover Beach" the imagery is constant because each reader will view the scene in a similar way.

B-11   Images are constant or "fixed" because every reader will experience a similar response to them, even though the experiences of readers vary greatly. In "Dover Beach," for example, the imagery does not allow the reader's imagination to wander or bring distracting additional sensations to the scene; so we say that the imagery is fixed or constant.

B-12   Fixed imagery permits only a calculated response to be evoked,with a minimum of distracting sensations brought in by readers. What Arnold attempts to do in "Dover Beach" with fixed imagery is to achieve unity within his scene and to give the reader a foothold in the poem before Arnold takes off into his theme.

B-13   Although fixed imagery gives the poem unity and makes the reader comfortable with it, poets do not always fix their images. With fixed imagery the image is formed for the reader and all he must do is to evoke the responses to accompany it. But with "free" imagery not only must the reader evoke the response, but he must first create the image.

B-14   When the image requires that the reader form it in addition to forming the experience which surrounds it, then we say that the image is free. With fixed images the reader need only depict the scene and recall what he felt when he experienced it, but with free images the word merely suggests the image which the reader must then form.

B-15   In the following stanzas, for example, there is brilliant description which creates vivid images for most readers, but the images formed by one reader will not be the same as those formed by the next, because the reader must use his imagination and whatever related experiences he can recall to form the imagery.

> "Beyond the shadow of the ship,
> I watched the water-snakes:
> They moved in tracks of shining white,
> And when they reared, the elfish light
> Fell off in hoary flakes.

> "Within the shadow of the ship
> I watched their rich attire:
> Blue glossy green, and velvet black,
> They coiled and swam; and every track
> Was a flash of golden fire.

FROM: THE RIME OF THE ANCIENT MARINER
SAMUEL TAYLOR COLERIDGE

The images in these stanzas are free in the sense that an exact vision of the water-snakes must be formed by the reader's imagination after being triggered by numerous suggestions from the poet. But after the poet has made the suggestions he has no control over what the reader does with them, whereas with fixed images he is controlling the reader's formation of the image.

B-16   We can say, then, that with fixed images the poet is controlling the formation of the image to a greater degree than he is with free imagery, which does not necessarily mean that he has greater or lesser control of the reader's emotional response to whatever image is formed.

Uses for Free Images

B-17   When a poet uses fixed images, he is probably doing one or more of several things: setting a mood or scene in which the thought or action can occur; giving the reader something to cling to as the poem becomes more complex; establishing realism; searching for universality; or commenting on society.

B-18   The reader is not asked to form or create the fixed image, only to see what the poet has created for him, but he is asked to take from the image whatever the poet has formed and to bring to it his own set of responses.

B-19   When the poet requires that the reader take his own set of experiences as a background for forming an individual and unique personal image, then the poet is using free imagery. In theory, free imagery is more meaningful to the reader because the poet merely triggers the reader's mind to form its own image, thereby making the image, and thus the poem, more personal.

B-20   Images which are formed by the reader and not the poet should be more personal since they rely on the reader's experiences and not the poet's, thereby potentially making the poem more relevant and meaningful. In this way, the reader might tend to become more involved with the poem because he has not been forced to channel his identification; he, in theory, makes the poem conform to his own needs and experiences. But imagery which is truly "free" cannot really be used in poetry because the poet has not formed it.

B-21   In spite of the problems with control, however, many modern poets like to use free images as far as possible because they seem to be more significant for an age which is caught up in existential probings.

B-22   Perhaps because the modern age has become obsessed with the existential question, "who am I?" free images seem more relevant and significant, since they require the reader to project himself into creating the image before examining his responses to it.

B-23   Poets who make liberal use of free images will quite likely be asking the reader to look into the depths of his own being for the answers to perplexing universal and personal questions, while poems which use fixed images will probably be turning to nature or to the experience of the poet (rather than the reader) for answers.

Mixing Free and Fixed Images

B-24   Most poems use a combination of both types, or images which fall into neither category. In poems which use a combination of both, the poet will allow some freedom with some images while rigidly controlling the reader with others. By using a combination of freedom and control, the poet can cause the reader to direct his thoughts while allowing him to probe for the most meaningful aspects in them.

B-25   In the following poem, for example, the poet allows a good deal of imagistic freedom, but finally controls the reader.

> *And yet one arrives somehow,*
> *finds himself loosening the hooks of*
> *her dress*
> *in a strange bedroom —*
> *feels the autumn*   5
> *dropping its silk and linen leaves*
> *about her ankles.*
> *The tawdry veined body emerges*
> *twisted upon itself*
> *like a winter wind . . . !*   10

ARRIVAL
WILLIAM CARLOS WILLIAMS

B-25 (1)   Without giving us any idea as to what the arrival is, the poet places us in a situation in which we must begin forming images; we are not given the luxury of much dramatic situation before we are required to cope with images. This is unlike "Stopping by Woods on a Snowy Evening," which places us firmly into the situation first.

B-25 (2)   The first line is quite free, yet suggestive enough to make most readers remember how they felt when they found themselves doing something which they did not expect they would do. The image in line 1 is so free as to almost not be an image; yet it does ask the reader to recall a moment out of his past when he suddenly arrived unexpectedly in a situation or place.

B-25 (3)   Lines 2 and 3 suggest a scene familiar to all men aware of sexual associations with women; yet the poet has allowed the reader some flexibility in forming the image because the persona "finds himself loosening the hooks," not unzipping the zipper or unsnapping snaps.

B-25 (4)   Since the reader cannot tell exactly what motions are being performed with the hooks, he injects whatever he would be doing, which makes him become a part of the poem, and because the arrival in line 1 is an arrival which the reader would remember out of his own life, and because line 2 allows the reader to continue projecting his actions into the poem, the persona and the reader are now increasingly blended as one; the poem has seduced the reader into placing his own experiences into the poem, so that he is now committed to it.

B-25 (5)   The arrival, the woman, and the bedroom (lines 1-4) are all personal (free) images which the poet has "drawn out" of the reader. The poet cannot at this point have any exact idea what the reader is seeing, because he has made no attempt to control it; yet he is prepared to interpret the reader's images for him by using a more complex but fixed image as a point of comparison, and lines 5-7 take the individualized situation and compare it to another image: that of leaves falling in autumn.

B-25 (6)   The image of falling leaves by itself is fairly fixed, but the feeling which readers would have during autumn is quite free, so that in lines 5 and 6 we are both seeing the leaves fall and recalling our own emotions toward that image. The image in these lines is thus both fixed and free as the reader is led out of the bedroom into autumn.

B-25 (7)   The leaves in our personal image, however, are not the poet's leaves at all, for he has transformed them into garments which the woman is wearing, so that we are forced into superimposing our second image on the first. The woman, then, has become like the autumn and whatever emotions we have about the season will be applied to the arrival scene of the poem.

B-25 (8)   By the end of line 7 the poet has taken the reader deep into understanding what one feels after arriving, and he is now ready to fix the free images and evoke a particular response from us. In line 8 the image of a veined body twisted upon itself suggests the structure of a tree bare of leaves, and it is consistent with the preceeding image of the autumn. But it is also consistent with the image of the woman who is like the autumn, and this final fixed image is positive and forceful. Since what emerges from the soft dress is ugly and twisted, the image of the winter wind serves to describe the body, but it also portrays the speaker's response to seeing the body, and we know that his amorous desires have been chilled by the horrible nakedness.

B-25 (9)   Thus, by fixing the free images which involved the reader earlier in the poem, the poet causes the reader to superimpose the emotions of one on the other so that the poet is able finally to control the reader's response to the poem.

For a partial explication of imagery and allusion, refer to the critical essay of James Dickey's "In the Mountain Tent," pp. 237-240.

⊲‖⊳ Metaphor

The quality of a poem can be greatly influenced by the quality of its *metaphors*. One brilliant metaphor can sometimes make a poem succeed even amid a host of mediocre metaphors, while one bad metaphor can ruin a host of good ones. The success of metaphors depends on how good the images (B-1 ff) are, and how well the comparison of images conveys profundity, wit, or observations about life.

HOW METAPHORS WORK

B-26   Because images must be used in consistent patterns to develop ideas, it follows that images which are associated with one idea would necessarily become associated with each other.

B-27   Because the images associated with a central idea are necessarily associated with each other, and because rational men formulate ideas by analogy, poets frequently create new images and ideas through comparison. When one object in a poem is identified with another so that some of the properties of one are associated with the other, then we call the comparison a metaphor; metaphors may demonstrate either *similar* or *dissimilar* properties.

B-28   The object in the metaphor which is of initial importance is called the *tenor;* the element which reflects or illustrates the tenor is called the *vehicle.*

B-29   Metaphors are thus divided into two parts corresponding to the images or objects: the tenor and vehicle. The vehicle reflects on the tenor and provides the means by which we understand the properties of the tenor better.

For example, in the line:

> *My love is like a red, red rose*

the poet is attributing the qualities of the rose to his love, and so the rose becomes the vehicle reflecting on his lover, who is the tenor in the metaphor.

B-30   The tenor and vehicle are not always so clearly stated, and the tenor may not be mentioned at all, only *implied* (B-35). When this occurs the metaphor often becomes obscure, and, if so, finding the tenor will often lead to understanding the poem.

Similes

B-31   When the tenor and vehicle are both stated and are associated by a connecting word such as "like" and "as," then we call the comparison a simile. Similes are metaphors in which both the tenor and vehicle are stated and connected by a comparative word.

Relationship to Images

B-32   Metaphors must contain images, although images need not be metaphorical. For example, there is little poetical advantage in saying, "she is like a tree," because the reader cannot form any specific image for a tree, which is the vehicle of the metaphor. But if the poet says that his love's hair is like wheat fields blowing, then we have some idea about the color and texture of her hair because it is possible to form an image of wheat fields blowing.

Problems with Metaphors

B-33   One of the problems in writing and explicating metaphors is that, in addition to the rigid requirement for acceptable logic, the relationship between the images must be made clear by the context of the poem. However, the poet cannot always work with obvious associations since he is attempting to show the reader something different about life; so metaphors do not always seem consistent with the context.

B-34   Poets frequently work with unusual relationships, and for many readers this seems to imply consistency or a violation of logic, but often the apparent inconsistency is the key to thematic development, as is the case with *conceits* (B-38), and readers should pay close attention to such inconsistencies.

B-35   In addition to working with unusual relationships, the poet may also demand that the reader create an implied metaphor within the vehicle in order to make sense out of the stated metaphor, which further complicates consistency. For example, if the poet says:

her breath is like the smell of fresh cut grass

he does not mean that her breath literally smells like grass. He means, of course, that the smell of fresh cut grass is sweet, or refreshing, or like the spring, or whatever the image implies, and that her breath possesses these qualities.

B-36   The analogy, then, is implied, since the properties of grass and women are not similar. The implication is that since the smell of grass is sweet, and we are told that she is like the grass, then her breath must also be sweet. Frequently, the logic of such a metaphor is unclear, which further complicates the relationship between metaphor and theme.

B-37   So there are two basic problems when explicating metaphor: determining what the tenor and vehicle are, and finding their common properties.

Conceits

B-38   When the analogies involve eccentric or highly intellectualized properties, we call the resulting metaphor a *conceit*, and they can be fully understood only after thorough study and rationalization.

Example/self-check

B-39   For example, with the metaphor:

> *When the evening is spread out against the sky*
> *Like a patient etherized upon a table,*

FROM: THE LOVE SONG OF J. ALFRED PRUFROCK
T. S. ELIOT

the reader must closely examine the association before it can be completely understood. Looking at some of its possibilities, we can form the following kinds of statements:

B-39 (a) Just as a patient who is _____ is under the control of his doctor, the evening (twilight) is controlled by the sun.	etherized
B-39 (b) Just as the patient is deadened in a state between life and death, the evening is between light and _____.	darkness
B-39 (c) Just as the table is the backdrop for the patient, the sky is the backdrop for the _____.	evening
B-39 (d) Since the image of the patient upon a table suggests an operation — suggesting that the patient will be taken apart or dissected — then through this conceit the reader begins to sense that anyone who participates or associates with the evening may also be _____.	dissected
B-39 (e) By understanding the relationship between the patient and the evening as described in analogy statements (a), (b), and (c), above, we will be prepared to take the logic of the conceit one step further and conclude that whoever participates or associates with the _____ has been projected into the role of one being operated upon.	evening
B-39 (f) While the terms of the metaphor make a comparison between the evening and a _____, the point of the analogy seems not directed at a dissection of an evening as a total environment, but at dissection of particular persons or aspects associated with it. Because there is thus more than a direct one-to-one relationship between the elements of this analogy, the metaphor may be considered a _____.	patient conceit

Free Images in Conceits

B-40   In many conceits, especially those found in modern poetry, at least one of the images will be free, with the fixed image defining the free one. That one or both of the images is free (as above, the evening) further complicates the conceit, since we as readers are attempting to find an analogy between them and therefore must first discover their common qualities.

For example, in the lines:

> *Streets that follow like a tedious*
> *argument*
> *Of insidious intent*

FROM: THE LOVE SONG OF J. ALFRED PRUFROCK
T. S. ELIOT

the clearest tenor/vehicle arrangement is not used. Had Eliot said that a tedious argument is like winding, narrow streets, we would have had a fixed image serving as the vehicle, and it would have been easy to understand the metaphor, but as it stands now, we must first understand the vehicle, which is a free image, before we can see what Eliot is getting at.

B-41   It would seem as though the poet would lose control over his readers with conceits which depend heavily on free imagery, but in fact, the opposite usually occurs; the reader will finally come to the association which the poet is seeking, because only there can the reader find the greatest number and "best" common qualities on which to form the basis for the analogy.

Use for Conceits

B-42   Poets commonly use conceits for one of two reasons: (a) to make the reader stop and think about a particular aspect of the poem, thereby focusing on it, and (b) to shock the reader into vivid imagery by showing him an analogy which he may have never before considered.

B-43   The conceit, then, serves as both a focusing and shocking device, but in both cases the conceit must be worked out intellectually by the reader. Obviously, if the poet is using the conceit for shock in order to create vivid imagery, it will also function as a focusing device, although the reverse is not necessarily true. Often, the thematic key to a poem, especially metaphysical poetry, is the conceit.

B-44   Because conceits demand so much attention from the reader, few poems are able to hold more than one or two conceits, unless they are particularly long poems containing complex characters. Another limiting factor on conceits is that good conceits, like good metaphors, are difficult to conceive, and unless the conceit is worked brilliantly, and in the right proportion to theme, character, and situation, readers will consider it absurd or boring. Consequently, good poets are very careful in their use of conceits, so the appearance of a conceit gives the explicator a central place to begin studying theme.

EXTENDED METAPHORS

B-45   Sometimes one metaphor will convey the image which the poet is constructing; at other times the poet may have to pile metaphor upon metaphor in order to fully describe the tenor. When metaphors are piled up so that they run in a series, the vehicle of the former becoming the tenor of the later, we call it an extended metaphor.

B-46   In the following poem, for example; the first word, *she*, is the tenor of the poem; everything else is the vehicle. But within the vehicle there are sub-tenors and vehicles.

> *She is as in a field a silken tent*
> *At midday when a sunny summer breeze*
> *Has dried the dew and all its ropes relent,*
> *So that in guys it gently sways at ease,*
> *And its supporting central cedar pole,*
> *That is its pinnacle to heavenward*
> *And signifies the sureness of the soul,*
> *Seems to owe naught to any single cord,*
> *But strictly held by none, is loosely bound*
> *By countless silken ties of love and thought*
> *To everything on earth the compass round,*
> *And only by one's going slightly taut*
> *In the capriciousness of summer air*
> *Is of the slightest bondage made aware.*

> THE SILKEN TENT
> ROBERT FROST

B-47   Diagramming each metaphor in the poem (refer to page 53 for the diagram) we can see that the poet has taken us through a series of changing tenors and vehicles. The central metaphor of the poem is "she is like a silken tent," but within the basic metaphor is the extended metaphor which shows us how the relationship takes place.

B-48   Had Frost used only the basic metaphor without including the extended metaphor, the relationship between "She" and "tent" would have been more difficult to see because the reader would have had to intellectualize the missing steps. When the poet wishes to avoid a conceit, (B-38) it is possible for him to do so by using an extended metaphor to point out how the analogy is working, although most extended metaphors used for this purpose aren't as long or involved as "The Silken Tent."

B-49   Not all extended metaphors are circular as is the one in "The Silken Tent," and in most instances the change of vehicle to tenor will not be so clear. However, while most extended metaphors are not circular, many of them will have "loop-like" structures within the vehicle in order to give emphasis to a particular association.

B-50   For example, note (in the adjoining diagram showing the metaphorical structure of "The Silken Tent") how Frost's metaphor number 7 "loops around" to return to metaphor number 1. Because a loop of this kind does occur, we should anticipate in the early stages of our explication that an important element in the theme will lie here, since the poet has chosen to emphasize this particular association.

B-51   The term "extended metaphor" has been loosely used to included metaphors which are not technically extended but simply have a number of vehicles which describe the tenor. But if the metaphor is extended, there is a good chance that it will contain a loop, and if it does, it is important to look for theme at that point.

Summary

B-52   The term metaphor simply implies that a comparison is being made, and the types of metaphors which have been standard in poetry — similies, extended metaphors, and conceits — are merely terms to denote the type and degree of complexity of the metaphor.

B-53   Because bad metaphors will ruin a poem, and since good metaphors are so hard to come by, poets normally use care and discretion in choosing metaphors. So whenever any form of metaphor appears, it is probable that the poet considers it vital to developing his theme; therefore metaphors provide a good foundation for explication.

B-54   Determining the complexity of a metaphor and its use in the poem is essential in explication, since the analogy will generally lead to and must be consistent with the theme.

REVERSE METAPHORS

B-55   While most metaphors work with the common properties of images, some work with the excluded properties.

B-56   When the poet draws a comparison between those properties which are exclusive (unalike), he is creating a reverse metaphor. For example, in "The Silken Tent," the soul is *unlike* a single cord. The reverse metaphor functions like the metaphor, except that the association between the images is likely to be clearer. For example, in the line:

> *My mistress' eyes are nothing like the sun*

it is clear how eyes could be compared to the sun while it is not so clear how *she* can be compared to a tent. In other words, before the poet will usually compare dissimilar qualities, he will first make certain that the similar qualities are understood.

B-57   Before reverse metaphors can be successful, the similar qualities of the images must be understood. In "The Silken Tent" the reverse metaphors are clear only because they are in context with the positive metaphors which surround and explain them, while the comparison between the sun and a woman's eyes is clear even out of context. The properties of

METAPHORICAL DIAGRAM OF "THE SILKEN TENT"

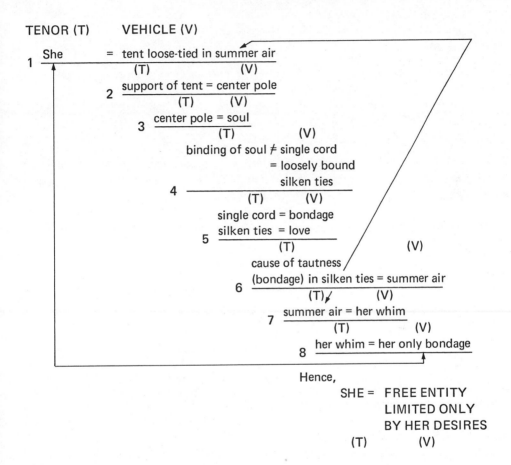

TENOR (T)   VEHICLE (V)

1 $\dfrac{\text{She} \quad = \text{ tent loose-tied in summer air}}{\text{(T)} \qquad\qquad \text{(V)}}$

2 $\dfrac{\text{support of tent} = \text{center pole}}{\text{(T)} \qquad \text{(V)}}$

3 $\dfrac{\text{center pole} = \text{soul}}{\text{(T)} \qquad\qquad \text{(V)}}$

binding of soul $\ne$ single cord
= loosely bound
silken ties

4 $\dfrac{\qquad\qquad\qquad\qquad}{\text{(T)} \qquad \text{(V)}}$

single cord = bondage
silken ties = love

5 $\dfrac{\qquad\qquad}{\text{(T)} \qquad\qquad\qquad \text{(V)}}$

cause of tautness
(bondage) in silken ties = summer air

6 $\dfrac{\qquad\qquad\qquad\qquad}{\text{(T)} \qquad\qquad \text{(V)}}$

7 $\dfrac{\text{summer air} = \text{her whim}}{\text{(T)} \qquad\qquad \text{(V)}}$

8 $\dfrac{\text{her whim} = \text{her only bondage}}{}$

Hence,

SHE = FREE ENTITY
LIMITED ONLY
BY HER DESIRES

(T)   (V)

METAPHORICAL ANALYSIS

She is a tent loose-tied in the summer air. The support of the tent is its center pole. The center pole is the soul. The binding of the soul is not a single cord; rather, it is loosely bound silken ties. The cause of tautness in the silken ties is the summer air. The summer air represents her whim, which is her only bondage. Hence, the poem says that she is a free entity limited only by her desires.

reverse metaphors, then must either be inherently similar, or made similar by the context before their reverse properties become clear.

◀▮▮▶ IMAGERY AS A STRUCTURAL DEVICE: CONTROLLING METAPHORS

B-58   Just as a poem may include as structural devices form, theme, action, or dramatic situation, it may also use imagery for structure. When an image does exist which runs throughout the poem, giving unity to smaller images or ideas, it is called a controlling image, and functions as an important structural device. Controlling metaphors are important to the explicator because the central idea usually develops out of or parallel to it.

B-59   Notice how, in the following poem, the imagery in each stanza revolves around weaving. While the cloth is being woven, the soul, metaphorically, is becoming complete and finished, so that by the end of the poem the woven product is not cloth spun from thread and dyed, but a pure soul spun from understanding, good will, and affections. The controlling metaphor binds the stanzas together structurally, evolving the theme at the same time.

> Make me, O Lord, thy Spinning Wheele compleate.
>   Thy Holy Worde my Distaff make for mee.
> Make mine Affections thy Swift Flyers neate
>   And make my Soule thy holy Spoole to bee.
>   My Conversation make to be thy Reele
>   And reele the yarn thereon spun of thy Wheele.
>
> Make me thy Loome then, knit therein this Twine:
>   And make thy Holy Spirit, Lord, winde quills:
> Then weave the Webb thyselfe. The yarn is fine.
>   Thine Ordinances make my Fulling Mills.
>   Then dy the same in Heavenly Colours Choice,
>   All pinkt with varnisht Flowers of Paradise.
>
> Then cloath therewith mine Understanding, Will,
>   Affections, Judgement, Conscience, Memory
> My Words, and Actions, that their shine may fill
>   My wayes with glory and thee glorify.
>   Then mine apparell shall display before yee
>   That I am Cloathd in Holy robes for glory.

HUSWIFERY
EDWARD TAYLOR

Example/self-check

B-60 Using only the imagery presented in the following fragment, describe in prose what the images depict, and determine whether the images are free or fixed, what the poet wants the reader to get from the imagery, how the metaphors function, and whether there is a controlling image.

> Now winter downs the dying of the year,
> And night is all a settlement of snow;
> From the soft street the rooms of houses show   3
> A gathered light, a shapen atmosphere,
> Like frozen-over lakes whose ice is thin
> And still allows some stirring down within.   6
>
> I've known the wind by water banks to shake
> The late leaves down, which frozen where they fell
> And held in ice as dancers in a spell   9
> Fluttered all winter long into a lake;
> Graved on the dark in gestures of descent,
> They seemed their own most perfect monument.   12

FROM: YEAR'S END
RICHARD WILBUR

B-60 (1)   The suggestion of a dying year may arouse some individual associations, but if so they are highly personalized and beyond the poem's control, thereby making the image completely _____ .

free (B-9)

B-60 (2)   Beginning with line 2, the poem is rich with imagery, line 2 itself suggesting at least two images:
(a) The snow and the night have become one, each containing the qualities of the other so that one cannot tell where the night ends and the _____ begins; there is no horizon, only a mixture of black and white, matter and nothingness.

snow

(b) The night and snow have become a *settlement*; i.e. they seem to have a kind of body or substance which has _____ upon the community, engulfing it in a protective manner (and with *winter downs* in line 1, there is a suggestion of a nesting, down-feathered, bird-like body).

settled down

B-60 (3)   Line 2 constitutes both a metaphor (night =
_____) and an image in which the metaphor becomes an image itself rather than remaining two separate
images.

snow

B-60 (4)   Line 3 conveys the image of the settled snow
on the _____ ; we feel the snow beneath our feet
as we stand looking into the lighted houses, and perhaps
see the fluff as it scatters while we walk.

street

B-60 (5)   The image from the street is both *mixed* and
free. We probably imagine other qualities about the night
as we stand in it, or as we remember having stood in a
cold night somewhere during our lives. Perhaps we see a
street light which illuminates the falling snow, or feel the
snow blowing against our faces, but we are outside the
world within the _____ atmosphere.

shapen

B-60 (6)   The houses and the people in them are on
display for us — they live in an atmosphere shaped for
them by shelter, heat, boundaries — while we are looking
at them from our seemingly unshaped _____ of
snow, cold, and dark, and whatever else the free images
have permitted.

atmosphere

B-60 (7)   We look at them through windows as they
move within, just as we peer at the marine life through
the _____ (line 6).

ice

B-60 (8)   The world beneath the water is like the
world within the houses — bound by time, space, and
nature. There is some _____ (line 6) down within,
but whatever freedom there is has been allowed by
some greater force.

stirring

B-60 (9)   The metaphoric comparison between the
world below the ice and the world within the _____
_____ attempts to make the reader feel a sense of
awesomeness; just as nature can freeze the lake, some
greater force can freeze the world.

shapen
atmosphere

B-60 (10)   With stanza 2 the image moves from the
settlement of snow to the _____ where the late
leaves fell and froze, but the overall controlling image
is still that of preservation through ice.

lake

B-60 (11)   Although the images change in stanza 2, there is still a _____ image which is that of pre-servation.

controlling

B-60 (12)   The fallen leaves, held where they fell by their icy weight, are motionless, like _____ who are spellbound in their art.

dancers

B-60 (13)   The graceful halting of nature is once again compared with the halting of _____ in the metaphor equating the leaves with dancers.

man

B-60 (14)   The image in the last two lines is one of burial; the lake, which is the shapen atmosphere for the leaves engulfs them in a tomb, just as the night _____ the human atmosphere in stanza 1.

engulfed

B-60 (15)   The image in stanza 2 forms the monu-ment to the _____, and because the metaphor is so strong between the atmospheres in both stanzas, the reader cannot help wondering what his own monu-ment will be and the image of an all-encompassing universe begins to permeate the poem.

leaves

For a partial explication of imagery and allusion, see the critical essay following Frame M-26 of James Dickey's "In the Mountain Tent."

◄▌▌► A STUDENT EXPLICATION

Imagery in "Year's End" by Richard Wilbur

by John W. Metzger

Wilbur begins his poem in a rather customary manner with the creation of his first prevailing image. The snow image conveys the state or quality of existence unspoiled by time or use: downs *in line 1 initiates an image which Wilbur later complements in line 2 with* the settlement of snow. *The* down; *i.e., the soft fine feathers of a young bird, compares most favorably to the fresh snow still falling at the time. The metaphorical manner in which he casts the image is definitely an asset to the success and effectiveness of the image. Later he gives added emphasis to the metaphor with the* thin ice *in line 5. The* thin ice *is also quite suggestive of the season, winter, which has not yet exerted the full force of its potential. As the year is slowly ending, the image also suggests the diametrical opposition of the natural passage of time to the man-observed year.*

With the use of soft street *in line 3, Wilbur manages to create an almost mystic, dream-like atmosphere. It is from this vague and soothing, seemingly interminable perspective that the persona views the light harboring in nearby houses. The responses evoked by* gathered light *and* shapen atmosphere *are those of security and shelter. The houses and the events which occur within them are ablivious or indifferent to the falling snow intermingled with eternal darkness.*

Wilbur continues by effectively utilizing another metaphor in lines 5 and 6. The metaphor suggests the similarities between the shapen atmospheres *of the houses and the aura which pervades the area beneath the ice, which is much like a window. It is not all-encompassing, but acts merely as a temporary boundary between the* shapen atmospheres *and time. Time, however, could at any moment erase or erode these artificial boundaries. The metaphor depicts the security created by the* shapen atmospheres *as false.*

Just as Wilbur has pointed out the similarities existing between the two areas, the metaphor is extended to the people who exist in their houses, much like the creatures who inhabit the water. The people, then, are also subject to change as well as are the dwellings which they inhabit. Just as ice may form and melt, glass may be structured or broken.

Wilbur begins stanza two by applying two solidly fixed images within a metaphor. The leaves twirl and flutter from their perches upon the trees, and because they are late to fall, they become fixed within the ice when it forms. The leaves are perfectly preserved in the crystalline ice, creating an image much like a ballet dancer who strikes a fixed pose in the intense shaft of light projected by the spots. They are a perfect monument to their previous existence, yet while they are being preserved temporarily in the ice their state is quite purgatorial, in that it resembles a punishment for their remaining intact on the trees out of season.

Stanza 3 makes use of simple implied metaphors to suggest the inherent similarities between the deaths and plights of the small delicate ferns and the large, omnipotent mammoths. Both expired in an abrupt and untimely manner. There also is a portrayal of likeness between the changeless lands of ice *and the ashes which covered Pompeii. Both the ashes and the ice entombed a creature which was totally unaware of the impending disaster. Like the leaves, their unawareness is also punished by an extended purgatorial existence before their final descent.*

The organic images portrayed in the poem are all "shapen" by similar phenomenal occurences. The images which are acted upon share the characteristics of organic matter; they have all experienced unheralded disasters, and they have all perished.

Through the use of a controlling metaphor, i.e., the idea of unawareness and complacency, Wilbur is relating the plights of other living creatures, big and small, thinking and merely existing, and an actual sector of the human race, to the plight of all men.

He also emphasizes the horror involved in entering such an abysmal existence through the images aroused in random hands *and* loose, unready eyes. *His use of* sun *in line 23 also seems to suggest that the men of Pompeii were quite complacent creatures. The sun not only serves as a daily counterpart to life, but also to all civilizations as the very essence of eternity.*

The phrase shapely things *in line 24 is capable of creating multiple images. The men of Pompeii were in need of another day, more time, doubtlessly to continue to be unprepared and indifferent to forces which at any time could claim them. This is the first image used by Wilbur to convey a bleak outlook for the future.*

In stanza 5 Wilbur is calling upon us to create images for ourselves. We must look at the sudden ends *which have claimed so much in the past, and envision such an occurence stopping ourselves. He utilizes another metaphor, a rope dangling, to symbolize existence. The very essence of life is that rope dangling loosely. His warning to us is also conveyed in an intricately clever manner. As tapestries are woven quite skillfully, so we must weave the rope, our lives, keeping it taut at all times. Then we can complete those tasks which the men of Pompeii were never able to do.*

The recurring images of snow and the New Year again turn our attention to the shapen atmospheres. Just as anything organic in the poem ignored time and was conquered by it, so time quietly passes over the New Year accompanied by the infinite snow and darkness.

The muffled radio suggests a medium which is not capable of transmitting a message, yet cannot, or will not, be tuned in. From the radio come the muffled yet learned voices of all who have passed on before and never had the opportunity to weave the rope or do the shapely things. *Unfortunately, they are crying out a message from a muted tomb.*

◀▐▌▶ Symbol

When *images* (B-1 ff) take on meanings which are not inherent to their sensual qualities, then they can become symbols, contributing to theme in ways different from images or metephors. Determining the poet's use of symbol is sometimes not easy, especially in modern poetry when poets not only use traditional symbols but may also create obscure symbolism of their own. The first problem for the explicator is recognizing that a symbol is being used; then it is determining the symbol's source and implications, and finally relating it to the theme of the poem.

C-1   When a poet evokes an image, he is asking the reader to imagine a sensuous scene; i.e., the reader is expected in his imagination to see, hear, smell, taste, or feel the presence of physical objects.

C-2   When Wilbur writes:

> From the soft street the rooms of houses show
> A gathered light, a shapen atmosphere,
> Like frozen-over lakes whose ice is thin
> And still allows some stirring down within.

he clearly demands that the reader see the snow, lights and houses, and feel the cold and the slow stirring down within; perhaps he is also demanding an image of quietness which is associated with the calm of snow.

C-3   All these things are related to the image being formed, and the reader, through his own experience — either actual or intellectual — projects himself into the scene.

C-4   The image may arouse particular emotions for the reader which will affect his interpretation of the image. For example, if the reader associates snow with sleigh rides, then whenever the image of snow is evoked the reader will envision lightheartedness until the poem forces him to dismiss that notion. But the reader's emotion, whether consistent with the poet's use of the image or not, is part of and influences the way the reader perceives the image. However, the image does not take the place of the emotion, although one may remain after the other is gone. Indeed, arousing an emotion through the use of an image, then dismissing the image but allowing the emotion to remain throughout the poem is a subtle technique which brilliant poetry achieves.

C-5   If the poet can create a strong enough emotion which the reader will feel throughout the poem, without a continuation of the image which aroused it, then he can play against it, using it as a base almost as he uses as *base meter* (D-29) for *counterpoint* (D-62, H-32) and *emphasis* (D-17).

C-6   Assuming the image does not replace or displace the emotion, but arouses emotion so that it remains, then the poet can use the emotion as a base and play further ideas against it, thereby creating complementary or conflicting emotions which give emphasis to his theme. However, if the image with its associated emotions comes to stand for something else which has an entirely different set of connotations and emotions, then the image becomes a *symbol*.

C-7   If, for example, in "Year's End" the metaphors of the frozen lake and the slow stirring come to stand for man's fragility, then the image is a *symbol* in addition to being an image, and an entire new set of associations arise. Everything which the reader has ever considered about mortality, death, preservation; also everything that he might recall about fish being frozen in blocks of ice, or the Ice Age; all this will become part of the symbol although it is not a part of the image.

C-8   Symbols, then, do not replace images but work in addition to them, and because the symbol does embody such vast connotations, symbolism can add dimension and richness to the theme, both emotionally and intellectually, when it can be focused and controlled.

C-9   An image, therefore, may be working on two levels, as an image and as a symbol, developing the poem in two different but consistent ways. If there is conflict between the image and symbol it must be for a reason, which is usually to demonstrate a conflict within the theme.

C-10   Notice how the image in the following lines progresses into symbol:

> *I am hearing the shape of the rain*
> *Take the shape of the tent and believe it,*

> FROM: IN THE MOUNTAIN TENT
> JAMES DICKEY

The dramatic situation is that the persona is in a tent listening to the rain as it runs down the canvas. The image is formed because of an intermingling of sound and sight; the taut canvas allows the narrator to hear every trickle of water, and because the rain does follow the curves of the tent the water takes the same shape. What we begin to see is a tent of water; the canvas overhead seems to disappear so that the narrator feels enclosed in the water, not in the tent. Because the image in the context of the poem does make the reader feel enclosed, almost submerged, the image enlarges itself to make us feel that our enclosure in water is something like baptismal submersion, and once this link is formed between the image and the enlarged image, the rain becomes symbolic of the baptismal ritual and all of its religious connotations. While the image of the tent in the rain does not disappear, the image does become symbolic when the reader begins to associate the water image in the tent with the water image of the baptismal ritual, and once the reader forms this metaphor the image becomes significant on several levels.

The image, then, suggests the symbol, and in this example, it is necessary before the symbol is possible.

Developing Symbols

C-11   The formation of an image is limited by the senses. For example, the image of a rose is restricted to the physical characteristics of the rose; we can place it in its various stages in a variety of situations, but we are still restricted by what the rose can physically be.

C-12   Because images are sensory responses they are restricted by how our senses can regard them. The physical characteristics of the object trigger the senses which perceive it, and when a word suggests that image, we associate physical properties with it. The physical characteristics of the rose become part of the image, along with our associated emotions at the time we perceived it, but nothing else is included.

C-13   A symbol, on the other hand, is not restricted or limited in what it can become because it relies on intellectualization of the image rather than on sensation. The rose, for example, is restricted to what its physical properties are as an image, but as a symbol it can stand for love, or beauty, or God, or virginity; or for that matter, the moon, or death, or society, or anything else. Whatever the poet and reader are willing to agree upon can become intellectual properties associated with the image, and while the image usually suggests the symbolic properties; e.g. the rose symbolizing beauty, it does not have to.

C-14   We can say that images are formed by the senses while symbols are created by by the mind, and whatever the poet and reader agree upon can become symbolic.

◀❙❘❚▶ TRADITIONAL SYMBOLS

C-15   Symbols, then, are established by consensus, and are valid only when understood. Consequently, many symbols have become symbols through many years of use in which the symbolic properties were slowly evolved and established by consensus. Some images, for example, have become symbols through their use in religion and folklore. The cross, for instance, was once part of the image of the crucifixion, and as it came to stand for the religious implications associated with the crucifixion, people agreed through common usage what the symbol could stand for.

C-16   Symbols which evolve out of religion or folklore, or out of natural imagery, such as the tide (which symbolizes, among other things, time and eternity), become symbols by the consensus of a large number of people who frequently come in contact with particular associations of the image which produced the symbol.

C-17   Symbols which have grown out of common usage, like the cross, or out of common understanding, like the tide, or which have been used frequently enough so that every reasonably informed reader will recognize them are usually referred to as *traditional symbols.*

C-18   A cross, for example, has come to symbolize the Christian ideal because it has been used for that purpose for a long time, while the tide symbolizes eternity because most people feel that response when they see the ocean. There is common understanding in the image since so many people have noted the never-ending cyclic recurrence of the sea. Symbols which arise out of natural imagery, whether traditional or non-traditional (C-24), are sometimes referred to as natural symbols. *Natural traditional symbols* (seasons, gardens, tides, the sun) tend to permit the poet much more flexibility than the more fixed symbols representing ideals (anchor of hope, the cross, the crown, etc.).

C-19   Traditional symbols, then, have been so frequently used in a particular way that it is difficult for the poet to change their usage. The cross, for example, will always carry Christian associations no matter what the poet does to dispel them.

Use for Emphasis

C-20   Traditional symbols will evoke traditional associations which the poet cannot dispel; thus, whenever the poet uses a traditional symbol, he does so knowing the reader's response.

C-21   Although traditional symbols evoke traditional responses, the poet may not be using his symbol in the same sense that it was originated. The cross, for example, traditionally brings to mind the passion and beauty of Christian suffering and forbearance, and the poet may be using it for this purpose. But he might just as easily be using it as a base for counterpointing or for satire.

C-22   Another use for traditional symbolism, apart from its traditional use, is to comment on the myth from which the symbol is derived. In other words, the poet uses a symbol which represents the myth, and then comments on the myth rather than using the myth to comment on something else.

C-23   Although there must be an understanding between poet and reader before a symbol becomes valid, traditional symbols no longer have the force that they once possessed in the hands of Dante, Shakespeare, Milton and many others. One of the reasons for this, of course, is that the traditional symbols were used so well that they have now become platitudes rather than meaningful concepts, and poets will not use them in their commonly accepted symbolic sense. Poetry which depended upon traditional symbols has not survived except in rare instances (and in books which are dear to little old ladies' hearts); so when we find them in serious poetry, there is a good chance that they are being used for satire or because the myth from which they were derived remains important. But for most poetry, especially modern poetry, traditional symbolism will not be used at all.

NON-TRADITIONAL SYMBOLS

C-24   If poets refuse to use commonly accepted symbols, then they must create some substitute to take the place of traditional symbols. The problem with non-traditional symbols, however, is that readers do not inherently understand them. Since a symbol can work only when there is a consensus of meaning between poet and reader, the poet must create his own symbols, using the context of the poem to make them clear.

C-25   While the properties of traditional symbols find consensus through common usage or understanding, non-traditional symbols find consensus through the context into which they are placed. In "Year's End," for example, the leaves in the ice become symbolic of preservation — a symbol which is in itself fairly traditional. However, it is the context which shapes the full dimensions of this symbol; otherwise, the ice in Wilbur's poem would be the same as the ice, for example, in Dante's inferno.

C-26   In order to create fresh, unique, appropriate symbols, poets have come to reply on academic symbols as well as those which arise out of tradition and natural imagery.

C-27   With cultural symbols (those arising out of events) the image which once accompanied the symbol may have dropped out; e.g., with the cross the image of the crucifixion is not necessary for the symbol to be understood.

C-28   With traditional symbols the image may or may not remain with the symbol, as with the tide; but with non-traditional natural symbols, such as leaves preserved in ice, the image will accompany the symbol. However, with academic or intellectual symbols (a type of non-traditional symbol) there are no accompanying images as there are with the other two types, because the symbol stands for an abstract concept. For example, with the atom, which has come to symbolize the progressiveness of the age, there is little or no imagistic connection between the object and the symbolized concepts.

C-29   Poetry which uses academic symbolism strives to force the reader to consider intellectual rather than sensual concepts, although one may lead to the other. When explicating, it is sometimes helpful to determine the type of symbol being used in order to establish the type of reaction the poet is expecting from his reader. Anticipating the expected reaction may in turn lead to an understanding of how the poet hopes to control the reaction.

Determining Non-traditional Symbols

C-30   Because they create their own base for consensus, non-traditional symbols can be used without regard for traditional symbolic practices. As a result, those poets taking great liberties with non-traditional symbols have generated much confusion, frustration, and misunderstanding because of their use of modern symbolism. Deciding what is being used symbolically and how far it can be taken is a major task for the explicator. Readers should be suspicious of almost every word in the poem, and attempt to see its symbolic possibilities.

C-31   Although every word in a modern poem is potentially the basis for an image that may become a symbol, the reader should be "tough" and accept nothing as a symbol unless it will prove consistent with the overall theme of the poem. If it looks as though a word or image may become a symbol standing for a concept beyond the literal meaning, the reader should attempt to fit the symbolized concept into the overall theme. If there is some possibility for a symbolized meaning in that context, even if it is not a "perfect fit," the possibility should not be dismissed.

Thus, because almost all words have potential for use as symbols in some kind of context, readers must remain skeptical of each possibility until it proves to add meaning and depth to the poem. On the other hand, the reader must be open-minded enough to accept various levels of interpretation once he has accepted that symbolism is valid within the poem.

C-32   Since symbols become meaningful when a reader can understand them and find identity with them, some readers will find symbols where others won't, and many unhappy arguments have been perpetrated, and many poems destroyed for readers, through elaborated symbolic interpretation.

C-33   One example of a symbolic dispute is over a Freudian interpretation of *Hamlet*. After the publication of Freud's work showing the relationship between sex and symbols, a number of critics applied Freudian symbols to the play and produced a new level of meaning, (and this did prove consistent with the earlier interpretations). But the idea of seeing *Hamlet* in sexual terms shocked so many people that there was immediate reaction against it.

C-34   This type of reaction, combined with modern poetry's liberal and sometimes invalid use of and dependency upon symbols, has created concern and distrust for symbolic interpretation, even to the point that satirists have interpreted "Jack and Jill' and "Little Red Riding Hood" in sexual symbolic terms to demonstrate the absurdity of symbolism.

C-35   Thus the conscientious explicator must examine all the possibilities for symbols and search for those which may not be obvious without using symbolism as a crutch for his explication. But at the same time, since no poem can exist by symbol alone, and since symbols are used only to enrich poetry, not to create it, the explication cannot be centered on a purely symbolic interpretation. Yet, clearly, symbolism does add meaning and importance to a poem, and the explicator must open up any prospects which the poem might contain by considering all aspects of the symbol.

C-36   Although explicating symbolism is difficult, there are some rules which will help. Notice the approach to explicating symbolism in the following example.

> *Does the Eagle know what is in the pit?*
> *Or wilt thou go ask the Mole?*
> *Can Wisdom be put in a silver Rod?*
> *Or Love in a golden Bowl?*

FROM: THE BOOK OF THEL
WILLIAM BLAKE

C-36 (a)   Since a great number of symbols are created by nouns, the first step is to look at all the nouns and their associated adjectives. In the example the seven nouns are: Eagle, pit, Mole, Wisdom, Rod, Love, and Bowl.

C-36 (b)   If the poet has not given many clues as to what the nouns might symbolize, as in the example, then we as readers and explicators should make a list of all possibilities, and re-examine the symbol as the poem progresses; as the poet begins to involve the symbol into his theme, we will be able to eliminate some of the possibilities.

C-36 (c)   Looking at the example again, we can list some of the obvious symbolic possibilities for the nouns.

Eagle: power, freedom, holiness, God, arrogance, fate, majesty, immortality.

Pit: hell, evil, death, decay, vagina, earth, trap.

Mole: creature of earth (in contrast to the eagle which is a creature of the skies), humility, destruction, filth, blindness, narrowmindedness.

silver Rod: power, authority, enslavement, phallus.

golden Bowl: purity, beauty, vagina, holiness, Baptismal font, confinement.

Wisdom;   Abstract ideas like these become the concepts for which symbols stand, and they are seldom symbols themselves although something such as hate may connote, but not be a symbol for, evil.

C-36 (d)   Obviously not all the possibilities in our list will apply to the poem, and we will certainly discover more as the poet creates them for us, but by beginning with a fairly complete list on this level, we can at least begin to understand what may have seemed nonsense before.

C-37   Since symbols are concrete things representing concepts, the nouns which denote concepts are not themselves symbols but may lead the reader to the symbols. *Wisdom* and *Love* in "Thel's Motto," for example, are nouns, but they are not symbols because they are already abstractions. Only concrete nouns are normally used for symbols.

C-38   Symbols which are not nouns usually stem from images or metaphors, and any time a poem emphasizes sensory response the explicator should be on the alert for symbols. Colors, for example, are particularly symbolic, since people respond so strongly to them.

C-39   Occasionally, words which act as though they might be symbols do not function as such but function as implications; i.e., they imply but do not symbolize. Whiskey, for example, may be used to imply that a given character is a dissolute or a bum, but it does not symbolize evil *until* the poet chooses to explore the concept relative to that theme. *Implication,* then, is not yet symbol, because it has not presented to the poem a complete concept which can be explored; its function is to give breadth, not depth, to the dramatic situation.

C-40   A symbol must be directly related to the theme or else it remains an image or implication, which may enhance the poem without changing the level of interpretation. Possibilities for symbols do not become symbols until they directly affect the theme, at which time they will add a new level of interpretation to the poem, but a level which must be consistent with the other levels.

REINFORCING SYMBOLS

C-41   Since non-traditional symbols must be created within the poem's full context, it is likely that the symbolic level of interpretation will be consistent with the more literal level. This likelihood serves us as a good check when we are deciding what is functioning as symbol. If the symbol possibility does not fit comfortably, it should not be forced unless it is certain that the symbol adds a valid dimension to the theme.

C-42   Once the poet has established a symbol, he will reinforce it with other symbols or images, or he will begin changing the symbol in order to show how the change relates to the theme. Symbols are never randomly introduced into the poem, and they will always be reinforced by other symbols or images.

C-43   Although they will always be reinforced, symbols may or may not remain constant throughout the poem, and it is possible that the symbol will change abruptly or gradually by thematic development. In either case the concept for which the symbol stands is likely to appear again, and if it does, it is important to the explication because a comparison can be made between the first appearance and the second, and the comparison will reflect on thematic development.

C-44   As with meter, (D-1 ff), pattern is a key to understanding how symbol works in a poem, and the pattern of symbolic development should run parallel to dramatic development. Normally there is a controlling symbol just as there may be a controlling image, (B-58) around which other symbols and images will work.

C-45   In the following stanza, let us carefully describe the dramatic situation, (A-1), list the images (B-1), and then discuss all possibilities for symbol (C-1) or implication (C-39).

> *"Is there anybody there?" said the Traveller,*
> *Knocking on the moonlit door;*
> *And his horse in the silence champed the grasses*   3
> *Of the forest's ferny floor:*
> *And a bird flew up out of the turret,*
> *Above the Traveller's head:*   6
> *And he smote upon the door again a second time;*
> *"Is anybody there?" he said.*

FROM: THE LISTENERS
WALTER de la MARE

C-45 (1)   Apparently the Traveller has ridden through the forest and has arrived at some sort of castle, where he is knocking on the door. His horse is waiting impatiently, champing the grasses around the castle. The Traveller speaks out to anyone who might be inside; he has knocked and spoken out twice. Only his voice, the knocking, the horse's champing, and the bird break the silence of the forest.

C-45 (2)   The images in this stanza are free, but since most readers' experience of moonlit castles in the forest come out of fiction, the image and the scene probably produce an atmosphere of mystery and suspense. With very little description, the images are basically free, yet they produce a fairly clear picture of the scene, since the author can probably assume that most readers share the same idea of castles in the forest.

C-45 (3)   There are a number of potentially vivid images which seem mysterious and suspenseful even though they have not been described as such:

the door: Reflecting ominously in the moonlight, the door is heavy, and is probably ornate with great hinges and latches to keep people out. It will probably creak when opened, perhaps by a doorman or guard.

the sounds: We hear the knocking and champing echoing through the forest, and the Traveller's voice haunts the scene. When the bird flies out of the turret we hear the flapping of his frantic wings.

the forest: Thick with trees; deep and dark but not a jungle; there are no paths through the forest. The Traveller may have been guided by spirits and wasn't lost when he found the castle.

the castle: Large and deserted, it probably is a maze of cobwebs inside and has spirits which haunt it. The turret might have once been a prison or place of confinement for a member of a royal family who lived there, but it has long been abandoned so that birds now build nests here. Most likely the bird is a bat or owl or some kind of night bird who inhabits the castle with the spirits.

the Traveller: The horse and the word "smote" suggest that he is some kind of knight, and while we are not given an image of swords and armor, the scene taken as a whole may evoke this idea. On the other hand, knights are not generally referred to as "travellers," so it may be difficult to form an image of him at this point in the poem. In any event, he is determined and pounds hard on the door.

the horse: If the traveller is indeed a knight, his horse is probably a heavy charger, all decked out in armour and fancy trimmings.

C-45 (4)   The poem is full of symbolic possibilities, and although it is easy to be trapped by such blatant symbolism, it is a good idea to list everything which might apply and eliminate later.

Traveller: mutability, vulnerability, unrest, purpose, lack of purpose, Christ, Childe Harold, stranger, searcher.

door: barrier, divider, way to the other world, secret of life.

castle: place of the dead, past civilization, artifact of man, other world, afterlife, spirit of mystery, abode of truth.

forest: artifact, gateway to the spirits, place of the spirits, barrier between men and spirits; the grasses could symbolize abandoned civilization and cultivation.

moon: mystery, suspense, partial illumination

bird and horse: link to the spirits (they know more than man; the bird could possess a good or evil spirit, the horse and bird could be symbolic counterparts since one feels comfortable and the other doesn't).

knocking: desire, fear, death, moment of departure, search.

second time: (Leading to the third time?) — betrayal, the crucifixion, futility, insistence, perseverance.

C-45 (5)   The reader-explicator's decision to develop an interpretation based on any of these possibilities or implications, or to accept any of these as a presentation of a poetic symbol, will depend completely on their reinforcement in further portions of the complete poem. As these or new possibilities are more fully developed, the explicator will be able to review more possible connections among the many thematic threads building up here, and so arrive at a coherent and consistent approach to interpreting key symbols as they are embodied in the total experience of this poem.

◀▐▐▶ A STUDENT EXPLICATION

Robert Frost's Use of Symbol in "After Apple-Picking"

by Doug Schroeder

In "After Apple-Picking," Frost's copious use of poetic device is dominated by symbol, the most important single poetic device employed by Frost in this poem. It becomes necessary, then, to center any complete explication of this poem around Frost's use of symbol, and to seek to comprehend this poem in light of this usage.

In recognizing and comprehending the many symbols in "After Apple-Picking," the reader is able to form an intelligent, concise, yet almost totally abstract opinion of what Frost attempts to convey to the reader. Although many of Frost's symbols are traditional, the reader is not compelled to compute traditional "symbolic equations." Through Frost's unique use of symbol, the reader may use his imagination to guide him through "After Apple-Picking."

As is the case in the majority of Frost's poetry, most of the nouns in "After Apple-Picking" become symbols, creating an abstract image or idea from a physical image.

For the narrator, the long two-pointed ladder sticking through a tree/Toward heaven still *is the vehicle from which he lived and the vehicle from which he would hope to live after death. The* two-pointed ladder *also suggests to the reader an image of outstretched arms, reaching toward heaven. Although not necessarily a Christian symbol, this is the first religious symbol to appear in the poem and precedes other traditional Christian and non-Christian symbols.*

The apple plays an important role as a symbol in "After Apple-Picking." For Frost, the actual time spent picking apples represents his mortal life, his physical years as a mortal. The physical presence of apples and the memory of those apples also represent to the narrator his failures and achievements. For example, in line three there is a barrel of apples which he didn't fill, probably something which the narrator feels he left unfinished. In line five the apples left unpicked upon some bough may be those goals which the narrator has not achieved. In lines thirty and thirty-one, the reader realizes the many challenges which the narrator faced and the passion with which he set about to accomplish them in the statement, "There were ten thousand thousand fruit to touch,/Cherish in hand, lift down, and not let fall."

Frost's religious tone is revealed to the reader if he chooses to interpret apples and apple-picking as religious symbols. Traditionally, the apple and apple-picking represent the fall of mankind into a mortal existence. When Adam and Eve picked the forbidden fruit, they and mankind were forever banished from the Garden of Eden. If apple-picking represents the narrator's life, is it possible that Frost views death, or after apple-picking, as a form of banishment from the garden? Because Frost may use apples either as traditional religious symbols, or as non-traditional symbols of achievement and failure, or both, the final possibilities of this symbol are still not completely clear.

Another important symbol appears in lines nine through twelve. Looking through a pane of glass (in this case a sheet of ice skimmed from the drinking trough) is a traditional symbol for seeing things on a conceptual rather than real level. Frost, after seeing the "World of hoary grass," or the natural world, in conceptual terms, cannot rub this new vision from his eyes, even after the icy pane of glass melts, falls and breaks, even after reality again presents itself to his sight.

Apples again appear in lines eighteen and nineteen, but this time in Frost's dreaming. As part of his past, apples appear in minute detail and disappear in his restless, troubled sleep.

In lines twenty-four through thirty-six, the reader again discerns the weariness in Frost's tone. Through symbol, the poet expresses the magnitude of his weariness. It seems there were thousands of moments in the poets life that he could grasp and cherish. Those moments which were not firmly grasped by the poet were lost to him as of no worth; the apples were symbolically spiked with stubble. It is important to note, however, that the apples did not go to the cider heap, worthless, but "as of no worth." Even though these apples were symbolically lost to Frost, the knowledge and experience gained in the loss were retained by the poet.

The woodchuck is probably one of the most important single symbols in "After Apple-Picking." Interpreting the woodchuck symbolically is a key to a total comprehension of the poem. Although the woodchuck appears on the surface as a nontraditional religious symbol, it is important that this symbol be fully understood. As a religious symbol, the woodchuck may be a Christ figure. "Were he not gone," communication and understanding of death would be possible to the poet, also the knowledge of what sleep to expect.

What is hidden beneath the religious qualities of the woodchuck symbol and the entire poem is the meaning Frost so subtly concealed with the obvious. Frost uses the woodchuck to refute traditional Christian symbols which he has seduced the reader into accepting throughout the poem. In reality, the woodchuck cannot conceive of death because he lacks imagination. Therefore his sleep is only sleep, and it is only through imagination that man can conceive of death. But just as the reader used his imagination to "miscreate" symbols, so all men may misinterpret their lives to establish conceptions about death. Thus "After Apple-Picking" becomes a poem about imagination, not a moralistic statement about living life to its fullest, and this is the theme that is revealed to the careful reader at the end of the poem through the rather thick crust of religious symbolism.

THE EMOTIONAL TOOLS

Meter

Rhythm is heavily influenced by the internal maneuvering of the *line* (I-1ff), and it is essential that readers trying to understand *meter* should refer to the sections which discuss the *foot* (D-60ff and H-1ff) and *caesura* (I-8ff).

RHYTHM IN LIFE AND IN ART

D-1   For most of mankind, lives are defined by the passing of time which leads to a physical death, and the common, primal instinct which all men share is that all respond in some way to that passing. Our lives and civilizations are a result of our typical modes of response.

D-2   One of the manifestations of our response to passing time is rhythm. Our bodily movements and intellectual perceptions are somehow in tune, or out of tune, with some kind of primal rhythm. How well we imitate the flow of time as we perceive it, and how we find some harmony with it, will in part determine our happiness. Rhythm is an essential element in man's life because it gives order — a framework — to the passing of time, and man will create rhythm in nature where there is none in order to preserve his sanity.

D-3   Rhythm in art attempts to imitate rhythm in nature. The type of art form — painting, sculpture, prose, poetry, music, dance — will determine the type and extent of imitation possible. Art imitates the passing of time in a response which we call rhythm.

Rhythm in Literature

D-4   Written art forms — prose and poetry — are able to combine the rhythm of nature (imitating natural rhythm in its language) with the meaning of words. In prose, meaning is more important than rhythm, with most of the emphasis in prose resulting from the connotative and denotative use of words rather than their sound. In poetry, the meaning and rhythm are inseparable, and rhythm is essential to any understanding of meaning. Both of the written art forms are dependent upon rhythm to convey meaning, but in poetry the rhythm is absolutely essential.

FROM PROSE TO POETRY

D-5   When rhythm is closely associated with meaning, it is frequently difficult to distinguish between or clearly separate meaning and rhythm. When this association is close, but not quite inseparable, the result is called *prose-poetry*. It is possible to say that the meaning in prose-poetry is *partially* dependent upon the rhythm.

D-6   Usually, the rhythm in prose-poetry is closely associated with the voice of emotion or passion. Because rhythm conveys emotion the more emotional the voice becomes in prose-poetry, the more likely it is to rely on rhythm.

D-7   In the following example of prose-poetry, rhythm is used extensively, and the result is that the narrating voice conveys considerable emotion.

> *And light came and went and came again —*
> *but now not quite the same as it had*
> *done before. The boy saw the pattern of*
> *familiar shapes and knew that they were*
> *just the same as they had always been.*

FROM: THE LOST BOY

THOMAS WOLFE

If the first sentence of this prose-poetry passage had been written: "Light was present, then it disappeared, then came again," the narrating voice would have sounded more matter-of-fact, and less emotional, whereas emotion or passion in this Wolfe passage is by the rhythm.

D-8   The rhythm in the prose-poetry passage is derived from several elements: the pattern which the words form in the sentence, the repetition of words and patterns, the emphasis placed on particular words, and the sound of the words themselves.

D-9   *Pattern, repetition, emphasis,* and *sound* are the principal elements which give prose-poetry its rhythm or emotion. In "And light came and went and came again," the word "and" occurs three times, and the word "came" occurs two times. But more important than the repetition of words is the pattern into which the repeated words fall. The verbs "came, went, came" are separated by the conjunction "and," and "because." Each of the verbs requires equal emphasis, and because they are connected in a pattern, the phrase is rhythmical.

D-10   In this example —

cáme aňd ẃent aňd cáme

we have a patterned rhythmical phrase, with more emphasis, or stress, placed on the verbs than on the conjunctions. We can say that the verbs *came, went, came* are similarly stressed, and that relative to each other in this line, similar emphasis is placed on each verb.

D-11   When more emphasis is placed on one word in a pattern of words than on another, we say that the emphasized word is stressed. But what we are saying when we determine that a syllable in a line is stressed is that relative to the other syllables, this syllable demands more emphasis.

D-12 There are many factors which contribute to the amount of relative stress placed on a syllable, and understanding how relative stress works is the single most important aspect of understanding rhythm and emphasis.

D-13 In the example,

cáme aňd weht aňd cáme ǎgdin

came, went, came, /gain have relatively equal stress, while *and, and, a/* also have relatively equal stress (or unstress). Because the strongest relative stresses are placed on every other syllable, the line forms a pattern of relative stress, which makes it rhythmical.

D-14 Because the relative stresses form a pattern, the first condition for rhythm in language has been met. But another major factor contributes to rhythm: the pattern in which relative stresses and unstresses associate themselves (see Frames D-60 ff, H-1 ff, for a discussion of the *foot*).

D-15 In the example, the word *again,* placed at the end of the phrase, breaks the syntactical pattern of a verb plus a conjunction (*came and went and came*). However, *again* does not break the pattern of relative stress and unstress, because we place more emphasis on the second syllable of *again* than we do on the first syllable, thereby maintaining the pattern of unstresses to stresses. However, the reader will tend to combine the syllable *a* with the second *came* in the line (*came and went and came a*), and the result is that the cadence, or rhythmic speed, picks up at the end.

Although the *a* in *again* associates itself with the second *came* because of the relative stresses, *a* also associates itself with */gain*. This adds an additional tempo to the line, thus accelerating the cadence.

D-16 It is the amount of relative stress/unstress on *a/gain*, however, that makes it possible for the cadence, and eventually the rhythm, to change. Had the relative stress on */gain* been equal to or greater than the stress on *came* and *went,* the rhythm at the end of the line would have been noticeably different from what it is.

MAINTAINING PATTERN IN RHYTHM

D-17 Regular rhythm, then, is established by a *pattern* of word sounds. A sound pattern is the orderly repetition of relative stresses and unstresses. Emphasis normally falls on those words in the pattern which have the greatest relative stress.

D-18 In the example, Wolfe chooses to break the verb-conjunction-verb pattern, but he still maintains his relative stress/unstress pattern with *again* because the reader has established a rhythmical pattern which would have been altered tremendously with syllables having a different stress/unstress combination.

D-19 Because readers come to expect certain patterns once they have been established, poets will maintain the expected pattern unless there seems to be a particular reason not to. "Agreeing" to break an expected meter only when particular reasons require it, and not randomly breaking the meter, is sometimes called the "metrical contract."

D-20   The remainder of the first sentence in the previous example runs thus:

bŭt nów nŏt qu'ite thĕ same ăs ĭt h̆ad

dŏne bĕ/fóre

It also falls into the pattern of stressing every other word. Notice, however, that even among the stressed syllables some syllables demand more attention than others. The greatest relative stress is on *now* and *quite,* with lesser emphasis on *it, done, /fore.* Among the lesser stressed syllables, there is much more emphasis on *not* than on the others. If a syllable does not have enough pressure to be considered a stress, yet it is too strong to be an unstress (see Frames D-70 ff for a discussion about the problems and advantages of using stresses and unstresses rather than a more elaborate system of relative stress) — as with *not* in the example — then we may call it a *secondary stress* in order to distinguish its degree of relative stress. Secondary stresses are normally denoted by two slanted lines (*//*).

D-21   The pattern of relative stress determines both the rhythm and emphasis of the line; rhythm and emphasis affect each other and constitute an important relation in the written arm forms, especially in poetry.

D-22   If the prose-poetry segment from Wolfe's short story had been written this way —

bŭt nów nŏt qu'ite the sáme ăs befóre

then the rhythmical pattern would have been broken. The more often a pattern is broken, the less possibility there is to use rhythm for emphasis, and it is for this reason that the relation between rhythm and meaning is less important in prose than poetry.

RHYTHM IN VERSE

D-23   The rhythmic pattern in poetry is important because it affects our emotional response to the poem, and frequently moulds our intellectual reading of it. One of the principal differences between prose and poetry is that poetry absolutely depends on meter in order to elicit particular responses from the reader, whereas prose is much less dependent on meter and relies on character and dramatic situation.

D-24   It is necessary to make a distinction between poetry and verse because readers frequently identify any rhythmical composition which has poetical form as poetry. Any composition which establishes a rhythmical pattern within a line may be called "verse," but the mere presence of a pattern does not create poetry. Poetry results only when the rhythmical pattern is used to influence the emotion conveyed in the line. Verse in which rhythmic patterns aid memorization but do not affect meaning is called *mnemonic verse.*

D-25   For example, if we compare the following examples, we can tell a distinct difference in the manner in which emotion is conveyed.

> *Example A: Our life runs down in sending up the clock. The brook runs down in
> sending up our life. The sun runs down in sending up the brook. And
> there is something sending up the sun.*

> *Example B: Part of you died each year when the leaves fell from the trees and
> their branches were bare against the wind and the cold wintry light.*

In Example A the first part of each sentence is stressed, then the emphasis declines in the
middle, and is stressed again at the end. This "running down" in the middle is consistent
with meaning. Example B describes the sadness which the narrator feels in the fall, and
the passage is written to convey this emotion. The author, however, relies on the natural
rhythm of the language (rather than on an organized pattern rhythm) and on denotation
to build the emotional response, and although the passage is emotional and beautiful, it
capitalizes on the techniques of prose rather than on the techniques of poetry.

From Rhythm to Meter

D-26   We can say then, that poetry results when the natural rhythmical cadences of
colloquial speech are heightened, organized, and regulated so that a pattern emerges from
the relatively haphazard rhythm of everyday speech. In poetry, this established rhythmical pattern is called *meter*. If, for instance, we rearrange Example A above into poetical
form, we can see how the lines are heightened, organized, and regulated.

> *Our   life   runs down in sending up the   clock.*
> *The   brook   runs down in sending up our   life.*
> *The   sun   runs down in sending up the   brook.*
> *And   there   is something sending up the   sun.*

Obviously, the words have been organized so their position is important to the meaning.
When the established pattern is broken in line 4, emphasis is placed on the *something*
which is sending up the sun.

D-27   We do not normally heighten, organize, and regulate colloquial speech, and the
result is that usually the rhythm does not consciously affect the meaning. But in poetry,
where the rhythm is an essential part of the emotion — and usually meaning — the language will be heightened, organized, and regulated. In traditional poetry, this language is
called *meter*, but even in *free verse* (K-153 ff), which is often thought of as having no
meter, the patterns which syllables form on the page (rather than in a line) become essential.

D-28   The regularity and rhythmical patterns of meter may vary considerably from poem
to poem, depending upon how the poet chooses to use the meter, but in all poetry the
pattern is, to some extent, important to the meaning and emotion.

BASE METER

D-29   Although it is possible for the meter of each line in a poem to differ, every line establishes its own rhythmical pattern, so there can be only one basic meter in each line. However, it is possible for the meter in a poem to change from line to line, so that strictly speaking, we can only talk about meter as it appears in one line. It is customary, however, for a poem to maintain the same meter throughout many of the lines, and when there are a number of lines with similar meter, we can talk about the *base meter* of the poem.

D-30   Determining the base meter of a poem is important because it can help explain where the poet wishes to place emphasis. This in turn may help us decide what the poem means. Without first establishing the base meter, it is not easy to locate the places where the expected pattern of stress and unstress has been altered in order to emphasis a particular word or phrase.

D-31   Establishing the base meter is simply a matter of finding the pattern of relative stress, but since there are several different types of rhythmical bases available to poets, and because hearing the relativity of stresses can be difficult, the base meter is frequently elusive.

TYPES OF RHYTHMICAL SYSTEMS

D-32   Measuring the line for its rhythmic pattern, which consists of placing the relative stress on the syllables in the line, is called scansion. However, since there are four basic systems of meter, there are four methods of scansion, in English — one method for each type of meter. They are accentual, syllabic, accentual-syllabic, and quantitative. Rhythmical patterns must be seen in relation to the type of metrical system which the poet is using.

The Accentual System

D-33   *Accentual meter* is a system in which the occurrence of a syllable marked by a stress determines the basic unit, regardless of the number of unstressed syllables. In other words, it is the stresses and not the unstresses that determine the metrical base; thus, when scanning a line for accentual meter, we mark only the stresses. For example, we can scan the following line for accentual meter:

> *They're out of the dark's ragbag, these two*
>
> FROM: BLUE MOLES
> SYLVIA PLATH

We see that there are five stresses, and if the poem is using accentual meter, we can expect to find five-stress lines recurring throughout the poem.

D-34   We can say, then, that the example line is a five-stress line, and if by scanning the remainder of the poem we see that there is no pattern of stresses and unstresses, we can say that the poet is using accentual meter. If the metrical base of an accentual poem is the five-stress line, then we can expect the five-stress to recur. However, if the poet chooses to deviate from his metrical base and let his line have a different number of stresses, then he wants that line to have a different effect on emotion or emphasis.

D-35   Accentual meter does, then, establish a pattern, but the metrical base is derived from the number of stresses rather than the pattern of stress and unstresses. We could, of course, wildly speculate that this line

They're out of the dark's ragbag, these two

sets up a pattern of alternating two stresses and two unstresses, but in English, where the natural pattern is an unstress to a stress, we would have to justify our speculative pattern by looking at the rest of the poem.

D-36   Although each line in a poem can theoretically have a different meter, no poems apply the theory because the poet would lose his power to vary the meter for the sake of emotion or emphasis, and in all traditional poems, no matter what system of meter is used, some sort of metrical base will be established. Taking the next three lines from "Blue Moles," it is easy to see that accentual meter is being used, with the five-stress line as the base.

They're out of the dark's ragbag, these two

Moles dead in the pebbled rut,

Shapeless as flung gloves, a few feet apart-

Blue suede a dog or fox has chewed.

None of the lines form a definite pattern of stresses and unstresses, and all the lines have a different number of syllables, but three of the four have five-stresses, and we feel the force of the five-stress line holding the poem together metrically.

Old English Versification

D-37   The most extensive use of accentual meter came in Old English (before 1100) poetry, in which the line rather than the stanza served as the basic verse unit, since no end rhyme was used. The Old English line was composed of four stressed syllables with a varying number of unstressed syllables; the line was normally divided into two parts (each half line is called a hemistich), separated by a caesura (pause), with two of the four stressed syllables falling on each side of the line. The hemistichs are bound by *alliteration* (E-30), with the stressed syllables falling on the alliterated syllables. The two stresses in the first hemistich often alliterate with each other, and at least one must alliterate with the first stressed syllable (the third in the line) in the second hemistich. In Old English the alliteration may not be continued to the fourth syllable, although in Middle English verse it frequently does. In Middle English alliterated verse, the rules were loosened, but the following line from *Piers Plowman* is similar to the Old English line form.

In a súmmer séason   when sóft was the sún.

Not only are the number of stresses per line important, but also the position in which they fall. The unstressed syllables, however, are not used for measuring the line. After the French conquest (1066), during the period between 1100 and 1300, poets began counting the number of syllables per line (see Frames D-49 ff). By the time Chaucer wrote the *Canterbury Tales,* poetry had begun settling into a four-stress line with eight or nine syllables, or a five-stress line with ten or eleven syllables. The extensive use of poetry counting both accents and syllables was to follow soon. Use of the four-stress line continued, however, especially in popular verse and nursery rhymes. Notice the following examples which are close to Old English versification, though somewhat loosened.

Thís is the cóck   that crowéd in the mórn

That wakéd the príest   all sháven and shórn

That márried the mán   all táttered and tórn

That wóoed the máiden   áll forlórn

Wíre, bríar, lúmber lóck,

Thrée géese ín a flóck.

Óne flew éast and óne flew wést

And óne flew óver the cúckoo's nést.

Sprung Rhythm

D-38   If accentual poetry is taken to its extreme, one can never predict the patterns of succeeding stresses and unstresses; all that will be possible to predict will be a prescribed number of stresses per line. This extreme of unpredictability characterizes *sprung rhythm,* first described near the end of the Nineteenth Century by Gerald Manley Hopkins. In sprung rhythm, "any two stresses may either follow one another running, or be divided by one, two, or three slack syllables." Thus, in sprung rhythm, there can be, and usually is, a tendency toward grouping stresses.

D-39   Stressed syllables are often grouped together as follows:

shéer plód makes ploúgh doẃn síllión

Shíne,

FROM: THE WINDHOVER
G. M. HOPKINS

This tends to make the reader spring from one stress to the next because there are few slack stresses to give pause or relief to the stresses. Groups of stresses occurring together in a line create tension, and Hopkins often uses sprung rhythm for describing his tenseness or excitement for an image or idea.

D-40   While the unpredictability of stresses in sprung rhythm makes it impossible for the poet to set up expectations, there is a pattern to this type of *accentual meter* (D-33), and once the reader determines that a poet is using Hopkin's sprung rhythm, he is better prepared to discover what the poet is attempting through the tension of the line, and he should compare the poem to Hopkins' work.

The Syllabic System

D-41   The second system of meter is *syllabic* meter. Syllabic prosody measures only the number of syllables per line, without regard to the stress of the syllables relative to each other, and while a syllabic line in English does have stressed and unstressed syllables, it is the number of syllables and not the pattern of stresses and unstresses that account for the metrical base.

D-42   In some languages, such as French and some oriental languages, there is much less difference between the stressed and unstressed syllables than there is in the Germanic-based languages, and counting the number of syllables rather than the stressed syllables establishes the base. In English, however, many syllables have a strong natural tendency toward heavy stresses, and English poetry cannot be syllabic in the same sense that French and Japanese are syllabic. However, since some of the techniques of early English prosody came into the language through French, it is sometimes useful to see English lines in terms of their syllabic meter.

D-43   Although most English poetry will have a stress/unstress pattern, some may not, and it is sometimes useful to talk about the number of syllables per line if no pattern exists, or if the syllable count helps to explain the existing pattern. For example, consider the following line from "Fern Hill" by Dylan Thomas:

1   2 3 4   5   6   7 8 9   10 11   12 13   14
Now as I was young and ea/sy un/der the ap/ple boughs

There are fourteen syllables, and it may be helpful to count the syllables without regard to their relative stress (although it is apparent that the syllables do create different emphasis and rhythm) or to attempt to group syllables into patterns.

D-44   For example, consider these lines:

Noth/ing I cared in the lamb white days, that

time would take me

Up to the swal/low thronged loft by the

sha/dow of my hand

FROM: FERN HILL
DYLAN THOMAS

Here it is possible to establish where the stresses and unstresses should be placed, but there is apparently no pattern to them. The rhythm does, however, seem to indicate some relationship between the lines which cannot be explained by the stress/unstress pattern or by accentual meter, and it is only when we count the syllables that we can see why the lines are associated.

1   2   3   4   5   6   7   8   9
Noth/ing I cared, in the lamb white days,

10   11   12   13   14
that time would take me

1   2   3   4   5   6   7   8   9
Up to the swal/low thronged loft by the

10   11   12   13   14
sha/dow of my hand

D-45   A syllabic line is named according to its syllable count. For example, a ten syllable line is called decasyllabic, an eight syllable line is octasyllabic. Lines of more that twelve syllables are called by their English numerical count; e.g., fourteener, fifteener. The Greek prefixes for the names of syllabic lines are as follows:

mono = one	*penta* = five	*nona* = nine
di = two	*hexa* = six	*deca* = ten
tri = three	*hepta* = seven	*hendeca* = eleven
tetra = four	*octa* = eight	*dodeca* = twelve

Review/self-check

D-46   Established rhythmical pattern in poetry is called _____ . Meter results when natural rhythmical language is heightened, _____ and _____ .

meter (D-25)
organized & regulated (D-25).

D-47   A metrical base is established so that the poet can deviate from it when he wishes to place _____ on a particular word.

emphasis or stress (D-30)

D-48 In the following lines a base meter is established in lines 1, 2, and 3 because a pattern of unstress/stress is clear.

$$\text{In every cry of every man}$$

$$\text{In every infant's cry of fear,}$$

$$\text{In every voice, in every ban,}$$

$$\text{The mind-forged manacles I hear.}$$

D-49 In line 4, however, the poet deviates from the _____ of unstress/stress. Because of this deviation the words _____ and _____ are stresses. Placing the stresses and unstresses correctly in a line is important because a change in _____ may cause a change in meaning.

pattern
forged, I

emphasis or stress (D-30, D-34)

D-50 If there is doubt as to whether a syllable is stressed, the _____ _____ may help in determining the solution.

base meter, or metrical base (D-29)

D-51 Scansion is the method by which we measure the _____ of a line.

meter (D-32)

D-52 In accentual poetry, scansion consists of counting _____ without regard to the number of unstresses.

stresses (D-33)

D-53 The following line of accentual poetry is called a _____ - _____ line.

five-stress (D-33)

$$\text{They're out of the dark's ragbag, these two}$$

FROM: BLUE MOLES
SYLVIA PLATH

D-54 The use of consecutive accents in the following line (as in the line in D-35) makes it an example of _____ rhythm.

sprung (D-38)

$$\text{Sheer plod makes plough down sillion shine,}$$

FROM: THE WINDHOVER
G. M. HOPKINS

D-55   If in English we naturally place a heavy stress on approximately every other syllable, then syllabic meter (is, is not) readily adaptable to English poetry.

is not (D-41)

D-56   Because the stresses are not important in syllabic poetry, only the number of _____ are counted.

syllables (D-42)

D-57   The following line would be called _____ in the syllabic system, and a _____ _____ line in the accentual system.

nonasyllabic (D-45)
five-stress

/ v / v v / / / v
Tells with si/lence the last light break/ing
1   2   3   4   5   6 7   8   9

FROM: A REFUSAL TO MOURN THE
DEATH, BY FIRE, OF A CHILD
IN LONDON
DYLAN THOMAS

The Accentual-Syllabic System

D-58   With the exception of a smaller number of purely accentual poems, and even fewer syllabic poems, the meter of English poetry can be measured by the pattern of stresses relative to the unstresses. This type of meter is called accentual-syllabic meter. In other words, it is the association of stresses and unstresses that creates the meter in most English poetry.

D-59   Because stressed syllables dominate unstressed syllables in the accentual-syllabic system, it is common to show the association of unstresses to the stresses. For example, in reading the following line,

I am there like the dead or the beast

FROM: IN THE MOUNTAIN TENT
JAMES DICKEY

our speech patterns tend to section the line into three parts:

I am there/ like the dead/ or the beast

so that we associate the first two unstressed syllables with the third stressed syllable:

v v /   v v /   v v /
I am there/ like the dead/ or the beast

D-60   In English poetry the stressed syllables dominate the unstressed syllables, and our speech patterns tend to group the unstressed syllables around the stressed syllables. This natural speech occurrence creates groups of associated unstresses and stresses within the line. Each of these groups is called a foot. In the line:

I am there like the dead, or the beast,

the three feet are these:

(1) I am there (2) like the dead (3) or the beast

D-61   The type of base meter in accentual-syllabic poems will be determined by the type of foot which dominates the poem, and by the length of the line. For example, a poem which is dominated by *iambic* feet (v /) (see H-10) and which generally contains five feet per line will have an *iambic pentameter* (I-4) base meter. That is not to say that all the lines will have five feet or that all the feet will be iambs, but that for the purpose of explaining where the poem's emphasis lies, we can consider the base meter as iambic pentameter.

D-62   The important reason for looking at the base meter in an accentual-syllabic poem is that it is essential for explaining emphasis. Whenever a poet establishes a base meter, then deviates from it, he is breaking the "metrical contract" (D-19) because he wants to call attention to the deviation. The regularity (D-17) of the line moves the reader along until the poet wants the reader to note a particular place in the poem, at which point he will alter the base meter. Creating emphasis is not the only reason a poet will alter his base meter, but it is by far the most important reason, and the reader should become sensitive to alterations in the base. Altering the base meter so that a foot, or the entire line, changes from rising to falling, or vice-versa, is called *counterpointing*.

D-63   We can say, then, that the base meter helps us know where the poet wishes to place emphasis or to regulate sound, which in turn will help us understand his theme. For example, suppose Shakespeare had written this:

My mistress' eyes are like the sun;

instead of this:

My mistress' eyes are nothing like the sun;

FROM: SONNET 130

We can tell by *scanning* (D-32) the supposed line that the word *like* is stressed:

My mĭs/trĕss' eyĕs/ ăre likĕ/ thĕ sún;

while with Shakespeare's line, the relative strength of *like* is diminished considerably by the strength of *nothing.*

My mĭs/trĕss' eyĕs/ ăre nóth/ĭng likĕ/ thĕ sún

By taking the stress away from *like*, in a position which we know from the base meter should take a stress, Shakespeare has emphasized the absence of comparison, and we can assume at this point the absence will be important to the meaning of the poem.

D-64   We knew (or assumed) that the base of the line was iambic, and that a word coming in the position of *like* should be stressed, but the relative stress of *nothing like* takes the stress off *like,* and because of this we can infer something about emphasis. However, with the first foot (D-60) in the line, *my mis/,* it is impossible for us to tell whether Shakespeare wants us to place strong relative stress on *My* and secondary stresses (D-20) on the first syllable in *mistress* to say this:

$$\acute{My} \; mi\overset{//}{s}/tr\overset{//}{e}ss'$$

or to place less relative stress on *my* and more stress on *mis/* in *mistress* to say this:

$$\overset{\vee}{My} \; mi\acute{s}/tr\overset{\vee}{e}ss' \; e\acute{y}es$$

and we can solve this problem only by looking at the base meter of the poem rather than the base of the line. By comparing deviations in this line to other deviations (once the base meter is established), we should be able to resolve the problem because we know (as Shakespeare knew) how to apply base meter to theme.

LEARNING TO SCAN

D-65   Learning to scan poetry is oftentimes difficult, and there is no satisfactory way of teaching it, but given that meter and meaning influence each other, it is possible by trial and error to scan a poem correctly. Readers who have an ear for meter can listen and hear where stresses fall, and everyone should attempt to place stresses naturally before going through the following steps which analyze those elements which bring pressure to a syllable. But if you find scanning difficult, then you can attempt scansion through analysis, which is fairly reliable though not as satisfactory as being able to hear natural rhythms and stresses.

Steps for Scanning

D-66   After reading the poem enough times so that it can be read smoothly, go through each line and mark the syllables on which there is no doubt that they should be accented. If the stress of a syllable is questionable, do not mark it during this initial scansion.

D-67   The first step in a difficult scansion is to mark those syllables which take heavy accents. There is no way to instruct people how to hear strong accents, but almost everyone should be able to pick out one or two in a line by concentrating on the rhythm and by remembering where the natural accents of words fall. We can expect accents on nouns, verbs (except auxiliary verbs), adjectives (but not usually monosyllabic, attributive adjectives) and adverbs, but we should not expect stresses on articles, conjunctions, or prepositions. These are only expectations, of course, and forcing a syllable into a metrical pattern can change its natural stress, but in many cases the part of speech of the word containing the syllable will influence the stress. Another helpful observation is that most English surnames are accented on the first syllable, and that many two-syllable English words, particularly those ending in resonating consonants, are accented on the initial syllable (E-4).

D-68   Given this knowledge of English words, we can apply it to the consonants which we find in particular lines to determine the stress of many syllables. Take the first two lines of "Luke Havergal."

> *Go to the western gate, Luke Havergal,*
> *There where the vines cling crimson on the wall.*

Let us perform an initial scansion, accenting only those syllables which we can be sure of.

D-68 (1)   The rhythm of the first three syllables is a little complicated because of the short duration of each syllable and because *to* and *the* tend to run together. There is however, only one possibility with *western* since the first syllable is always accented; the harsh *g* and plosive *t* in *gate* also give it a heavy stress, though not quite as heavy as the *west/* in *western* because of the meter established by the first part of the line.

D-68 (2)   *Havergal* is an English surname with the accent on the first syllable, but the pressure on *Hav/* is increased because the plosive *k* in *Luke* takes the reader's breath, and in order to have enough air to pronounce *Havergal*, (*h*'s are pronounced by an escape of air, making them harder to say), the reader forces his remaining breath out, and *Hav/* is pronounced with some force. The initial scansion of line 1, then, is this:

> /a   /b   /a
> *Go to the western gate, Luke Havergal*

where a denotes stronger pressure than b. (Consonants are discussed in E1-13.)

D-68 (3)   Scanning the second line:

> *There where the vines cling crimson on the wall,*

we again sense that it may be difficult to determine the pressure on the first two syllables, so we skip them until the next reading. However, the resonating *n*, the exhaustive *s*, the plosive *v*, the absence of pressure before *vines* (*the* seldom takes any pressure at all), and the fact that it is an important noun in the line, all give *vines* considerable pressure. Likewise, the plosive *c* and highly resonating *ng* in *cling* give it major pressure, but not quite as much as *vines.*

D-68 (4)   After the two stresses on *vines* and *cling*, which include both resonating and exhaustive consonants, the reader is short of breath, but he is again asked to stress *crimson*. The harsh *c* and resonating *m* demand a full stress, in addition to the fact that it is the only adjective (and an important adjective) in the line.

D-68 (5)   The sudden drop in */son* causes the reader to run *-on* in *crimson* and the word *on* together; the *-on* in *crimson* and *on* set up a cadence which is maintained through *the* so that there is very little stress after *crim/* until we reach *wall*. The *l*'s in *wall* give the final syllable some stress, but not a great deal, so our initial scansion of "sure" stresses in line 2 is this:

$$\overset{/a}{There}\ where\ the\ \overset{/b}{vines}\ \overset{/a}{cling}\ crimson\ on\ the\ \overset{/b}{wall}$$

D-69 Now that the obvious major stresses have been applied we can begin figuring out poetically what we cannot be sure of phonically. But first we must reckon with and come to believe in the principle of *relative stress* (D-11). Relative stress states that once the dominant stress in the line or poem has been determined, then every other syllable can be given a stress factor relative to the dominant syllable.

D-70 The stress factor is created by several aspects of prosody and word structure, and it may be more accurate to talk about the pressure brought on a syllable rather than the stress. The position of the syllable in the line, the position of the syllable in its word, the surrounding syllables, the type of vowels and consonants which constitute the syllable, and the syllable's relation to the foot, base meter, and caesura all contribute to the pressures which determine the amount of stress. Since every syllable will have a different stress factor, we could assign as many values as there are syllables in the poem, but there is no advantage to this when explicating.

   For many years prosodists divided syllables into two major groups: stresses and un-stresses, and for some poems which are insensible to exact pressure (such as some limer-icks), only two groups are needed. Many critics agree, however, that most serious poems require at least three groups: stresses, secondary stresses, and unstresses.

D-71 As the name implies, *secondary stresses* are stresses — not an intermediary be-tween stress and unstress — but they are stresses which do not command as much pres-sure as primary stresses. In the following line, for example:

$$\overset{//}{I}\ \overset{\vee}{am}\ \overset{/}{there}\ like\ \overset{\vee}{the}\ \overset{\vee}{dead,}\ \overset{/}{or}\ \overset{\vee}{the}\ \overset{\vee}{beast}$$

FROM: IN THE MOUNTAIN TENT
JAMES DICKEY

the base meter will not permit *I* to take a full stress, but it may be more forceful that the unaccented syllables, in which case we could give it a secondary stress (//).

D-72 Using three categories of relative stress is usually adequate for understanding how a line is working, but for close work on the phonics and rhythm of a line, more categor-ies must be established, and the explicator can make as many as he needs. With "Luke Havergal" we have begun with a system which recognizes two stresses /a and /b; by adding secondary stresses — a step below our stress *b/* — and unstresses, we should be able to scan the poem to our satisfaction.

D-73 Returning to lines 1 and 2, we can now complete the scansion. Thus far we have this in line 1:

$$Go\ to\ the\ \overset{/a}{western}\ \overset{/b}{gate,}\ Luke\ \overset{/a}{Havergal,}$$

If we are unable to place phonically any more stresses with certainty, the next step is to decide rationally the relationship between stress and meter, and between stress and meaning. One good place to begin is with base meter, if it can be established. Based on the general feeling of a two-beat rising line, even amid the host of substitutions, and on the strict ten syllable line throughout the poem, we can assume an iambic base as a place to begin in "Luke Havergal."

D-74   Because we can feel a basic two-beat rising line in "Luke Havergal," which indicates an iambic base, and because of the strict adherence to a ten syllable line, we can assume an iambic pentameter base, as long as we recognize that this may vary or change. Dividing the line into feet containing two syllables in order to test how the base might be working, we get this:

$$\overset{\lor}{Go}\ \overset{/}{to}/\ \overset{\lor}{the}\ \overset{/}{west}/\overset{\lor}{ern}\ \overset{/}{gate},/\ Luke\ \overset{/}{Ha}/vergal$$
$$1\qquad 2\qquad 3\qquad 4\qquad 5$$

Since we have already established that *the* and /*ern* are unstressed, feet 2 and 3 are iambic.

D-75   Even from a cursory reading we know that the poem concerns whether or not Luke will go to the gate, and because of this and because the first line is a command, we can be sure that *Go* and not *to* will be stressed in foot 1. In addition to knowing that *Go* is accented because the meaning of the line indicates that it would be, we also know that trochaic and spondaic substitutions are very common in the first foot of a line; so it makes sense that there is a substitution in this line.

D-76   *Luke* in foot 4 is not too much of a problem, since it comes between two full stresses and after a caesura. Clearly we can feel that it has less pressure than *Hav*/ although it might have similar pressure to *gate* were it not for the caesura which forces a pause, and the plosive "t" which makes us take another breath. The two full stresses, the *-t* in *gate*, and the caesura reduce the pressure on *Luke*, but the long *u* and the plosive *k* give it some pressure; so the word should take a secondary stress.

D-77   We can go through the same analytical process with foot 5 (or any foot once the base meter is established). Since syllable 8 is stressed, and since syllable 9 is part of the last foot, which is usually not spondaic or trochaic when the syllable immediately preceeding it is stressed, it is reasonable to assume that foot 5 is either pyrrhic or iambic. The *-er* in *Havergal* moves quickly and takes very little unaccent while *-gal* has considerably more stress because of the harsh *g* and liquid *l*. This last foot, however, takes less pressure than the heavy middle of the line so that the natural emphasis of the line has been altered.

D-78   If we scan the line this way:

$$\overset{/b}{Go}\ \overset{\lor}{to}/\ \overset{\lor}{the}\ \overset{/a}{Wes}/tern\ \overset{\lor}{\ }\ \overset{/b}{gate},/\ \overset{//}{Luke}\ \overset{/a}{Hav}/\overset{\lor}{er}\overset{/b}{gal},$$
$$1\qquad 2\qquad 3\qquad 4\qquad 5$$

we should stop and examine what has been done. Since we have figured out rationally what we could not hear, we should assume that what we have is correct, and if we find that our rationale is not fitting a particular line, we know that the poet has deviated from standard technique for a particular reason, in which case we will have a lead to theme. At this point, however, the line looks reasonable: the normal trochaic substitution in foot 1 sets up the command; the two consecutive unaccents in *to the* set up the heavy *west* and return to the basic iamb. The line is full of harsh and plosive consonants, but they fall where the accents are natural.

D-79   Looking at line 2, we should proceed on the same assumption that we made with line 1: that there is a basic iambic pentameter meter. Dividing into feet again,

$$\underset{1}{\text{There where}}/\underset{2}{\overset{/b}{\text{the vines}}}/\underset{3}{\overset{/b}{\text{cling crim}}}\underset{4}{\overset{/a}{\text{son on}}}/\underset{5}{\overset{/b}{\text{the wall}}}$$

we see right away that there is a spondaic substitution in foot 3, and whenever a line contains a spondaic foot, there is a good chance that a pyrrhic foot will follow, particularly if the second syllable in the spondaic foot is the first half of a two syllable word.

D-80   Since there are three consecutive stresses in the line, and because pyrrhic feet often follow spondaic feet, and because there is no reason to stress *on*, we can assume that foot 4 is pyrrhic. Also since *the* is seldom stressed, and because it runs together with *on*, we know that foot 5 is iambic.

D-81   In foot 1 we are faced with an internal rhyme, which usually takes equal stress if the syllables are of similar duration. This is the case with *There where* which makes the foot spondaic, although *There* takes a little more stress than *where*.

D-82   The lack of stress on *the* in foot 2 picks up a quicker cadence after the long duration of the internal rhyme, and the line scans this way:

$$\overset{/a}{\text{There}}\ \overset{/b}{\text{where}}/\ \overset{v}{\text{the}}\ \overset{/a}{\text{vines}}/\ \overset{/b}{\text{cling}}\ \overset{/a}{\text{crim}}/\overset{v}{\text{son}}\ \overset{v}{\text{on}}/\ \overset{v}{\text{the}}\ \overset{/b}{\text{wall}}$$

Applying the Scansion to Meaning

D-83   After scanning each line, we should go back through the poem and determine how the use of caesura and substitution influence emphasis, if we haven't done so already. The caesura in line 1 helped to reduce the pressure brought on *Luke*. That every line is end-stopped in stanzas 1 and 4, that many lines have full stops, and that many lines contain internal caesuras, all indicates that the poet is using the *natural emphasis of the line* as a base for his own emphasis. Another prosodic device which Robinson uses is to repeat phrases but change their emphasis and sound with a caesura. For example, the internal rhyme, *There where* in line 2, placed similar stress on both syllables, but in line 11 the same internal rhyme is broken with a caesura:

$$\overset{v}{\text{But}}\ \overset{/}{\text{there}},\ \overset{v}{\text{where}}\ \overset{/}{\text{west}}\overset{v}{\text{ern}}\ \overset{/}{\text{glooms}}\ \overset{v}{\text{are}}\ \overset{/}{\text{gath}}\overset{v}{\text{er}}\overset{v}{\text{ing}}$$

and this, combined with the heavy accent on *west,* gives *where* in line 11 an unaccent.

THE QUANTITATIVE SYSTEM

D-84   The fourth system of meter is *quantitative meter,* the principal system of versification for ancient Greek poetry. Quantitative meter is measured by the duration, or quantity, with which the syllable is pronounced. In other words, syllables of the same quantitative length would take the same amount of time to pronounce.

D-85   While there have been a few attempts in English to imitate quantitative meter, the language does not adapt satisfactorily to the system. Quantity is, however, frequently useful in noting the durational qualities of English syllables. For example, the word *column* is a two-syllable word:

$$\overset{\prime}{col}/\overset{\smile}{umn}$$

with an unstress on the second syllable. The second syllable, however, has a long durational stress, and sounds as though it carries equal stress with the first syllable. This long durational stress accounts for the emphasis which might be placed on the second syllable in a line. Other, and perhaps better examples are: *morphine, cognate, vengeance, ribald, standard, purists,* and *anguished.* Compare the following lines from two different poems:

1. *Within/ be fed,/ without/ be rich/ no more.*

FROM: SONNET 141
WILLIAM SHAKESPEARE

2. *These sud/den ends/ of time/ must give/ us pause*

FROM: YEAR'S END
RICHARD WILBUR

Both lines have five feet and both are written in iambs, but line 2 takes longer to read than line 1. One reason for this is that the *s* sounds take longer to pronounce than do the others. Another reason is that line 2 also has some hard consonant clusters: *-nds-* *-mm-* (time must) *-stg-*.

D-86   The effect which long durational stresses have on a line is to slow the meter and make the stressed syllables less prominent. In the two previous examples, the first line seems to be more heavily stressed than does the second, although both lines have the same number of stressed syllables. The reason is that three of the five unstressed syllables in the second line (*These, must, us*) are of long duration and sound as though they should carry equal stress, which makes the line sound more even than the first line, where every other syllable is stressed heavily.

D-87   Poets do choose their words according to the quantity of the syllable as well as to the number of syllables and meaning of the word. Quantitative stress can alter the tone and meter, and quantity (duration) is as much a part of poetry as the foot. In this line —

When Ă/jăx strĭves/ hĭs rock's/ vast weight/ tŏ throw

FROM: AN ESSAY ON CRITICISM
ALEXANDER POPE

there is no way to show all metrical effects except by quantity, as determined by long vowels and consonant clusters. The presence of consonant clusters is the main means of determining length; the second means is long vowels.

Hovering Stress

D-88   When two syllables have long durational stresses and appear to carry similar stress, although one of the syllables may be scanned as unstressed in the accentual-syllabic system, we have a "quantitative dilemma" which some metricists like to refer to as a *hovering stress,* thereby indicating the strength of the syllables.

D-89   There can, of course, be no absolute rule for scanning quantitatively, and within established limits, what best serves the particular poem should be used. A mixture of all four metrical systems is certainly possible and could be most useful, but it is absolutely essential that prosodic consistency be maintained throughout the poem, or at least throughout a section of it.

D-90   It should be remembered that the types of metrical systems are only descriptions of what happens to rhythm when it is channeled into poetry. These systems help us understand how rhythm is created, but they are limited in their ability to describe the rhythmic magic of good poetry.

◄‖►Sound

In some poems the poet aims to give pleasure primarily through the sound, while other poems give pleasure through their ideas or images, but all poems depend to some extent upon all three elements, and almost by definition poetry depends upon sound to achieve its ends. Poets achieve the sounds they desire through meter (D-1 ff), rhyme (I-63 ff), and the *sound of words*.

VOWELS, CONSONANTS, AND SYLLABLES

E-1 In poetry it is, of course, the sound of the words which determines the ultimate success or failure of the work. The sound of a word is determined by the order in which certain vowels and consonants form syllables, and by the number and relative stress of the syllables in the word.

E-2 It is possible, and often advantageous, to analyze how the poet is using vowels, consonants, and relative stress to create sound in his poem, and frequently, understanding how sound is working will aid the reader in his explication because it may reveal the poet's attitude toward his subject (see Tone: F-1 ff). For example, consider the following lines:

> *You must plant your ecstacies*
> *With hearts of hook. All right my love. I'll walk*   2
> *On spikes for you. I'll snake out a line to cling*
> *In fire around your throat and jerk you back*   4
> *To me. I'll bite blood from you, I'll stalk*
> *And corner your dark joy.*   6
>
>   FROM: THE CROOKED MILE
>   JACK BUTLER

The poet pushes hard on the *plosive consonants* (E-9) *t* and *k* so that these lines become hard and foreboding. When he softens line 3 with *l*'s, that is, with *liquid consonants* (E-6), we feel his grip tightening around us rather than releasing our fears. The *h* (line 2) and *b* (line 5) *alliteration* (E-30) also contribute to the harshness, and the total effect achieves the horror which the poet wants us to feel.

TYPES OF CONSONANTS

E-3 Consonants are among the most important sound-producing devices, and there are five basic effects which certain consonants will produce: resonance, harshness, plosiveness, exhaustiveness, and liquidity. Resonance, exhaustiveness, and liquidity will tend to give the word — and consequently the line if several of these consonants are used — a soft-sound effect, while plosiveness and harshness tend to create tension.

92

E-4   Resonance is the property of long duration produced by nasals, such as *n, m, ng,* and voiced fricating consonants, such as *z, zh, v,* and the voiced *th* as in *them.* Compare, for example, the length of time it takes to pronounce *man* and *cat.* Resonating words tend to ring throughout the line, and they can be used to establish either harmony or cacophony.

E-5   Exhaustiveness is created by the voiceless fricating consonants and consonant combinations, such as *h, f,* the voiceless *th, s, sh.* The length of exhaustive consonants, if enough are grouped together, will force the reader to pause in order to catch his breath. For example, when we read this line —

These sudden ends of time must give us pause.

FROM: YEAR'S END
RICHARD WILBUR

we must pause before continuing, which, in this case, reinforces the meaning. In other cases a group of exhaustive consonants may be used to establish an attitude of the persona.

E-6   Liquidity results from using the liquids and semi-vowels: *l*'s, *r*'s, *w*'s and *y*'s. When these are placed in the word, the consonant seems lengthened. For example, the *l* in *silken* seems to flow for a long duration. (D-84) When a line possesses liquidity it usually seems smooth and sensuous. When liquid consonants hover between syllables, as in *solemn*, they seem especially flowing, and it is difficult to tell which syllable the consonant lies in.

E-7   When resonant, exhaustive, and liquid words are formed together, they give the line a soft, sensuous quality, as follows:

The summer palaces on slopes, the terraces.

FROM: JOURNEY OF THE MAGI
T. S. ELIOT

E-8   Although consonants serve many functions in creating sounds, some consistently require particular reactions when read. Resonating consonants, for example, resonate long after they occur in the word, and a group of resonating consonants can make the line ring, creating either a sense of harmony as when bells ring in time with each other, or of disharmony as when bells ring out of time.

When a number of exhaustive consonants are grouped together, they force the reader to pause, but when a few are included in a line they tend to soften it.

E-9   Plosiveness occurs when certain consonants create a stoppage of breath before releasing it. The consonants *b, p, t, d, g* and *k* as well as *ch* and *j*, are plosives. Their aspiration (release of air) is especially noticeable in terminal positions, as in *top, putt,* or *tag.*

E-10   When certain consonants create a stoppage of breath before allowing it to be released, they are plosive, and make the word sound hard and restrained. The harsh consonants, *k, g,* are also plosive in most words, but when they come initially or terminally they are especially harsh. When plosive and harsh consonants are formed together, the line reverberates with bitterness, as in this example:

> *Six hands at an open door dicing for pieces of silver,*
> *and feet kicking the empty wine-skins.*

> FROM: JOURNEY OF THE MAGI
> T. S. ELIOT

In the example, the plosive consonants in the first line are *t, p, d, d, p.*

E-11 It is not valid to generalize and say that liquid consonants are used exclusively for soft lines and plosive consonants for hard lines, although a large number of either will produce these effects. Usually a line will contain a mixture of both, and unless the poet is really pushing a point, he will not rely on any particular kind of consonant, but a mixture which will produce the effect he wants. In the following example there are a number of harsh and plosive consonants, but they are overpowered by the softer consonants so that the line is extremely sensuous and smooth.

> *With jellies smoother than the creamy curd,*
> *And lucent syrups, tinct with cinnamon.*

> FROM: THE EVE OF ST. AGNES
> JOHN KEATS

Consonant Groupings

E-12 Poets frequently use consonant groupings to create special sounds in the line, and the critic should be careful to note how consonant groups work. For example, in the line:

> *The mind-forged manacles, I hear*

> FROM: LONDON
> WILLIAM BLAKE

mind-forged has two resonating and two plosive sounds, an exhaustive, a liquid, and an affricative sound; *manacles* has a plosive *c.* This combination creates tremendous strain on the reader, and exhausts him.

E-13 When the poet makes such a deliberate attempt to establish an effect, it will be for a particular reason, and it is important to determine the reason in order to completely understand the poem.

SYLLABLES

E-14 Another important factor which influences the sound of a word is the number and length of syllables in it. In English many words were adopted from non-Germanic sources, and the result is that we possess many words which are polysyllabic.

Polysyllabic Words

E-15   Words adopted from the Romance languages (referred to as "Latinate" words) tend to be polysyllabic, fluid, and soft; while the words adopted from German are often monosyllabic or disyllabic, relying more often on plosive and harsh consonants. Thus many poems endeavoring to be conventionally sensuous might use polysyllabic rather than monosyllabic words.

E-16   Because Latinate words are very effective in softening the line without straining consonant groupings, English poets like to use them, but the problem is that polysyllabic words do not fit easily into the strong iambic base of English, especially when a number of them are needed in a stanza.

E-17   Polysyllabic words generally have the same effect on a line as the soft consonants, and poets like to use polysyllabic words because they give variety to prevent an over-abundance of soft consonants. Poems which use a number of polysyllabic words will usually be trying to create smooth or pleasing sounds rather than abrupt or cacophonous ones, although the poet may use the pleasant sound for irony.

E-18   In the following line there are three polysyllabic words.

Monuments of unageing intellect.

In spite of so many polysyllabic words in the line, it still maintains a pentameter base, divided as follows:

Monu/ments of/ unag/ing in/tellect.

FROM SAILING TO BYZANTIUM
W. B. YEATS

Placed within an iambic or trochaic base, polysyllabic words will, of course, have to be split, and unless the poet is careful the split foot (H-20) might counteract the softness of the word. But by the same logic, and set in a different situation, the split, poly-syllabic words might establish a special tone — one which plays the tension created by the split foot against the sound of the word — and the effect could be most useful.

WRENCHED ACCENTS AND "PROBLEM POLYSYLLABLES"

E-19   It is sometimes necessary to take certain liberties with polysyllabic words if we are to scan them in the confines of a strict accentual-syllabic base meter. For example, in an iambic poem in which multiple (multi-syllable) substitutions (H-25) are not other-wise found, it is often possible to "adjust" pronunciations to fit the meter. If the poet has such adjustments in mind, he may or may not give hints to the reader; often a strictly maintained base meter is hint enough. When the poet does intend for a syllable to be pronounced differently from its customary usage, that syllable is called a "wrenched accent." Wrenched accents are created by *elision* (E-20) and *syncope* (E-21).

Elisions

E-20   Poets who attempt to maintain a *regular* (D-17) *accentual-syllabic* (D-58) *base meter* (D-29) will sometimes join two vowels into a single vowel in order to make a polysyllabic word fit evenly. For example, in this line:

> *Of man's first disobedience, and the fruit*

FROM: PARADISE LOST
JOHN MILTON

the *ie* in disobedience is pronounced as a *y* ("ye") so that the word reads *dis/o/bed/yence*, thereby making a five-syllable word into a four-syllable word. This process of forming one vowel out of two is called *synaeresis* or *elision*. Elisions can serve several purposes: poems which contain elisions bring the reader's attention to the fact that the poet is especially sensitive to his metrical base, and even though many poems containing elisions will have lines with fewer or extra syllables, we can assume that variations on the base are important. Notice the use of elision in the following lines:

> *True ease in writing comes from art, not chance,*
> *As those move easiest who have learned to dance.*   2
> *'T is not enough no harshness gives offense,*
> *The sound must seem an echo to the sense:*   4

FROM: AN ESSAY ON CRITICISM
ALEXANDER POPE

Line 1 is fairly regular, containing ten syllables, while in line 2, Pope adds a syllable, makes frequent *substitutions* (H-25) and dances through his meter gracefully in order to reinforce the meaning of lines 3 and 4. Pope deliberately does not elide *easiest* in line 2, and the elision in line 3, which allows the line to have ten syllables, emphasizes the misconceived idea that ten syllable lines are likely not to give offense. When we contrast the beauty of line 2 with the starkness of line 3, we realize what Pope thinks about metrical technique. Thus, by using elisions, the poet can call attention to lines with fewer or extra syllables.

Another use for elision is simply to change the sound of a word, to spell words as they are pronounced, or to indicate some kind of dialect. It is rare to find poets using elision in these ways, but it is a possibility.

Syncope

E-21   Another technique similar to synaeresis which creates the same effect is *syncope*. Syncope occurs when a syllable is dropped altogether (rather than combining two vowels into one), as in *nat'ral* for *natural* or *hast'ning* for *hastening*. Both syncope and synaeresis are commonly called elision, and both indicate that the poet is adhering rigidly to his base meter.

Polysyllabic Words in Modern Poetry

E-22 For most modern poetry, synaeresis and syncope seem artificial and out of tune with the freedom which the age enjoys. Poets must therefore be exceptionally careful when they use polysyllabic words, but the poets who use them best seem to be the best poets. Notice the skill with which the poet handles the following polysyllabic words while maintaining a strict pentameter line.

> She says,/ "But in/ content/ment I/ still feel
> The need/ of some/ impe/risha/ble bliss."

> FROM: SUNDAY MORNING
> WALLACE STEVENS

"VOWEL MUSIC" POETRY

E-23 Through the use of polysyllabic words or particular consonant and vowel patterns, a number of poets, especially during the present century, have experimented with creating new musical effects in poetry. What resulted was not really musical poetry, but a softening of the language, and much of this "vowel music" poetry has been very successful. Although poetry creating musical effects is not new (most of the masters used it, especially Milton), its resurgence in the twentieth century is of special importance because of the poets' conscious attempts to compose "musical poetry," and because the present century has been characterised as an age of machinery, which creates noises far removed from that of vowel music.

Characteristics of "Vowel Music"

E-24 While there is a high correlation between the number of vowels and vowel music poetry, the softening effect is not created only by the vowels but also by the use of words which soften the harsh (E-10) and plosive (E-9) consonants, by the use of fluid (E-6) and resonating (E-4, E-8) words, by frequent pyrrhic (H-17) and anapestic (H-13) substitutions, and by polysyllabic (E-15) words. (This much variation makes blank verse [K-173] a favorite form.)

Notice how these factors are working in the following vowel music stanza.

> Complacencies of the peignoir, and late
> Coffee and oranges in a sunny chair,
> And the green freedom of a cockatoo
> Upon a rug mingle to dissipate
> The holy hush of ancient sacrifice.
> She dreams a little, and she feels the dark
> Encroachment of that old catastrophe,
> As a calm darkens among water-lights.
> The pungent oranges and bright, green wings
> Seem things in some procession of the dead,

Winding across wide water, without sound,
The day is like wide-water, without sound,
Stilled for the passing of her dreaming feet
Over the seas to silent Palestine,
Dominion of the blood and sepulchre.

FROM: SUNDAY MORNING
WALLACE STEVENS

The entire stanza is not — could not be — composed of only soft words and sounds, but the general feeling of the poem is one of softness. When the plosive consonants do appear, they call attention to themselves:

Upon a rug mingle to dissipate

This is a very effective method for emphasis in vowel music.

E-25   One general tendency which vowel music poems seem to have is a kinship to accentual and syllabic meter rather than to accentual-syllabic meter. This is not to say that vowel music poetry is either accentual or syllabic, but notice the lack of accentual-syllabic influence in the first three lines of the sample stanza.

Complacencies of the peignoir and late

Coffee and oranges in a sunny chair,

And the green freedom of a cockatoo

The lack of any pattern suggests that vowel music patterns may be closely akin to syllabic or accentual meter rather than to the foot system, although it is reasonable to scan these lines noting frequent substitutions.

Compla/cencies/ of the/ peignor,/ and late

Coffee/ and or/anges/ in a sun/ny chair

And the/ green free/dom of/ a cock/atoo

E-26   As evidence in this passage, polysyllabic (E-15) words aggravate the problem of scansion (D-32). Obviously there is not identical stress (D-11) on both the third and fourth syllables of *complacencies*. They can be scanned as relative unstresses, but the dictionary pronunciation of this word places a secondary stress on the final syllable.

com/pla/cen/cies

If we scan the word using secondary stresses (D-20), the iambic base of the poem becomes much more evident:

"complá/cenciès/ ... and or/anges ... a cock/atoo"

Thus, eight of the fifteen feet in these lines can be scanned as iambic, establishing the poem's claim to a base meter. Secondary stresses, then, help give vowel music its more sensuous sounds, while granting the poet the luxury of a base meter.

E-27   Through enjambment (I-20), substitution (H-25), and polysyllabic words, vowel music poetry attempts to eliminate whatever artificial tone highly structured poetry might have. Clearly vowel music in poetry is a contrived effect, but the tone and mood of this poetry seem to make it less artificial.

E-27   Another device which makes vowel music seem less formal is its reliance on repetition of words, rather than on formal rhythms. For example, here:

> Remote on heaven's hill, that has endured
> As April's green endures; or will endure
> Like her remembrance of awakened birds,
> Or her desire for June and evening, tipped
> By the consummation of the swallow's wings.
>
> FROM: SUNDAY MORNING
> WALLACE STEVENS

Still another characteristic of vowel music poetry is the repetition of consonants and vowels. Notice the repetition of the consonant sounds c and p in the lines in Frame E-24.

E-28   Thus repetition, both of words and consonants, along with frequent use of substitutions, enjambment, and polysyllabic words, are the primary means by which vowel music poetry, without a strongly emphasized foot, achieves a decisive rhetorical effect with an extremely informal tone.

E-29   The explicator should remember that vowel music poetry is dependent upon its sound and mood, and that emphasis is usually achieved through consonants rather than through substitution. Three types of sound association which give emphasis and effect to vowel music are *alliteration* (E-30), *consonance* (E-32), and *assonance* (E-34).

ALLITERATION

E-30   When consonant repetition is focused at the beginnings of syllables, the repetition is called alliteration, as in:

> Large mannered motions of his mythy mind.

In vowel music alliteration is sometimes used to stress words or sentences, and there is a curious correlation among words which are stressed by alliteration. ·

E-31   While internal repetition of consonants is not usually called alliteration, it has the same effect as initial repetition when it begins a syllable within the word. Consider this line:

Encroachment of that old catastrophe

Here the first *c* in *Encroachment* is alliterative with the *c* in *catastrophe* because it begins the middle syllable of *En-croach-ment*. Alliteration is a useful device when the poet wishes to focus on the details of a sequence of words. A reader cannot simply skim over an alliterative line, and it will therefore become conspicuous and emphasized if alliteration has not been overdone in the poem.

CONSONANCE AND ASSONANCE

E-32   When the final consonants of stressed syllables agree, but the preceeding vowels are different, *consonance* occurs. Chair/star is an example of consonance, since both end with *r* which is preceeded by different vowels. Terminal consonance creates *half rhyme* (I-73) or *slant rhyme*. Consonance differs from alliteration in that the final consonants are repeated rather than the initial consonants.

E-33   Since vowel music poetry is generally unrhymed, consonance plays an important function in forming associations. Internal consonance also assists in establishing the rhetoric toward which vowel music poetry usually strives.

E-34   Another technique used to create vowel music is *assonance,* in which identical vowels are followed by different consonants in two or more stressed syllables. For example, the *-pla-* in *complacencies* assonates with the *la/* in *late* in this line:

Complacencies of the peignoir, and late

Also there is assonance between *g* ree *n and f* ree *dom* in this line:

The green freedom of a cockatoo.

In assonance there is approximate sound between words, whereas in rhyme there is exact sound. When assonating words come at the end of two lines, they form *half rhyme* (I-73).

Assonance as Syllabic Binder

E-35   When assonance occurs in consecutive syllables, as between *g* ree *n* and *f* ree *dom:*

The green freedom of a cockatoo

then the syllables are "bound together" in a way that gives greater emphasis to the unit. When assonance binds consecutive syllables, it is called a *syllabic binder*. Syllabic binders give even greater emphasis to a relationship than does alliteration or consonance.

Review/self-check

E-36 (a)   Sound is determined by the type and order into which vowels and consonants fall. Identify the types of consonants italicized in each of the following examples:

1. a*m*azing
2. *c*oagulate
3. *slush*
4. mi*lli*on
5. *sp*it

1. resonating (E-4)
2. harsh (E-10)
3. exhaustive (E-5)
4. liquid (E-6)
5. plosive (E-9)

E-36 (b)   In the following lines, identify the consonant types.

> *Then how should I begin*
> *To spit out all the butt ends of my days and ways.*

FROM: THE LOVE SONG OF J. ALFRED PRUFROCK
T. S. ELIOT

resonating:

way*s*	*th*en
day*s*	begi*n*
e*n*ds	

harsh: begin
liquid: a*ll*   *w*ays
exhaustive: *s*pit   *sh*ould
plosive: *b*egin   s*p*it
                  ou*t*   *b*utt
                  *d*ays   *t*o
                  shoul*d*

E-37   What seems to be the function of the liquid consonant placed amid the plosive ones in the example?

to emphasize that everything cannot be spit out

E-38   *S* alliteration is one of the most common means for making a line _____.

soft (E-7)

E-39   When a poem contains polysyllabic words, it is probably trying to achieve a _____ mood, although this mood may be dispelled in the next line.

soft (E-15)

E-40   When explicating a line containing polysyllabic words, determine how they fit into the _____ _____.

base meter (E-18)

E-41   Vowel music is not a separate genre of poetry, but utilizes sound in order to create a _____ effect.

musical (E-23)

E-42   While vowel music may be accurately approached from an accentual-syllabic point of view (if liberal substitution is allowed), it also possesses some properties of _____ and _____ meter.

accentual/syllabic (E-25)

E-43   The base meter of poems containing polysyllabic words can be best seen by scanning extensively with _____ stresses.

secondary (E-26)

E-44 (a)   In the following lines from a vowel music poem, identify examples of the elements common to vowel music.

> Supple and turbulent, a ring of men
> Shall chant in orgy on a summer morn
> Their boisterous devotion to the sun,
> Not as a god, but as a god might be,
> Naked among them, like a savage source.
> Their chant shall be a chant of paradise,

FROM: SUNDAY MORNING
WALLACE STEVENS

slant rhyme:	men, mourn, sun
syllabic binders:	supple-turbulent
resonating consonants:	ring, men, summer, morn
liquid consonants:	shall, supple, turbulent
alliteration:	shall-summer-supple
	savage-source
plosiveness for emphasis:	Not as a god, but as a
	god might be
repetition:	god, chant
polysyllabic words:	turbulent
	boisterous
	devotion
	paradise

E-44 (b)   Note the following examples of liberal substitution:

> Supple/ and tur/bulent/ a ring/ of men
> Shall chant/ in or/gy on/ a sum/mer morn
> Their bois/terous/ devo/tion to/ the sun,
> Not as/ a god,/ but as/ a god/ might be,
> Naked/ among/ them, like/ a sav/age source.
> Their chant/ shall be/ a chant/ of par/adise.

Tone
and
Meaning

◀‖▶

Tone is dependent upon the *sound of words* (E-1 ff), and is closely related to *paradox* (G-1), *hyperbole* (G-9), and *irony* (G-13). Before tone can be understood, the *point of view* (A-19 ff) must be defined clearly.

A DEFINITION

F-1 Tone is usually defined by modern critics as the reflection of the author's attitude toward his subject, his persona, himself, or his audience. We can say, then, that tone is the *expression* or *reflection of attitude,* and if we accept this definition, tone is the most important single element of any art, since the ultimate aim of art is to control emotions and attitudes.

F-2 If tone is a reflection of attitude, and if the ultimate aim of art is to control emotions and attitudes, then whatever goes into establishing tone may be one of the most important elements in poetry. However, the usual definition of tone is really too inclusive to mean a great deal. Yet since the word is one of the most frequently used in poetry, perhaps it is best to accept it on its own terms and examine the elements of it.

F-3 Tone is created in one of two ways or by a combination of both: tone is established through the meaning of words, either *denotatively* (F-4) or *connotatively* (F-4), and tone is established through the sound of words.

DENOTATION AND CONNOTATION

F-4 Words "mean" in two ways: through *denotation* and *connotation.* When we denote the properties of a word without considering its emotional associations, we have a denotative meaning; denotation is, in effect, the formal definition of the word. In order to determine a denotative meaning we need only look up the word in an authoritative dictionary, where the primary definitions will be the denotative meanings (though the dictionary may also provide information about the associations of the words, and hence provide clues to emotional associations). The standard dictionary for complete historical meanings of English words is *The Oxford English Dictionary* (formerly the *New English Dictionary,* and now available in various abridged or compressed editions), which gives all known definitions, both modern and historical, with a tracing of the word's origins.

Connotation, on the other hand, refers to the associations which surround the word, and they are almost always unwritten until they become part of the formal definition. The word "mercenary," for example, simply means denotatively a soldier who is paid to fight by an army not of his own region. But the connotations which accompany the word are numerous, and "mercenary" has come to mean much more than its original denotative definition. However, when those connotative elements of a word become universally accepted, then the connotative meaning becomes a new denotative variation in the definition, and there are, of course, many definitions to many words.

Uses for Denotation

F-5   Poets delight in using words which are rich in both denotative and connotative associations, and while the skillful use of rich words invariably results in pleasurable poetry, it presents problems for the explicator.

F-6   Denotative problems result not only from the various definitions possible for a word, but also from the parts of speech for which the word can be used. For example, the noun *mark* has a number of definitions ranging from the starting point in a race (*on your mark*) to a feature of a person's character. But in addition to its various definitions when used as a noun, *mark* can also be used as a verb and adjective. We *mark a book* meaning to make marks in it, or that we *mark a person* meaning to single him out. Using the word as an adjective, we speak of *a man marked for greatness,* meaning that he is predestined to become great. Having examined the differing definitions and their possibilities, we must then put the word into context and see how these affect the potential tone. For example, consider the following stanza:

> *I wander through each chartered street,*
> *Near where the chartered Thames does flow,*
> *And mark in every face I meet*
> *Marks of weakness, marks of woe.*
>
> FROM: LONDON
> WILLIAM BLAKE

The explicator must decide what the poet is trying to do with the word *mark*. In order to determine the denotative meanings the explicator must first establish dramatic situation and point of view.

F-7   In the stanza above, the narrator is wandering through the streets of London looking at the situation, particularly the faces of the people he meets. From the dramatic situation it is clear that when he says he *marks in every face,* he means that he *notes* or *sees* in every face. But *mark* in line 3 might also mean that the bard figuratively places a mark upon the people who see him because his influence in some way perhaps hurts them. In line 4 the use of the word shifts from a verb to a noun; the repetition emphasizes its importance and creates an effect through its sound. Then, too, *marks of weakness* can be seen as character traits, while *marks of woe* are evidently reactions to environmental conditions; that is, one is created within the human mind, the other without.

F-8   Thus, the denotative problems are twofold: determining which meanings of the word are applicable, and determining how a shift in the use affects meaning and emphasis. When explicating, it is essential that all definitions be considered and that any one of them having any association with the poem be explained, even if it is not at first clear how it applies.

EQUIVOCATION AND DOUBLE MEANING

F-9   When several meanings of a word can apply to one situation, *equivocation* results, and because of equivocation it is essential that every possible definition be considered. Equivocation frequently indicates that the poem is working on several levels of interpretation. Seeing how each meaning fits into the poem will lead to an understanding on all levels. (Refer to G-1 ff for a discussion of words which have conflicting meanings.)

Puns

F-10   Another technique which is associated with tone is the *pun*, which occurs when words which have similar pronunciations have entirely different meanings. With equivocation the same word has different meanings; with the pun entirely different words are pronounced similarly, though there is normally no relation between their meanings. Thus by use of a pun the speaker establishes a deliberate, but apparently accidental, connection between two meanings that the reader/listener would not ordinarily associate together. The result may be a surprise recognition of an unusual or striking connection, or more often, a (hopefully) humorous accidental connection.

F-11   Thus with puns, one word will suggest another meaning which may enrich the poem. But the pun, as has equivocation, has fallen in bad hands during various periods, and as a result is seldom used in modern poetry for serious purpose. "Bad puns" make poems absurd and ridiculous, but there are some "good puns." The following is an example of a pun which might have once pleased readers, but only revolts modern critics: "They went and told the sexton and the sexton tolled the bell" (the second meaning in this case has not much point, and so the humor evaporates rapidly).

F-12   Puns rely on the reader's recognition, and they are usually easy to spot because of the sound similarity between two different words which will be located within proximity of each other (as at the end of F-11 above). On the other hand, if the pun is obvious, only one of the spellings may be explicitly included if the other is sure to come to mind. For example, on a sign marking a well-known lovers leap: "Into this chasm, many a great lover has heaved his size" (where "sighs" is an obvious assumption).

F-13   Because the pun is often absurd and ridiculous, poets are careful in their use of it, and when one occurs it is usually to characterize or stereotype a situation. Determine how the poet wants his pun to be taken and any effect which one word's definition might have on the other, and there should be no trouble with it.

PLACING TONE IN ITS CONTEXT

F-14   An important consideration with tone is seeing the poem in context with its age. In other words, tone, as the expression of attitude, will depend in part upon how words were used when the poem was written, as well as on how they are used now; thus the entire tone may change from age to age as the use of the words changes. With Shakespeare, for example, passages which we now read as serious and meditative were read in the Elizabethan period as hilarious and bawdy. So when explicating tone, we must place the poem in its period and try to look at it objectively — in the same way that a reader of that period would look at it, and although it is impossible to look objectively at a poem outside our own period, it is necessary to try if we are to be fair to the poem and if we are attempting to understand why it was written.

F-15   Looking at a poem in its own period is important if we are to understand why it was written, but the tone must also be looked at in modern terms since the aim of poetry is, after all, controlling the emotions of the reader. If the meanings of words have changed so that Shakespeare's bawdy is now serious and meditative, then to the modern readers they are serious and meditative whether they were ever anything else. So tone changes as meanings change, and whatever the words denote and connote now is what they mean unless we choose to read the poem entirely in its own period.

F-16   What this means is that tone is finally determined by the reader, not by the poet, although he has at his disposal a number of devices for controlling tone. So when a reader honestly decides, after placing the poem in context with its age, that a pun is flippant and obnoxious, then the pun is flippant and obnoxious, and if the poet did not intend it that way, then he has lost control of his reader.

F-17   Obviously tone is a problem for the poet since he has no control over how words will change after he is dead, and many good poems have been lost to an evolving language. Almost without exception the poetry which has survived is that whose tone has been able to maintain fair stability and consistency within the changing language.

STABILIZING TONE WITH SOUND

F-18   What this means, of course, is that poets must, if their poetry is to be both excellent in this age and lasting in others, use other means in addition to denotation and connotation for producing tone. More stable elements (though not especially stable) such as imagery (B-1) and allusion (M-1 ff) give a wider spectrum through which tone can be seen, and if the poet can incorporate enough stable elements into his poem, the principal tone will remain constant even though some passages may get lost, as with Shakespeare. But there is no such thing as a completely stable device, so the poet must use as many as he can in hopes that not all of them will change.

F-19   Although vowels vary from age to age and even from region to region, one very stable device which is available to the poet is sound, and poets will capitalize on it as much as possible. When explicating first look for sound, then for the total effect of all the other devices, and finally for specific connotative and denotative meanings.

CONNOTATION

F-20   Connotation presents even a greater problem for the explicator than denotation since there is no standard use for it and no reference material which can help. Yet all poets work under connotative influence since they do not work in a vacuum or out of a dictionary, and the explicator must deal with the emotional associations of the word.

F-21   The explicator's job is made even more difficult because English poetry is so widely read and written, and because of this he must be very liberal and open-minded when dealing with connotative problems in contemporary poetry. Because there is no standard source for connotative meanings, and because connotations are derived in so many various parts of the English speaking world, the explicator simply cannot afford to pass up any possibility for exploring possible connotations. For example, if the explicator suspects that it is possible for the word "mother" to be pejoratively used, then he must consider that possibility until he can prove conclusively that it could not have that connotation in his particular poem.

F-22   There will, of course, be times when the explicator simply cannot know that a word is being used in a certain connotative way, and he will necessarily make some mistakes, but in considering all known possibilities and admitting ignorance for others, the explicator has done all he can do.

DICTION

F-23   The language used most commonly by the people is called "colloquial." When the colloquial or vernacular takes on emotional associations, it has connotative meaning; when the connotative meaning becomes standard, then there is denotative meaning, but colloquial itself means only that the word is in common use.

F-24   When vernacular is used in poetry it greatly affects the tone because even in our age of liberated art, poetry remains the medium of elevated language, and when the poet uses less than elevated language there is a contrast which we did not expect.

F-25   Because "vernacular" implies less than elevated language, it affects the tone because we did not expect to hear it in the poem. "Vernacular" does not, however, necessarily imply that the language being used is slang, though it may be. Slang may be a part of the colloquial or vernacular, but in poetry it does not have to be. "Vernacular" simply means that the language is of a lower diction than we have come to expect in poetry or from a particular dramatic situation (A-1).

F-26   When we understand a dramatic situation we may have expectations as to what sort of language should accompany it, and when the language is of a lower diction than what we expect, vernacular is being used. For example, when we agree to hear the Christmas story, we expect that it will be told in *King James'* language because that's the way it is always told, but the voice speaking to us in the following stanza is not that of the wiseman's voice we have always imagined.

> *'A cold coming we had of it,*
> *Just the worst time of the year*
> *For a journey, and such a long journey:*
> *The ways deep and the weather sharp,*
> *The very dead of winter.'*
> *And the camels galled, sore-footed, refractory,*
> *Lying down in the melting snow.*

There were times we regretted
The summer palaces on slopes, the terraces,
And the silken girls bringing sherbet.
Then the camel men cursing and grumbling
And running away, and wanting their liquor and women,
And the night-fires going out, and the lack of shelters,
And the cities hostile and the towns unfriendly
And the villages dirty and charging high prices:
A hard time we had of it.
At the end we preferred to travel all night,
Sleeping in snatches,
With the voices singing in our ears, saying
That this was all folly.

FROM: JOURNEY OF THE MAGI
T. S. ELIOT

Certainly there is nothing common about the Magus' language; he speaks in beautiful and elevated diction, but he speaks in modern English, not in King James English, and the difference between what we expect to hear and the language that is used makes the tone a central device in this poem.

F-27   Because the Magus makes no mention of "mangers" or "Bethlehem" or guiding stars, and because the language is modern, the poet establishes an attitude toward the event which becomes essential to the understanding of the poem. It is the difference, then, between the voice which is expected by the reader because of the dramatic situation and the voice which actually speaks that determines the level of the diction.

F-28   In "Church Going," (A-75) for example, the narrator's diction in stanza 1 tells us that he is not a man of this church, and probably not of any church, but does it reveal his attitude toward churches? In line 1 ("Once I am sure there's nothing going on,") there are words which strongly suggest the tone: "sure, there's nothing going on." Since "sure" and "there's" are associated with natural, everyday speech, they reduce the elevation of diction, while "nothing going on" gives a clear indication of attitude for two reasons:

F-29   First, if there is "nothing" happening now, "something" must happen at other times; yet Christians believe that formal church proceedings – the *something* to which the narrator indirectly refers – do not constitute the backbone of religion. Although formal proceedings are not supposed to be the basis for the church, the narrator feels that unless something is happening, "nothing" is going on. For the narrator, as for the reader, the something may be part of the ritual as a service or wedding, or it may be part of the non-ritualistic function as a tea or kindergarden. What the poet has very casually implied is that in the decline of the Church people have come to confuse what was fundamental to Christian doctrine with what is really unimportant; that to the modern churchman the times when "nothing" happens is unimportant, and the times when "something" happens is important beyond all perspective, thus reversing the doctrine of the early church. Although the narrator doesn't realize what he has done, he has subtly condemned the modern church through his use of the word "nothing."

F-30   The second implication of "nothing going on" is that the narrator does not really understand what happens in churches. Things "go on" but he is removed from them.

F-31   What the tone in the first line does, then, is to establish an attitude of indifference for the church which contrasts with the narrator's concern for holiness later in the poem, and it is the narrator's attitude toward the church that makes his concern for holiness effective.

F-32   Although there are only three other especially modern or vernacular terms in the poem — "stuff," "holy end," "Brewed God knows how long" in stanza 1 — and while the diction in the rest of the poem is quite elevated, line 1 is enough to permeate throughout the poem and establish its tone.

TONE AND SOUND

F-33   In addition to the effect which the meaning of words has on tone, both denotatively and connotatively, tone is also influenced by the sound of the lines. There are five basic elements which determine a line's sound: stress (D-11), duration (D-84), vowels and consonants (E-3), meter (D-25), and rhyme (I-63 ff).

F-34   Although it is possible to analyze the tone of every line in the poem through an analysis of the basic elements, it is usually unnecessary to do so because in most places the tone will be clearly defined by the other elements as well. If, however, the tone is too subtle to recognize through reading, and if it seems important to the explication, then look at the five elements individually, then relative to each other, and finally in relation to the entire stanza or poem.

F-35   Generalizations which can be made about each of the elements apply to the tone of that particular line, but it is the combination of these elements which finally determines sound or tone. While each element contributes to sound, not any one of the elements can individually create tone, and it is the combination of all of them that finally establishes the poet's attitude.

F-36   Since there are a great number of possible combinations, and therefore a great many different sounds, no helpful generalizations can be made about how the sound of a line is created, but it is usually not difficult to see how the poet is working. Taking the following stanza out of context (which is not really possible when working with tone) as an example, we can analyze it for sound.

I grow old . . . I grow old . . .
I shall wear the bottoms of my trousers rolled.

FROM: THE LOVE SONG OF J. ALFRED PRUFROCK
T. S. ELIOT

F-36 (1)   Looking only at line 1, we can feel a progression of lengthening duration which results in fatigue: the harsh g followed by the long *o* and liquid *w* give "grow" more duration (D-84) than "I".

Example/self-check

F-36 (2) The long _____ in "old" creates a syllabic binder (E-35) with "grow," and this combined with the duration of the word gives equal pressure to it.	*o*
F-36 (3) The liquid *l* in "old" and the plosive *d* give the word considerably longer _____ than the first two, which, when combined with the _____ binder brings equal pressure (D-70) on "old."	duration (D-84) syllabic
F-36 (4) Because "old" does have a _____ *l*, and because "I grow old" has a progressive durational lengthening, "old" reverberates throughout the line, but because of the relatively equal _____ on all three words, "old" does not dominate.	liquid (E-6) pressure
F-36 (5) What this reverberation does in an atmosphere of lacking dominance is to suggest a mood of sadness and introspection.	
F-36 (6) The absence of a dominating word, and the _____ of "old" suggest a sad and introspective tone, and because the cadence of the line is slow and deliberate, when "I grow old" is repeated, it is clear that the tone is one of despairing resignation.	reverberation
F-36 (7) In addition to the sound of the consonants and vowels, the slow, deliberate _____ influences the tone.	cadence
F-36 (8) The sound, the cadence, and the repetition of "I grow old" suggest a tone of _____ _____.	despairing resignation

Review:

F-37 Tone is a reflection of the author's _____; it is established through both the _____ and _____ of words.	attitude (F-1) meaning (F-3) sound
F-38 Words mean in two ways, through _____ and connotation. Denotation is a description of the	denotation (F-4)

meaning of a word without considering its _____ associations.

F-39   The explication problems surrounding denotation are that a word can have numerous _____ and can be used as different _____ _____ _____.

F-40   Before the denotative and connotative properties can be confirmed, both the dramatic situation and _____ _____ _____ must be established.

F-41   When two or more definitions of a word can apply to one situation, _____ results.

F-42   Equivocation is a good indication that the poem is working on several _____ of interpretation.

F-43   Puns work because different words have similar _____, so that the meaning of one word is associated with the other word, and in some way the shifted meaning is pleasurable.

F-44   Placing a poem in its period is important because the meaning of words _____ from period to period.

F-90   It is important to look at a poem in both its own period and in our own in order to understand how it attempts to control _____.

F-91   That the tone of the poem changes substantiates the theory that tone is created by the _____, not the poet, and what a poem means to the reader is what the poem means.

F-92   In order to control change in tone, poets use other devices so that tone will not be completely dependent on the meaning of words. One of the most stable devices which the poet can use is _____.

F-93   Elements which influence sound are: _____, _____, _____, _____, _____, _____.

It is, however, the _____ of all five which produces tone.

emotional (F-4)

meanings or definitions
parts of speech (F-6)

point of view (F-6)

equivocation (F-9)

levels (F-9)

pronunciations (F-10)

changes (F-14)

emotions (F-15)

reader (F-16)

sound (F-19)

stress
duration, consonants &
vowels, meter, rhyme
(F-33)
combination (F-35)

One situation in which poetical vernacular occurs is when there is a difference between the diction used and the diction anticipated because of _____ _____.

dramatic situation (F-25)

Paradox, II▸ Hyperbole, and Irony

When a poet has made skillful use of paradox, hyperbole, or irony, these aspects of poetry may be among the most difficult for readers to respond to fully or to explicate carefully, partly because there seem to be no hard and fast rules for readers to apply in a simple way for understanding them. It is only through a very open awareness and perceptiveness and a certain amount of sophistication that readers can confidently appreciate what poets may be doing with these devices. However, we can begin to get at these undertones of a poem through sensitive attention to the effects of *sound* (E-1 ff) and to the poem's literal sense.

PARADOX

G-1 Paradox is a statement of apparently contradictory ideas within one assertion which, when reduced to a certain base level, will show that some implications of the seemingly contradictory ideas can in fact reach a common level of far-reaching truth.

G-2 Paradox, then, consists of at least two opposing statements which can be shown to have a common truth which is not obvious when first considered. For example, when we first hear that "a little learning is a dangerous thing," we are puzzled at how learning could be *dangerous* until we consider it further.

G-3 The value of paradox lies in its power of emphasizing itself, and in doing so, causing the reader to think about an apparent absurdity which leads to a deeper truth.

G-4 The basic properties of paradox are that on the first level the two statements are totally contrary and unresolvable, while at their base level the contraries contain a common element of truth which demonstrates something more profound. For example, when the Renaissance poets spoke of dying to create life (men "died" sexually, and in giving of themselves conceived life), they were using paradox to reduce contraries to a common truth: that death and life take their existence from the same source.

G-5 Prophets, such as Christ, frequently spoke in paradox to show that truth is not always apparent; poets who use paradox must have as a premise to their philosophy that there is some basic level of universal truth, and most likely their poetry will be in search of it. One good example is the principal Christian paradox, that Christ died to give men life, which suggests like the Renaissance, life coming through a kind of death.

G-6 Whenever a poem relies on paradox, there is a good chance that it will be in search of some universal truth; it is the explicator's job to take the paradox to its roots and discover the common truth. When the explicator has discovered what truth the poet wants us to see in the paradox, he can then relate it to the theme of the poem (oftentimes the truth and the theme will be the same).

113

Oxymoron: A Variation on Paradox

G-7 Closely related to paradox is *oxymoron,* which occurs when two paradoxical words are placed in juxtaposition, such as *devilish angel* or *wise fool.* Oxymorons are normally used to call attention to a line rather than for discovering a common truth.

G-8 An oxymoron is neither as profound nor as important as paradox, and it is not used for calling attention to a new level of truth so much as it is to call attention to the line or section of the poem which contains it.

HYPERBOLE

G-9 Hyperbole (overstatement) and understatement, as well as irony, are devices which depend upon the reader's awareness that they cannot be taken as literal truth. In other words, the poet deliberately misstates, underplays, or exaggerates, but in doing so knows that the reader is aware of what he is doing. Consider the following poem, for example.

> *He clasps the crag with crooked hands;*
> *Close to the sun in lonely lands,*
> *Ringed with the azure world, he stands.*
>
> *The wrinkled sea beneath him crawls;*
> *He watches from the mountain walls,*
> *And like a thunderbolt he falls.*

THE EAGLE
ALFRED, LORD TENNYSON

We know that an eagle cannot get close to the sun (though he looks as though he is from the ground) and that he can't fall with the swiftness of a thunderbolt, but by incorporating hyperbole into a metaphor, the image is made vivid and forceful.

G-10 As with irony, hyperbole and understatement work because the reader can perceive the difference between the importance of the dramatic situation and the manner in which it is said.

G-11 In "The Eagle," hyperbole helps us to understand the awe which the narrator feels for the eagle, and we come to understand him and the dramatic situation through it. Hyperbole and understatement usually cause the reader to understand or identify with the narrator, and because of this they affect tone rather than directly affecting theme.

G-12 When explicating hyperbole, then, the important thing to look for is the difference between what the dramatic situation calls for and how it is said. This should lead to a better understanding of its effect on *tone* (F-1) and *point of view* (A-19).

IRONY

G-13 Irony (which may or may not be used for satire) works with the discrepancies between what the words say and what the narrator means. Just as with hyperbole, irony depends on the reader's recognition of the difference between what is said and what is done or meant. There are three basic types of poetical irony:

(1)   the difference between what the speaker says and what he means,
(2)   the difference between what happens and what should have happened,
(3)   the difference between what the speaker knows (and says) and what the poet knows.

G-14   Irony is pleasurable for the reader because he eventually comes to the discovery that he understands why the difference is important, and he is willing to accept it, or at least to think about it, because he has come to it himself, rather than having it pointed out. The problem, of course, is that the reader may not discover that there is a discrepancy and may miss the point of the poem entirely; this is complicated by the problem that the best irony is often that which is most subtle and hardest to detect. If the reader doesn't discover that the poet is using irony, he may miss the point altogether since the ironic poem often says just the opposite of what it means.

Irony (1)

G-15   *Irony (1): The difference between what is said and what is meant.* For an example of this type of irony, in the following poem a good portion of the meaning and most of the pleasure is derived from the ironic closing which the rest of the poem builds to.

> My long two-pointed ladder's sticking through a tree
> Toward heaven still
> And there's a barrel that I didn't fill
> Beside it, and there may be two or three
> Apples I didn't pick upon some bough.   5
> But I am done with apple-picking now.
> Essence of winter sleep is on the night,
> The scent of apples: I am drowsing off.
> I cannot rub the strangeness from my sight
> I got from looking through a pane of glass   10
> I skimmed this morning from the drinking trough
> And held against the world of hoary grass.
> It melted, and I let it fall and break.
> But I was well
> Upon my way to sleep before it fell,   15
> And I could tell
> What form my dreaming was about to take.
> Magnified apples appear and disappear,
> Stem end and blossom end,
> And every fleck of russet showing clear.   20
> My instep arch not only keeps the ache,
> It keeps the pressure of a ladder-round.
> I feel the ladder sway as the boughs bend.
> And I keep hearing from the cellar bend

> The rumbling sound   25
> Of load on load of apples coming in.
> For I have had too much
> Of apple-picking: I am overtired
> Of the great harvest I myself desired.
> There were ten thousand thousand fruit to touch,   30
> Cherish in hand, lift down, and not let fall.
> For all
> That struck the earth,
> No matter if not bruised or spiked with stubble,
> Went surely to the cider-apple heap   35
> As of no worth.
> One can see what will trouble
> This sleep of mine, whatever sleep it is.
> Were he not gone.
> The woodchuck could say whether it's like his   40
> Long sleep, as I describe its coming on,
> Or just some human sleep.

AFTER APPLE-PICKING
ROBERT FROST

G-15 (1)   Although the poem centers on the physical activity of apple-picking, it seems to be more about sleep or dreaming than about apples, since sleeping is specifically referred to in lines 8, 15, 17, 38, 41, 42, and implied in many other places.

G-15 (2)   Apples are normally harvested in late fall, and it is now after apple-picking; so we know that the season which is approaching is winter, which in nature suggests a dormant period of hibernation.

G-15 (3)   Apple-picking, then, is a physical activity which will dominate the sleep which the narrator will have during the winter, and through line 37 the poem describes what the dream will be like. But the *symbols* (C-1) which Frost has gently pushed throughout the poem begin to haunt us, and we start to realize that while *unfilled barrels* in line 3 are unfinished responsibilities, and that *apples* are experience, this is not a poem only about apple-picking or one's duties in life. *Sleep* comes to mean *death*, and the *woodchuck*, who is a ground-hog, thus becomes a corpse.

G-15 (4)   Beginning with line 38 the poem turns strangely ironic, and what has seemed to have been a perfectly normal description of and reaction to apple-picking becomes the theme of the poem; *one* cannot see what will trouble his sleep unless he can see that the poem is not about apple-picking or even about dreaming, but is about man's intellectual process of changing physical events into metaphysical experience through imagination.

G-15 (5)   Unless the reader has imagination enough to make the leap from the physical description to metaphysical concepts he will not be able to see what *sleep it is*. But this in itself does not constitute the full irony; Frost once again turns to the feeling of hibernation which he suggested in the poem's beginning, this time openly using the image of an animal which does hibernate. Were the woodchuck not gone (away and to sleep) he could say whether the dreams were alike, but by this time the reader knows that the woodchuck could not say because he does not suffer from the imagination which impairs man's sleep.

G-15 (6)   When in lines 37-38 Frost says, "One can see what will trouble/ This sleep of mine, whatever sleep it is," the reader isn't fully prepared for the irony because he hasn't met the woodchuck. But once the narrator compares himself to the animal, the reader can understand that what troubles the narrator, unlike the woodchuck, is that he can question what sleep is and compare it to death.

G-15 (7)   The last line *or just some human sleep,* is an example of understatement, (G-9) but in this context it also becomes ironic because the reader knows that it is not just some human sleep; indeed, it is not sleep at all as the woodchuck sleeps, but an awareness of life and death magnified by imagination. (See pp. 70-71 for a complete explication.)

Irony (2)

G-16   *Irony (3): The difference between what is known and what is revealed; between what has happened and what we "know" should happen.*

   In "After Apple-Picking," the irony comes in the discrepancies between what the speaker says and what he means, whereas in the following poem, the other two types of irony work impressively.

> *I met a traveller, from an antique land*
> *Who said: Two vast and trunkless legs of stone*
> *Stand in the desert . . . Near them, on the sand,*
> *Half sunk, a shattered visage lies, whose frown,*
> *And wrinkled lip, and sneer of cold command,*
> *Tell that its sculptor well those passions read*
> *Which yet survive, stamped on these lifeless things,*
> *The hand that mocked them, and the heart that fed;*
> *And on the pedestal these words appear:*
> *"My name is Ozymandias, king of kings:*
> *Look on my works, ye Mighty, and despair!"*
> *Nothing beside remains. Round the decay*
> *Of that colossal wreck, boundless and bare*
> *The lone and level sands stretch far away.*
>
> OZYMANDIAS
> P. B. SHELLEY

G-16 (1)   The most prominent irony, and that which forms the basis for the poem falls in the third category: the difference between what Ozymandias expected would happen and what actually happened; his kingdom which conquered kings was itself destroyed.

Irony (3)

G-16 (2)   *Irony (3): The difference between what one speaker knows or says and what the poet (or another narrator) lets the reader see;* this type is conventionally known as *dramatic irony.*

Irony (3) is illustrated with the quote from the pedestal. The traveller, and in any case the narrator, and possibly even the sculptor of the pedestal, knew what Ozymandias the king could not imagine, namely the collapse of the kingdom. It is further irony that the sculptor's work, not Ozymandias', is the last remaining evidence that the kingdom ever existed. (See pp. 27-28 for a full discussion of "Ozymandias.")

G-17   Irony, then, usually seduces the reader into thinking in a certain direction, then reverses what it has originally proposed. When explicating irony it is a good idea to show how a literal reading will not be consistent with the poem, while showing how the reversal will. Obviously, irony is quite dependent on the effectiveness of point of view.

Example/self-check

G-18   How does irony function in the following poem?

> When my mother died I was very young,
> And my father sold me while yet my tongue
> Could scarcely cry " 'weep! 'weep! 'weep! 'weep!"
> So your chimneys I sweep, and in soot I sleep.   4
>
> There's little Tom Dacre, who cried when his head,
> That curled like a lamb's back, was shaved; so I said,
> "Hush, Tom! never mind it, for when your head's bare,
> You know that the soot cannot spoil your white hair."   8
>
> And so he was quiet, and that very night,
> As Tom was asleeping, he had such a sight!
> That thousands of sweepers, Dick, Joe, Ned, and Jack,
> Were all of them locked up in coffins of black.   12
>
> And by came an Angel who had a bright key,
> And he opened the coffins and set them all free;
> Then down a green plain leaping, laughing, they run,
> And wash in a river, and shine in the sun.   16
>
> Then naked and white, all their bags left behind,
> They rise upon clouds and sport in the wind;
> And the Angel told Tom, if he'd be a good boy,
> He'd have God for his father, and never want joy.   20
>
> And so Tom awoke, and we rose in the dark,
> And got with our bags and our brushes to work.
> Though the morning was cold, Tom was happy and warm;
> So if all do their duty they need not fear harm.   24

> THE CHIMNEY SWEEPER
> WILLIAM BLAKE

G-18 (1)   In lines 7 and 8 the narrator tells Tom not to mind being bald because the soot won't spoil his hair this way. What type of irony is this?

the difference between what is and what should be (type 2)

G-18 (2)   Tom dreams that an Angel will set him free. What are the chances for this?

unlikely

G-18 (3)   Why is this ironic?

because the narrator believes that it will happen while the reader knows it won't

G-18 (4)   Obviously the narrator has learned about Angels through religious teachings, probably from the Church and his parents. Why is this ironic?

because his parents, who must profess Christianity, sold him, and because the Church allows these conditions to exist while teaching ideals

G-18 (5)   How does the equivocation with *want* (line 20) become ironical?

it implies (equivocally) that one should not want or desire joy when near God

G-18 (6)   To whom must duty be done?

chimney masters and to the God that churches teach

G-18 (7)   Why is this ironic?

it equates the Church's God and the masters, as well as equating the nature of the duty

G-18 (8)   What will happen to the sweepers if they continue doing their duty?

they are likely to die from lung diseases

G-18 (9)   What will happen if they don't do their duty?

they are likely to be beaten, killed, sold, or set free

G-18 (10)   By analogy, what may the reader infer from the fact that Tom is happy and warm because of believing the Angel will save him?

the Church may be making our lives miserable too, but making us content in our misery

G-18 (11)   The boys clearly state that if they do their duty they will be saved by God. What does the poet believe?

that the boys are being abused by the Church and society, and unless something is done about it many more of them will die

G-18 (12)   What types of irony does the poem use?

type (3), the difference between what the speaker knows and what the poet knows; also type (2), the difference between what situation exists and what should exist.

THE POET'S METRICAL TOOLS

The
Foot

The foot is a devised unit for explaining how the *accentual-syllabic* system (D-58) is working. In order to understand the foot more fully, refer to *relative stress* (D-11, D-76), *metrical contract* (D-19), and *base meter* (D-35).

THE NATURE OF THE FOOT IN POETRY

H-1   Looking at the relative stress of syllables will help the explicator who is trying to explain how the emphasis of a line is achieved. Unless readers can accept that no two syllables carry equal stress or *pressure* (D-77), they will have a difficult time explaining the effects of meter and sound.

H-2   Although it is always best to work with relative stress, the nature of the accentual-syllabic system, in which most English poems are written, encourages readers to hear beats; i.e., a pattern of stresses and unstresses. This fact has a useful effect for the poet who is trying to develop patterns of emphasis, and for the reader who is trying to pick them out.

H-3   Because the accentual-syllabic system encourages readers to associate unstresses with stresses, the poet can take that expectation and change it to create emphasis.

H-4   In other words, the base meter establishes the expectation of a stress/unstress pattern, and when the poet changes that expectation, he creates emphasis, thus opening up a place where he can hammer at theme.

H-5   In order to explain how breaking the stress/unstress pattern creates tension or emphasis, metricists have devised methods for talking about the accentual-syllabic system, the most important of which is the foot.

H-6   In the accentual-syllabic system, unstressed syllables tend to group themselves around stressed syllables; so what metricists have done is to assume that in all accentual-syllabic poems there is a regular pattern of stress/unstress groupings. For example, consider this line:

And hell/ is more/ than half/ of par/adise.

FROM: LUKE HAVERGAL
E. A. ROBINSON

121

The first unstress seems to cling around the first stress, the second unstress around the second stress, and so on throughout the line. This set pattern makes this a *regular line* (D-17), and it is easy to see where the unstress/stress groups fall.

H-7   Metricists "assume" that all poems are regular (which isn't literally true, of course) so that they can have a valid basis for talking about associated stresses and unstresses. When unstresses are associated with stresses in the accentual-syllabic system, metricists call the group a foot. Consider this example:

$$\breve{}\quad\breve{}\quad/\quad\breve{}\quad\breve{}\quad/\quad\breve{}\quad\breve{}\quad/$$
With the sift/ed, harmon/ious pause,

> FROM: IN THE MOUNTAIN TENT
> JAMES DICKEY

There are two unstresses associated with each stress, and so this line consists of three feet which group themselves as (vv/).

BASIC TYPES OF FEET

H-8   What metricists have done is to examine the bulk of poetry to see how many combinations of stress/unstress patterns are possible, and while many metrical arguments have arisen from the search for kinds of feet, metricists have agreed on at least six varieties in English poetry:

iamb (v/)	dactyl (/vv)
trochee (/v)	spondee (//)
anapest (vv/)	pyrrhus (vv)

Examples/self-check

H-9   There are a number of combinations of unstresses/ stresses which may be formed. In other words, there are several different types of feet, depending upon the association of _____ to _____.

unstresses to stresses (H-7)

The Iamb

H-10   The result of the natural tendency of English to place a stress on every other syllable is that the basic foot in English consists of one unstress and one stress (v/). This basic _____ is called an iamb.

foot (H-7)

H-11   The following line is composed of iambs:

$$\breve{}\;/\quad\breve{}\;/\quad\breve{}\quad/\quad\breve{}\;/\quad\breve{}\;/$$
So long/ as men/ can breath/ or eyes/ can see,

> FROM: SONNET 18
> WILLIAM SHAKESPEARE

There are _____ iambic feet in each line.

An iamb is a foot in which _____ unstress and _____ stress are associated.

In English the iamb is the _____ foot, and most poetry is written primarily in iambs.

five

one
one (H-10)

basic

The Trochee

H-12   Another common foot in English is the trochee, which is the reverse of an iamb: stress/unstress (/v). Consider this line:

$$\overset{v}{A} \overset{/}{cold}/ \overset{/}{coming}/ \overset{v}{we} \overset{/}{had}/ \overset{v}{of} \overset{/}{it}$$

FROM: JOURNEY OF THE MAGI
T. S. ELIOT

There are four feet: three are iambic and _____.
The base meter of the line is _____.
Consider this line:

one is trochaic
iambic

$$\overset{/}{Double}/ \overset{v}{double},/ \overset{/}{toil} \overset{v}{and}/ \overset{/}{trouble}$$

FROM: MACBETH
WILLIAM SHAKESPEARE

There are _____ trochaic feet, and the base meter is _____.

four
trochaic

The Anapest

H-13   A third common foot, the anapest, forms the following pattern: unstress - unstress - stress (vv/). Consider this line:

$$\overset{v}{With} \overset{v}{the} \overset{/}{sift}/ \overset{v}{ed}, \overset{v}{harmon}/ \overset{vv}{ious} \overset{/}{pause},$$

There are three _____ feet.

anapestic

H-14   The unstress/stress patterns for the following feet are these:

iamb	( )
trochee	( )
anapest	( )

(v/)
(/v)
(vv/)

The three most common feet in English are the _____,   iamb
_____, and _____.   trochee, anapest

The Dactyl

H-15   The *dactyl,* formed of a stress followed by two
unstresses (/vv), is fairly common in isolated words,
but when this pattern is included in a line of poetry it
tends to break down and rearrange itself into compon-
ents of other types of feet. Consider, for example, how
to *scan* (D-32) this word:

$$\overset{/}{mean}\text{-}\overset{v}{ing}\text{-}\overset{v}{less}$$

The stress pattern forms a foot which is a _____.   dactyl
But when the pattern is incorporated into a line, we get
this:

$$\overset{v}{Po}\overset{/}{lite}/ \overset{/}{mean}\overset{v}{ing}/\overset{v}{less} \overset{/}{words}$$

FROM: EASTER 1916
W. B. YEATS

the dactyl is formed into a trochee and an _____.   iamb

Nonetheless, a few dactylic poems do exist; the base meter of the following line is dactylic:

$$\overset{/}{Af}\overset{v}{ter} \overset{v}{the}/ \overset{/}{pangs} \overset{v}{of} \overset{v}{a}/ \overset{/}{des}\overset{v}{per}\overset{v}{ate}/ \overset{/}{lo}\overset{v}{ver}$$

FEET INVOLVING RELATIVE STRESS

H-16   While the foot can best be conceived of as the grouping of unstresses around a
stress, the problem of relative stress arises which cannot be explained by the stress/
unstress method. In other words, two syllables in a foot may appear to have equal stress,
as in a spondee (foot 5 below), or a pyrrhus (foot 4). Yet, as a metrical unit, they are
forced together despite whatever relative unstress they may have. When explicating it is
sometimes helpful to compare a system of relative stress (D-69) with a simpler foot division to see where discrepancies lie.

$$\overset{v}{Ap}\overset{/}{pear}/ \overset{v}{and} \overset{/}{dis}/\overset{v}{ap}\overset{/}{pear}/ \overset{v}{in} \overset{v}{the}/ \overset{/}{blue} \overset{/}{depth}/ \overset{v}{of} \overset{v}{the} \overset{/}{sky}$$
$$\quad 1 \qquad 2 \qquad 3 \qquad 4 \qquad 5 \qquad 6$$

FROM: THE MAGI
W. B. YEATS

The relative unstress of the syllables in foot 4 is similar, and the relative stress of the
syllables in foot 5 is similar.

The Pyrrhus

H-17   When two relative unstresses (vv) appear in a foot, as in foot 4, the foot is called a pyrrhus.

The Spondee

H-18   When two relatively stressed syllables (//) appear together in a foot, as in foot 5, the foot is called a spondee.

Greek Feet

H-19   In Greek literature, from which the poetical foot originates, there are a number of other types of feet. In English, however, the presence of a strong duple base meter tends to cause the Greek feet to divide into the major English feet, and it is doubtful whether any of the Greek feet exist in English poetry. For example, in a line the Greek antipast (v//v) might divide into an iamb (v/) and a trochee (/v).

The amphibrach, however, has some claim to consideration as a pattern in English. In a poem like "How They Brought the Good News from Aix to Ghent," there may be Greek feet, especially the *amphibrach* (v/v), as in the word *ro-man-tic* (a stress between two unstresses).

SPLITTING THE FOOT

H-20   The purpose of dividing a line into feet is to help explain where the tension in the line lies. There are two principal means by which the poet creates tension with his use of feet: (1) by splitting the foot in such a way as to cause disharmony between the natural rhythm and poetical meter, and (2) by substituting a different type of foot from the one expected. Consider this line:

$$\text{And sends/ the froz/en-ground-/swell un/der it}$$

FROM: MENDING WALL
ROBERT FROST

There seems to be tension (almost a swelling sensation) after the word *swell*, which makes the line very effective. The poet has split the foot to create this tension.

H-21   A splitting of the foot occurs when the natural rhythm of a word is changed because of the force of the meter in a line of poetry. For example, the base meter (D-29) of the line:

$$\text{And sends/ the froz/en-ground-swell un/der it}$$

is iambic, and because the preceeding lines in the poem have also been iambic, the reader has set his expectations (D-19). However, when he comes to *frozen-ground-swell*, tension is created because the reader anticipates hearing *ground-swell* as a word group, but instead, when *ground* associates itself with *frozen* rather than *swell,* tension is established. Because we attempt to hook *swell* into *ground,* and are denied, there is a verbal "swelling."

H-22   In other words, tension has been created because the normal grouping *ground-swell* has been split. Had the line been this:

$$\acute{A}nd\ \overset{v}{it}|\ s\acute{e}nds\ \overset{v}{the}|\ \overset{v}{frozen}|\ gr\acute{o}und\ \overset{v}{swell}|\ \acute{u}nder|\overset{v}{it}$$

then the fourth foot would not have been split, and there would have been less tension.
   The following line is a less dramatic example of splitting foot:

$$\overset{v}{My}\ l\acute{o}ng|\ tw\acute{o}\text{-}p\acute{o}int|ed\ l\acute{a}d|d\overset{v}{er}\text{'s}\ st\acute{i}ck|\overset{v}{ing}\ thr\acute{o}ugh|\overset{v}{a}\ tr\acute{e}e$$
$$\quad\text{1}\qquad\text{2}\qquad\quad\text{3}\qquad\quad\text{4}\qquad\quad\text{5}\qquad\quad\text{6}$$

FROM: AFTER APPLE-PICKING
ROBERT FROST

The natural rhythm which comes from a complete word is broken in feet 2, 3, and 4; meanwhile, there is a trochaic rhythm normally created by these words:

$$p\acute{o}int|\overset{v}{ed}\qquad\qquad l\acute{a}d|d\overset{v}{er}\qquad\qquad st\acute{i}ck|\overset{v}{ing}$$

but these are forced into iambic base, and the result is a slight uncertainty or tension in the line.

RISING AND FALLING RHYTHM

H-23   Consider these words:

$$p\acute{o}int|\overset{v}{ed}\qquad\qquad l\acute{a}d|d\overset{v}{er}\qquad\qquad st\acute{i}ck|\overset{v}{ing}$$

They have what is called natural *falling rhythm* because their last syllable is unstressed. The meter of the poem, on the other hand, is rising; it is iambic and leads to the expectation of a stressed syllable at the end of each syllable group. Thus, the falling rhythm of *pointed, ladder,* and *sticking* must be fit into an iambic base meter, and it is this disparity between rhythm and meter which causes the tension of splitting the foot.

H-24   *Rising meter,* then, is a meter in which the feet end with a stressed syllable; anapests, for example, normally create rising rhythm, while dactyls create falling rhythms.

SUBSTITUTION

H-25   *Substitution* is one of the most common and most effective methods by which the poet can emphasize a foot. Substitution occurs when one type of foot is replaced with another. For example, a line which has five feet and an iambic base meter might have four iambic feet and one trochaic foot. We would say, then, that the trochaic foot had been substituted for one of the iambic feet. Such a substitution occurs in foot 3 of the following line:

$$\breve{His}\; \acute{sil}/v\breve{er}\; sk\acute{in}/\; l\acute{aced}\; w\breve{ith}/\; h\breve{is}\; g\acute{ol}/d\breve{en}\; bl\acute{ood}$$

1   2   3   4   5

FROM: MACBETH
SHAKESPEARE

H-26   Any foot may be substituted for another foot, but before substitution is possible, a base meter must have been established. The reader's expectations must have been heightened by an established base meter so that a change in those expectations will have effect. Look at the following line, for example:

$$\acute{one}\; h\acute{and}/d\acute{id}\; n\breve{oth}/\breve{ing}\; \acute{on}/\; th\breve{e}\; v\acute{est}$$

FROM: A MAN WHO HAD FALLEN
AMONG THIEVES
E. E. CUMMINGS

There are three different types of feet (spondaic, pyrrhic, and iambic); were the poet depending on substitution for effect in the next line, he could not get it, because no base meter has been established.

In the following line, however, observe:

$$\breve{Thy}\; l\acute{ife}/\; \breve{a}\; l\acute{ong}/\; d\acute{ead}\; c\acute{alm}/\; \breve{of}\; f\acute{ixed}/\; r\breve{e}p\acute{ose},$$

1   2   3   4   5

FROM: ELOISE TO ABELARD
ALEXANDER POPE

There is a substitution in the third foot which we can identify because a base meter of iambic feet is established.

H-27   In order to have substitutions, there must first be a base meter established. The base meter may consist of any type of foot, but the base must be strong enough so that the reader anticipates a continuation of that meter. When the base rhythm is broken with a different kind of foot from the base foot, a substitution has taken place. Consider this line:

$$\breve{But}\; sl\acute{ept}/\; th\breve{e}\; d\acute{eep}/\breve{er}\; \breve{as}/\; th\breve{e}\; \breve{ash}/\breve{es}\; r\acute{ose}$$

1   2   3   4   5

FROM: YEAR'S END
RICHARD WILBUR

The base meter is iambic, and a pyrrhic substitution occurs in the third foot.

Types of Substitution

H-28   Though many studies have analyzed numerous complexities of substitution, we can analyze most poems quite effectively by distinguishing three basic types of substitution: (1) substitution of stressed syllables without expected intervening unstressed syllables; (2) substitution of unexpected unstressed syllables; (3) substitution for the purpose of temporarily reversing the rhythm. Each of these types creates different characteristic effects.

H-29   The substitution of *unexpected stressed syllables* can create a sense of strength, heavy labor, or weightiness. Uninterrupted stress syllables tend to slow down the line, as in this example:

When A̐/jax strives/some rock's/ vast weight/to throw,

The line/ too la/bors, and/ the words/ move slow;

FROM: AN ESSAY ON CRITICISM
ALEXANDER POPE

The spondaic substitution in foot 4 of line 1 helps slow the line and make us feel the difficulty of the labor, while the spondees in line 2 reinforce the meaning.

H-30   We can say, then, that spondaic substitutions tend to create a sense of strength or weightiness, and a succession of spondaic substitutions will make a line move slowly. On the other hand, unstressed syllables can be substituted to give a line the feeling of lightness and cause the meter to move quickly. Pyrrhic substitutions almost always give lightness and quick movement, as in line 2 of the following example:

Not so/ when swift/ Camill/a scours/ the plain,

Flies over/ the unbend/ing corn,/ and skims/ along/

the main.

FROM: AN ESSAY ON CRITICISM
ALEXANDER POPE

H-31   Besides pyrrhic substitution, almost any triple substitution (an anapest or a dactyl) in a duple base meter (iambic or trochaic) will give similar lightness, particularly since triple meters are associated with dance tempos, as here:

Like the skip/ping of rab/bits by moon/light-

three/ slim shapes,

FROM: FRA LIPPO LIPPI
ROBERT BROWING

We find anapestic substitutions in the first three feet. Notice the contrast between the movement of the first part of the line and the last; the spondaic substitution, combined with the caesura, (I-8 ff) slows down the last part considerably.

H-32   The third type of substitution, the *unexpected reversal of rhythym,* can create far more complex effects. This type of substitution often marks unanticipated movement, discovery, change, new force or direction of power. Whatever it suggests, it is almost always accompanied by the release of some emotion. Generally, because of the prevalence of the iamb in English, the characteristic reversal is achieved by a trochaic substitution, particularly in the first foot, but any type of counterpointing will achieve a similar effect. Look at the following stanza, for example:

$$\text{my fa/ther moved/ through dooms/ of love}$$

$$\text{through sames/ of am/ through haves/ of give,}$$

$$\text{sing/ing each/ morning/ out of/ each night}$$

$$\text{my fa/ther moved/ through depths/ of height}$$

FROM: my father moved through
dooms of love
e. e. cummings

The first two lines establish a *regular* (D-17) iambic tetrameter base meter, but in line 3 there are several metrical variations which vastly alter the meter of the line. The initial stressed syllable in line 3 sets up a *falling rhythm* (H-23) which is continued by the two trochaic substitutions, and finally culminated by the spondee. The results of these metrical changes is that line 3 becomes quite emotional. Some readers would be tempted to scan the third line:

$$\text{singing/ each morn/ing out/ of each night}$$

But the meaning demands that *each* take a stress. (See frames H-42 ff for a discussion of how to decide between different possible scansions.)

CATALEXIS

H-33 One means by which the poet can achieve metrical variation and give emphasis to either the end or beginning of a line is by use of *catalexis,* or a truncated foot. A truncated foot occurs when one or two unaccented syllables have been deleted from the first or last foot of a line.

H-34 Obviously, initial catalexis (a "headless" foot) will be characteristic of rising meters, and can be used to change the rhythm from rising to falling. For example, notice these lines:

Whereon/ a doz/en staunch/ and leal
cit/izens/ did graze/ at pause

FROM: a man who had fallen
among thieves
e. e. cummings

A headless foot occurs in the second line. The effect of the headless is a bit unusual because it de-emphasizes the split foot (H-20) while effecting a falling rhythm. Notice how the relative stress and rhythm changes if we write the line:

$$\text{the cít/izens/ díd gráze/ and páuse}$$

The *duration* (D-85) of the word *citizens* becomes greater in the rewritten line, and be-cause there is not a headless, a bit more stress can be given to the last syllable in *citizens*. This change in relative stress permits us to place less stress on *did* in the rewritten line, thus causing less tension. However, here is the example as it was originally written:

$$\text{cít/izens/ díd gráze/ and páuse}$$

Here *citizens* moves very quickly because of the headless and enjambment between the lines, taking any stress off the last syllable in *citizens*.

H-35   Terminal catalexis, known simply as truncation, is characteristic of falling rhythms. Truncation affects only the end of the line, occurring when the last, unstressed syllable of a falling line is omitted. Consider the following line, for example.

$$\text{Týger,/ Týger/ búrning/ bright}$$

FROM: THE TYGER
WILLIAM BLAKE

The last foot is truncated, although it is possible to read the first foot as a headless (see Frames H-43 (9) ff for a discussion example of distinguishing headless and truncated feet).

H-36   Often, in rhymed poems in falling meters, the rhyme will demand truncation so that there will be no preponderance of feminine or multiple rhymes which would lighten an otherwise serious poem. Consider this stanza:

$$\text{Óne móre ún/fórtunàte}$$

$$\text{Wéary óf/ bréath,}$$

$$\text{Ráshly ím/pórtunàte}$$

$$\text{Góne to hér/ déath}$$

FROM: THE BRIDGE OF SIGHS
THOMAS HOOD

The base meter is dactylic, and because dactylic rhyme throughout the poem might ren-der it ridiculous, the last foot in the second and fourth lines has been truncated. Because of rhyming problems, terminal catalexis occurs much more frequently in English poetry than does initial catalexis.

ANACRUSIS

H-37 The opposite of truncation is *anacrusis,* generally defined as an extra unstressed syllable at the beginning of a line, although it is acceptable to say that in anacrusis the extra syllable can occur at the end of the line. For example, for this line —

their shoul/ders held/ the sky/ suspended

FROM: EPITAPH ON AN ARMY OF MERCENARIES
A. E. HOUSMAN

— we describe the line as iambic tetrameter with terminal anacrusis.

H-38 Just as initial catalexis may change the metrical character of a line from rising to falling, initial anacrusis may change a line from falling meter to rising. For example, anacrusis at the beginning of a trochaic line will make it appear iambic; anacrusis at the beginning of a dactylic line may make it appear anapestic.

H-39 Because of the frequency of initial dactylic anacrusis, and terminal dactylic catalexis, many say that true dactylic meter does not exist in English; that all triple meters are anapestic.

H-40 Terminal anacrusis on rising meters will create a falling ending, known as a feminine ending; feminine endings, particularly in rhymed poems, are frequently used for soft, soothing endings.

H-41 Variant masculine and feminine endings may result from truncation or anacrusis. The following line exemplifies masculine endings caused by terminal catalexis.

Down the/ rivers/ of the/ windfall/ light

FROM: FERN HILL
DYLAN THOMAS

OPTIONS IN SCANNING

H-42 Obviously, anacrusis, catalexis, and foot divisions are subjective and sometimes arbitrary, and it is not uncommon to find metricists scanning the same line differently. Many problems confront the reader as he attempts to examine meter closely, and he will have to make judgments about rhythm based on the entire explication. That is to say that a reader cannot isolate meter from the other parts of the poem, but must consider it as a contributing factor to images, sound, and the other elements which make up the poem. But just as symbols can help the reader explain theme, meter can too, and it is always necessary for the explicator to study its function in the poem.

If the rhythmic patterns of the meter are part of the essence of the poem, it will be worthwhile to analyze the possibilities carefully for any one poem, even though there may be room for differences among the efforts of different analysts. (See H-44 below.)

H-43   Let us analyze the following stanza to discover what might be our major options in scanning, and which analysis might do most in helping to explain the basic rhythmic patterns of the poem.

> Today we have naming of parts. Yesterday
> We had daily cleaning. And tomorrow morning
> We shall have what to do after firing. But today
> Today we have naming of parts. Japonica
> Glistens like coral in all of the neighboring
>   gardens,
> And today we have naming of parts.

FROM: THE NAMING OF PARTS
HENRY REED

H-43 (1)   While it is common for poets to establish a firm base meter in the first line of the poem, Reed begins immediately with substitutions and an odd number of syllables (11 in line 1).

$$\overset{\lor}{\text{To}}\overset{/}{\text{day}}|\ \overset{//}{\text{we have}}|\ \overset{/}{\text{na}}\overset{}{\text{ming}}|\ \overset{/}{\text{of}}\ \overset{\lor}{\text{parts.}}|\ \overset{/}{\text{Yes}}\overset{\lor}{\text{ter}}\overset{//}{\text{day}}$$

1   2   3   4   5

It is fairly clear that the line is divided into feet which have two syllables, and we can probably even say that the base meter of the line is iambic. The trochaic substitutions in foot 3 and foot 5 counterpoint whatever rising rhythm the iambs might have created, and although foot 3 is a trochee, the iambic foot 4 permits us to feel a dactyl slipping into the meter (this usually occurs when a trochee is followed by an iamb or a pyrrhus).

It is also probable that the last foot is trochaic, and that the final secondary stress is a masculine ending caused by terminal catalexis (H-41) rather than part of the fifth foot, but we can't tell at this point.

H-43 (2)   Just as line 1 is composed of duple feet (two syllable feet), line 2 is clearly a duple foot line, but it differs from line 1 considerably.

$$\overset{\lor}{\text{To}}\overset{/}{\text{day}}|\ \overset{\lor}{\text{we}}\ \overset{/}{\text{have}}|\ \overset{/}{\text{na}}\overset{\lor}{\text{ming}}|\ \overset{\lor}{\text{of}}\ \overset{/}{\text{parts.}}|\ \overset{/}{\text{Yes}}\overset{\lor}{\text{ter}}\overset{//}{\text{day}}$$

1   2   3   4   5

$$\overset{\lor}{\text{We}}\ \overset{/}{\text{had}}|\ \overset{/}{\text{dai}}\overset{\lor}{\text{ly}}|\ \overset{/}{\text{clea}}\overset{\lor}{\text{ning.}}|\ \overset{//}{\text{And}}\ \overset{\lor}{\text{to}}|\overset{/}{\text{mor}}\overset{\lor}{\text{row}}|\ \overset{/}{\text{mor}}\overset{\lor}{\text{ning}}$$

1   2   3   4   5   6

The most noticeable difference is that line 2 is a falling (H-23) line, and while this was anticipated by line 1, a trochaic base meter was not established. The only substitution is in the first foot, and the full stop after *cleaning* reinforces the falling meter. But the most definitive metrical quality is that the line ends with a trochee. There is no catalexis as there is in line 1. This causes the line to come to a natural pause, unlike line 1 in which the unfinished foot caused us to move more quickly to the second line.

H-43 (3)   The third line presents more of a problem than the first two, and it is important that we see how the poet has used his meter, since this line is overtly different metrically from the others.

Today/ we have/naming/ of parts./ Yester/day

We had/ daily/ cleaning./ And to/morrow/ morning
1   2   3   4   5   6

We shall have what to do after firing. But today

Looking at the first two lines, it is possible to scan the third line in duple feet:

We shall/ have what/ to do/ after/ firing./ But today
1   2   3   4   5   6

The fact that the second line is a full six foot line makes this scansion reasonable. However, when we read the line, grouping the natural unstresses to the stresses, the meter is anapestic rather than trochaic with some substitutions.

We shall have/ what to do/ after/ firing./ But today
1   2   3   4   5

H-43 (4)   What the explicator must decide is why the poet shifted into anapests in line 3, if the line is to be read as triple meter. In order to speculate on the rhythm, we must turn to the *dramatic situation* (A-1).

H-43 (5)   The person speaking in the first four lines seems to be talking about guns, and from his jargon we can say that he is probably an army sergeant lecturing to the recruits. In good military form, the sergeant outlines what has happened in the past and what will happen in the future, repeating what is important for today — the naming of parts. After the caesura in line 4, the voice changes, and we look at the situation from a recruit's point of view; the theme of the poem somehow centers on the discrepancy between what the sergeant sees and what the recruit sees in the same dramatic situation.

H-43 (6)   The sergeant's rhythm is mechanical, like the mechanical rhythm of the bolt action of guns. He is not without rhythm; it is only that his rhythm is stilted so that he is unable to see the natural rhythm of the bees in the garden. When the sergeant lapses into anapests in line 3, it is as close to sexual rhythm as he can come, while the recruit in line 5 contrasts the sergeant's mechanical rhythm with his own sensual rhythm. But it is important that we see line 3 as anapestic if we are to counterpoint it with line 5.

H-43 (7)   Line 4 repeats the meter of line 1 until the end of foot 4, when the recruit begins to speak.

Today/ we have/naming/ of parts./ Yester/day
1   2   3   4   5

We had/ daily/ cleaning./ And to/morrow/ morning,
1   2   3   4   5   6

We shall have/ what to do/ after/ firing./ But today,
1   2   3   4   5

$$\overset{\smallsmile}{Today}/\ \overset{\smallsmile}{we}\ \overset{/}{have}/\ \overset{/}{naming}/\ \overset{/}{of}\ \overset{\smallsmile}{parts}./\ \overset{\smallsmile}{Japon}/ica$$

Today/ we have/ naming/ of parts./ Japon/ica
  1   2   3   4   5

The last two feet, however, mark important differences from the catalectic foot in line 1. First, *Japonica* is a four syllable word which is soft because of its number of syllables (E-15) and its unstressed last syllables (H-40). It fits metrically into two feet so that no tension is created by a split foot (H-20); the last two syllables form a pyrrhic foot, the first we've seen in the poem. And while the trochaic foot at the end of line 2 created a natural pause, especially when followed in line 3 by an anapestic foot, the pyrrhic in *Japonica* (line 4) establishes a strong enjambment which is picked up by the initial stress in *Glistens* (line 5).

H-43 (8)   To summarize line 4, we can say that the sergeant's rhythm which opens the poem continues until we reach the caesura, at which point we find the first four syllable word in the poem, and also the first pyrrhic foot (H-17). The end of line 4, when seen in relation to the last foot in lines 1 and 2, sets us up for a meter which will counterpoint the sergeant's.

H-43 (9)   If we were to isolate line 5 and try to scan it, there would be several possibilities. The first tempting scansion is to read the first stress as a headless (H-34):

(It) Glis/tens like/ coral/ in all/ of the/ neighboring/ gardens
       1   2   3   4   5   6   7

But when this foot is put into the context of the rest of the stanza, several considerations appear which show why it is not a headless. First, headless lines normally contain fewer syllables than the other lines, the headless foot making the line shorter, whereas here in line 5 there are more syllables than in any other line. Second, headless feet are normally used for counterpointing, and since no firm iambic base has been established, the headless can't counterpoint as it did in the example in frame H-34:

whereon/ a doz/en staunch/ and leal
cit/izens/ did graze/ at pause

Third, it is obvious that the pyrrhic in line 4 would lose its effect were it followed by an unstress, and we know that the poet is setting us up for a stronger falling rhythm than a headless would create.

H-43 (10)   Another tempting way of scanning the line (once we have decided that the first foot is not a headless) is to read it as having a dactylic base meter with one substitution:

Glistens like/ coral in/ all of the/ neighboring/ gardens

But the problem with this is that while the recruit is speaking with a different meter than the sergeant's, it is just as regular. The reason that a dactylic scansion is especially

problematic and important is that a regular meter in line 5 may be just the effect the poet
is looking for. Obviously, it makes a tremendous difference to our explication if the poet
feels the same way toward the recruit as he does toward the sergeant.

Scanning the fifth line as dactylic can be repudiated on two bases. First, the only images
in the stanza are contained in this line, and the meter must best convey the metaphor:
"Japonica glistens like coral." If the first two feet are dactyls, the quickness (H-31) with
which we breeze across the syllables takes the emphasis off *Glistens* and *coral.* Second,
the enjambment between lines 4 and 5 makes the stress in *Glistens* cling more closely to
Japonica than to *like,* and our natural reading of these lines will not permit us to include
like in the first foot.

H-43 (11)   This leaves us with a third possibility — one which is derived from the first
two: scanning the first part of the line to focus on the metaphor, and the last part as
anapests with a feminine ending:

$$\text{Glistens/ like co/ral in all/ of the neigh/boring gardens}$$

But this doesn't seem too likely a possibility since the poet is setting up a dichotomy between what is outside in the garden and inside at the lecture, and the anapests would recall the sergeant's meter. Also, a feminine ending to the line would anticipate enjambment
(I-20), or a strong relationship to the following line, but neither occurs as the last line returns us to the lecture.

H-43 (12)   There is finally a fourth possibility, which seems most likely:

$$\text{Glistens/ like cor/al in/ all of the/ neighboring/ gardens}$$

This scansion places emphasis on the metaphor, permits a pause after *in,* ends the line
with a complete foot, and provides a noticeable contrast to the sergeant's rhythm. The
recruit speaks with a passion that the sergeant lacks.

H-43 (13)   The last line of the stanza, which is metrically shorter than any of the other
lines, brings the stanza to a close by showing us the recruit's opinion of naming parts.
The conjunction *And* tells us the relationship between the gardens and the lecture; so it
must be scanned with a secondary stress, making the last line weakly catalectic:

$$\text{And/ today/ we have/ naming/ of parts.}$$

H-43 (14)   The entire stanza is thus scanned:

$$\text{Today/ we have/ naming/ of parts./ Yesterday,}$$

$$\text{We had/ daily/ cleaning./ And to/morrow/ morning,}$$

$$\text{We shall have/ what to do/ after/ firing./ But today,}$$

$$\text{Today/ we have/ naming/ of parts./ Japonica}$$

/ ˇ   // / ˇ ˇ   / ˇ ˇ   /   ˇ ˇ   / ˇ
Glistens/ like co/ral in/ all of the/ neighboring/ gardens,

// ˇ /   ˇ / / ˇ   ˇ /
And/ today/ we have/ naming/ of parts.

H-44   If there are several possible scansions for a line which are reasonable and consistent within traditional prosodic techniques, what difference does it make how we scan the line and assign the foot divisions? There is only one answer to that question.

Dividing the line into feet *can* make a difference in one important way: it can help explain the counterpoint and tension of the line. Let us look at another example:

ˇ / / / ˇ / ˇ / ˇ / ˇ /
My long/ two-point/ed lad/der's stick/ing through/ a tree

The base is iambic with only one substitution, yet the line feels as though it is falling, which creates an unbalance that can be explained by the split feet (H-20).

Similarly, foot divisions help explain associated syllables. Theoretically, the way in which syllables are associated will help determine with what rhythm the line is to be read, in addition to how it should be stressed.

In the example: "I am hearing the shape of the rain," we can see how associated syllables affect the reading. With the anapestic base we read thus:

// ˇ / ˇ / ˇ ˇ /
I am hear/ing the shape/ of the rain

Now *hear* is included in foot 1 while *-ing* is associated with *the* in foot 2. Since *hearing* is split by the foot, it creates some tension and reduces the pressure on *shape*. With a duple base, however, we would read thus:

// ˇ / ˇ ˇ / ˇ ˇ /
I am/ hearing/ the shape/ of the/ rain

There is enough of a pause between feet 1 and 2 to give *hear, shape,* and *rain* more pressure, as well as to reduce the general tension of the line.

Scansion and Meaning

H-45   What the explicator must do, then, after distinguishing the various metrical possibilities is to determine how each possibility affects meaning. Usually foot divisions affect meaning through tension, which in turn affects tone and feeling.

H-46   There are a couple of rules of thumb to follow when approaching base meter: (1) Remember that most poems are written in iambs with frequent substitutions. Indeed, some critics argue that all English poetry is iambic and that variation comes because iambs vary. (2) By reading the poem in a natural manner, the rhythm of the words will force enough cadence so that the reader can tell whether there are more accents or unaccents. If there is a quickness to the line, the base is either anapestic or iambic with anapestic or pyrric substitutions.

For example, the following line should give no trouble with foot division, even though there are two substitutions, because the meter works a basic beat every other syllable.

But with other lines, foot divisions may not be so clearly established and can be determined only after the poem has been carefully studied.

For example, consider this line:

I am hearing the shape of the rain

There is a quickness which suggests the presence of anapests, and since the accents are clearly marked, we can scan the line without difficulty:

$$\overset{//}{I} \overset{v}{am} \overset{/}{hear} / \overset{v}{ing} \overset{v}{the} \overset{/}{shape} / \overset{v}{of} \overset{v}{the} \overset{/}{rain}$$
$$\qquad 1 \qquad\qquad 2 \qquad\qquad 3$$

We can say that the base is anapestic trimeter with a substitution in foot 1 (if we are willing to admit that // v / is a valid English foot).

H-47   One good way to approach scansion is to assume a two syllable foot as soon as the obvious stresses have been marked. If the two syllable foot doesn't work, go to an *alternate base* (D-32 ff) see if it helps to explain tension and emphasis. If this doesn't work, it will be necessary to shift to an accentual and/or syllabic system, which usually helps — even with free verse.

DEPRESSED FEET

H-48   Occasionally, two syllables occur in a pattern in such a way as to be taken as one syllable without actually being an elision (E-20), thus creating a *depressed foot*. For example, consider these lines:

$$\overset{v}{We} \overset{/}{keep} / \overset{v}{the} \overset{/}{wall} / \overset{v}{between} / \overset{v}{us} \overset{/}{as} / \overset{v}{we} \overset{/}{go}.$$

$$\overset{v}{To} \overset{/}{each} / \overset{v}{the} \overset{/}{boul} / \overset{v}{ders} \overset{v}{(that} \overset{v}{have})} \overset{/}{fallen} / \overset{v}{to} \overset{/}{each}$$

FROM: MENDING WALL
ROBERT FROST

The base meter consists of five iambic feet. But in the second line there is an extra syllable which disrupts the meter but does not break it. *Have* in foot 3 might be read as depressed so that it is pronounced in combination with *that*. *That have* functions as the stressed half of the iambic foot. Clearly there are three syllables in the foot, but the lingual quality of *that have* allows it to be depressed into the iambic base, and the meter can be maintained. Another metrical possibility is for *have* not to be depressed and for *fallen* to be elided into *fall'n*.

H-49   Thus when one syllable is depressed into another, the resulting combination is called a *depressed foot*. The effect of a depressed foot is to change the balance of the line, and it serves as an effective means by which the meter can be interrupted without being broken.

REVIEWING THE SCANNING PROCESS

H-50   The important thing to remember about the accentual-syllabic system (foot system) is that it is designed to assist in explaining the emphasis in a poem. There may, indeed, be several ways to scan a line (H-42 to H-44), in which case the critic must choose the method which will best aid him.

   Splitting the foot (H-20), substitution (H-25), anacrusis (H-37), and catalexis (H-33) are all important means of varying the base meter in the accentual-syllabic system of meter, and the explicator must use these concepts to show where the poet intends the reader to place emphasis.

Review/self-check

H-51   In English, unstressed syllables are dominated by _____ syllables, and the unstresses group themselves around a stress.

stressed (H-6)

H-52   Group the unstresses around the stresses.

ˇ   ˇ   /   ˇ   ˇ   /   ˇ   ˇ   /
I have passed with a nod of the head

ˇ ˇ /
I have passed/
ˇ ˇ /
with a nod/
ˇ ˇ /
of the head

H-53   A metrical grouping of stresses and unstresses is called a _____ .

foot (H-7)

H-54   The line "I have passed with a nod of the head" (is, is not) regular. It contains _____ feet.

is/three

H-55   Identify the types of feet in the following:

/   ˇ   ˇ   /   ˇ   ˇ   /   /
This is/ no coun/try for/ old men

trochaic
iambic (H-8)
pyrrhic
spondaic

H-56   Feet help to explain why a line has _____ . Two means by which the foot gives tension are:

tension (H-20)
splitting the foot or word substitution (H-20)

H-57   Consider the following lines:

ˇ   /   ˇ   /   ˇ   /   ˇ   /
then fired/by hy/perciv/ic zeal

/   /   ˇ   /   ˇ   ˇ   ˇ   /
sought new/er pas/tures or/because

swád/dlĕd with/ ă fróz/ĕn bróok

ŏf pínk/ĕst vóm/ĭt óut/ŏf éyes

FROM: a man who had fallen
among thieves
e. e. cummings

H-57 (a)   There are _____ feet per line.   four

H-57 (b)   There are _____ regular lines, lines   two
_____ and _____.   one and four

H-57 (c)   The base meter is _____, and there   iambic
are substitutions in line _____.   two

H-57 (d)   The iambs have been substituted by a
_____ in foot _____.   spondee, one

H-57 (e)   They have been substituted by a _____   pyrrhus
in foot _____.   three

H-57 (f)   Foot one of line three is a _____ foot.   headless (H-34)

Punctuation

The three basic devices poets have for regulating meter and sound, and showing the relationship between ideas are these: the *line* (I-1 ff), *caesura* (I-8 ff), and *rhyme* (I-63 ff). Each of these devices must be seen in relation to the others and to the *foot* (H-1 ff).

THE LINE

I-1   Because the nature of the line varies considerably from poem to poem, one of the most disputed critical aspects of modern poetry is the function of the line. It is generally agreed, however, that in serious poetry there must exist some reason for creating a particular line as it is, and on this assumption it is possible to demonstrate a number of functions which the line can serve.

I-2   A line may be defined as a poetical unit characterized by the presence of meter. It is an individual unit which is part of a larger unit, and every line must contain some particular meaning or purpose which contributes to the whole poem. The line is a typographical unit, but it must have more reason for existing than sheer typography.

I-3   A line, while characterized by the presence of particular meter, must also make a contribution to the whole poem. One line has no real poetical function by itself, and must be placed into context before it can be properly considered. However, we do take lines out of context in order to show some general characteristics.

The Accentual-Syllabic Line

I-4   The meter of an accentual-syllabic poem is measured by the predominant type of foot which the line contains and is named according to the type and number of feet. A line which has a predominant number of iambic feet would be called an iambic line: a predominant number of anapestic feet would be an anapestic line.

number of feet	name of line
1	monometer
2	dimeter
3	trimeter
4	tetrameter
5	pentameter
6	hexameter (Alexandrine)
7	heptameter (Fourteener)

Note that six-foot iambic lines are often called "Alexandrines," while seven-foot lines are usually called "fourteeners."

Review/self-check

I-5 (a) A line which contains four iambic feet is called iambic tetrameter. A line containing five trochaic feet would be called _____ _____.

trochaic pentameter

I-5 (b) The following line is _____ _____:

iambic trimeter

$$\breve{U}pon/ \ the \ sl\breve{i}/my \ sea$$

The Line's Natural Emphasis

I-6 As an autonomous unit, the line normally places more emphasis at its beginning and end than in the middle. For example, consider this line:

Rough winds do shake the darling buds of May

We tend to remember *Rough winds* and *May* more vividly than we do the remainder of the line, although there is no more stress on one part than on another.

I-7 Because of the natural emphasis at the beginning and end of the line, the poet has an important regularity which he can use for emphasis; he can play the natural emphasis created by the beginning and end of the line against other less regular elements of his poetical emphasis in order to change the focus.

THE CAESURA

Caesuras are effective when the poet uses them to alter the natural emphasis of the line. For other techniques of variation related to altering the emphasis, refer to *base meter* (D-29), *metrical contract* (D-19), and the *line* (I-1).

I-8 When the poet achieves a pause or break in his poem, he is said to have used a device called a *caesura*. Although "caesura" is the accepted term for any kind of pause in the line, no matter how it is achieved, some type of punctuation mark is generally used at the pause. A caesura may be created by any form of punctuation, or by no punctuation at all; however, the most commonly used punctuation mark for marking a caesura is the comma.

I-9 For example, Keats (or his editors or printers) used punctuation marks to create pauses in the following lines:

Was it a vision, or a waking dream?
Fled is that music: — Do I wake or sleep?

FROM: ODE TO A NIGHTINGALE
JOHN KEATS

I-10 The comma, question marks, colon, and dash all serve to signal the reader where to pause, and they are each properly termed a caesura. However even though pauses, or caesuras, are most frequently denoted by punctuation marks, the poet can also establish pauses through syntax, the line and meter, rhyme, and the sound and meaning of the words he chooses.

I-11   The type of punctuation determines the length of the pause. Periods and question marks demand full stops; colons take almost a full stop; semicolons take a long pause; commas take a short pause. The end of a line usually demands a pause even if there is no punctuation; however, the pause at the end of the line where there is not a punctuation is seldom termed "caesura," and even with punctuation, the term is normally reserved for internal pauses. At non-punctuated spots in a line which demands a pause, common speech usage will determine the length of the caesura.

I-12   Caesuras, whether punctuated or not, are really an imposition of prose rhythm on meter for the purpose of changing the natural emphasis of the line, and while there are numerous ways a poet can achieve caesura, the reason is always to alter the sound and rhythm, or to emphasize a particular portion of a line or section of the poem.

I-13   Since the line normally places more natural emphasis on its beginning and end, the line contains an important inherent quality which the poet can use to his advantage. Through the use of caesuras, the poet can change to natural emphasis of the line, making it either weaker or stronger. For example, consider the example from Shakespeare:

Rough winds do shake the darling buds of May

SONNET 18

The natural emphasis is on *Rough winds* and *May* and without the presence of a caesura in the line – either through punctuation marks or other means – the reader will tend to remember the first and last words. Notice that in addition to the natural emphasis at the beginning, the line was also strengthened by a spondaic substitution in the first foot. In the following first line, however, Milton uses caesuras – not substitution – to alter the natural emphasis:

Avenge, Oh Lord, thy slaughtered saints, whose bones
Lie scattered on the Alpine mountains cold;

FROM: ON THE LATE MASSACRE AT PIEDMONT
JOHN MILTON

The commas after *Avenge* and *Lord* emphasize both the first and second feet, and the comma after *saints*, combined with the *-s* alliteration (E-30) and substitution in foot 3, gives a great deal of emphasis to *slaughtered saints* in a position in the line which does not normally take much emphasis. Likewise, the last foot is set off by a caesura and further emphasized by the *-s* alliteration. Milton has achieved his effect by breaking up the line with caesuras.

I-14   We can say, then, that the caesura is really an imposition of rhythm on the meter of the line for the purpose of changing the emphasis, and whenever the poet is depending on his caesuras for emphasis, it is the explicator's job to determine what effect the altered rhythm has on the poem.

PUNCTUATION — ITS EFFECT ON MEANING

Example/self-check

I-15   Caesuras can be used for so many different effects that we cannot say that the presence of a caesura means that the poet is attempting to emphasize a particular word, as in the example from Milton. We can say, however, that the caesura imposes itself on the _____ of the line and that by altering the expected rhythm, the poet alters emphasis.

rhythm (I-14)

I-16   It is the relationship, then, between natural rhythm and imposed rhythm that alters the expected _____ of the line or section of the poem, and while we cannot attempt to rationalize every pause, we can and should talk about the effect of the caesuras when we explicate the poem.

emphasis (I-15)

I-17   Looking at the caesuras in the following passage, analyze the *general* effect of the pauses.

> What are the roots that clutch, what branches grow
> Out of this stony rubbish? Son of man,
> You cannot say, or guess, for you know only
> A heap of broken images, where the sun beats,   4
> And the dead tree gives no shelter, the cricket no relief,
> And the dry stone no sound of water. Only
> There is shadow under this red rock,
> (Come in under the shadows of this red rock),   8
> And I will show you something different from either
> Your shadow at morning striding behind you
> Or your shadow at evening rising to meet you;
> I will show you fear in a handful of dust.   12

FROM: THE WASTE LAND
T. S. ELIOT

I-17 (1)   In the first six lines, the position of many of the caesuras is in the _____ of the line, forcing us to pause and alter the rhythm with which we are reading.

middle

I-17 (2)   The internal caesuras recreate the clutching roots and heaps of broken images, and the pauses and substitutions wear at the reader and make him realize the harshness of the land. When we reach lines 7 and 8, however, the lines seem to pause at their natural place at the _____ of the line, and we don't feel as plagued by the internal breaks. It is almost as though the full lines tell us that we will, indeed, find comfort under the shadow of the rock.

end

I-17 (3) Beginning with line 7, the diction is smoother and the tone less frantic than in the first six lines because of the use of caesura and the sound of the words; lines 7 and 8 sound almost as though they are trying to seduce us out of the sun into something comforting, and we are soothed until the end of line 9 when we begin to realize that the absence of caesuras may be as exhausting as the presence of them, and the comfort of lines 7 and 8 begins to fade. By the end of line 11 we are again exhausted; the full stop at the end of line 11 sets up line 12, giving the reader the first chance to pause after three of the longest lines in the stanza. The full stop at line 11, however, permits a sinking feeling to permeate the exhaustion, and even without reading line 12, the reader can sense the despair which is to follow. In contrast to the frantic voice of the first six lines, however, the voice of line 12 is diabolical, and the seduction out of the desert land into something worse is complete.

Caesura Segments

I-18   The effect of the caesura is to break the metrical pattern, thereby changing the emphasis of the line, and in so doing, the line is divided into sections. For example,

She says, "I am content when wakened birds,

FROM: SUNDAY MORNING
WALLACE STEVENS

If the line were written without the first caesura, the beginning of the line would be stressed; but the caesura breaks the meter so that additional stress falls on *I*. The poem's next line works similarly:

Before they fly, test the reality

The trochaic substitution in foot 3 and the caesura place a good deal of emphasis on *test*.

I-19   By sectioning the line into smaller speech groups, a poet can achieve variety, since emphasis is usually placed at the beginning and end of each group. A line which has no caesuras is itself a speech group.

ENJAMBMENT

I-20   Punctuation which comes at the end of a line forces the reader to stop, thereby placing more emphasis on the latter part of the line than if there were no punctuation.

When a punctuated pause occurs at the end of the line, the line is said to be *end-stopped*.

I-21   When the end of the line signifies the end of a complete statement, the line is said to be *autonomous* even if there is no punctuation indicating end-stop. For example, consider these lines:

> *O sages standing in God's holy fire*
> *As in the gold mosaic of a wall,*
>
> FROM: SAILING TO BYZANTIUM
> W. B. YEATS

Line 1 completes a statement which is complemented by line 2. Line 1, then, is said to be autonomous even though there is no punctuation after *fire*; line 2 is end-stopped.

I-22   When a line is not end-stopped, so that it carries over into the following line, the line is said to be *enjambed*. Consider this example:

> *She says, "I am content when wakened birds,*
> *Before they fly, test the reality*
> *Of misty fields, by the sweet questionings;*
>
> FROM: SUNDAY MORNING
> WALLACE STEVENS

There is enjambment between lines 2 and 3.
In these lines, line 1 is enjambed:

> *Avenge, O Lord, thy slaughtered saints, whose bones*
> *Lie scattered on the Alpine mountains cold;*
>
> JOHN MILTON

The caesuras in line 1 of Milton's poem are used to place emphasis on the command to avenge the slaughtered saints, and to establish the most suitable meter to emphasize the horror of the slaughter. By breaking up the natural emphasis at the beginning and end of the line with caesuras, Milton has managed to place emphasis on all three sections of the line. For example, by setting off *thy slaughtered saints* with caesuras, Milton has emphasized this portion of the line although it comes in the middle.

I-23   In addition to using caesuras, which change the natural emphasis of the line, the poet can use enjambment and substitution to give variation.

> *Avenge,/O Lord,/ thy slaugh/tered saints,/ whose bones*
>
> *Lie scat/tered on/ the Al/pine moun/tains cold;*

The enjambment between the lines helps force more stress on *Lie,* thereby causing a spondaic substitution in foot 1. What the poet is trying to do with caesuras, enjambment, and substitution is to give variation to his iambic pentameter base.

I-24   With caesura and enjambment the poet can create many variations, even within a strict base meter. Examine the following stanza for use of caesura and substitution:

> There wǎs/ perféc/tiǒn ǐn/ thě déath/ ǒf férns
>
> Whǐch láid/ thěir frá/gǐlě chéeks/ agáinst/ thě stóne
>
> Ǎ míl/lǐon yéars./ Gréat mám/mǒths ǒ/vérthrówn
>
> Compós/ědlý/ hǎve máde/ thěir lóng/ sojóurns,
>
> Lǐke pál/acěs/ ǒf pá/tǐence, ǐn/ thě gráy
>
> Ǎnd chánge/ lěss lánds/ ǒf íce./ Ǎnd ǎt/ Pompéii

FROM: YEAR'S END
RICHARD WILBUR

The base meter of the stanza is iambic pentameter. Line 1 is autonomous with no caesuras, and one substitution in foot 3. Line 2 is enjambed with no caesuras and no substitutions. Line 3 is enjambed with a full-stop caesura after foot 2; foot 3 is spondaic. Line 4 is end-stopped, with no internal caesuras and no substitutions. Line 5 is enjambed and has a caesura which breaks foot 4; a pyrrhic substitution occurs in foot 2. There is one caesura in line 6, and a pyrrhic substitution in foot 4.

   With an almost perfectly regular iambic pentameter meter (only 6 substitutions), the poet has created great variations within the stanza. Notice the caesura in line 3. Although there is a full stop, the regularity of the meter and the long durational stress on *years* form an association between *years* and *Great,* almost like a bridge which spans the million years.

TYPES OF CAESURAS

I-25   There are five basic types of caesuras, and from these five types a great number of metrical variations can be achieved when combined with enjambment, end-stops and substitution. The first two types are (1) caesuras which break the foot, and (2) caesuras which come after the foot. In addition to these caesura types marked by punctuation, there are three caesura-like pauses created by (3) omitting a word, (4) by long durational stresses, and (5) by syntactical construction.

END-STOPS

I-26   If a line is *end-stopped* (I-20) the reason usually is to indicate a more prominent break between the meaning of the lines than when there is no end-stop. End-stops aid the poet in showing the relationship between lines, indicating a prominent break between one line and the next. For example, look at these lines:

> Some say the world will end in fire,
> Some say in ice.
> From what I've tasted of desire
> I hold with those who favor fire.

FROM: FIRE AND ICE
ROBERT FROST

The caesura at the end of line 1 indicates that the poet expects some break in thought between lines 1 and 2, and a major break between lines 2 and 3. But between lines 3 and 4 there appears to be a stronger unity in meaning than between any of the other lines. All of the lines in the stanza are building toward a unified end, but some of the lines are more closely associated than others and should be read together.

I-27   Other frequent uses for end-stopping are either to create the type of pause giving the most advantageous emphasis for that line or the one following, or else to increase the natural emphasis at the end of the line. Thus, for example:

> About, about, in real and rout
> The death-fires danced at night;
> The water, like a witch's oils,
> Burnt green, and blue, and white.

FROM: THE RIME OF THE
ANCIENT MARINER
SAMUEL TAYLOR COLERIDGE

The end-stop causes a pause after *oils*, and gives full emphasis to the long durational stress of the word, so that the image of the witch's oils works a mystifying effect. After making the meter quick-moving in lines 1 and 2 and then slowing the reader down — with the internal rhyme and end-stopping caesura in line 3, with the two internal caesuras in line 4, and also the long durational stress on the words *witch's, oils, burnt,* and *green,* — the stanza has focused on the mysterious image of flames dancing slowly in an almost surrealistic manner.

End-Stops and Rhyme

I-28   Although end-stopping is not considered a caesura, pauses at the ends of line are extremely important. End-stopping, or autonomous lines without an end-stop, serve two primary functions: to show the association between lines, and to create stress or emphasis on particular words or on a particular line.

I-29   Because end-stopped lines increase the stress placed on the end of the line, poets must be very careful about their use of rhyme. When added to end-stop, the extra emphasis of rhyme causes the reader to become exceedingly aware of rhyming words at the end of the line. In the following lines, for example, the end-stops call attention to rhymes which do not seem particularly important or effective:

> *With a soul as strong as a mountain river,*
> *Pouring out praise to the Almighty Giver,*

I-30   The result of the additional emphasis placed on the rhymes by the end-stops is that the reader becomes aware of this poetical device, and unless the rhymes are especially important and deserve attention, or can be used very skillfully to give pleasure, as in much Eighteenth century poetry, end-stops should not be used.

I-31   With enjambed lines the poet can reduce the attention which the reader gives to the rhymes while maintaining the effectiveness of rhymed lines. In the following lines, for example:

> *And then, the simpering Byzantines*
> *Fled, with a noise like tambourines.*

FROM: PETER QUINCE AT THE CLAVIER
WALLACE STEVENS

The rhyme is de-emphasized because the enjambment and caesura in line 2 reduce the stress at the end of the line and place greater emphasis at the beginning of the following line.

I-32   Rhymed words always call attention to themselves, but the emphasis on them can be reduced through enjambment. This method is quite effective when the poet wants to maintain the associative power of rhymes without calling attention to them.

Review/self-check

I-33   Lines are characterized by the presence of meter, and accentual-syllabic lines are named according to the
_____ and _____ of predominant feet   type and number (I-4)
within the line.

I-34   Poetry is characterized by the presence of lines. A line which contains a unit of thought within itself is said to be autonomous; when the line is continued or runs over into the next line, the line is said to be

_____ .   enjambed (I-22)

I-35   The line is of special importance because it carries with it natural emphasis at its beginning and end. By increasing, decreasing, or interfering with this natural emphasis, the poet can create different effects. One

principal means by which the poet changes the natural
emphasis is by the use of _____.

caesuras (I-12)

I-36   We can define caesura as a pause or _____
in the metrical pattern. Usually punctuation marks are
used to indicate caesuras. Arrange the following punctuation marks in order, according to the duration of the
caesura created (beginning with the longest):
   colons, commas, semicolons, periods

break (I-8)

periods (I-11)
colons
semicolons
commas

I-37   Lines which end with a punctuation mark are
said to be _____; lines which are complete but
which have no final punctuation are said to be autonomous.

end-stopped (I-20)

I-38   The devices which poets frequently use to give
variation to lines are these: caesuras, _____, and
_____. One effect of enjambment is to (increase/
decrease) the emphasis at the end of the line, and to
(increase/decrease) the emphasis at the beginning of the
next line.

enjambment
substitution (I-23)
decrease
increase (I-31)

I-39   Two principal functions of end-stops are these:
   (1)   (2)

(1) to show associated
lines
(2) to emphasize the
end of the line (I-28)

RHYTHMIC VARIATIONS WITH CAESURAS

Caesuras Which Split Feet

I-40   Caesuras accomplish a variety of purposes (I-25). Caesuras which break feet in rising meters (H-23) are frequently used to create a falling rhythm within the line, although
they are not limited to this function. Similarly, caesuras breaking feet in falling meters
create rising rhythms, though the practice seems to be used with more general effectiveness in rising meters.

I-40   Consider the following lines:

Just as my fingers on these keys

Make mu/sic, so/ the self/ same sounds

FROM: PETER QUINCE AT THE CLAVIER
WALLACE STEVENS

The caesura breaks the iambic foot (line 2, foot 2) thereby emphasizing the falling
rhythm of *music,* and suggesting that the rest of the line continues a falling character.

When a caesura breaks an iambic foot, a falling rhythm is created within the line.

I-41   In this example, the first half of foot 2 attaches itself rhythmically to the previous foot, while the second half of the foot, the stressed half, attaches itself to the following foot. The result is that the remainder of the line maintains a falling rhythm which would read as follows:

$$\text{só the/ sélfsame/ sóunds}$$

Notice the similar effect of the caesuras in the following lines:

$$\text{For Í/ have knówn/ them áll/ alréad/y, knówn/ them áll:}$$

$$\text{Have knówn/ the éve/nings, mórn/ings, áf/ternoóns,}$$

FROM: THE LOVE SONG OF J. ALFRED PRUFROCK
T. S. ELIOT

Coming near the end of an iambic hexameter line, the first caesura (combined with the long line) creates a soft, exhaustive mood which is followed in line 2 with two caesuras that break iambic feet. Here the long line and the reinforced falling rhythm help establish a mood of boredom or defeat.

Splitting Triple Feet

I-42   Ceasuras, of course, can be used to break up not only iambs, but other types of feet, and in most instances the result is a disparity between the rhythm and the base meter. All breaks in feet cause a modification of rhythm so that rhythm does not exactly coincide with the base meter.

Generally, caesuras breaking duple feet (iambic or trochaic) have a more noticeable effect than caesuras dividing triple feet. This is true because a break in duple meter will change the rhythm from obviously rising to obviously falling, or vice-versa. Comparable changes in triple meters are less successful because the presence of more unaccented syllables makes such a reversal less obvious. Consider this line:

$$\text{With the síft/ed, harmón/ious páuse}$$

It exemplifies the position that caesuras which break iambic and trochaic feet usually have a more dramatic effect on the line than caesuras which break anapestic feet.

Caesuras Coming After the Foot: (Dieresis)

I-43   Caesuras which come after the foot (called *dieresis* in discussions of classical meters to distinguish them from caesuras which break the foot) can be used to create long pauses in the line, and they are often used to prepare the line for enjambment. Dieresis which is being used to create a long pause usually comes after words of long durational stress, and it comes in a metrical situation in which the reader would tend to pause anyway. For example, look at these lines:

More time, more time. Barrages of applause
Come muffled from a buried radio.

FROM: YEAR'S END
RICHARD WILBUR

The caesuras (the word "dieresis" is seldom used and so the reader should be aware that "caesura" includes both caesura and dieresis) in line 1 indicate the length of pause which comes from the natural pause created by the long duration of *more time*.

I-44   Any caesura creates a pause (by definition), but dieresis tends to create longer pauses because there is not the strong metrical unity of the foot to overcome as there is when the foot is broken. Instead, dieresis tends to give the foot more unity by separating it from the feet around it.

I-45   A dieresis pause is most effective in creating a long pause when it comes after a foot which contains syllables of long duration. But it is also very effective when it separates different types of feet. For example, in the line below, the long pause after *Listen* is made longer because the dieresis separates a trochaic foot from an iambic foot:

$$\text{Lís} \breve{\text{ten}}, / \text{ the } \text{háy-} / \text{bèlls } \text{tínk} / \breve{\text{le}} \text{ ăs} / \text{ thĕ } \text{cárt}$$

FROM: THE HOLY INNOCENTS
ROBERT LOWELL

But what if the line had been this way?

$$\text{Lís} \breve{\text{ten}}, / \text{hŏw } \text{théy} / \text{ tĭnkle} / \text{ăs thĕ} / \text{cárt}$$

The caesura then would not have been as long, because the continual falling rhythm would have maintained some rhythmic momentum.

I-46   A dieresis pause which separates different types of feet creates longer pauses than one which separates similar feet, because with similar feet the rhythm maintains momentum. We can say then, that caesuras which come after the foot can create long pauses; but when they do, it is usually in conjunction with durational stresses or substitutions.

The effects of dieresis are to slow down the line and to emphasize that particular foot.

Syntactical Pauses:

I-47   In addition to natural pauses which might occur in the line, the poet can use syntax to force caesuras which might not otherwise occur, or to strengthen those which do. For example, consider this line:

Avenge,/ O Lord,/ thy slaught/ered saints,/ whose bones
   1   2   3   4   5

The caesuras emphasize the first, second, and fifth feet, but Milton is also taking advantage of the rules of grammar, which dictate that an apostrophe (the address to the Lord) be set off even more. This results in greater emphasis on both the first and second feet. Compare Milton's line with the following:

O Lord, avenge thy slaughtered saints, whose bones

Of the two options, Milton chose the one bringing the greater pressure on the words which expressed his sentiments most strongly.

Here is another example:

Music is feeling, then, not sound;

The poet is emphasizing the dichotomy between feeling and sound by balancing the first part of the line against the last through the use of his caesura. Syntactically, *then* must be set off by commas, which forces the desired stress effect. Perhaps the line might have read this way:

Then music is feeling, not sound;

No commas would have been syntactically necessary, and the balance would not have been quite as effective.

Caesuras and Enjambment

I-48   Because the end of a line usually signifies a pause, and because the poet does not always want the reader to pause at the end of a line, caesuras are used to set up enjambment. Consider the following lines:

> *Forget not: in Thy book record their groans*
> *Who were Thy sheep and in their ancient fold*
> *Slain by the bloody Piedmontese, that rolled*
> *Mother with infant down the rocks. Their moans*
> *The vales redouble to the hills, and they*
> *To Heaven.*
>
> FROM: ON THE LATE MASSACRE AT PIEDMONT
> JOHN MILTON

There is a pause after autonomous line 1, but between lines 2 and 3, 3 and 4, 4 and 5, and 5 and 6 there is enjambment. In the last three instances enjambment has been set up by caesuras which come before the last foot in each line.

I-49   While it is not necessary for enjambment to be set up by caesuras which come before the last foot, lines which set up enjambment with a caesura near the end of the line tend to be more strongly enjambed than lines which have no caesura, or caesuras which come near the beginning of the line. This is not to say that all caesuras near the end of a line create enjambment, nor does it imply that in order to have enjambment there must be a caesura, but the enjambed lines which move the reader most quickly to the next line often have a pause near the end in order to give the reader wind to continue and a warning that enjambment is about to take place. For example, consider these lines:

> *Slain by the bloody Piedmontese, that rolled*
> *Mother with infant down the rocks. Their moans*

The enjambment moves rapidly because the caesura comes before the last foot, but in the example:

> *Fade far/ away,/ dissolve,/ and quite/ forget*
> *What thou among the leaves hast never known,*

> FROM: ODE TO A NIGHTINGALE
> JOHN KEATS

The caesura is two feet from the end of the first line, and the result is that the enjambment is not especially commanding. But in another example from the same poem, there is strong enjambment even though the caesura comes early in the line.

> *My heart/ aches, and/ a drow/sy numb/ness pains*
>
> *My sense, as though of hemlock I had drunk.*

Notice, however, that unlike the earlier line, the caesura breaks a trochee (foot 2), and the effect is to make the line fall away after the caesura. In effect, the line reads:

> *and a/ drowsy/ numbness/ pains*

The momentum of the falling line forces us into the following line with little pause, and in addition to the falling rhythm, the caesura after the first foot in the second line tends to associate itself closely with the preceding line, thereby strengthening the enjambment even more.

Effect of Enjambment

I-50   One effect of commanding (or strong) enjambment is to reduce both the attention which rhyme normally calls to itself and the natural emphasis which comes at the end of a line.

For example, let us look at these lines again:

> *Forget not: in Thy book record their groans*
> *Who were Thy sheep and in their ancient fold*
> *Slain by the bloody Piedmontese, that rolled*
> *Mother with infant down the rocks. Their moans*
> *The vales redouble to the hills, and they*
> *To Heaven.*

Lines 1 and 4 have strong masculine rhyming words: *groans, moans;* as do lines 2 and 3: *fold, rolled.* But in reading the poem, we find the rhymes are hardly noticeable because the enjambed lines reduce both the emphasis which normally comes at the end of a line and the attention which rhymed words call to themselves. (Refer to I-63 ff for a complete discussion of rhyme.)

Durational Pauses

I-51   Caesuras which are not punctuated, but which are formed by long durational stresses, or by certain combinations of feet or of syntax, can function in the same way as a comma functions. For example,

$$\overset{\smallsmile}{The}\ \overset{\prime}{mind}/\text{-}for\overset{\prime\prime}{ged}\ man/\overset{\prime}{acles}/\ \overset{\smallsmile\smallsmile}{I}\ \overset{\prime\prime}{hear}.$$
$$\quad 1 \qquad\quad 2 \qquad\quad 3 \quad\ 4$$

The line has an effective pause after *manacles* because of the long duration of *-cles* in combination with the spondaic substitution. Also contributing is a reversal of the usual subject-object syntactical relationship (I-47).

In another example, the syntactical pattern set up in the first half of the line causes a strong metrical caesura:

$$Does\ the/\ eagle/\ know//\ what\ is/\ in\ the/\ pit?$$

FROM: THEL'S MOTTO
WILLIAM BLAKE

If the poem were trochaic, the only explanation for this caesura after *know* could be seen by scanning the line as if it were two lines of trochaic trimeter, each with a terminal *anacrusis* (H-37):

$$Does\ the/\ Eagle/\ know$$

$$What\ is/\ in\ the/\ pit?$$

In other words, the caesura acts as a replacement for an unaccented syllable. In this isolated line, the momentum of the trochaic meter can be maintained only by inserting this pause, which the reader feels automatically.

What has actually occurred is that the combination of feet has played against the reader's metrical expectations, and a caesura after *know* has resulted.

On the other hand, if the line occurs in a poem whose base meter is rising iambic with frequent anapestic substitutions, the scansion could be as a four foot rising line:

$$Does\ the\ Ea/gle\ know/\ what\ is\ in/\ the\ pit?$$

In this case the middle foot is not split at all, thus reducing the shock of the pause. Scanned as iambic-anapestic, the pause after *know* is a more natural break, created by the foot rather than the syntax, while in the trochaic base the syntax jars the reader's sense of rhythm.

I-52   We can conclude, then, by saying that caesuras, whether denoted by punctuation or forced by syntax, duration, or a combination of certain feet, give variety, emphasis, and tension to the line.

Review/self-check

I-53   Caesuras which break iambic feet usually create a falling rhythm within the iambic base. For example, consider this line:

Then fly/ our greet/ings, fly/ our speech/ and smiles!
  1   2   3   4   5

The caesura breaks foot _____, thereby placing more emphasis on the words _____ and _____ than they would normally take. Although the line maintains a strict iambic base meter, the part after the caesura has a falling rhythm.

    Place the best effective stress pattern and falling feet divisions on this part of the line:

        fly our speech and smiles

3
greetings
fly

fly our/ speech and/
smiles (I-49)

I-54   Caesuras which break _____ feet usually have a more dramatic effect than caesuras which break triple feet because they tend to alter the effective meter of the line.

duple (I-42)

I-55   Caesuras which come after the foot (dieresis) are used to create long pauses or to prepare the line for _____.

enjambment (I-43)

I-56   One reason that dieresis is more effective in creating long pauses than caesuras which break the foot is that dieresis does not have to overcome the strong metrical unity of the _____.

foot (I-44)

I-57   Dieresis which separates different types of feet causes a longer pause than dieresis which separates the same type of feet, because an established meter maintains _____.

momentum (I-46)

I-58   The effect of a long pause after a foot is to:

emphasize that foot or change the natural cadence of the line (I-46)

I-59   The end of a line signifies a pause even if there is no end stop. If the poet wishes to reduce the length of this natural pause, he can do so by _____.

enjambment (I-48)

I-60   Enjambment is frequently set up by _____. Generally, the strongest enjambed lines are those which have caesuras near the _____ of the line, or those which have a strong _____ rhythm in the latter part of the line.

caesuras (I-48)

end (I-49)
falling (I-49)

I-61   Caesuras without punctuation can be formed by long _____ stresses, a combination of _____, or _____.

durational, feet
syntax (I-51)

I-62   Caesuras are important prosodic tools because they give _____ and _____ to the line.

variety/emphasis and
tension (I-52)

Rhyme

A large body of scholarship about *rhyme* has managed to prove only that it is a complex device that varies greatly from one poem to the next. While we cannot delve into the complexities of why rhyme works as it does, for the purpose of basic understanding and explicating we can make some helpful generalizations about rhyme as a device essential to the *sound* of poetry (E-1 ff) and as closely related to *structure* (L-1 ff), *caesura* (I-8 ff) and *stanza form* (J-1 ff).

THE FUNCTIONS AND TYPES OF RHYME

I-63   One function of rhyme is to create pleasure for the reader through the sounds which it makes. When one sound is already echoing in the reader's consciousness, and the poem reinforces that sound with a similar one, the reader derives pleasure from it. Not all associated sounds are pleasurable, of course, nor should they be, since the poet attempts to find rhymes which convey the sort of sounds that he wishes in order to produce a particular emotional response.

Rhyme and Meaning

I-64   In addition to the sounds of rhymes, meter and meaning are also quite important contributors to establishing pleasurable rhymes. Let us look at these lines:

> *I saw a man without a hat,*
> *And close beside a large, grey cat.*

Here the rhyme gives very little pleasure because the meter is too regular, the rhymes too commonplace, and the association between the rhymed words too absurd. Regularity of meter and predictability of rhyme tend to make rhyming less pleasurable.

We can say then, that some of the factors which influence the success of rhymes are the ingenuity of the rhymes, the meter of the line, and the intellectual connotation and logic of the rhyming words. Consider the following lines, for example:

> *For I have known them all already, known them all:*
> *Have known the evenings, mornings, afternoons,*
> *I have measured out my life with coffee spoons;*

FROM: THE LOVE SONG OF J. ALFRED PRUFROCK

There is something very pleasurable about associating *afternoons* with *coffee spoons*, especially when they are in the context of a poem which is about a proper society that spends its afternoons over coffee and cakes.

One reason that *afternoons* and *spoons* is a pleasurable rhyme whereas *hat* and *cat* or *moon* and *June* are not so pleasurable is the logical association between the words. In the example, hats and cats here have nothing to do with each other; and the *moon - June* rhyme has been so overworked that it causes a negative reaction. However, the sound of clinking spoons during polite tea parties is set easily in the afternoon.

Rhyming words to be effective must have reasonable intellectual association and freshness as well as pleasurable sound associations, and while the right sort of expectations in rhyme will give pleasure when fulfilled, poets try to avoid overworked or obvious rhymes. With Alexander Pope, we are all likely to be annoyed with the banal and all too predictable rhyme:

> *Where'er you find "the cooling western breeze,"*
> *In the next line, it "whispers through the trees";*

FROM: AN ESSAY ON CRITICISM

I-66   Closely associated to reasonableness and freshness of rhyme is the appropriateness of the image with which the rhyme is associated. The following lines make a good example:

> *I have seen the moment of my greatness flicker,*
> *And I have seen the eternal Footman hold my coat, and snicker.*

FROM: THE LOVE SONG OF J. ALFRED PRUFROCK
T. S. ELIOT

Here *snicker* is a pleasurable rhyming word because the image of Death (the Eternal Footman) snickering is both horrifying and amusing, and with *flicker* already echoing in our memory, the rhyme gives pleasure. There is pleasure here, too, because of the metrical distance one must travel in order to link *flicker* with *snicker*.

I-67   We can say that one of the primary purposes of rhyme is to give pleasure. Rhyme can achieve pleasure through its sound when one ingenious word is reinforced by another.

I-68   When explicating a poem, the reader should remember that the repetition of sounds calls attention to the rhyming words; hence, the rhymes must be chosen to emphasize words of importance to the development and meaning of the poem. It is also helpful to try to discover why the pleasurable rhymes give pleasure, or why the unpleasurable lines are irritating. The poet may be attempting a number of things with his rhyme: focusing on an image or idea, establishing harmony or disharmony, creating a particular tone, or simply forcing associations between lines. If the reader can establish how the rhyme functions, he will be better able to determine where the emphasis lies, and how the poet feels toward the subject of the poem.

Types of Rhyme

I-69   The function which a rhyme serves depends in part upon its type. There are several different types, ranging from full rhymes (as: *hat, rat*) to words which have only slight rhyming association (as: *smart, retort*). Types of rhymes are classified according to: (1) the sound relationship between rhyming words, (2) the position of the rhyming words within the line, and (3) the number and position of the syllables within rhyming words.

RHYME CLASSIFIED BY SOUND

Full Rhyme

I-70   The most common traditional rhyming is done with full rhymes. *Full rhyme* is defined as two or more words which have the same vowel sound, followed by the same consonant or consonants in their last stressed syllable, and in which all succeeding syllables are phonetically identical (they may be spelled differently as long as the sounds are identical). For example, *hat* and *cat* are full rhymes, as are *laughter* and *after*.

I-71   A second type of frequently used rhyme is formed by words whose sounds only approximate each other; approximate rhymes may be either assonances or half (slant) rhymes.

Assonance

I-72   *Assonances* have identical *vowel sound* clusters in their stressed syllables but different succeeding consonant sounds. For example, *stars, arms, park* assonate, though they don't fully rhyme.

Slant Rhyme (Consonance)

I-73   *Slant,* or *half rhymes,* on the other hand, have different (though often phonetically contiguous) vowel sounds in their final stressed syllables; it is the succeeding *consonant sound* clusters which are identical. For example, *fall, pal, well* are related to each other as half or slant rhymes.

I-74   *Table* and *bauble* constitute half rhymes; *law, cough,* and *fawn* assonate; *daughter* and *water* are full rhymes. The following lines have alternating terminal assonances:

> *Brushing from whom the stiffened puke*
> *i put him all into my arms*
> *and staggered banged with terror through*
> *a million billion trillion stars*

> FROM: a man who had fallen among thieves
> e. e. cummings

Alliterative Rhyme

I-75   Assonance and half rhyme are only two types of approximate rhyme; another approximate rhyme is *alliteration.* Here the initial consonant sounds of stressed syllables are identical, while succeeding sounds may vary. For example, *fling* and *flair* form alliterative half rhyme if each occurs at the end of its line. If similar examples are found within lines, they are known simply as alliteration (see frame E-30 ff for a discussion of alliteration).

I-76   The following two stanzas use approximate rhyme; the first stanza uses alternating alliterative half rhymes; the second uses alternating half rhymes (consonance I-73).

> *It was not Frost, for on my Flesh*
> *I felt Siroccos — crawl —*
> *Nor Fire — for just my Marble feet*
> *Could keep a Chancel, cool —*
>
> *And yet, it tasted, like them all,*
> *The Figures I have seen*
> *Set orderly, for Burial,*
> *Reminded me, of mine —*

FROM: IT WAS NOT DEATH
EMILY DICKINSON

In the first stanza we can say that lines 1 and 3, and 2 and 4 form alliterative half rhymes because the first consonants of the last word in the line recall each other. In the second stanza the final sounds of the last word in lines 5 and 7, as well as 6 and 8, recall each other, and because the preceeding vowel sounds differ, the words consonate. Also, notice that in addition to alliterating, *crawl* and *cool* in stanza 1 consonate.

Uses for Approximate Rhyme

I-77   Generally, approximate rhyme is not so satisfying as full rhyme, and it is frequently frustrating for the reader because it approaches rhyming without actually achieving it. For this same reason, however, assonances and half rhymes are well suited for poems in which despair or anxiety are important. In "a man who had fallen among thieves" (I-74), for example, the five preceeding stanzas use full rhyme, but by the sixth stanza, the persona has degenerated into a state of despair, which the incomplete rhyming of the assonances reinforce.

I-78   While approximate rhymes are very adaptable to poems connoting anxiety or despair, they do not necessarily have to be used in this way, and poets will sometimes use good half rhymes rather than mediocre full rhymes. This is especially true in stanza forms which are particularly demanding on rhyme (see Sections J and K for discussion of these stanza forms).

Light Rhyme

I-79   Words whose final stressed vowels and all succeeding consonants are identical, but whose stressed syllables do not correspond, are known as *light rhymes*. Light rhyme is comparable to full rhyme except that the rhyming syllables are usually not primary stresses in all the words involved. For example, *pant* and *ignorant* form a light rhyme, as do *sing* and *beckoning*.

Eye Rhyme

I-80   Words which only appear identical (because of their spelling) but sound different, are known as eye rhyme. For example, *bough, enough,* and *cough* are eye rhymes. Because of changes in pronunciation, many traditional poems appear to have eye rhymes in words which were once full rhymes. For example, *wind* (meaning the noun describing moving air) once rhymed with *bind* and *find.* Eye rhymes which are intentional and do not result from a change in pronunciation are often used for a disconcerting effect.

Identical Rhyme

I-81   Identical rhyme in which the entire final stressed syllables contain exactly the same sounds (e.g., *break, brake*) can be successful only if employed sparingly. Exact rhymes are usually unpleasing, and force problems with *puns* (F-10). Examples of other identical rhymes would include *bear* (noun), *bear* (verb), *bare* (adjective), and *bare* (verb), or a repetition of the same word in the same sense.

I-82   Usually identical rhyme is used to indicate weariness, defeat, or dullness, and for this effect it can be quite good if skillfully handled. Notice the use of identical rhyme in the following lines:

> There passed a weary time. Each throat
> Was parched, and glazed each eye.
> A weary time! a weary time!
> How glazed each weary eye.

FROM: THE RIME OF THE ANCIENT MARINER
SAMUEL TAYLOR COLERIDGE

In Chaucer's time, however, identical rhyme was used somewhat indiscriminately for a variety of purposes, but by the Renaissance was used more cautiously.

RHYME CLASSIFIED BY POSITION

I-83   Besides classification according to the sound relationships between rhyming words, a second classification examines the position of rhyming words in the line. On the basis of the position of the rhymed words, there are end rhyme, internal rhyme, and initial rhyme.

End Rhyme

I-84   *End rhyme* (or terminal rhyme) occurs when the last words of two lines rhyme whether or not the rhymes are full or approximate. The following is an example of end rhyme:

> So long as men can breathe or eyes can see,
> So long lives this, and this gives life to thee,

FROM: SONNET 18
WILLIAM SHAKESPEARE

It is not necessary, however, for the lines to be consecutive in order to have end rhyme.

I-85   One of the effects of end rhyme is to bind or associate lines. By using the associative power of rhyming words, the poet can force a strong association between complete lines through the use of the rhymed words; this is true even if the lines are somewhat separated within the poem.

I-86   End rhyme is especially effective in binding lines together. This binding effect allows the poet to form a close association between the content of the lines through the sounds of the lines. Regular lines of equal length with an end-stop (I-20, I-26) place the greatest emphasis on the rhyme, and form the most rigid association.

I-87   We can generalize and say that the lines which form the closest association are contiguous, are of the same length with regular meter, have strong end rhymes, and are end-stopped. An example of two closely associated lines is this:

> *This lock the Muse shall consecrate to fame,*
> *And 'midst the stars inscribe Belinda's name.*

FROM: THE RAPE OF THE LOCK
ALEXANDER POPE

I-88   Long poems which use highly regularized lines with strong end rhymes become monotonous for most modern readers and are difficult to sustain without repeating rhymes or using ineffective ones, unless the rhyming is very skillfully handled. However, end-stopped end rhymes assist in memorizing poetry, and our most mnemonic (D-24) verse tends to employ them as in this example:

> *A little learning is a dangerous thing:*
> *Drink deep or taste not that Pierian spring.*

FROM: AN ESSAY ON CRITICISM
ALEXANDER POPE

I-89   It is quite easy to reduce the starkness of end rhyme while maintaining its binding qualities by the use of the caesura (I-20, I-8) and enjambment (I-20). In the following lines, which have a regular iambic pentameter base as do the lines in the preceeding example, there is strong end rhyme, but it is hardly noticeable because of the skillful use of caesura and enjambment.

> *That's my last Duchess painted on the wall,*
> *Looking as if she were alive. I call*
> *That piece a wonder, now: Fra Pandolf's hands*
> *Worked busily a day, and there she stands.*

FROM: MY LAST DUCHESS
ROBERT BROWNING

In addition to caesura and enjambment, the poet can use substitution (H-25 ff) or vary the length of the lines to reduce the irritating qualities of strong end rhyme while retaining the desirable qualities. The following lines are an example of varying the the line length to reduce end-rhyme starkness.

> *It melted, and I let it fall and break.*
> *But I was well*
> *Upon my way to sleep before it fell,*
> *And I could tell*
> *What form my dreaming was about to take.*

FROM: AFTER APPLE-PICKING
ROBERT FROST

I-90   Besides enjambment, substitution, caesura, and line length, approximate rhyme is a valuable tool in reducing the starkness of end rhyme, as in the example in I-76.

Internal Rhyme

I-91   A second type of rhyme according to position of words is *internal rhyme.* When two words located somewhere after the beginning of a line and before the end recall each other through their sound, internal rhyme occurs. The words may occur in the same line, or in contiguous lines. Generally, only full rhyme is recognized as internal rhyming; nevertheless, internal approximate rhymes contribute to binding the parts of lines tightly, and help create *vowel music* (E-23).

An example of internal rhyme is the following:

> *Wet, below the snow line, smelling of vegetation*

FROM: JOURNEY OF THE MAGI
T. S. ELIOT

where *below* and *snow* rhyme.

I-92   While there are some variations on the formal definition of internal rhyme, these nevertheless function in the same way that internal rhyme functions, and they should be considered within this type of rhyme. An example is this line:

> *About, about, in reel and rout*

FROM: THE RIME OF THE ANCIENT
MARINER
SAMUEL TAYLOR COLERIDGE

where the rhyming words do not fall between the beginning and end of the line, but at the beginning and end. Here is another example:

> *And mark in every face I meet,*
> *Marks of weakness, marks of woe.*

FROM: LONDON
WILLIAM BLAKE

Here *meet* at the end of line 1 assonates (I-72) with *weak* in the middle of line 2. Within a broad definition, we can say that internal rhyme occurs when either of the rhyming words occurs somewhere other than at the end or the beginning of the lines.

Thus, for example, consider this stanza:

> *Swiftly, swiftly flew the ship,*
> *Yet she sailed softly too:*
> *Sweetly, sweetly blew the breeze-*
> *On me alone it blew.*

FROM: THE RIME OF THE ANCIENT
MARINER

We can say that *flew* in line 1 forms an internal rhyme with *too* in line 2 and *blew* in lines 3 and 4, but the rhyme formed by *too* in line 2 and *blew* in line 4 is not internal because both words come at the end of the line; *too* and *blew* (line 4) form an end rhyme (line 2).

I-93   The effect of internal rhyme can vary, but generally it is used to give greater unity to a line, or to several lines. When used in conjunction with end rhyme, it creates very tight lines; when used in the absence of end rhyme, it subtly knits portions of lines together. Internal rhyme can also be used effectively to give the line a more musical or rhythmic quality than it might normally have. For example, consider this line:

> *About, about, in reel and rout,*

The three rhyming words — *about, about, rout* — (as well as the *r*- alliteration in *reel* and *rout*) suggest the dancing motion of the poem's death fires which dance at night.

I-94   When an internal word rhymes with the end word in the same line, the general effect is for the line to be split in two, as in this example:

> *Ah, distinctly I remember it was in the bleak December.*

FROM: THE RAVEN
EDGAR ALLAN POE

Initial Rhyme

I-95   The third type of rhyme according to position of the word within the line is initial rhyme, which occurs when the rhymed words come at the beginning of lines. An example of beginning rhyme is this:

Wind the whirlpool
Blind and certain;
Dark as the dark there,
Stark, you shall disturb.

In lines 1 and 2, and 3 and 4, there is initial rhyme. In addition to the initial rhymes, line 3 contains an identical rhyme (I-81).

I-96   Initial rhyme is rarely used, and there are no major poems which depend solely upon it for any sustained period. One problem with using initial rhyme exclusively is that unless the rhyme occurs on the first syllable in the word (as does the rhyme *dark/ stark* in the example), beginning rhyme does not have the same binding quality as does end rhyme. When used in conjunction with end rhyme, or in enjambed lines, it has the same binding quality as internal rhyme (I-91).

Review/self-check

I-97   Rhyme functions to create _____ in poetry through the _____ which it makes.

pleasure (I-63)
sound

I-98   Since rhymed words are closely associated with each other, the logical association between them must be meaningful. We can say, then, that the meaning as well as the _____ of the words will, in part, determine the success of the rhyme.

sound (I-63)

I-99   The types of rhyme according to the position of the words, in the line are _____, _____ and _____,

initial, internal, end (terminal) (I-83)

I-100   End rhymes are especially effective in _____ lines together.

binding (I-85)

I-101   The type of line which places greatest emphasis on its rhyme is _____.

a regular, end-stopped line of equal length to the line with which it rhymes.(I-87)

I-102   The starkness of end rhyme can be reduced by use of _____, and _____, or by varying the _____ of the lines.

caesuras, enjambment length (I-90)

I-103   Approximate rhymes may be either _____ or _____.

assonances (I-71)
half (slant) rhymes

I-104   Half rhymes are especially good for conveying feelings of _____ because their closeness to rhyme without actually rhyming tends to frustrate the reader.

despair or anxiety
(I-77)

I-105   Internal rhyme gives greater _____ to the line, and can be used to create _____ effects.

unity (I-93)
musical

I-106   Consider the following stanza from "The Rime of the Ancient Mariner":

> In mist or cloud, on mast or shroud,
> It perched for vespers nine;
> Whiles all the night, through fog-smoke white,
> Glimmered the white Moon-shine.

There are several types of rhyme used. Internal rhymes come in lines _____ and _____. They are: _____ / _____ ; _____ / _____ .

1 and 3
cloud/shroud
night/white

I-107 (a)   Generally the effect of an internal word rhyming with the final word in the same line is _____ .

to divide the line in two (I-94)

I-107 (b)   In other words, if we examine this line:

> In mist or cloud, on mast or shroud,

it could work effectively as two *dimeter* (I-4) lines, written as follows: _____ / _____ .

In mist or cloud,
On mast or shroud,

I-107 (c)   In addition to the internal rhyme, line 1 is also made tighter by the repetition of the word *or*, by parallel structure on both sides of the caesura, and by the closeness of the sounds of the words _____ and _____ . The end-rhymed lines are _____ and _____ .

mist/mast
2 and 4

I-108   Comment on the use of rhyme in the following poem, identifying each type and showing how it gives unity to the poem (the principal rhymes have been marked).

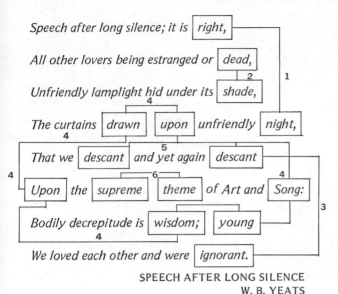

SPEECH AFTER LONG SILENCE
W. B. YEATS

1. *Full end rhyme* (I-84), bind-ing the first four lines as a quatrain. (Compare the strength of the first four lines to the last four.)

2. *Approximate end rhyme* (I-73), called half rhyme. Binds lines 2 and 3 loosely.

3. *Light rhyme* (I-79); would be full rhyme except that *descant* is a masculine word (I-110) and *ignorant* a femi-nine (I-112). The rhyme jars our expectations, ending the poem with a falling meter (H-23, I-40).

4. *Half rhyme* serving the same function as item #2 above, but which is also turned inter-nally into assonance (I-72). The result is an extraordin-arily tightly bound quatrain.

5. *Identical rhyme* (I-81); reinforces the exhaustion the persona feels.

6. *Internal rhyme* or a sylla-bic binder (I-91) used to con-vey a facetious tone.

RHYME CLASSIFIED BY NUMBER OF SYLLABLES

I-109   Besides the sound relationship between rhyming words, and the position of rhymes within the line, a third type of classification involves the number of syllables in the rhyme words. On the basis of the number of syllables in the rhymed words, there are three types of rhyme: masculine, feminine, and multiple. These are classified according to the number of rhyming syllables.

Masculine Rhyme

I-110   *Masculine rhyme* occurs when the correspondence of sound is restricted to the final accented syllable. For example, notice this line:

> So shalt thou feed on death, that feeds on men,
> And death once dead, there's no more dying then.

FROM: SONNET 146
WILLIAM SHAKESPEARE

Here *men* and *then* are final-accented rhymes, and are therefore called masculine rhymes.

The final word, however, need not necessarily contain only one syllable. For example, notice these lines:

> *Have known the evenings, mornings, afternoons,*
> *I have measured out my life with coffee spoons;*
>
> FROM: THE LOVE SONG OF J. ALFRED PRUFROCK
> T. S. ELIOT

Here *afternoons* contains three syllables while *spoons* is monosyllabic, but since the final stressed syllables rhyme, the rhyme is masculine.

I-111   Masculine rhyme is generally more forceful than the other two types — feminine and multiple — and while it has a variety of uses, it generally gives authority and assurance to the line, especially when the final syllables are of short duration.

Feminine Rhyme

I-112   *Feminine rhyme* occurs when the final accented syllable is followed by a single unaccented syllable. The accented syllables rhyme, while the unaccented syllables are phonically identical, as in this example:

> *I have seen the moment of my greatness flicker,*
> *And I have seen the eternal Footman hold my coat, and snicker*
>
> FROM: THE LOVE SONG OF J. ALFRED PRUFROCK

Here the accented syllables in *flick-er* and *snick-er* rhyme, and the following unaccented syllables are identical.

The following lines have feminine rhyme, although the last word of line 1 has two syllables while the last word of line 2 has three syllables.

> *Smoothed by long fingers,*
> *Asleep . . . tired . . . or it malingers,*
>
> FROM: THE LOVE SONG OF J. ALFRED PRUFROCK

The rhyming syllables in *fingers* and *malingers* are *fin-gers/lin-gers.*

Uses for Masculine and Feminine Rhymes

I-113   Feminine rhymes are often used for lightness in tone and delicacy in movement, and whereas masculine rhyme is forceful and sure, feminine rhyme seems soft. This softness may or may not indicate a lack of assuredness, but it does indicate a lack of brusqueness and brutality.

I-114   When feminine rhymes occur, they often convey lightness and delicacy, partially because the final syllable is unstressed, which creates a falling rhythm (H-23, I-40), and partially because polysyllabic words are softer (E-15). Feminine rhymes may also be used to add humor.

I-115   Rhymes in which the correspondence of sound comes only in a final unstressed syllable which is preceded by another unstressed syllable are called neither masculine nor feminine, but are referred to as falling rhymes (feminine rhymes involve the final unstressed syllable preceded by a stressed syllable).

Multiple Rhymes

I-116   Multiple rhyme occurs when more than the last two syllables rhyme, as in this example:

> *Deferential, glad to be of use,*
> *Politic, cautious, and meticulous;*
> *Full of high sentence, but a bit obtuse;*
> *At times, indeed, almost ridiculous —*

FROM: THE LOVE SONG OF J. ALFRED PRUFROCK

Here lines 2 and 4 have triple rhymes. The rhyming syllables in *meticulous* and *ridiculous* are *tic-u-lous/dic-u-lous.*

I-117   Multiple rhymes can be used only sparingly for poems of a serious nature because they tend to produce a comic effect. However, when used appropriately, multiple rhymes can reinforce pathos or defeat.

I-118   The complete description of a rhyme includes an analysis according to each of the three types of rhyming classification (sound, position, and number of syllables). Thus, a rhyme may be full masculine end rhyme, or light masculine internal rhyme, etc.

Review/self-check

I-119   Rhyme is classified according to the _____ of the word in the line, and to the number of final rhyming _____.

position

syllables (I-69)

I-120   Two effects of end rhyme are _____.

to bind lines together (I-85); to place greater stress on the end of the line

I-121   Two effects of internal rhyme are _____.

to give unity to the line; to create musical effects (I-93)

I-122   Half rhymes occur when there is (exact, approximate) correspondence of sound between the vowels.

approximate (I-73)

I-123   One effect of masculine rhyme is _____ while the effect of feminine rhyme is to soften or lighten the tone.
    Consider the following example:

to give assurance (I-111)

> *These, in the day when heaven was falling,*
>   *The hour when earth's foundations fled,*
> *Followed their mercenary calling*
>   *And took their wages and are dead.*

>   FROM: EPITAPH ON AN ARMY OF
>   MERCENARIES
>   A. E. HOUSMAN

The rhymes in lines 1 and 3 are _____, and in 2 and 4 are _____.

full feminine end-rhyme
full masculine end-rhyme

Form

The effects of both rhyme (I-63 ff) and meaning cause lines to become associated into groups of varying size, and by using these groupings the poet produces certain divisions within the poem known as *stanzas*. Stanzas, in turn, can be used to structure and develop theme, so that the type of stanza used becomes important to the explicator. Refer to the discussions of the influence of the stanza on structure (L-1 ff), and the types of stanza forms (K-1 ff) that are available to the poet.

UNIT PATTERNS IN VERSE

J-1   In terms of understanding a poem, one of the most important functions of analyzing rhyme is to help establish the form of the poem. Rhyme suggests associations between lines which should be considered together, as in this stanza:

> *I was angry with my friend:*
> *I told my wrath, my wrath did end.*
> *I was angry with my foe:*
> *I told it not, my wrath did grow.*

> FROM: THE POISON TREE
> WILLIAM BLAKE

The first rhyming lines signify a complete idea which contrasts with the next set of rhyming lines.

We can say, then, that rhyme can function as a type of "punctuation" for larger units of thoughts, which then become stanzas, verse paragraphs, or divisions therein.

J-2   Of course, most associations formed by rhyme are not as simple or straightforward as those in the preceeding example; indeed, one of the assets of using rhyme is that subtle associations can be achieved which would otherwise not be established in the reader's mind.

J-3   When successive lines rhyme, as in the example above, they usually have some direct association. Non-successive rhyming lines, however, may not have direct association, but may be used to bind several ideas together, as in this example:

> *Shall I compare thee to a summer's day?*
> *Thou art more lovely and more temperate:*
> *Rough winds do shake the darling buds of May,*
> *And summer's lease hath all too short a date.*

> FROM: SONNET 18
> WILLIAM SHAKESPEARE

Lines 2, 3, and 4 constitute the comparison to the summer, and therefore have a logical association. The rhyme *temperate/date* binds the three lines together. But the three lines must also be bound to the initial question, which the rhyme *day/May* achieves; so that the total effect is to make the four lines an interwoven unit.

J-4   Rhyme, then, can show the association between two lines, or can bind a number of lines into an interwoven unit. Notice that even though lines 2 and 4 are light masculine end rhymes (I-79, I-110) (lines 1 and 3 are full masculine end rhymes), the binding force is still strong.

An established pattern of rhyme, then, acts as a larger unit of punctuation than the period, holding a group of lines together. For example, consider the line group below:

> *We listened and looked sideways up!*
> *Fear at my heart, as at a cup,*
> *My life-blood seemed to sip!*
> *The stars were dim, and thick the night,*
> *The steersman's face by his lamp gleamed white;*
> *From the sails the dew did drip —*
> *Till clomb above the eastern bar*
> *The hornèd moon, with one bright star*
> *Within the nether tip.*

FROM: THE RIME OF THE ANCIENT MARINER
SAMUEL TAYLOR COLERIDGE

The rhyme is so interwoven that it is obvious that we should take these lines as a unit.

STANZAS

J-5   When rhymed lines are meant to be taken as a unit, and the unit recurs in the major divisions of the poem, that unit is called a stanza. There may be several smaller groups of associated lines within the stanza, but they all contribute to the main stanza unit.

J-6   Poems may be generally differentiated according to their reliance on the stanza as the basic unit of division in the poem. Poems which are divided into fairly regular and patterned stanzas are called *strophic.* Poems in which there is no predictable stanza form or length are called *stichic.*

J-7   Since rhyme is the binding element which gives unity to most stanza forms, it should be obvious that most strophic poems are rhymed, while most stichic poems are unrhymed.

J-8   Both strophic and stichic units represent a logical division within the poem, and the difference between them lies in the formality of the pattern which is formed by the interwoven unit.

Strophic Units

J-9   Accentual-syllabic poems which have recurring units of similar length, and which have metrical pattern and rhyme pattern, are said to be *strophic,* as in this example from "The Rime of the Ancient Mariner:"

> *All in a hot and copper sky,*
> *The bloody sun, at noon,*
> *Right up above the mast did stand,*
> *No bigger than the moon.*
>
> *Day after day, day after day,*
> *We struck, nor breath nor motion;*
> *As idle as a painted ship*
> *Upon a painted ocean.*

Strophic divisions (stanzas) are approximately the same length, and have recurring metrical and rhyme patterns.

Although not every stanza need have exactly the same form for the poem to be considered strophic, some basic form is necessary. In "The Ancient Mariner," for example, there are 5, 6, and 9 line stanzas intermingled within the 4 line stanzas, but the poem is strophic because these are only variations on the basic 4 line stanza.

Uses for Strophic Divisions

J-10   Short stanzas are generally most appropriate for concentrated ideas or moments of emotion, or for narration when the action is steadily progressing. Short stanzas also give the impression of organized thought or emotion as opposed to more spontaneous thought or emotion expressed in long strophic or stichic divisions.

J-11   We can say, then, that short stanzas usually connote a logical progression of action or thought, and that the emotion contained within the stanza is less spontaneous than that in longer strophic or stichic units. This is not to say that short stanzas are unemotional, only that the emotion in each stanza is more often controlled. We can therefore expect that in a strophic poem which is composed of a series of short stanzas, the unifying element will come either through the action, or through the total effect of a number of quick emotional glimpses.

STICHIC UNITS

J-12   In *stichic* organization the lines are grouped with no formal arrangement as to the number of lines or rhyme pattern (if any exists). A stichic poem can have divisions (called "verse paragraphs"), but they may be few, and each stichic unit may contain a large body of thought and action.

J-13   A stichic poem may have divisions which have different number of lines. For example, a stichic poem of 1000 lines might have three divisions, one 200 lines long, one

500 lines, and one 300 lines. Within these large divisions, however, there may be sub-groups of associated lines, but they are part of the larger unit and are not separated physically from other lines.

J-14   Although some poems are composed of long stichic divisions, like *Paradise Lost,* stichic verse need not necessarily have a vast number of lines. Each stichic division will, however, have an unpredictable number of lines.

J-15   Stichic organization has been most successfully used for large, expansive narration, or for long meditative or dramatic action.

Because strophic verse allows pauses at regular intervals, the climactic effect is usually created by a fusion of all the parts, whereas with stichic divisions the reader is not allowed expectations of pauses, and the poet can build the material to climax at any point or at as many points as he likes.

J-16   We can say, then, that one of the principal differences between strophic and stichic stanzas lies in the expectation of where climactic events or emotions are likely to take place.

J-17   Every division, either stanzas in strophic verse, or verse paragraphs in stichic verse, will often complete some major idea in the poem, so that the unit helps build toward the high point of the idea. With strophic divisions it is likely that the focus on the idea will come at the end of the stanza, since there is relatively little space for development.

LARGER DIVISIONS THAN STANZAS

J-18   Some poems, both strophic and stichic, need larger divisions than stanzas or verse paragraphs, in which case such divisions may be signified by Roman numerals, letters of the alphabet, "books," or cantos, depending on the size.

J-19   When a poem contains books or Roman numerals it is because lines and stanzas have not provided large enough divisions to handle a large number of ideas or an expanse of action. Generally a major division (denoted by letters, numbers, or books) will maintain similar stanza forms although the stanza form may differ from division to division (as in "Peter Quince at the Clavier"). There are some poems, however, which use both strophic and stichic organization in the same large division (as in "The Marriage of Heaven & Hell").

When a mixture of stanza forms occurs, it usually denotes that complex — sometimes almost psychotic — thoughts and actions are transpiring, and the mixed forms reflect the complexity of thought. Also, if the poet changes moods or type of action, he may change stanza forms within a major division.

EXAMINING RHYME SCHEMES

J-20   When stanzas establish some sort of pattern of rhyme, we say that the stanza has a rhyme scheme. We designate the pattern of a rhyme scheme by assigning a letter to each end-rhyme unit, beginning with the first unit and using the same letter each time the rhyme is repeated. Let us examine an example to see how this works.

Example/self-check

J-21 Consider the following lines:

> *That time of year thou mayst in me behold*
> *When yellow leaves, or none, or few, do hang*
> *Upon those boughs which shake against the cold,*
> *Bare ruined choirs, where late the sweet birds sang.*

FROM: SONNET 73
WILLIAM SHAKESPEARE

We tag *behold* at the end of the first line as "a." Since the second line does not rhyme with the first, we tag it as "b." The third line, however, rhymes with the first; so we tag it "a," and the fourth line rhymes with the second; we we tag it _____. The rhyme _____ of this stanza, then, is *abab*.	"b", scheme

J-22 The rhyme scheme of the following stanza is _____.

Are those her ribs through which the sun	a
Did peer, as through a grate?	b
And is that woman all her crew?	c
Is that a Death? and are there two?	c
Is Death that woman's mate?	b

FROM: THE RIME OF THE ANCIENT MARINER

J-23 The rhyme scheme of the following stanza is _____ .

We listened and looked sideways up!	
Fear at my heart, as at a cup,	
My life-blood seemed to sip!	
The stars were dim, and thick the night,	
The steersman's face by his lamp gleamed white;	
From the sails the dew did drip —	
Till clomb above the eastern bar	
The horned moon, with one bright star	
Within the nether tip.	*aabccbddb*

FROM: THE RIME OF THE ANCIENT MARINER

THE LANGUAGE AND TRADITION

Traditional Stanzas

Some stanza forms are used so frequently, or have been used with such force and success that they are recognized as unique types and have special names.

When explicating a poem which uses one of the standard stanza forms, it is important to compare the traditional use of the form with the use which the poet in question is making of it, because the differences or similarities may give a clue as to what the poem is about. Traditional stanza forms are determined by the *rhyme* (I-63 ff), and type of *line* (I-1 ff) and *foot* (H-1 ff) used.

THE FUNCTION OF STANZA TRADITIONS

K-1 Stanza forms which have been consistently used in a certain way, or forms which have been used with force or success, carry connotations which must be considered and compared to the poem which is being explicated, because a comparison of the similarities and differences of the forms being considered may indicate what the poet is attempting to do.

K-2 Some of the standard forms, such as the couplet and triplet may stand by themselves as a stanza, or may be incorporated into a larger stanza and simply act as a unit, while other standard forms, such as the Spenserian, always stand by themselves, constituting an entire stanza.

TWO LINE STANZAS: COUPLETS

K-3 A *couplet* occurs when two succeeding lines rhyme, as here:

> *I was angry with my friend.*
> *I told my wrath, my wrath did end.*
>
> FROM: THE POISON TREE
> WILLIAM BLAKE

When two successive lines rhyme, the pair is called a couplet. Although the two lines in a couplet do not have to be the same length or have the same meter, they frequently do.

K-4 One of the most commonly used couplets is constructed of two lines of iambic pentameter. When two successive, rhyming lines of iambic pentameter occur, the pair is called a *decasyllabic couplet*, as in Browning's "My Last Duchess":

> *That's my last Duchess painted on the wall,*
> *Looking as if she were alive. I call*
> *That piece a wonder now: . . .*

176

An end-stopped (I-20) decasyllabic couplet is called an *Heroic couplet,* named because its stately form has often been used to sing the praise of heroes.

K-5   However, since the Heroic couplet is so closely associated with heroes, it sets itself up for satire, and many poets have used the form for that purpose in "Mock heroic verse." For example:

> *Whether some nymph shall break Diana's law,*
> *Or some frail china jar receive a flaw;*
> *Or stain her honor, or her new brocade,*
> *Forget her pray'rs, or miss a masquerade;*

FROM: THE RAPE OF THE LOCK
ALEXANDER POPE

K-6   The Heroic couplet was the form most often chosen by the Neo-Classical poets of the eighteenth century. The Heroic couplet lends itself to the pithy, aphoristic, ordered statement so prized by that century because of its earlier use as the stanza form of heroes. The Heroic couplet also lends itself to monotony if not varied masterfully; some of our greatest poets proved their metrical skills by making the Heroic couplet brilliantly fresh.

K-7   Another commonly used couplet is the octasyllabic couplet, formed from two lines of iambic tetrameter, as in the following lines from "L'Allegro" by John Milton:

> *Come, and trip it as we go*
> *On the light fantastic toe,*

Although practiced by many serious poets, the octasyllabic couplet was made popular during the seventeenth century by Samuel Butler, who wrote one of the most famous of all satires, called "Hudibras." The form of this poem, much varied octasyllabic couplets, has since become known as "Hudibrastic verse."

K-8   Hudibrastic verse consists of rhymed iambic tetrameter lines, but the variations in Hudibrastic verse include free use of feminine and multiple rhyming, as well as unexpected or ludicrous rhyme words. For example:

> *For he by geometric scale*
> *Could take the size of pots of ale . . .*
> *And wisely tell what hour of the day*
> *The clock does strike by algebra.*
> *Besides, he was a shrewd philosopher*
> *And had read every text and gloss over.*

FROM: HUDIBRAS
SAMUEL BUTLER

K-9   When there is an end-stop on the second line of a couplet, the couplet is said to be closed; if there is enjambment on the second line the couple is said to be open. The following is an example of a decasyllabic open couplet:

> *The sire then shook the honours of his head,*
> *And from his brows champs of oblivion shed*
> *Full on the filial dullness:*

Open couplets occur when the second line in the couplet is not end-stopped.

K-10   Because the rhymes immediately follow each other in couplets, the juxtaposition of closely associated lines sets up an opportunity for witty antithesis or observation; i.e., the poet can make a statement and then, with identical form, make a comment on it or contrast something with it. For example, Pope says:

> *Laugh where we must, be candid where we can,*

and then he makes an observation as to what we must do:

> *But vindicate the ways of God to man.*

K-11   When a couplet is used to break another rhyme scheme, it generally has a summing up effect, and contains about it an air of profundity. For example, Shakespeare closes his sonnets (which have alternating rhyme) with a couplet in order to give the poem a final note of authority and purpose.

THREE LINE STANZAS

K-12   Stanzas which consist of three lines are either triplets, tristichs or tercets.

Triplets

K-13   Triplets are three rhyming lines (*aaa*) as in:

> *As for Venice and her people, merely born to bloom and drop,*
> *Here on earth they bore their fruitage, mirth and folly were the crop:*
> *What of soul was left, I wonder, when the kissing had to stop?*

FROM: A TOCCATA OF GALUPPI'S
ROBERT BROWNING

K-14   Triplets are three lines of any length which rhyme *aaa*. In English poetry triplets are difficult to sustain because they usually result in a comic or supernatural effect. In serious English poetry triplets are also rare, although they have been used in an attempt to catch musical tempo. Triplets have, however, been very successfully used for satire or for parts in verse plays when a comic character speaks.

K-15   We can say, then, that a few poets have been able to use triplets to approximate musical rhythms, but in most instances triplets are associated with comedy. However, by varying the length of the line in a triplet, or by sandwiching the triplet between other rhymes, the poet can reduce the starkness as in the following example:

It melted, and I let it fall and break.
But I was well
Upon my way to sleep before it fell,
And I could tell
What form my dreaming was about to take.

FROM: AFTER APPLE-PICKING
ROBERT FROST

Tristichs

K-16 *Tristichs* are three unrhymed lines which form a stanza. Except as an occasional breaker in stichic poems, tristichs are seldom used.

Tercets

K-17 Three line stanzas which have interlocking rhyme are called *tercets.* The following example is a tercet stanza.

They felt by its beats her heart expand —	a
As one at each ear and both in a breath	b
Whispered, "The Great-Duke Ferdinand."	a

FROM: THE STATUE AND THE BUST
ROBERT BROWNING

In a tercet, the first and third lines interlock around the second line.

Terza Rima

K-18 When the first line of the following tercet rhymes with the middle line of the previous tercet, the interlocking stanzas are called *terza rima*. For example, the next stanza in the above Browning poem is this:

That selfsame instant underneath,	b
The Duke rode past in his idle way,	c
Empty and fine like a swordless sheath.	b

Here *breath* in the first stanza rhymes with *underneath* and *sheath* in the second stanza.

K-19 Terza rima is a form which occurs when the middle line of the first tercet rhymes with the first line of the second tercet. The rhyme scheme of the third tercet in Browning's poem above would be *cdc*. Since the rhyme of one stanza can be completed only by adding the next stanza, terza rima tends to project itself forward. Because of this strong sense of forward motion, terza rima is well suited to long narration; it can maintain a feeling of unity even though the poem is composed of short strophic stanzas.

K-20   Terza rima has strong forward momentum because the rhyme is never complete in a tercet until the following tercet fulfills it.

The final stanza of a poem in terza rima is usually a couplet or quatrain completing the rhyme anticipated in the last tercet. Thus, the final couplet gives a note of authority (K-11).

K-21   Usually short stanzas create their effect through the total effect of disunified stanzas, but with Terza Rima there is a strong feeling of unity.

FOUR LINE STANZAS: QUATRAINS

K-22   The most common stanza type aside from the couplet is the quatrain, of which there are eight prominent iambic variations: (1) ballad (2) short ballad (3) long ballad (4) Heroic quatrain (5) "In Memoriam" stanza (6) brace stanza (7) Rubaiyat stanza (8) unrhymed quatrain.

K-23   A *quatrain* is any four-line stanza. When a quatrain has lines of a certain length arranged in a particular rhyme scheme, it may fall into one of the basic categories. The type of quatrain will depend upon the length of its lines and its rhyme scheme.

K-24   The quatrain's popularity among both unsophisticated and sophisticated readers suggests that there is something inherently pleasing about the form; something even in the arrangement of four line stanzas on a page makes people think of poetry. For most readers, poetry and quatrains are almost synonymous. Balance and antithesis, contrast and significance of statement not possible in tercets and five-line stanzas seem possible in quatrains.

TYPES OF BALLAD QUATRAIN STANZAS

K-25   The *ballad stanza,* a type of quatrain, may have alternating (*abab*) rhyme, or it may rhyme *abcb*. Lines 1 and 3 are iambic tetrameter; lines 2 and 4 are often iambic trimeter. An example of a ballad stanza with alternating rhyme is this:

> *A slumber did my spirit seal;*   a
> *I had no human fears:*   b
> *She seemed a thing that could not feel*   a
> *The touch of earthly years.*   b

FROM: A SLUMBER DID MY SPIRIT SEAL
WILLIAM WORDSWORTH

The following ballad stanza rhymes *abcb*, but has alternating tetrameter/trimeter lines, just as the preceding stanza does:

> *The very deep did rot: O Christ!*   a
> *That ever this should be!*   b

> *Yea, slimy things did crawl with legs*   c
> *Upon the slimy sea.*   b

FROM: THE RIME OF THE ANCIENT
MARINER

Thus ballad stanzas are always iambic quatrains with lines 1 and 3 tetrameter, 2 and 4 often trimeter, and with a rhyme scheme of either *abab* or *abcb*. The advantage of using the ballad rhyming *abcb* is that the stanza maintains all of the connotations associated with the *abab* form without forcing too much rhyme.

Long Ballads

K-26   The *long ballad* stanza contains four iambic tetrameter lines rhyming *abab* or *abcb*. The following stanza is a long ballad rhyming *abcb*.

> *And sang within the bloody wood*
> *When Agamemnon cried aloud,*
> *And let their liquid siftings fall*
> *To stain the stiff dishonoured shroud.*

FROM: SWEENY AMONG THE NIGHTINGALES
T. S. ELIOT

The difference between a ballad and a long ballad is that in the long ballad all four lines are tetrameter.

Short Ballads

K-27   The short ballad stanza has three lines of trimeter (1, 2, and 4) and one line of tetrameter (3). Short ballads usually rhyme *abcb*. The following stanza is a short ballad:

> *My girl, thou gazest much*
> *Upon the golden skies:*
> *Would I were heaven! I would behold*
> *Thee then with all mine eyes!*

Popular Ballads

K-28   Ballad stanzas, which are highly *mnemonic* (D-24), take their origin from verse adapted to singing. For this reason the ballad is well suited for the presentation of simple narration or exciting episodes. Popular ballads are songs or verse which tell simple tales, usually impersonal, and they usually imply the wisdom of the folk: supernatural events, courage, and love are frequent themes, but any experience which appeals to common people is acceptable material.

Art Ballads

K-29   When the ballad stanza occurs in written literature, usually called an "art ballad," it is usually in connection with a story which is oftentimes mysterious or apocalyptic. By using the ballad form the poet can establish expectations of simplicity and suspense.

Hymns

K-30   The ballad stanza has also been frequently used for hymns (it is as often called "hymn stanza" as "ballad stanza"), as in the following example:

> *Oh! for a closer walk with God,*
> *A calm and heavenly frame;*
> *A light to shine upon the road*
> *That leads me to the Lamb!*

Likewise, the long ballad has often been used for hymns, as in:

> *When I survey the wonderous cross*
> *On which the Prince of Glory died,*
> *My richest gain I count but loss,*
> *And pour contempt on all my pride.*

Because the ballad has been closely associated with hymns, it carries with it the connotation of openness and sincerity, and when the ballad stanza is used for highly sophisticated purposes, the form sets a foil for high irony.

K-31   Ballad stanzas, then, set up expectations for simple tales which are sincere, open, mysterious, or apocalyptic. Appropriate themes for a ballad stanza would be romance, adventure, or religious experience.

OTHER QUATRAIN STANZAS

Heroic Quatrains

K-32   An Heroic quatrain contains four lines of iambic pentameter with alternating rhyme (*abab*). An example of an Heroic quatrain is this:

> *The curfew tolls the knell of parting day,*
> *The lowing herd wind slowly o'er the lea,*
> *The plowman homeward plods his weary way,*
> *And leaves the world to darkness and to me.*

FROM: ELEGY, WRITTEN IN A COUNTRY CHURCHYARD
THOMAS GRAY

The effect of the additional foot to the long ballad stanza is to add weight and solemnity to the stanza, and frequently the Heroic quatrain is used for subjects about death, war, or unrequited love. (For further discussion of the elegy, see Appendix A.)

"In Memoriam" Stanza

K-33   Closely related to the lamentation or seriousness of the Heroic quatrain is the *"In Memoriam" stanza*, which consists of four tetrameter lines rhyming *abba*. The following is an example of an "In Memoriam" stanza:

> *Tonight the winds begin to rise*   a
> *And roar from yonder dropping day;*   b
> *The last red leaf is whirled away,*   b
> *The rooks are blown about the skies;*   a

FROM: IN MEMORIAM
A. LORD TENNYSON

One of the most important characteristics of the "In Memoriam" stanza (which takes its name from the title of a poem by Tennyson) is the rhyme scheme, which is *abba*. The effect created by an external couplet gripping an internal couplet is to give the stanza a feeling of restraint or introversion, which makes the "In Memoriam" stanza well suited for introspective or meditative subjects.

K-34   Because of the couplet arrangement and the shortness of the lines, the third line of the "In Memoriam" stanza demands great emphasis, giving the poet a natural area of focus. When explicating a poem using the "In Memoriam" stanza the reader must give careful attention to the third line.

Brace Stanza

K-35   The *brace stanza* consists of four lines of iambic pentameter rhyming *abba*. The form is seldom used except in Italian sonnets (K-107) because it has a tendency to cause the poem to build toward a climax very quickly, and unless some resolution is found after two or three stanzas the reader becomes quite frustrated. But for the purpose of quickly moving to a resolution, the brace stanza is ideal though difficult to write. The following is an example of a brace stanza:

> *The sea that bares her bosom to the moon;*
> *The winds that will be howling at all hours,*
> *And are up-gathered now like sleeping flowers*
> *For this, for everything, we are out of tune:*

FROM: THE WORLD IS TOO MUCH WITH US
WILLIAM WORDSWORTH

"Rubaiyat" Stanza

K-36   "Rubaiyat" stanzas contain four lines of iambic pentameter which rhyme *aaba*. The following is an example of a "Rubaiyat" stanza.

> *Then to the Lip of this poor earthen Urn*
> *I leaned, the Secret of my Life to learn;*

> And Lip to Lip it murmured — "While you live,
> Drink — for once dead, you never shall return."

FROM: THE RUBÁIYÁT OF OMAR KHAYYÁM
EDWARD FITZGERALD

Like "In Memoriam" stanzas, the most important characteristic of the Rubaiyat stanza is the effect which the rhyme scheme (*aaba*) has on the emphasis.

In Fitzgerald's rendering of the *Rubáiyát of Omar Khayyám,* from which the stanza takes its name, the fourth line is usually used to make some profound observation about life and death (as in the examples). For the purpose of profundity the "Rubaiyat" stanza works well because of the return to the original rhyme after the stanza has been built to crescendo in the third line.

K-37   One reason why the "Rubaiyat" stanza works to make the last line ideal for profound observation is that after the initial couplet the third line line breaks the established rhyme and builds the stanza to a climax. When the fourth line returns to the original rhyme, it seems to be reflecting on the situation, creating a climax to what was presented in the first three lines.

K-38   Because the "Rubaiyat" stanza is so rigidly associated with one particular poem whose theme is commonly construed to be "eat, drink, and be merry," and because the last line in the stanza purports to be profound, the Rubaiyat stanza is seldom used successfully except as satire or for comic effect.

Unrhymed Quatrains

K-39   Unrhymed quatrains include any unrhymed four line stanzas. This form has not been especially popular because some rhyme seems necessary in lyrical poems or in narratives which use rhyme as a mnemonic device. Since poems which use quatrains tend to be either lyrical or narrative, and because both of these need rhyme to accomplish their purpose, unrhymed quatrains have not often been used except as breakers in long poems containing other stanza forms.

Quatrain Variations

K-40   There are numerous variations on the eight basic quatrain stanza forms which poets use for particular effects. For example, in the following ballad variation:

> O what can ail thee, knight-at-arms,
>   Alone and palely loitering?
> The sedge has withered from the lake,
>   And no birds sing.

FROM: LA BELLE DAME SANS MERCI
JOHN KEATS

Here the poet uses a dimeter fourth line which, in this poem, creates a stark, harsh effect meant to convey despair.

K-41   When a poet deviates from one of the eight standard quatrain patterns, it is usually for a reason, and when explicating a poem which has quatrain variations it is a good idea to explore possible reasons why deviations have been made, although there is no certain way to find the answer.

K-42   A careful poet deviates from the standard stanza forms in order to create a particular effect, and recognizing the difference between the standard form and the form in the poem will help to determine meaning. Remember, however, that most four line stanzas (e.g., alternating dimeter with pentameter) are not ballad variations, but are just unnamed stanzas.

K-43   Quatrains can, of course, consist of any number and any type of feet in any rhyme scheme; the word "quatrain" merely refers to the number of lines in the stanza. However, when a poet uses one of the basic stanza forms there are particular connotations that accompany it — connotations utilized by good poets and recognized by good critics and careful readers.

K-44   In addition to the eight basic iambic quatrains, trochaic quatrains have also been quite successful. Trochaic quatrains, called Anacreontic from the Greek poet Anacreon, are almost always tetrameters and rhyme *abab* or *aabb*. Blake used the form to give lightness and innocence to his poems, as in this example:

> *Piping down the valleys wild,*
> *Piping songs of pleasant glee,*
> *On a cloud I saw a child,*
> *And he laughing said to me:*

> FROM: THE BARD'S SONG

But Blake also used trochaic quatrains to create a sense of awesomeness as in these lines:

> *What the hammer? what the chain?*
> *In what furnance was thy brain?*
> *What the anvil? What dread grasp*
> *Dare its deadly terrors clasp?*

> FROM: THE TYGER

Although Blake achieved awe in the trochaic quatrain, the falling rhythm tends to make the stanza soft and musical. Many songs are written in this form.

Review/self-check

K-45   Stanza forms which have been consistently used in a particular way, or forms which have been used with force or success carry _____ with them.

connotations (K-1)

K-46   A couplet consists of _____ successively
rhymed lines. The lines of a couplet (do, do not) have
to be of equal length; couplets (may, may not)
be part of a larger stanza.

two
do not (K-3)
may

K-47   One type of tetrameter couplet which was successfully used to satirize heroes was _____ verse.

Hudibrastic (K-7)

K-48   Couplets are ideally suited for setting up _____.
When interspersed with other stanza forms, couplets give
a feeling of _____ to the poem.

antithesis (K-10)

authority (K-11)

K-49   Triplets are particularly well suited for satire or
for parts in verse plays as speech for _____ characters.

comic (K-14)

K-50   Terza rima is unusual for short strophic stanzas
in that it maintains forward momentum through its interlocking _____.

rhyme (K-18)

K-51   Some of the connotations associated with the
ballad are _____, _____, _____

simplicity, mystery, sin-
cerity, romance, adventure,
the supernatural (K-28)

K-52   In "Rubaiyat" and "In Memoriam" stanzas, the
_____ _____ creates emphasis on particular
lines. The profound statement in the Rubaiyat stanza
comes in the _____ line; the focus in "In Memoriam" stanzas comes in line _____.

rhyme scheme (K-36, K-31)

fourth (K-37)
three (K-34)

K-53   What is the rhyme scheme for the following
stanza types:

    Heroic quatrain (   )
    terza rima   (   )
    ballad   (   )
    "Rubaiyat"   (   )
    "In Memoriam"(   )

(*abab*) K-32
(*aba bcb*) K-18
(*abcb*) K-25
(*aaba*) K-36
(*abba*) K-33

K-54   What connotations does the following stanza
form carry?

    Now fades the glimmering landscape on the sight,
    And all the air a solemn stillness holds,

The heroic quatrain indi-
cates solemnity; it often
takes death or unrequited
love as its subject (K-32)

Save where the beetle wheels his droning flight,
And drowsy tinklings lull the distant folds;

FROM: ELEGY, WRITTEN IN A COUNTRY CHURCHYARD
THOMAS GRAY

FIVE LINE STANZAS

K-55   Although five line stanzas have been used in a variety of ways, there are only two types which can be considered standard: the mad-song and the limerick.

Mad-Songs

K-56   The mad-song — verse uttered by the presumably insane — usually connotes a happy, harmless, inventive sort of insanity, and whenever the mad song form is used the reader will immediately tend to associate it with madness because of its simplistic sound and form.

K-57   The mad-song rhyme scheme is *abccb*, and the unrhymed first line gives much of the "madness" to the form, since it controverts the usual expectation. The standard mad-song is patterned this way: lines 1, 2, and 5 are iambic trimeter; lines 3 and 4 are iambic dimeter — the shortness of the lines also accounts for the madness, since simple people are associated with uncomplicated sentence patterns. Frequently, lines 2 and 5 will have feminine rhyme (I-112), and any of the lines may contain anapestic substitutions. The following is an example of a mad-song.

I'll sail upon the dog-star,
And then pursue the morning;
I'll chase the moon
Til it be noon
But I'll make her leave her horning.

FROM: MADSONG
THOMAS D'URFEY

K-58   The longest line in the mad song has three feet; the shortest line two feet. The shortness of the lines, the feminine rhymes, the anapestic substitutions, and the absence of a rhyme for the first line (which leaves the reader with a sense of incompleteness) all give the mad-song a harmless, semi-aimless, happy tone.

Limericks

K-59   The limerick differs from the mad-song in its type of base foot, in its rhyme scheme (*aabba*), and in the length of its lines. The limerick's anapestic base makes the verse sound silly rather than mad, and limericks are almost invariably associated with bizarre indecency, or with anti-ethnic or anti-clerical jokes. The following is an example of a limerick.

> *There once was a girl from Saint Paul,*
> *Who wore a newspaper gown to a ball.*
> *The dress caught on fire*
> *And burned her attire,*
> *Front page, sporting section, and all.*

Other Cinquains

K-60   As breakers for serious poetry written in quatrains, five-line stanzas have been successful, but entire poems written in cinquains (five-line stanza) are rare before the twentieth century.

K-61   Poets who intermingle cinquains with quatrains have no set pattern for doing so, but generally the cinquain is merely a ballad quatrain with an extra rhyming line added to the middle of it. In the following stanza we have an example:

> *Beyond the shadow of the ship,*   a
> *I watched the water-snakes:*   b
> *They moved in tracks of shining white,*   c
> *And when they reared, the elfish light*   c
> *Fell off in hoary flakes.*   b
>
> FROM: THE RIME OF THE ANCIENT MARINER

Here the poet has expanded the third line of his ballad stanza, and constructed a fourth line rhyming with it.

K-62   Five line stanzas are rare in the English tradition, and when they occur they are usually some variation on the ballad stanza. In addition to being used as a breaker for quatrain stanzas, the cinquain is useful when the poet wishes to postpone the climax of the stanza. If the poet has established expectations as to where the climax will come by using quatrains, the cinquain will very effectively use these expectations to place new emphasis on itself as a variation on the normal climax.

K-63   When the cinquain is structured in a way similar to the above example, using an internal couplet or other forceful rhyme to heighten the climax, the cinquain works as an impressive breaker, but it can only be used sparingly. However, poets must be careful of using the cinquain because of its tendency to sound mad or silly. In the following cinquain, one reason the poet might not have rhymed his lines is that he is using an anapestic base, and the combination of rhyme and anapests might recall the limerick, in which case the poet would have a hard time writing about serious matters.

> *I am hearing the shape of the rain*
> *Take the shape of the tent and believe it,*
> *Laying down all around where I lie*

A profound, unspeakable law.
I obey and am free-falling slowly

FROM: IN THE MOUNTAIN TENT
JAMES DICKEY

K-64   If the heroic couplet (K-4) was a fitting verse form for the eighteenth century because the rigidity of the couplet reflected the attitudes and ambitions of the society, then
it may be significant that the five line stanza has become popular for serious poetry since
World War II. It can be argued that stanzas containing five or seven lines project a sense
of imbalance and uncertainty, particularly if the lines are rhymed. Look at the following
poem, for example:

Home is so sad. It stays as it was left,
Shaped to the comfort of the last to go
As if to win them back. Instead, bereft
Of anyone to please, it withers so,
Having no heart to put aside the theft

And turn again to what it started as,
A joyous shot at how things ought to be,
Long fallen wide. You can see how it was:
Look at the pictures and the cutlery.
The music in the piano stool. That vase.

HOME IS SO SAD
PHILIP LARKIN

Although no precedent has been set in the poem to make us expect a sixth line which
rhymes with *go* and *so*, we are still left uneasy and dangling after the fifth line; as readers
of traditional poetry, and perhaps as beings who thrive on rhythm and symmetry, we feel
that the sixth line is necessary if order is to be restored to the stanza. In "Home Is So Sad"
it is clear that the meaning is reinforced by the uneasiness and incompleteness of the cinquain, and for social critics who hold that the world is in a precarious, nervous state, the
five line stanza does seem appropriate.

K-65   The question which poets and critics must ask is whether five line rhymed stanzas
are inherently imbalanced, no matter what the rhyme scheme, or whether modern men are
simply attuned to thinking that. For many decades after Byron used ottava rima (K-80) as
the stanza form for "Don Juan" people felt that the form was inherently designed for
comedy; this expectation was later undermined with such serious ottava rima poems as
"Among School Children" (W. B. Yeats). So we may be too close to the cinquain to make
judgments about it, or there may not have yet been a brilliant enough poet to change the
connotations, but it is likely that until the imbalance created by the cinquain is refuted,
modern poets will continue using it as the stanza form of despair.

SIX LINE STANZAS

K-66   The most common six line stanzas consist of either three couplets (*aabbcc*), alternating rhyme (*ababab*), or an alternating quatrain plus a couplet (*ababcc*).

Stave of Six

K-66   The stanza form rhyming *ababcc* is commonly called a *stave of six*, when written in iambic tetrameter, and the stave is the most frequently used of the six line stanzas. The following is an example of a stave:

> *I wandered lonely as a cloud*
> *That floats on high o'er vales and hills,*
> *When all at once I saw a crowd,*
> *A host of golden daffodils;*
> *Beside the lake, beneath the trees,*
> *Fluttering and dancing in the breeze.*

FROM: I WANDERED LONELY AS A CLOUD
WILLIAM WORDSWORTH

"Venus and Adonis"

When a foot is added to each line of the stave of six, making all the lines pentameter (and recalling the Heroic quatrain), the stanza is called *"Venus and Adonis,"* named for Shakespeare's poem by that title.

The "Venus and Adonis" stanza works something like the last six lines of the Shakespearean sonnet (K-110), in which the couplet is used to make a profound observation on the three previous quatrains. However, in the "Venus and Adonis" stanza the one quatrain generally does not provide enough space to build a situation which can sustain an impressive couplet. Therefore, poets who are trying to use the "Venus and Adonis" stanza seriously will use the couplet as an extension of the quatrain rather than as commentary or paradox on the quatrain.

K-67   Since the "Venus and Adonis" stanza is not long enough to build a complex situation, the couplet is not normally used to make a profound observation. For this reason the "Venus and Adonis" stanza is usually used with other stanzas of the same kind which constitute a long work.

K-68   The reason that the couplet cannot be successfully used for profundity or witty observation in the "Venus and Adonis" stanza is that this stanza develops a stately quality, because of the pentameter lines that recall the Heroic quatrain, and whatever observation is made cannot be flippant or hasty, but seems to demand a continuation of the wisdom and grandeur of the first four lines.

K-69   The stave of six and the "Venus and Adonis" stanzas have the advantage of giving the impression of possessing more body than the quatrain, and while the couplet cannot be successfully used for commentary, it does have a summing-up effect, thereby giving a quality of finality to the stanza which is lacking in the quatrain.

These six line stanzas, then, are effective in building a number of serious events and ideas toward a whole, but with each stanza functioning fairly independently since each is pretty well concluded with the couplet.

Rime Couée

K-70 Another type of six line stanza which has been popular is *rime couée* (also called "tail rhyme"). The standard form for this stanza is *aabccb* where the *a* and *c* lines are tetrameter and the *b* lines trimeter. The form is made highly flexible by adding as many *a* and *c* lines as desired while maintaining the *b* lines as shown. The following stanza is a variation of rime couée, rhyming *aaaabcccb*.

> *A bow-shot from her bower-eaves,*
> *He rode between the barley-sheaves*
> *The sun came dazzling through the leaves,*
> *And flamed upon the brazen greaves*
> *Of bold Sir Lancelot.*
> *A red-cross knight forever kneeled*
> *To a lady in his shield,*
> *That sparkled on the yellow field,*
> *Beside remote Shalott.*

FROM: THE LADY OF SHALOTT
ALFRED LORD TENNYSON

K-71 Because the *b* lines are a foot shorter, and because they break the established rhyme, they call attention to themselves, and they are frequently used for a punch-line effect. In serious poetry, as in "The Charge of the Light Brigade," the *b* lines — particularly the final *b* line — are used to evoke an emotional response or profound comment to the material which has been presented in the stanza.

K-72 Thus rime couée, basically a six line stanza, permits many variations by adding *a* and *c* lines. In this stanza the *b* lines call attention to themselves because they are shorter, and because they break the rhyme pattern.

It is very likely that the *b* lines in rime couée will be used to reflect on the *a* and *c* lines, especially when the stanza is longer than six lines. In serious poetry the *b* lines may be used to evoke an emotional response to the material presented. Frequent substitutions (H-25) to effect a falling (H-23, I-40) or triple (H-31) meter is one characteristic method of creating emotion in rime couée, as in Tennyson's "The Charge of the Light Brigade."

K-73 In light verse, the deflation of the tail-rhyme can be devastating, as in Thomas Gray's "On the Death of a Favorite Cat, Drowned in a Tub of Goldfishes."

> *The hapless nymph with wonder saw:*
> *A whisker first, and then a claw,*

> *With many an ardent wish,*
> *She stretched to reach the prize,*
> *What female heart can gold despise ?*
> *What cat's averse to fish?*

Standard Habbie

K-74   Another six line stanza, a variation of tail rhyme, is the *Standard Habbie,* which consists of six lines rhyming *aaabab,* where the *a* lines are iambic tetrameter and the *b* lines are dimeter. The flourish of rhyming tetrameter lines (the *a* lines, which include a triplet) contrasted by the dimeter lines often creates a ridiculous effect.

K-75   The great master of the Standard Habbie, Robert Burns, was able to use it to portray everything from open freshness to impudent irony. His freshness is evident in this stanza from "To a Mountain Daisy, on Turning One Down with a Plow in April, 1786":

> *There in thy scanty mantle clad,*
> *Thy snowie bosum sun-ward spread,*
> *Thou lifts thy unassuming head*
> *   In humble guise;*
> *But now the share upturns thy bed*
> *   And low thou lies!*

The humorous irony, a prevalent characteristic in Burns, can also be seen in the following stanza from "To a Mouse On Seeing One On a Lady's Bonnet At Church":

> *Ye ugly, creeping, blastit wonner,*
> *Detested, shunn'd by saunt an' sinner,*
> *How dare ye set your fit upon her,*
> *   Sae fine a lady?*
> *Gae somewhere else, and seek your dinner*
> *   On some poor body.*

The "b" lines in the Standard Habbie are called "bobs" or "tails" since the form is re-garded as tail rhyme. The stanza, and especially the tails, are most often used for a comic effect.

SEVEN LINE STANZAS: RIME ROYAL

K-76   The only standard seven line stanza in English is *rime royal,* composed of iambic pentameter lines rhyming *ababbcc.* The following stanza is rime royal:

> *O hateful, vaporous, and foggy Night!*
> *Since thou art guilty of my cureless crime,*
> *Muster thy mists to meet the eastern light,*
> *Make war against proportion'd course of time;*

Of if thou wilt permit the sun to climb
His wonted height, yet ere he go to bed,
Knit poisonous clouds about his golden head.

FROM: THE RAPE OF LUCRECE
WILLIAM SHAKESPEARE

The only variation permitted in the rime royal stanza, seven lines of iambic pentameter rhyming *ababbcc*, is to make the last line in the stanza hexameter.

K-77   Rime royal is capable of great unity because of the central couplet (lines 4 and 5) and because the stanza seems to be composed of two fused quatrains (*abab* and *bbcc*) which are bound together by the fourth line; i.e., the fourth line (*aba* b *bcc*) seems to belong to both quatrains, thereby giving a natural unity to the stanza, the fourth line acting as a transition between the parts. Since the final couplet is not anticipated by the preceeding rhyme, it can act as an element of surprise or passion, which makes the form ideally suited for stories of romance.

K-78   Rime royal flourished during the period from 1375 to 1600, and it is closely associated with the imaginative world of romance, and with the narration of high and noble matters.

EIGHT LINE STANZAS

K-79   Eight line stanzas are quite common in English, though many of them are merely two consecutive quatrains concerning the same idea. A common rhyme scheme for these double quatrains might be *ababab*, although *ababcdcd* is more likely, since not so many demands on rhyme are made. The double quatrains have no special connotations which accompany them, and many variations with the form are possible.

Ottava Rima

K-80   The eight line stanza which does have special connotations is *ottava rima* — iambic pentameter lines rhyming *abababcc*. Probably the most famous English poem ever written in ottava rima is Byron's *Don Juan,* and because the poem was so successful as an hilarious spoof, the form has come to be associated with delightful heroi-sexual hijinks and sexual encounter. The stanza is very well suited to episode with commentary; the six lines of interlocking rhyme are adequate to build a situation on which the closing couplet can poke ridicule. The first six lines in ottava rima seem to inflate and swell, so that when they are followed by a couplet they tend to burst into mock heroic, as the following example illustrates:

Her glossy hair was clustered o'er a brow
Bright with intelligence, and fair, and smooth;
Her eyebrow's shape was like the aerial bow,
Her cheek all purple with the beams of youth,
Mounting, at times, to a transparent glow,

> *As if her veins ran lightning; she, in sooth,*
> *Possessed an air and grace by no means common:*
> *Her stature tall — I hate a dumpy woman.*

FROM: DON JUAN

K-81   Ottava rima is ideally suited for mock heroic (K-5, K-32) episodes which treat trivial subjects in a grand style and it works well for mock heroic because the couplet can be used to make a satirical or flippant comment on the first six lines.

K-82   While ottava rima has found its renown in the delightfully facetious *Don Juan*, the stanza has also been brilliantly used for just the opposite effect: seriousness and meditation (Yeats is the foremost practitioner). The stanza is long enough for detailed meditation as well as narration, and the couplet can be used for observation and profundity as well as for mock-heroics.

K-83   When ottava rima is serious and meditative the couplet can reflect on or create emotions about the material presented in the first six lines, and it can become quite lyrical and intense, as in the example:

> *Once out of nature I shall never take*
> *My bodily form from any natural thing,*
> *But such a form as Grecian goldsmiths make*
> *Of hammered gold and gold enamelling*
> *To keep a drowsy Emperor awake;*
> *Or set upon a golden bough to sing*
> *To lords and ladies of Byzantium*
> *Of what is past, or passing, or to come.*

FROM: SAILING TO BYZANTIUM
W. B. YEATS

K-84   Ottava rima, then, has traditionally been flippant and satirical, but in the hands of Yeats and others, it has also become lyrical, intense, and meditative.

   If it is difficult to tell from the subject matter and tone of an isolated ottava rima stanza whether the poet is using the form lyrically or for satire, the rhymes may give a clue as to which he is doing. Since it is frequently difficult to find exact rhymes which fit meditative verse rhyming *ababab,* the poet will use appropriate or light rhymes (I-73) (as in the above example) rather than ridiculous full rhymes. In mock epic the ridiculous situations often forced full rhymes to enhance the satire.

K-85   It should be obvious from an entire poem whether ottava rime is being used for satire or meditation, but in an isolated stanza, it is usually possible to determine how the form is being used by its rhyme. Meditative ottava rima with probably have some approximate rhymes while mock-heroic ottava rima will be able to force enough full rhymes to satisfy the scheme.

NINE LINES: THE SPENSERIAN STANZA

K-86   The only standard nine line stanza in English is the Spenserian, which contains eight lines of iambic pentameter plus an alexandrine (a hexameter line) rhyming *ababbcbcc*. The Spenserian stanza is so long and the pentameter lines so taxing that the form brings the reader to fatigue before it is over, so that the reader feels that he has come to the end of his journey by the end of the stanza. The result may be either fatigue or fulfillment, but the latter has been the main end desired in the traditional uses of the stanza. The end couplet gives a sense of satisfaction and feeling of completeness, especially since the hexameter line closes the stanza. Also, since the *c* rhyme has been used earlier, the couplet tends to draw the reader back into the details of the stanza so that great unity is achieved.

K-87   The Spenserian stanza is thus highly unified, because the final couplet gives a feeling of completeness and because the hexameter line tends to make the reader return to the details presented throughout the stanza. However, poets have found the Spenserian difficult to use because of the demanding rhyme and because it is difficult to shape an image or thought of sufficient magnitude for nine lines. The form works quite satisfactorily, though, for a long, meditative story; it is seldom used for any other purpose. The following is a Spenserian stanza:

Anon his heart revives: her vespers done,	a
Of all its wreathed pearls her hair she frees;	b
Unclasps her warmed jewels one by one;	a
Loosens her fragrant bodice; by degrees	b
Her rich attire creeps rustling to her knees:	b
Half-hidden, like a mermaid in sea-weed,	c
Pensive awhile she dreams awake, and sees,	b
In fancy, fair St. Agnes in her bed,	c
But dares not look behind, or all the charm is fled.	c

FROM: THE EVE OF ST. AGNES
JOHN KEATS

TEN AND THIRTEEN LINE STANZAS

K-88   With the exception of a few ten line stanzas which have no special associations, and a few French, Spanish, and Japanese forms (See Appendix A), there are no basic stanza or poetry forms between 10 and 13 lines lines. One of the most important of poetical forms, however, is a fourteen line poem called a sonnet (K-99 ff).

Review/self-check

K-89   Two five line stanzas which have a comic or silly effect are the _____ and _____ .

Limerick (K-59)
mad-song (K-56)

K-90   As breakers for poems written in quatrains, five line stanzas can be effectively used without the comedy or madness. Frequently the cinquain used in this manner will be a variation on the _____ quatrain by adding an identical line. When cinquains are interspersed with quatrains, they are effective in delaying the _____ of the stanza.

ballad (K-61)

climax (K-62)

K-91   The stave of six and the "Venus and Adonis" stanza rhyme _____.

ababcc (K-65, K-66)

K-92   The "Venus and Adonis" stanza is stately, the quatrain recalling the _____ quatrain. Both the stave and the "Venus and Adonis" stanza are suitable for serious moods and narration, but the "Venus and Adonis" stanza is heavier and more serene because of its _____ lines.

Heroic

pentameter (K-66)

K-93   "Bobs" and rime couée or "tail rhymes" are normally used for _____ effect, while the *b* lines in rime couée may be used to reflect on the previous lines or to evoke _____ .

comic (K-75)

emotion (K-71)

romance (K-78)

K-94   Rime royal is associated with stories of _____ and with the narration of high and noble matters.

K-95   The final couplet in rime royal is likely to be used for surprise or _____.

passion (K-77)

K-96   The most important eight-line stanza is _____ _____, which has been successfully used for both satire and _____.

ottava rima (K-80)

meditation (K-84)

K-97   Some characteristics of the Spenserian are its qualities of being long and _____; it is also highly _____ and gives a feeling of completeness; it is reflexive because _____ .. It is ideal for _____ .

taxing; unified

rhyme of the final hexameter line returns the reader to the stanza; long, meditative stories

POEMS WITH TRADITIONAL FORM

K-98   There exists in the tradition a number of poem-types which have been used so frequently that they, like frequently used stanza forms, have acquired a set of connotations which the explicator must consider. Poets choose one of the standard poem forms because of the connotations and because the forms posses certain qualities and technical possibilities which suit the poem's theme and emotional development. The most important traditional poem-form is the sonnet.

THE SONNET: GENERAL CHARACTERISTICS

K-99   Although there have been sonnets of more and fewer than fourteen lines, written in both tetrameter and hexameter, almost all sonnets are composed of fourteen lines of iambic pentameter with some form of alternating rhyme, and a turning point which divides the poem into two parts.

K-100   The advantages which the sonnet has over other poetical forms are that its length and structure allow it to present a problem and then reflect upon it; yet it is short enough to maintain an elevated state of emotion throughout the poem.

K-101   Because there have been so many sonnets written in the formal fourteen-line iambic pentameter form, and because much of the subject matter for these sonnets has been serious and aloof, the sonnet carries with its form a sense of seriousness and formality.

K-102   One of the characteristics of the sonnet is that it presents material and then interprets it. With the formality of its structure, then, the sonnet carries a connotation of reflective seriousness.

K-103   The most important characteristic of the sonnet is the "*turn*" which marks the point between two divisions in the poem. The section before the turn presents the problem or situation, and the section after the turn resolves it.

K-104   The "turn" in the sonnet is that point which comes between the presentation of the problem and the resolution. The turn is probably the one characteristic that has made the sonnet an attractive form for poets to use, since it provides a "countering" effect within a relatively short space to give the sonnet an exceptionally hard-hitting forcefulness.

K-105   It is the combination of forceful and serious reflection through the countering turn, along with an ideally balanced length, that has made the sonnet so appealing. It is long enough to present a detailed account, short enough to maintain elevated emotion, and divided enough to allow problems and resolutions. We can expect that the section after the turn will present the resolution to the problem presented earlier.

K-106   There are two basic sonnet types: the Petrarchan (Italian) and the Shakesperean (English). The most common variations are Spenserian and Miltonic. All four types have common characteristics, but each of the types functions to create different effects.

Petrarchan Sonnets

K-107   The Petrarchan (Italian) sonnet consists of an octave (the eight lines before the turn) and a sestet (The six lines after the turn) rhyming as follows:

	a							
	b	First						
	b	Quatrain						
OCTAVE	a							
	a							
	b	Second						
	b	Quatrain						
	a							

TURN

	c		c		c		c	c
	d		d		d		d	d
	c		e		e		c	d
SESTET	d	*or*	c	*or*	c	*or*	d	*or*	c
	c		d		e		e	e
	d		e		d		e	e

The octave presents material in the first quatrain and then complicates it in the second through argument, description, or imagery.

The turn represents an important change or emotional shift from the view presented in the octave.

K-108   While the octave in the Petrarchan sonnet is made up of two quatrains, the second of which complicates the first, the sestet is used to find a resolution to the problem presented in the octave. In the Petrarchan sonnet the sestet gradually diminishes the tension built by the octave until a final solution is achieved by the end of the sonnet.

Thus this form of the sonnet gradually defines and heightens the problem in the octave, then slowly diminishes it in the sestet so that by the end of the poem a satisfying resolution is achieved. Notice the building and diminishing effect in the following Petrarchan sonnet.

Much have I travelled in the realms of gold,	a
And many goodly states and kingdoms seen;	b
Round many western islands have I been	b
Which bards in fealty to Apollo hold.	a
Oft of one wide expanse had I been told	a
That deep-browed Homer ruled in his demesne;	b
Yet did I never breathe its pure serene	b
Till I heard Chapman speak out loud and bold:	a
Then felt I like some watcher of the skies	c
When a new planet swims into his ken;	d
Or like stout Cortez when with eagle eyes	c
He stared at the Pacific — and all his men	d
Looked at each other with a wild surmise —	c
Silent, upon a peak in Darien.	d

ON FIRST LOOKING INTO CHAPMAN'S HOMER
JOHN KEATS

K-109   The octave in the Petrarchan sonnet is very tight-knit because the two quatrains mold themselves together through the couplet in lines 4 and 5: *abbaabba*. If the poet works his craft well, lines 4 and 5 will have a close logical relationship so that the poem will have a smooth transition into the second quatrain. The second quatrain should extend — not repeat — the first quatrain in order to build to a climax at the turn.

K-110   One of the important characteristics of the Petrarchan sonnet involves the proportionate weight between the octave and sestet; the similar length of the two parts makes it possible for the problem or situation to be balanced by the resolution. The balance created in this sonnet makes the problem and resolution seem proportionate, which results in a satisfying ending.

The Shakespearean Sonnet

K-110   The Shakespearean, or English, sonnet is composed of three quatrains and a rhyming couplet. The "turn" occurs only after the third quatrain. Thus it creates an entirely different effect from the Italian sonnet because of the disproportion between the buildup of the "problem" and the "resolution," or the final couplet.

	a	
	b	First
	a	Quatrain
	b	
	c	
	d	Second
	c	Quatrain
	d	
	e	
	f	Third
	e	Quatrain
TURN	f	
	g	
	g	Couplet

Example/self-check

K-111   The Shakespearean sonnet consists of _____ quatrains and a _____ .
    The quatrains constitute the equivalent of the _____ in the Petrarchan sonnet, and the couplet is comparable to the _____ .

> three
> couplet
>
> octave
> sestet

K-112   In the Shakespearean sonnet the problem or situation can be presented in much more detail, while

the resolution must come in the short space of the
couplet; the turn in the Shakespearean sonnet comes
before the _____.

couplet

K-113   In the Petrarchan sonnet, where the problem
can be resolved by reason or perception over the space
of six lines, there is enough room for a gradual release of
tension, but in the Shakespearean sonnet, where the resolution must come in the space of _____ lines, the
resolution is likely to be achieved through wit, paradox,
or clever pseudo-profundity.

two (K-112)

K-114   Because the "sestet" equivalent in the English
sonnet is only a brief couplet, the resolution is likely
to be cleverly profound, paradoxical, or _____.

witty (K-113)

K-115   The advantage of not having to find a complete resolution is that the poet can be witty without
being trite; the disadvantage, of course, is the difficulty
in finding a comment for the couplet which is clever or
profound enough to balance the twelve lines presenting
the situation.

K-116   The couplet in the English sonnet allows the
poet to be witty without being _____ if he can
find material for the couplet which will _____
the quatrain.

trite
balance

Notice how the couplet balances with the quatrains in the following Shakespearean sonnet.

My mistress' eyes are nothing like the sun;	a
Coral is far more red than her lips' red;	b
If snow be white, why then her breasts are dun;	a
If hairs be wires, black wires grow on her head.	b
I have seen roses damasked, red and white,	c
But no such roses see I in her cheeks,	d
And in some perfumes is there more delight	c
Than in the breath that from my mistress reeks.	d
I love to hear her speak, yet well I know	e
That music hath a far more pleasing sound;	f
I grant I never saw a goddess go —	e
My mistress, when she walks, treads on the ground:	f
And yet, by heaven, I think my love as rare	g
As any she belied with false compare.	g

SONNET 130

K-117 It is not unusual in the Shakespearean sonnet for line 12 to break the logic of the quatrains in order to set up the reversal in the couplet.

K-118 In the ideal Shakespearean form, when the resolution can be contained within the couplet, line 12 will frequently break the logic of the quatrains in order to set up the resolution. However if the situation simply will not allow a resolution to come about in the couplet, there may be a preliminary turn at the end of the second quatrain, but it only anticipates the turn at the couplet and does not usually constitute the turn itself.

K-119 A preliminary turn may come at the end of the second quatrain when the couplet is incapable of containing a balanced resolution to the problem. When this situation occurs, the couplet is less likely to be witty or paradoxical as it frequently is when there is no preliminary turn. Notice the preliminary turn in the following sonnet.

Bright star, would I were steadfast as thou art —	a
Not in lone splendor hung aloft the night	b
And watching, with eternal lids apart,	a
Like nature's patient, sleepless eremite,	b
The moving waters at their priestlike task	c
Of pure ablution round earth's human shores,	d
Or gazing on the new soft-fallen mask	c
Of snow upon the mountains and the moors —	d — (preliminary turn)
No — yet still steadfast, still unchangeable,	e
Pillowed upon my fair love's ripening breast,	f
To feel forever its soft fall and swell,	e
Awake forever in a sweet unrest,	f — (turn)
Still, still to hear tender — taken breath,	g
And so live over — or else swoon to death.	g

BRIGHT STAR
JOHN KEATS

K-120 Even as a love poem, the sonnet, whether Petrarchan or Shakespearean, has a tendency to reflect rhetorical logic on an almost legalistic level. In the Petrarchan, a balanced problem-resolution structure is created; the Shakespearean more often catalogues characteristics. If the sonnet to be explicated lacks any trace of logical taint, this should certainly be noted.

Review/self-check

K-121 The length and structure of the sonnet allow it to maintain an elevated state of _____.

emotion

K-122 The standard sonnet forms — Shakespearean, Petrarchan, and the standard variations, Miltonic and Spenserian — contain _____ lines of iambic _____; the Shakespearean and Petrarchan sonnets differ from

fourteen, pentameter

each other in their _____ scheme and in the position of the _____ .

rhyme (K-99 to K-103)
turn

K-123   The countering effect of the turn within a relatively short space gives the sonnet tremendous force. In the Petrarchan sonnet, the section before the turn, which presents the _____ is called the _____ ; The section after the turn, which presents the _____ is called the _____ . The problem occupies _____ lines in the Petrarchan sonnet; _____ lines in the Shakespearean sonnet.

situation or problem; octave , resolution;
sestet; eight
twelve (K-107, K-108)

K-124   The second quatrain of the Petrarchan sonnet should _____ the first, not repeat it, as the quatrains in the Shakespearean sonnet should extend each other. The _____ between the octave and sestet in the Petrarchan allows a development of both situation and resolution.

extend (K-109)

balance (K-110)

K-125   The resolution in the English sonnet is likely to be witty, _____ or _____ .

paradoxical (K-113);
pseudoprofound

K-126   If the couplet will not permit a resolution which will balance the problem in the English sonnet, there may be a _____ .

preliminary turn (K-118)

K-127   Identify the type of sonnet in the following example and determine where the turn(s) come.

Let me not to the marriage of true minds
Admit impediments. Love is not love
Which alters when it alteration finds,
Or bands with the remover to remove:
Oh, no! it is an ever-fixed mark,
That looks on tempests and is never shaken;
It is the star to every wandering bark,
Whose worth's unknown, although his height be taken.
Love's not Time's fool, though rosy lips and cheeks
Within his bending sickle's compass come;
Love alters not with his brief hours and weeks,
But bears it out even to the edge of doom.
If this be error and upon me proved,
I never writ, nor no man ever loved.

Shakespearean; the only turn comes at the couplet

K-128   Trace the basic theme of each quatrain and the couplet:

1. Love does not alter just to follow fashion.
2. Love is as constant as a star.
3. Love does not alter with time.

TURN

If this can be proven wrong, love does not exist

Spenserian Sonnet

K-129   The Petrarchan and Shakespearean sonnets both have important variations, called Miltonic and Spenserian. The Spenserian sonnet, which is a variation on the English sonnet, attempts to interlock the quatrains through its internal couplets. The result is a very tightly bound exposition of the problem which demands an equally tight development of the situation.

	a	
	b	First Quatrain
	a	
	b	
		Internal couplet
12-line "octave"	b	
	c	Second Quatrain
	b	
	c	
		Internal Couplet
	c	
	d	Third Quatrain
	c	
	d	
TURN		
	e	
	e	Final Couplet

K-130   The Spenserian sonnet differs from the English in that it creates a very tight exposition through the use of internal couplets. Because the exposition is so tight-knit, the final couplet must present a resolution or reaction which is definitive enough to balance the "octave."

K-131   Developing a tight, definitive final couplet is a problem for poets using the Spenserian form, and except in the best Spenserian sonnets there is a tendency at the end of the second quatrain to anticipate the turn. But while the Shakespearean sonnet can get away with a preliminary turn because the quatrains are separate, the Spenserian sonnet cannot, and the reader will immediately perceive the shift, which is annoying because of the binding force which the internal couplet has on the quatrains.

K-132   Because it is difficult to balance such a tight-knit twelve-line "octave" with a couplet, and because the rhyme scheme is so demanding, the Spenserian sonnet form is very difficult to write. However, when an emotional response is forceful enough to balance an extremely tight octave, the Spenserian sonnet form is quite effective.

K-133   Two problems which face the Spenserian sonneteer are rhyme and balance. While the Petrarchan sonnet has a shorter octave and the English sonnet can accept a preliminary turn, the Spenserian sonnet demands tremendous unity throughout the long "octave." Notice how Spenser strives for unity in the following sonnet:

> Men call you fayre, and you doe credit it,
> For that your self ye dayly such doe see:
> But the trew fayre, that is the gentle wit,
> And vertuous mind, is much more praysd of me.
> For all the rest, how ever fayre it be,
> Shall turne to nought and loose that glorious hew:
> But onely that is permanent and free
> From frayle corruption, that doth flesh ensew.
> That is true beautie: that doth argue you
> To be divine and borne of heavenly seed:
> Derived from that fayre Spirit, from whom al true
> And perfect beauty did at first proceed.
> He onely fayre, and what he fayre hath made:
> All other fayre, lyke flowres, untymely fade.

SONNET 79
EDMUND SPENSER

K-134   Because of the tightness established by the rhyme and couplets, the Spenserian sonnet is likely to have an elevated emotional theme.

Miltonic Sonnet

K-135   The Miltonic sonnet is a variation of the Petrarchan sonnet. It maintains the same structure and rhyme scheme, and differs only in its frequent use of enjambment, especially at the end of the octave, and its positioning of the turn.

K-136   The Miltonic sonnet makes frequent use of enjambment, and places the turn somewhere between the ninth and eleventh lines.

  By not clearly defining where the turn will come, but by placing it at some point after the normal Petrarchan turn, the Miltonic sonnet attempts to overcome the expectation of an automatic shift in tone which the reader will make if he knows where the turn is located.

K-137   The result in reducing the force of the artistic shift is to help create a more natural resolution while working within the highly structured from of the Petrarchan sonnet. By using an undefined position for the turn (which reduces the possibility of an abrupt artistic shift) and by using enjambment and the undefined turn, which can come while maintaining all the advantages of the formal form) the Miltonic sonnet creates a more natural resolution, and the result is that the Miltonic sonnet tends to have an emotional rather than structural unity.

K-138   There are, of course, many advantages to having a defined position for the turn, but the less formal line created by enjambment and the undefined turn, which can come anywhere between the ninth and eleventh lines, give the Miltonic sonnet some flexibility in creating emotional surprise. Notice the use of enjambment and the turn in the following Miltonic sonnet.

> *Cromwell, our chief of men, who through a cloud*
> > *Not of war only, but detractions rude,*   2
> > *Guided by faith and matchless fortitude,*
> > *To peace and truth thy glorious way hast plowed,* 4
> *And on the neck of crownéd fortune proud*
> > *Hast reared God's trophies, and His work pursued,* 6
> > *While Darwen stream, with blood of Scots imbrued,*
> > *And Dunbar field, resounds thy praises loud,* 8
> *And Worcester's laureate wreath: yet much remains* *TURN*
> > *To conquer still; peace hath her victories* 10
> > *No less reknowned than war: new foes arise,*
> *Threatening to bind our souls with secular chains.* 12
> > *Help us to save free conscience from the paw*
> > *Of hireling wolves, whose gospel is their maw.* 14

> > TO THE LORD GENERAL CROMWELL
> > JOHN MILTON

Curtal Sonnets

K-139   Although a number of variations have been made on the English and Italian sonnet forms, none has distinguished itself enough to become standard except the Miltonic and the Spenserian. G. M. Hopkins, however, developed a new form which is separate from the English and Italian influence. It is called a *curtal* (curtailed) sonnet and consists of a six line "octave" rhyming *abcabc*, and a 4½ line "sestet" rhyming *dbcdc*. Hopkins wrote only two sonnets of this sort, both in "sprung rhythm" (D-38), and there have been no successful attempts to imitate the form.

LONGER POEM FORMS: THE SESTINA

K-140   There are no stanza forms in excess of fourteen lines which have been especially popular in English (refer to Appendix A for some foreign forms greater than fourteen lines). One form, however, the *sestina*, is important, though seldom used because of the difficulty in writing it well.

K-141   The sestina consists of six six-line stanzas and a final three-line stanza called an "envoi." All the stanzas are closely interwoven through the repetition of the six terminal words. There is no "rhyme" as such, merely the repetition of the six terminal words in each stanza.

K-142   The sestina is thus very closely knit because of the repetition of the final word in each line. All of the terminal words in the first stanza are repeated in varied patterns as the last words in each of the following stanzas. One pattern (used by Ezra Pound in "Sestina: Alta Forte") is *abcdef, faebdc, cfdabe, ecbfad, deacfb, bdfeca, eca.* Thus, each stanza repeats the terminal words of the immediately preceding stanza in the order, 6, 1, 5, 2, 4, 3. Another kind of order might be 6, 1, 4, 3, 2, 5, with a switch to 6, 1, 2, 3, 4, 5 in succeeding stanzas, as in the following example:

I saw my soul at rest upon a day	a
As a bird sleeping in the nest of night,	b
Among soft leaves that give the starlight way	c
To touch its wings but not its eyes with light	d
So that it knew as one in visions may,	e
And knew not as men waking, of delight.	f
This was the measure of my soul's delight;	f
It had no power of joy to fly by day,	a
Nor part in the large lordship of the light;	d
But in a secret moon-beholden way	c
Had all its will of dreams and pleasant night,	b
And all the love and life that sleepers may.	e
But such life's triumph as men waking may	e
It might not have to feed its faint delight,	f
Between the stars by night and sun by day,	a
Shut up with green leaves and a little light;	d
Because its way was as a lost star's way,	c
A world's not wholly known of day or night.	b

FROM: SESTINA
ALGERNON CHARLES SWINBURNE

Some poets have attempted "double sestinas," which contain twelve six line stanzas and an envoi. Beginning with stanza 7, the rhyme scheme repeats itself, and all six rhyme words are condensed into the envoi.

K-143   The repetition of the terminal words gives tremendous emphasis to them. The fact that the words are repeated in different stanzas makes the sestina well suited to the meditative study of an image which is continually reshaping itself as the mind and eye look at it. In other words, repeating the same terminal words gives the poet an opportunity to express the same image or idea in a different way while working within identical form. The difficulty of the sestina is, of course, providing enough variety to sustain the entire thirty-nine lines. Few English poets have been successful.

K-144   When explicating a sestina, look for a change in emotions as the change in images takes place, and try to discover how and where the image and emotion coincide. In many successful sestinas, the end words represent or contain the theme.

Review/self-check

K-144   Spenserian and Shakespearean sonnets are alike in having _____. They differ in that the Spenserian employs _____, which result in very tightly bound exposition.

a similar quatrain and couplet structure.
internal couplets linking quatrains

K-145   Miltonic and Petrarchan sonnets are alike in having _____. They differ in that the Miltonic links lines through _____, and also differs in the placement of its _____ in an (earlier/later) position, making the entire sonnet less _____ or _____.

similarly structured octaves and rhyme schemes.
enjambment, turn, later
rigid and/or predictable

K-146   Among the advantages of each of the sonnet forms are these: (a) the Petrarchan has great balance between the _____; (b) the Miltonic is less _____ than the Petrarchan; (c) the Shakespearean can be _____ in its conclusion after and elaborate _____. (d) the Spenserian encourages great density because of its _____.

situation and the resolution; rigid *or* logical *or* predictable; witty *or* decisive; exploration of the situation; tight-knit rhyme scheme

FIGURE VERSE AND ITS VARIATIONS

K-147   For all poems, the typography (how the lines are arranged on the page) is to some extent important, but in "Carmen figuratum," usually called *figure verse* or *pattern poetry,* the typography is essential because the poet is attempting a visual representation of the subject of the poem.

K-148   "Carmen figuratum" is a type of form in which the poem visually represents the theme. This example of Carmen figuratum is entitled, "For a Thirtieth Birthday, with a Bottle of Burgundy."

Drop by
Drop it
Empties
Now not
Even as
Our own
Tearful
Vintage
Gathering
Itself with
Such slowness
Gradually might
Widen at the bottom
Of some oblate vessel
But as when the pouring
Bottle now nearly half of
Its old wine spent delivers
The rest up in sobs rapidly
Tears years and wine expire
As tosspot Time sends after
His cellerer once more alas
Then let the darkling drops
Wept in a decent year along
The golden slopes elude for
A moment or so his horribly
Steady pouring hand and run
Into sparkling glasses still
Unshattered yes and undimmed.

Obviously the poet is visually representing a bottle; within the bottle the tone (F-1 ff) changes as the level of wine gets lower.

K-149   There cannot, of course, be any set form or rules for Carmen figuratum, and while there is some satisfaction derived from seeing how the picture affects the theme, the poet sacrifices both caesura and the advantages of the line. He can, however, work a relationship between his meaning and the poem's shape which other poems cannot. The rhythm, for example, of the first few lines of the poem, approximates the flow of wine from a bottle, although without the shape to give us a hint of this, and without the confined limits which the line must work in, this sound would not work.

K-150   By using Carmen figuratum, the poet sacrifices the advantages of the caesura and line, but by making the sacrifice, he gains something in the relationship between shape and meaning.

Variations on Figure Verse

K-151   Although there have not been very many successful Carmen figuratum poems, there are a number of poems in which words are placed on the page in order to visually demonstrate a point. In the following example the poet uses position to reinforce meaning.

Slow light turned massive,

Hanging

with potential force.

The grey

critical

mass

Pressing

$E = mc^2$

WALTON BEACHAM

Since there are no rules governing this sort of use of typography, one must approach an explication intuitively. Usually experiments in typography are straightforward, with sound and the position of the word in the line commanding special attention.

K-152   Another example of a poem which depends on the reader to recognize the position of the lines on the page is the following, in which the reader should notice that the poem is to be read forward and backwards, like a palindrome:

CEMETERY

With hardened eyes
granite angels
in the soothing darkness
would know
that
the gently carved letters
reflect only
the red city lights
At this dead end

CEMETERY
HOLLY ANNA JONES

The poet in "Cemetery" has opened up the possibility of presenting the same theme in two perspectives; the difference between the forward and reversed readings should lead the reader to an understanding of the poet's attitude.

FREE VERSE AND VARIABLE VERSE

K-153   The attempt to use line variation for the purpose of emphasis or informality has led to the creation of a new poetical genre called *free verse*. Free verse literally means that the line (verse) is free to do anything it wishes without regard for the other lines in the poem, but the genre has been so widely explored that the term has come to include many different definitions.

K-154   Some prosodists regard the regularity of the metrical pattern as the distinguishing factor between traditional and free verse: traditional verse depends upon metrical regularity whereas free verse depends on cadence.

K-155   There is no clear definition of free verse, and little agreement as to how it differs from traditional verse. Some approaches hold that the difference depends upon whether the poem depends on cadence or meter. Other definitions state that free verse means that the line is free from any prosodic devices, but this does not seem valid because, were it true, there would be no basis on which the effects of free verse could be explained, and the devices in many free verse poems can be explained by traditional prosodic techniques.

K-156   Many of the poems which are categorized as "free verse" seem to be based on conventional techniques, and are "free" only in the sense that they vary their techniques from line to line. Therefore, it is necessary to make a distinction between verse which is truly free from prosodic bonds — free verse — and verse which varies from line to line within some prosodic structure.

Distinctive Features of Variable Verse

K-157   If a poem contains prosodic techniques which set up some sort of expectations, or if the prosody affects the meaning or tone, then "free verse" means variable verse, not verse free from the bonds of prosody. We can say, then, that verse which does not form regular patterns but which does conform to some conventional prosodic devices should be categorized as variable verse rather than free verse. If, however, a poem relies primarily on imagery, metaphor, symbol, allusion, and dramatic situation without any substantial reliance on tension between sound and sense and meter, then the verse is relatively "free" from conventional prosody and may legitimately be called "free verse."

K-158   However, since no reader reads in a vacuum — since he has been trained to come to a poem knowing something of traditional methods — he will automatically make some conventional associations which may or may not be valid in the free verse poem. This will create some uncertainty in anticipating the effect of free verse for any group of readers.

For the explicator, the problem is to determine whether conventional methods are likely to be valid. In free verse poems, by definition, they will not be, although they may seem to work on occasion; in variable verse poems conventional methods are quite useful in determining how the poem is working. For the purpose of explication, if a poem has no base meter, or if there is no repetition in the number of feet per line, yet some conventional devices of prosody seem to be working, the poem should be approached as variable verse.

K-159   One reason a poet may use variable verse is that focus can be placed on images and ideas through a modification of tempo, and frequently understanding this function in a variable verse poem will reveal the meaning.

The tempo — which is, of course, regulated by the rhythm of the line — will be affected by the length of the line, and it is sometimes helpful to establish correlations between length, theme, and images.

K-160   Meter, or the absence of it, can be regulated according to the demands of the idea and image rather than having to conform to form. Polysyllabic words can be used without concern as to how they fit into the meter, and variable verse offers the opportunity for harshness through sudden variation; an effect which traditional verse achieves through substitution and the sound of words.

K-161   Some advantages of variable verse, then, are that the poet can use meter without being bound by it, and that he can use the length of the line for focus or to create a particular tone.

K-162   Under many definitions the following poem would be categorized as "free verse," but because anapestic and trochaic rhythms create some of the effect, and since the line is attempting to focus on various moods and ideas, the poem is not true free verse, although it does contain some free verse characteristics, such as the importance of imagery and the use of typography.

> *Green lilacs and the girl,*
> *And the days when lilacs of the mind could grow.*
> *My memory, through time, extorts these pleasures*
> *Of sweetness; I find the melancholy,*
> *Its mass expanded and trapped*
> *Like stranded whirlpools of light,*
> > *Standing in early morning mist,*
> *Slow light turned massive,*
>
> > *Hanging*
>
> > *with potential force.*
>
> > *The grey*
>
> > > *critical*
>
> > > > *mass*
>
> *Pressing*
>
> *To accelerate toward light, and motion, and presence.*
>
> *But the girl and the memory hold the grey, and me.*

$$E = mc^2$$
WALTON BEACHAM

K-163   With a variable verse poem, like the example above, the effect of the position of the words on the emphasis and imagery will lead to an understanding of the poem. In other variable verse poems, as in the following fragment, the position of the words is not as important as the use of the sound and rhythm of the words.

> *At the end we preferred to travel all night,*
> *Sleeping in snatches,*
> *With the voices singing in our ears, saying*
> *That this was all folly.*

FROM: JOURNEY OF THE MAGI
T. S. ELIOT

K-164   Obviously some variable verse poems are closer to traditional poetry than others, but at least some of the effects of the poem can be validly explained by prosodic conventions. For example, some practitioners of variable verse, such as T. S. Eliot, will insert within their varying verses some four-stress lines (similar to those used in Old English poetry) (D-37), and while in some instances the four-stress line results simply from a pyrrhic substitution, in other instances the four stresses played against a conventional accentual-syllabic base (D-58) will achieve special tensions and effects. Explaining such tensions in conventional prosodic terms may help the reader understand themes or moods.

K-165   If, however, no patterns in any of the four metrical systems are established *and,* if the line is not being used to give emphasis , then the poem is true free verse and the systems of prosody described in this book will not help in explicating the poem.

K-166   Two of the definitive characteristics of free verse are that no metrical patterns are established and that the line is not being used for emphasis. Another characteristic seems to be the high incidence of unstressed syllables. If a poem is true free verse then the prosodic methods applied to explicating traditional poems are invalid, and the explicator must turn to the poet's use of such devices as allusion and imagery to determine meaning.

Review/self-check

K-167   Typography is important to both _____ figuratum (pattern poetry) and _____ verse poems.

Carmen (K-147)
free

K-168   In using this kind of pattern poetry, the poet sacrifices the advantages of the line but gains in his relationship of meaning to _____.

shape (K-149)

K-169   Although the length of meter may vary from line to line, a poem is not true free verse unless it is free from _____ bonds.

prosodic (K-155)

K-170   Free verse poems rely on such devices as imagery, metaphor, symbol, allusion, and dramatic situation without relying on tension between sound and sense, or on _____.

meter (K-157)

K-171   Two advantages of variable verse are that meter can be used without being binding, and that the

length of the _____ can be changed for
focus.

line (K-161)

K-172   In true free verse there is an absence of
_____ and use of the _____ .

meter (K-166) line

BLANK VERSE

K-173   The previous material has been concerned with strophic verse forms; the following discussion will investigate the most common form of English stichic verse: unrhymed iambic pentameter, called *blank verse*.

K-174   Although many variations can occur on the meter of blank verse, its base meter is iambic pentameter. Blank verse lines are unrhymed, and are usually arranged in stichic form. The following lines are blank verse:

> *To be, or not to be, that is the question:*
> *Whether 'tis nobler in the mind to suffer*
> *The slings and arrows of outrageous fortune,*
> *Or to take arms against a sea of troubles,*
> *And by opposing end them? To die; to sleep;*
> *No more; and by a sleep to say we end*
> *The heart-ache and the thousand natural shocks*
> *That flesh is heir to, 'tis a consummation*
> *Devoutly to by wish'd. To die; to sleep;*
> *To sleep! perchance to dream: ay, there's the rub;*
> *For in that sleep of death what dreams may come,*
> *When we have shuffled off this mortal coil,*
> *Must give us pause: there's the respect*
> *That makes calamity of so long life;*

FROM: HAMLET
WILLIAM SHAKESPEARE

K-175   Blank verse adapts well to many moods and subjects, but it is often used for poems which require narration or reflection in addition to elevated emotion. (In drama, blank verse serves much less of a narrative function than in poetry.)

K-176   The base meter of blank verse is iambic pentameter, but the form is very flexible, and substitutions, enjambments, feminine endings, and extra syllables can remove any rigidity from the base. In fact, the flexibility of blank verse gives the poet an opportunity to do more within a formal structure than almost any other form, and many of the best lines in English — as exemplified in Shakespeare's work — are written in blank verse. One of the principal advantages of blank verse is its flexibility within a formal structure.

K-177   However, even with its great flexibility, blank verse is very taxing because it demands beauty without the benefit of rhymes. And in addition to this there is also the demand of expectation made by the historical success of the form. Because blank verse was used so brilliantly by Shakespeare, readers will subconsciously make comparisons to Shakespeare when they see this form, and this in itself can be a tremendous obstacle to overcome.

K-178   Because of the tremendous definitive influence which Shakespeare had on the form, readers of blank verse have come to expect beauty created by language which eventually leads to some acute observation about life or the self.

K-179   We can say, then, that the characteristics associated with blank verse are narration, elevated emotion, beauty of language, and profound observation.

K-180   A number of poems have been written which take great liberties with the historical blank verse form by adding or subtracting a foot or by interspersing three foot lines to vary the decasyllabic base. Poets who take such liberties usually maintain the iambic base, but vary the length of the line, and many variable verse (K-157) poems are formed in this way. The following stanza is an example of this variable blank verse. (The number of feet per line is indicated on the left.)

3	*Time present and time past*
5	*Are both perhaps present in time future,*
4½	*And time future contained in time past.*
5	*If all time is eternally present*
4	*All time is unredeemable.*
4½	*What might have been is an abstraction*
6	*Remaining a perpetual possibility*
5	*Only in a world of speculation.*
4	*What might have been and what has been*
5	*Point to one end, which is always present.*

FROM: BURNT NORTON
T. S. ELIOT

The liberties which poets have taken with blank verse have led some critics to classify the variable form as "free verse." Clearly this form is not "free," since it relies heavily on the iambic base for substitution, and should be approached as variable blank verse.

Review/self-check

K-181   Unrhymed iambic pentameter is called _____ .   blank verse (K-173)

K-182   Although blank verse is very flexible, it is difficult to use because of _____ .

the absence of rhyme; its brilliant tradition (K-177, 178)

K-183 When a poet uses blank verse, he may be trying to establish these expectations: (a) _____ ;
(b) _____ ; (c) _____ .

(a) beauty of language
(b) elevated emotion
(c) profound observation
(K-179)

K-184 Poems which have an iambic base but whose
lines vary in length though they seem to center on
the five foot line might best be considered _____
blank verse since they are usually attempting what
blank verse attempts.

variable (K-180)

K-185 What is the form of the following fragment?

Come, gentle night, come, loving, black-brow'd night,
Give me my Romeo; and, when he shall die,
Take him and cut him out in little stars,
And he will make the face of heaven so fine
That all the world will be in love with night
And pay no worship to the garish sun.

blank verse

K-186 Even without scanning the lines, the regular
lines stand out amidst the substitutions and variations
in the verse. Lines _____ and _____
are regular (D-17).

four and five

Stanza and Structure

In addition to drawing on the inherent qualities and connotations of traditional stanza forms, poets use stanzas to structure their poems. Recognizing this aids the reader in understanding the poem's progression and areas of emphasis.

L-1 Most poets do not consciously conceive the entire metrical structure of their poems, although they do consciously rework segments which sound wrong to them. When analyzing prosody, then, we cannot assume that metrical devices were deliberately put into the poem, and we must remain open and flexible to possibilities which the poet may or may not have meant. Nonetheless, in order to explicate, we must assume that the poem is exactly as the poet wished it, because only then can we explicate the contribution of individual techniques to the total effect. We need not see every spondee as deliberately thought out, but we must regard every device as intentional if we are to explicate at all.

L-2 For a large part, poems are subconsciously composed, but this does not imply that a poem is inferior because its metrics may have come "naturally " (as with experienced poets); it means only that every poem contains some elements which have been carefully considered and created and some elements which are a result of "untutored" genius.

L-3 Although poems do not necessarily mean to the reader what the poet thought they meant, it is helpful when explicating to look for those elements which the poet had to work on consciously because we can be certain that he meant to include them. The elements consciously conceived which all poems contain are structure, tension, point of view, dramatic situation, and tone. Other conscious elements which most poems contain are imagery, metaphor, symbol, allusion, irony, and paradox. If we can determine which of these elements are included and how they work relative to the prosody and other elements, we will have achieved most of our explication.

FORM AND STRUCTURE

L-4 *Structure* can be considered the underlying element or elements in the poem which give it unity. Although there are numerous devices which give a poem structure, the most obvious structural device is the form which the poem takes. Whenever a poet uses one of the standard stanza forms he is doing so for one of three reasons: (1) the characteristics of the form fit his material and approach to the poem; (2) the associations which accompany the form will enhance the poem; (3) the associations give him a standard from which he can deviate to achieve emphasis.

L-5 When the characteristics of the form fit the poet's material and approach, a standard form may be useful. For example, if the poet wishes to tell a long story in which there is a progression of individual events, he may choose to use the ballad stanza because that form has proven to be successful for his type of poem.

L-6   If the poem will be enhanced by the associations which accompany the form, the poet may also use a standard form. The ballad stanza, for example, can carry a degree of the supernatural about it, and would therefore be appropriate for a poem which included an adventure.

L-7   Although the poet may choose a standard form for its associations, he may also choose it in order to deviate from the accepted qualities. In other words, the form may set up expectations which the poem denies, thereby emphasizing the differences.

L-8   Many poems use standard stanza forms because they have proven to be successful for centuries, and because the poet is familiar and comfortable with the forms which he has known all his life. When a standard form is used, the explicator has a good place to begin. However, many poems — perhaps a majority of rhymed poems — do not use standard forms; yet they achieve unity even though their form may never have been used before, or never used so successfully that it has acquired associations. Such improvised poetic forms may be termed "nonce" forms.

L-9   Most poems will be constructed of either one or more stichic divisions (J-12), or two or more stanzas (J-9), and the development from division to division will help determine the structure, and perhaps the theme of the poem.

STROPHIC STANZA FORMS

L-10   If there are no stanza divisions — if the poem is one stichic unit — there may be some problems in determining structure, and the best hints may come from the *rhyme scheme* (J-20). If, however, there are stanza divisions, the explicator may be able to determine stanzaic progressions within the entire poem. Poems composed of strophic stanzas are sometimes easier to analyze structurally because the progressions are clearer.

L-11   In addition to progression, strophic stanzas may also show divisions in ideas or emotions. For example, consider the following poem:

> *Tree at my window, window tree,*
> *My sash is lowered when night comes on;*
> *But let there never be curtain drawn*
> *Between you and me.*
>
> *Vague dream-head lifted out of the ground,*
> *And thing next most diffuse to cloud,*
> *Not all your light tongues talking aloud*
> *Could be profound.*
>
> *But, tree, I have seen you taken and tossed,*
> *And if you have seen me when I slept,*
> *You have seen me when I was taken and swept*
> *And all but lost.*

> *That day she put our heads together,*
> *Fate had her imagination about her,*
> *Your head so much concerned with outer,*
> *Mine with inner, weather.*

TREE AT MY WINDOW
ROBERT FROST

There the stanzas form divisions in ideas which ultimately fuse in the final meaning of the poem; it is the divisions as well as the similarity between each stanza that gives the poem unity.

L-12   Strophic stanzas can form divisions or units which then interact to form the overall theme of the poem, and it is this division, as well as the similarities between the stanzas, that give the poem unity. For example, "Tree At My Window" is composed of four stanzas, which suggests that each stanza will give equal weight to each idea presented, and that there will be no surprises or sudden turns (refer to J-10 ff for the characteristics of strophic stanzas).

L-13   Short poems composed of strophic divisions will probably give equal weight to the idea presented in each stanza, and they will either develop in a step by step progression of ideas or events, or they will present separate ideas whose union forms a larger, more complete observation than any of the individual parts.

L-14   Looking at the example poem, we might extract these ideas from each stanza:

> Stanza 1.   *I close my window at night, but*
> *there should never be a curtain*
> *drawn between us.*
>
> Stanza 2.   *When I look at you I imagine that*
> *you are like a cloud, and I know*
> *that you cannot be as profound*
> *as I imagine you are.*
>
> Stanza 3.   *I have seen you in a storm, and*
> *you have seen me toss in a storm*
> *of dreams.*
>
> Stanza 4.   *You are necessarily concerned*
> *with that which affects you —*
> *outer weather — and I am concern-*
> *ed with that which affects me —*
> *inner weather (psychological), but*
> *our heads are the same in fate's*
> *imagination.*

L-14 (1)   Structurally the poem sets up a pattern for development. Stanza 1 suggests the idea of a boundary between man and nature (the tree), and in doing so anticipates that the poem will consider this boundary.

L-14 (2)   Stanza 2, however, seems to break from this idea, but in doing so suggests that imagination about nature might lead to profundity for man.

L-14 (3)   It is the union in Stanza 2, of man's imagination about nature combined with what is in nature that will lead to profundity for man.

L-14 (4)   Stanza 3 once again sets up the idea of a boundary between the tree and the man, but this time shows how they are alike in their separate domains.

L-14 (5)   Stanza 4, like Stanza 2, returns to the element which bridges the gap between the two.

L-14 (6)   The basic stanza by stanza structure of the poem, then, is this:

1. *A desire to bridge the separation between man and nature.*
2. *The notion that a* union *between the two will lead imaginative man to profundity.*
3. *A realization that in* separation *the crux of unity is similarity.*
4. *The recognition that the tenuous unity of similarity is the profundity about man and nature desired in Stanza 2.*

L-14 (7)   From the structure only we can tell that the poem is concerned with the dichotomy and parallelism between man and nature, which reinforces the poet's idea that only in separation is unity possible.

L-15   In addition to the development of ideas and events as they form patterns, we must also look at the stanza form. "Tree At My Window" is basically iambic tetrameter rhyming *abba*, with the last line containing only two feet and some lines containing an extra syllable. We can also say that, in spite of its irregularities, the form is a modified "In Memoriam" (K-33) stanza.

L-15 (1)   When a standard form is used, we should determine how it conforms to and deviates from standard usage. In "Tree At My Window" the standard form resembles the "In Memoriam" stanza, which is traditionally used for meditative or introspective subjects. Because of the central couplet, which is interlocked by rhyming lines, great emphasis is placed on line 3, which gives the form a natural focal point.

L-15 (2)   Frost maintains the full rhyme of the standard form but makes variations on the form by adding and reducing syllables; indeed, there are so many long lines that the stanza might almost be considered a brace were it not for the short last line which reduces the tension of the brace stanza (K-35).
The syllable count for each stanza is as follows:

I – 8	II – 9	III – 10	IV – 9
8	8	9	11
9	9	11	9
5	4	4	6

The third line of each stanza does command focus, particularly in stanza 3, but line 4 brings it quickly to a resolution. The shorter third line in stanza 4 and the longer fourth line help to give the poem less of a quick resolution and cause the reader to slow down and reflect. So Frost is using the basic advantages of the "In Memoriam" stanza while creating his own by varying cadence in order to balance the stanza as he wishes.

L-15 (3)   Certainly the characteristics of the form apply to Frost's poem, and if we can determine why he deviated from the standard "In Memoriam" stanza we will know quite a bit about where he wanted to place emphasis.

L-16   Of course not all poems have parallel structure or neat dichotomy as does "Tree At My Window," but even with poems which are not as neatly structured we can form some generalizations about structure which will help in explicating.
   Here are some helpful generalizations:

(a)   The beginning of a new stanza normally indicates a shift in idea, action, tone or mood.
(b)   When stanzas are of equal length, it is generally true that the poet is giving equal emphasis to the ideas, or that there is going to be a progression of action in which each event is of importance.
(c)   The strophic poem will, of course, build to a climax, and there will be some stanzas more important than others, but the poet does not want to single out any one part by varying the length of the stanza. In "Tree At My Window," for example, the stanzas are of equal length and similar structure because Frost wants to demonstrate the force of both the separation and union between man and nature.

L-17   While each stanza represents a unified action or idea, several stanzas may be very closely related, each one acting as a slight extension or reflection on the preceding one. Therefore, it is sometimes helpful, when trying to decide where the emphasis lies, to look for the relative distance between stanzas.

L-18   Stanzas which have equal weight, and which develop ideas or events in a steady, consistent evolution rather than in sudden jumps, are probably trying to achieve a total effect which is greater than the parts — rather than trying to create sudden emotional effects within the poem. Poems which strive toward creating a total effect might use a limited number of short stanzas which develop idea or events in a steady, consistent evolution. Poems which are not composed of equal stanzas usually attempt to create some effect or emphasis by calling attention to the different length of the stanza.

SHORT VARIABLE STANZAS VS. EQUAL STANZAS

L-19   By varying the length of their stanzas, poets are often attempting to affect the emphasis of the poem by changing its balance. In very short stanzas, where an idea or event cannot be fully developed, the poet may be relying on an emotional effect which either reflects back or acts as a transition into the next stanza. The emotional effect hinges on the balance between short and long stanzas.

L-20 Poems which may have very short stanzas mixed with longer ones rely on an emotional response, with the short stanza reflecting on the longer ones. It is the balance between long and short stanzas which creates this emotional response.

For example, consider the following poem:

> *Ten feet he stalks,*
> *Ten feet secure within,*
> *But there are those beyond*
> *His balk.*
> *The cat retreats,*
> *The chain pulls taut*
> *With a sudden end and the collar chokes,*
> *The guardian bark becomes a whine,*
> *The stake a hangman.*
>
> *The cat looks on and darts across his govern,*
> *She know no boundary to the ten foot world.*
>
> *The universe is circular, I've heard.*

BOUNDARIES
WALTON BEACHAM

The bulk of the situation is presented in the first division as the poet attempts to establish sympathy for the chained dog who is performing his duty within the boundaries over which he has no control. But in the second division, which is only two lines long, the poet attempts to balance the first, and in the last division attempts to overwhelm the reader emotionally with an analogy between man's boundaries and the dog's, and to tantalize him with the idea that there is a free element which is not bounded.

L-21 In "Boundaries" the poet uses short segments to shift the balance of the poem in order to arouse an emotional response. There is no development of idea which contributes to the whole, but instead there is a short statement which shocks the reader. With poems that have stanzas of equal length, the poet relies on the reader to fuse the ideas in each stanza; it is the fusion in each stanza which the reader has, himself, created that makes the poem so forceful. On the other hand, in the poem containing stanzas of varied length there is usually one particular stanza which gives the poem emotional power.

L-22 We can say, then, that when explicating short poems of equally lengthened stanzas, we should look for an idea outside the poem which comes from the fusion of the basic ideas presented in each stanza; in short poems containing stanzas of varied lengths we should look closely at the balance and emotional forcefulness of the shorter stanzas.

L-23 Sometimes the typographical distance between stanzas is important, especially in free verse and variable verse poems where the physical distance may determine associated lines or the length of a pause. In "Boundaries" there is more space between divisions 1 and 2 than between 2 and 3, which would indicate that the poet felt there was a closer association between 2 and 3 than between 1 and 2, which might influence emphasis.

L-24   If stanzas are not typographically spaced evenly apart, we can assume that the poet is concerned with either association on the length of pause. In either case balance is important and the poet wishes to call attention to it. *Tone* (F-lff) is usually very important in this type of poem.

Review/self-check

L-25   When explicating, it is helpful to look for those devices which the poet had to use _____ because we are likely to discover what he meant to put in the poem.

consciously (L-3)

L-26   Structure results from those elements which give the poem _____.

unity (L-4)

L-27   Poets use standard forms because:

(1)

(2)

(3)

(1) the characteristics of the form fit their material, (2) the associations of the form enhance their material, (3) the associations give them a standard from which they can deviate (L-4)

L-28   Both the form and length of the stanza affect the structure of the poem. Poems which rely on a final fusion of ideas, events, and emotions will probably be composed of _____ stanzas.

short, equal-length stanzas (L-21)

L-29   Why does Frost use such careful balance in "Tree At My Window?"

to reinforce the union and separation between man and nature (L-14 (7))

L-30   Short poems which alter the balance by varying the length of the stanzas are depending upon emotional force created by one of the stanzas, whereas poems using stanzas of equal length depend on the force of an idea not expressed directly in the poem but formed by the _____ after fusing the two separate ideas.

reader (L-21)

SYMMETRICAL STRUCTURES

L-31   One of the traditional ambitions of poetry has been to show order in what appears to be a chaotic universe. For this reason poets have been interested in imitating ordered form within the poem's structure, and there are a great many poems which are symmetrically structured.

L-32   Poems which are symmetrically structured are usually attempting to find order and balance in an unordered situation, as in "Tree At My Window," for example. Here Frost uses symmetrical structure in order to reinforce his idea that there is harmony between man and nature.

L-33   With short strophic poems (2-6 stanzas) it is common for the poet to use a balanced structure. With an even number of equal-length stanzas there will probably be a division in which half the stanzas work with or against the other half. Notice the structure in the following two-stanza poem:

> These, in the day when heaven was falling,
>   The hour when earth's foundations fled,
> Followed their mercenary calling
>   And took their wages and are dead.   4
>
> Their shoulders held the sky suspended;
>   They stood, and earth's foundations stay;
> What God abandoned, these defended,
>   And saved the sum of things for pay.   8

EPITAPH ON AN ARMY OF MERCENARIES
A. E. HOUSMAN

On an overall level, stanza 1 sets up the idea of the world falling apart while stanza 2 tells how it was held together. We can say that Housman's poem is symmetrically balanced since the second stanza forms a resolution to the first.

L-34   The symmetry, however, is more subtle and detailed than the general structure reveals. Notice how line 5 balances line 1: they hold the sky on their shoulders; line 6 balances line 2: they keep the foundations from falling; line 7 balances line 3: God has abandoned his calling while they have followed theirs; line 8 balances line 4: they saved the world while losing their lives.

L-35   In addition to the balance which comes between corresponding ideas in the lines in each stanza, there is symmetry in the endings of corresponding lines: lines 1 and 3 of each stanza have feminine endings while lines 2 and 4 of each stanza have masculine endings.

L-36   Obviously Housman is using balanced structure to reinforce the meaning of the poem, and in explaining why a poem is effective the explicator must consider structure. The effectiveness of good structure, however, works unconsciously in the reader's mind (although very deliberately constructed by the poet). In other words, the reader will not stop to think about structures as he will images and ideas, and for this reason structure can work subtle effects which would be blatant with any of the other devices.

L-37   Short poems which have an odd number of stanzas will normally have some sort of a turn, or will, in the central stanza, contain the idea on which the stanzas on either side of it will reflect.

L-38   Poems with an odd number (three or five) of stanzas of equal length will likely have a turn, the center stanza serving as the pivot point and central idea of the poem. In the following poem, for example, there is a turn in stanza 2 which creates a balance in which the first six lines contain the counterpart of the idea presented in the last six lines.

> *"Love seeketh not itself to please,*
> *Nor for itself hath any care,*
> *But for another gives its ease,*
> *And builds a heaven in hell's despair.*
>
> *So sung a little clod of clay,*
> *Trodden with the cattle's feet,*
> *But a pebble of the brook*
> *Warbled out these meters meet:*
>
> *"Love seeketh only self to please,*
> *To bind another to its delight,*
> *Joys in another's loss of ease,*
> *And builds a hell in heaven's despite."*

THE CLOD AND THE PEBBLE
WILLIAM BLAKE

L-39   Poets do not, of course, always use symmetrical structure, and there are many poems of both odd and even numbered stanzas which use a straight progression to move the reader from point to point. A linear structure will usually denote that an argument in logic is occurring, or that the order of events is important.

L-40   Short poems composed of short strophic stanzas may be structured so that part of the stanzas act as a counterpart to the other half; thus there is a turn or central point that the other stanzas reflect upon, or build up to (as in the example above), or use to form a straight progression to move the reader from point to point. Linear structure usually denotes that a logical argument is occurring or that the order of events is important.

DIVISION WITHIN LONG POEMS

L-41   Long poems which are composed of many stanzas tend to have a linear structure, since it is the narration which serves as the unifying element. When explicating long poems composed of many short strophic stanzas, we should look for unity of structure in the narration rather than in any balance of stanzas. There may, however, be within the linear structure several stanzas which form subgroups using balance among themselves.

For example, in the following exerpt from "The Rime of the Ancient Mariner" there is a progression which moves the reader (and the Mariner) from the moon to himself:

> *The moving Moon went up the sky,*
> *And nowhere did abide:*
> *Softly she was going up,*
> *And a star or two beside —*

Her beams bemocked the sultry main,
Like April hoar-frost spread;
But where the ship's huge shadow lay
The charméd water burned alway
A still and awful red.

Beyond the shadow of the ship,
I watched the water snakes:
They moved in tracks of shining white,
And when they reared, the elfish light
Fell off in hoary flakes.

Within the shadow of the ship
I watched their rich attire:
Blue, glossy green, and velvet black,
They coiled and swam; and every track
Was a flash of golden fire.

O happy living things! no tongue
Their beauty might declare:
A spring of love gushed from my heart,
And I blessed them unaware:
Sure my kind saint took pity on me,
And I blessed them unaware.

THE RIME OF THE ANCIENT MARINER
SAMUEL TAYLOR COLERIDGE

Following the spatial progression through the stanza structure, we note a pattern of location:

Stanza 1: description of the moon
Stanza 2: the moon's beams and shadows they form with the ship on the ocean's surface
Stanza 3: beyond the shadows
Stanza 4: within the shadows
Stanza 5: within the Mariner

L-41 (1)   The progression in these five stanzas is from the universal, represented by the moon and stars, to the particular, represented by the Mariner. However, within the linear progression, there is a subgroup; stanzas 3 and 4 balance each other, and the emphasis created by the subgroup suggests that the poet is attempting here to call attention to the fact that there is some balance between that which is beyond (the universe) and that which is within (the Mariner).

L-42   We can say, then, that when the poet uses subgroups within linear structure, he is attempting to emphasize ideas or events.

L-43   Poems composed of long stichic divisions (perhaps as long as several hundred lines) will usually be structured according to dramatic action. Within each segment of action there will be substructures just as there were subgroups within the long strophic poems.

L-44   Groups of lines which form a unified body of action or idea within the stichic poem are called *verse paragraphs*. Verse paragraphs in stichic poems are analogous to stanzas in strophic poems. However, in strophic poems several stanzas may be associated to form a subgroup, while in stichic poems the case is usually that certain lines are associated within a longer verse paragraph to create a subgroup.

L-45   A valid question, then, is whether stanzas can be made out of subgroups, if they function in a similar manner. There is a two part answer to this. First, they do not always function in a similar manner; usually subgroups will not have the force or the autonomy of a stanza. They are only a division within one basic event or idea, and cannot stand alone. Second, the poet does not wish to disassociate the subgroups from the groups on either side of it because a pause might cause the stanza to lose its emotional impact.

L-46   We can say, then, that subgroups are not the same as stanzas or verse paragraphs because they are not autonomous, but are only a division within the general idea. In addition to their need to be associated with other subgroups, subgroups which are separated would tend to lose their emotional impact because of the pauses which would come between subgroups.

SHORT STICHIC POEMS

L-47   Poems consisting of one relatively short stichic unit will be aiming toward a "punch effect" as opposed to a development of several complete ideas; i.e., the poet hopes to create an emotional rather than intellectual response.

L-48   The devices which the poet has to achieve structural variation in short (3-20 lines) stichic stanzas are meter, number of feet per line, rhyme, and subgroups.

Review Example/self-check

L-49   When explicating a poem structured with one stichic unit that runs from 3-20 lines, we should look for the poet's use of meter, number of feet per line, _____ , and subgroups. Examine these elements   rhyme
in the following poem.

> Some say the world will end in fire,
> Some say in ice.
> From what I've tasted of desire
> I hold with those who favor fire.
> But if it had to perish twice,
> I think I know enough of hate
> To say that for destruction ice

Is also great
And would suffice.

FIRE AND ICE
ROBERT FROST

L-49 (1)   The title of the poem, which suggests that
there will be a balance between fire and ice, and the fact
that the poem is _____ lines long, would indicate   nine
that the first and last four lines will center on line
_____ if the poem is to be symmetrically balanced.   five

L-49 (2)   This is not to say that the poem will necessarily be structured in this manner, but from first glance
it is reasonable to begin by assuming that the poem will
be balanced by its form (as opposed to balance which
comes through the weight of the ideas or emotions), and
that the turn or _____ idea will come in line 5.   central or main

L-49 (3)   The reason that we should begin by assuming
balance in form is that the poet is presenting antithetical
ideas, and were he to divide the poem into a 5-4 situation,
one of the two dichotomies would receive greater _____.   emphasis

L-49 (4)   Looking at the poem now, we can see that
Frost is balancing the dichotomies. Lines 1-4 are about
destruction through fire; lines _____ about destruc-   6-9
tion through ice.

L-49 (5)   Apparently Frost wants to give balance to his
poem since he has set up a 4-1-4 structure, but he has not
chosen a rhyme scheme which reflects delicate balance as
he might have had if he had chosen some different schemes:
ababcdede ababbcbcb, or *abbababba.* Instead, the rhyme
scheme is _____, which does not show exceptional   *abaabcbcb*
balance.

L-49 (6)   Yet the poem does possess great balance,
which can be explained by considering the rhyme scheme
relative to line length, and although the rhyme scheme of
"Fire and Ice" is not symmetrical, the poem is balanced
because Frost has correlated rhyme scheme with line
_____.   length

L-49 (7)   Assuming, for the moment, that Frost wants
to achieve his dichotomy within one verse paragraph
rather than two strophic _____, he must find some   stanzas

way to close the first four lines. A period at the end of
line 4 would, of course, accomplish a syntactical close,
but it would not give the section finality.

L-49 (8)   Because the meaning of the subject matter
requires a closing which gives the section impressive
_____ , a period at the end of line 4 is not forceful   finality
enough; the couplet, however, formed by lines 3 and 4
gives the authority (K-11) which the poet needs.

L-49 (9)   Frost manages to achieve a forceful close on
the subject of destruction by fire by putting a _____   couplet
at the end of the subgroups.

L-49 (10)   Line 5 ties the two sections together because it contains a rhyme common to both _____ .   subgroups
Because the couplet is forceful, line 5 tends to be more
closely associated with the second part than the first;
but once again Frost achieves balance, because line 5
is the first time the *b* rhyme has been repeated, which
gives it a strong associative power.

L-49 (11)   The imbalance which might occur because
the couplet makes line 5 cling to the second part rather
than the first is again balanced by the repetition for the
first time of the _____ rhyme.   *b*

L-49 (12)   Whenever a rhyming word has occured in a
rhymed poem, the reader expects that the sound will
occur again; and this expectation will establish strong
association power if the repetition of the _____   sound
comes within reasonable distance.

L-49 (13)   Frost has set up dichotomies in the poem,
which are discussed in the first and last four lines re-
spectively. Line 5 manages to hold the two parts together and mold one verse paragraph because it contains
a _____ common to both sections.   rhyme

L-49 (14)   Both parts seems to contain about the same
amount of weight in terms of the argument, but the last
four lines rhyme *cdcd*. If, by analogy, we are to assume
that Frost wants to give the same finality to the last part
as to the first, then we might ask why there is no _____   couplet
at the end of the poem.

L-49 (15)   One reason why Frost has not used a final couplet might be that it would tend to give finality only to the last section, and what he wants to achieve is a finality to the poem — to the fusion of both ideas, and not just to the last.

L-49 (16)   The problem with a couplet would be that it would tend to give finality only to the _____ part, not to the entire fusion; yet there must be final authority equal to the couplet.

second (last)

L-49 (17)   In order to achieve the finality he wants, Frost shortens the tetrameter lines to _____ , and the short lines coming after the longer lines makes the poem end very quickly; the suddenness gives abrupt finality to the entire poem as well as to the last section.

diameter

L-49 (18)   After line length has been established, a dramatic shortening of the line will create abrupt finality. However, unless the change has been anticipated, the abruptness will only annoy or shock the reader. In order to anticipate the poem's end, and to maintain balance, line 2 has been shortened. The fact that it comes so early in the poem and is not repeated until the end gives the dimeter line force. In addition to this, the *b* rhyme is first associated with the short line, and when it is repeated in the last short line the reader recalls its initial use.

L-49 (19)   Although the dimeter line and *b* rhyme in line 2 anticipate the last line, the two parts do maintain separate identity because the *a* rhyme is used in the first part while the *c* rhyme is used in the last.

L-49 (20)   In summary, we might diagram the structure of "Fire and Ice" as follows:

	line	length	rhyme	function
	1	tetrameter	a	
	2	dimeter	b	anticipates later dimeter lines; short *b* line helps to balance the three a rhymes
fire	3	tetrameter	a	couplet gives finality
quatrain	4	tetrameter	a	central line gives unity to the parts
	5	tetrameter	b	because of the binding *b* rhyme
ice				
quatrain	6	tetrameter	c	
	7	tetrameter	b	
	8	dimeter	c	dimeter lines give finality to both
	8	dimeter	b	the section and the poem

L-49 (21)   Obviously Frost has been very careful in working out the structure so that great balance would be achieved, and as we analyze the meaning, the balance will serve as a good basis for arguing that Frost intended to place equal emphasis on both methods of destruction. The structure also raises interesting questions about the center line on which the argument is centered, and from the evidence coming from structure, we could almost say that line 5 constitutes a basic hypothesis or statement around which the philosophy of the poem is based.

⊲∥⊳ Allusion

Allusion adds dimension and texture to many poems, and often, without understanding allusion, the reader is incapable of understanding the poem. Readers must constantly be on the lookout for allusion, and be able to explain how it enriches theme.

HOW ALLUSION WORKS

M-1   When a reference is made to an historical or literary event whose story or outcome adds dimension to the poem, then poetical allusion occurs. For example:

> *Some say the world will end in fire,*
> *Some say in ice.*
> *From what I've tasted of desire*
> *I hold with those who favor fire.*
> *But if it had to perish twice,*
> *I think I know enough of hate*
> *To say that for destruction ice*
> *Is also great*
> *And would suffice.*

FIRE AND ICE
ROBERT FROST

The subject in this context creates an allusion to the Biblical account of the flood and the prophesy that the next destruction will come by fire, not water. While the allusion refers to the Biblical story of the flood and the second destruction by fire, the poem plays on destruction by ice, which would come "if it had to perish twice." So Frost's order of destruction is fire then ice, while the Bible's is water then fire.

M-2   The theme of the poem is built around the allusion, and unless the reader knows the story of Noah and the surrounding associations of hate and desire, "Fire and Ice" cannot be as meaningful, although it will make sense on the literal reading.

M-3   In "Fire and Ice," then, Frost uses the story of Noah with the associations of hate and desire as a base from which he creates his own version; we say, therefore, that the poem alludes to the Biblical account. Thus any event or story which happened outside the realm of the poem but to which the poem has some reference can be called an *allusion*.

ADVANTAGES OF ALLUSION

M-4   The poetical advantage of allusion is immense: simply by mentioning or even suggesting reference to an outside event, the poet brings that complete story to bear on the poem. By using an allusion the poet can bring to the reader's mind an outside historical or literary event, thereby associating this event with the poem. Tremendous economy in imagery can be achieved through allusion because a poet need only mention or infer an event in order to have the entire incident brought to readers' minds and applied to his poem. With "Fire and Ice," for example, everything which the reader remembers about the Biblical account will serve as a foil to the poem, and for some readers, even Dante's "Inferno" will be meaningful.

DANGERS OF ALLUSION

M-5   There are, however, two dangers with allusion which the poet must seriously consider before using it. First, the reader may not recognize that an allusion is being used, and if the poem depends on it for effect, the poet would have been better off to have used another device.

M-6   Second, even if the reader does recognize the allusion, he may have misinterpreted that story, in which case it would be misapplied to the poem, or he may only have remembered unimportant aspects (unimportant to the poem at any rate) of the alluded story. An example of the later danger might be for a reader to remember the episode of Joseph's coat of many colors, when the poem's reference was to his attempted seduction by Potiphar's wife.

M-7   Although recognizing allusions is a problem in any poetry, it has become especially difficult in some modern poetry because poets have turned to obscure allusions, some of which are not even found in western culture. Because many allusions in modern poetry are obscure and difficult to understand even after being recognized, scholars have adopted the task of searching for the sources of allusions and making them available to readers in anthologies and annotated editions. By going to the source of an allusion, scholars can learn about the event and give the important aspects of it.

M-8   Inexperienced explicator-analysts, like professional scholars, must proceed by suspecting everything of being a potential allusion; they must check out every likely reference before making an assumption that it is or isn't an allusion. The most common allusions in English poetry may be found in the Bible, classical literature and mythology, and in other English poems or classics of world literature. But allusions are by no means restricted to these, and readers should search wherever necessary for the basic sources.

RECOGNIZING ALLUSION

M-9   There are two methods that will help the reader to begin recognizing allusion when it is used, but beyond these, the reader can only rely on his general knowledge and the knowledge of more experienced critics. (A good explicator must be familar with the Bible, Greek mythology, Shakespeare, and Milton before he can expect to do anything much with allusion. The reason for this is that most traditional poetry in English was written for a readership with the kind of classically educated background that would make for familiarity with these.)

M-10   In spite of the difficulties, the reader can first begin looking for allusion in proper names or synonyms for proper names. Since there is seldom much other advantage in giving names to personae in poems, proper names are usually used to indicate some allusion, except in poems which strive for an informal tone or in narrative poems. A second indication that allusion is being used occurs when something does not fit exactly into a literal reading of the poem. For example, consider the following two stanzas:

> *The host with someone indistinct*
> *Converses at the door apart,*
> *The nightingales are singing near*
> *The Convent of the Sacred Heart,*
>
> *And sang within the bloody wood*
> *When Agamemnon cried aloud,*
> *And let their liquid siftings fall*
> *To stain the stiff dishonoured shroud.*

FROM:
SWEENEY AMONG THE NIGHTINGALES
T. S. ELIOT

There are three places which are confusing on the literal level, and these along with *someone indistinct, nightingales, Convent,* and *Agamemnon* must be checked for allusion. They are: *door apart, sang within a bloody wood,* and *stiff dishonoured shroud.*

M-11   Since we do not usually think of conversations occurring in a door apart, or of singing occurring in a bloody wood, or of staining a dishonored shroud, we should suspect these unusual locutions of referring to some outside events, and we should check them. They may not be functioning as allusions here, but we must first check and disqualify them on that ground before assuming they are not allusions. Other obvious places for allusion would be *nightingales, Convent,* and *Agamemmon.*

M-12   Checking for elements of the dramatic situation which do not at first glance seem to fit together will help in recognizing allusions, along with checking on proper names.

APPLYING ALLUSION

M-13   Recognizing the allusion, however, is only the first (often unappreciated) step in explicating the poem; applying it is, of course, the real object in recognizing it.

M-14   In order to understand the allusion, the reader should go to its source, and while poets usually try to use the force of the entire event and not parts from it, the reader will gain great advantage in knowing enough details so that he can see what aspects of the allusion are important to the poem. However, in interpreting the allusion, the explicator should concentrate on the overall theme, purpose, and consequences of the allusion as related to the poem.

Some allusions are as important for the connotative value they have, or for the cumulative layers of reaction that our culture has built around the event alluded to, as much as for the details of the event itself. For example, in "Fire and Ice," the Biblical prophecy of another day of judgment or doomsday has overshadowed the Western world for so long that it has become the reason for the existence of several apocalyptic religious groups which anticipated world destruction, and the poem uses the weight of this fear as well as the tradition of the Flood to work its effectiveness. Thus the importance of the allusion is not only in the significance of the event, but also in the reaction which the culture has had to it. Explicators must be aware of both the event and the most general reactions to it. but usually they would interpret this in the most general rather than in special or specific terms.

FUNCTIONS OF ALLUSION

M-15   Usually allusion functions in a manner similar to symbol in that it affects the intellect rather than the senses; it usually operates on the level of an abstraction. Although the emotional effects of the poem may be influenced or even permeated with the general cultural reaction to the allusion being made, the allusion itself usually serves as indicator to the theme rather than contributor to the emotion. In that respect, its function may be similar to that of the symbol.

M-16   There are two principal ways in which allusion affects theme. The first, as in "Fire and Ice," occurs when the allusion acts as a foil (background) for the entire poem. When the poet uses the allusion as a foil, he attempts to use the similarities and differences between the poem and the original event to emphasize his theme.

M-17   Basic things to look for with allusions, then, are the similarities and differences between the poem and the event. The similarities and differences will usually emphasize those aspects of the theme which the poet deems important.

M-18   The second basic use of allusion — and it is possible for both uses to occur within the same allusion — is to enrich a particular section within the poem, rather than to act as a Foil to the entire poem.
       An example in which both uses occur is this:

> *With the voices singing in our ears, saying*
> *That this was all folly.*

FROM: JOURNEY OF THE MAGI
T. S. ELIOT

The Biblical account of the wise men's journey to the Nativity serves as a foil for the entire poem, but there is a particular section of the allusion which serves this particular section of the poem. We know from the Bible that the angels sang: "Glory to God in the Highest, and on Earth Peace, Goodwill to men." But in Eliot's account the "voices" (not angels) "said" that the journey was all Folly. The allusion serves this segment in two ways: first, the Biblical story is a foil to the poem's story, and the differences between the universal response to the Coming and that of Eliot's wise men reinforces the theme of the poem. Second, and more particularly, the difference between a specific part of the event and the poem emphasizes and supports what the Magi felt about the journey.

M-19   Image, metaphor, symbol, and allusion may function separately, each contributing to the poem in a different way, or one may function as all four. The allusion to the "voices" in "Journey of the Magi," for example forms the image of the angels singing to the shepherds watching their flocks by night; but they could also symbolize the Birth, the word of God, or the saving of man's soul, or the mockery of unbelieving mankind.

M-20   We can say that a suggestion from the poet can function in separate ways, or in four ways at the same time: as image, metaphor, symbol, and allusion.

   Image and metaphor rely principally on the reader's emotional response to sensory perception, while symbol and allusion depend upon the intellectual assocations which the reader can bring to the poem. Although one is by no means exclusive of the other, image and metaphor rely on emotion while symbol and allusion rely on the reader's intellectual response.

Example/self-check

M-21   Let us discuss the possibilities for allusion, symbol (C-6), and equivocation (F-9) in the following poem:

> Gather ye rose-buds while ye may,
>   Old Time is still a-flying;
> And this same flower that smiles to day
>   Tomorrow will be dying.
>
> The glorious lamp of heaven, the Sun,
>   The higher he's a-getting;
> The sooner will his race be run,
>   And nearer he's to setting.
>
> That age is best which is the first,
>   When youth and blood are warmer;
> But being spent, the worse, the worst
>   Times, still succeed the former.
>
> Then be not coy, but use your time;
>   And while ye may, go marry;
> For having lost but once your prime;
>   You may for ever tarry.

TO THE VIRGINS,
TO MAKE MUCH OF TIME
ROBERT HERRICK

M-22   Equivocation is the property of a word which allows several of its meanings to be applicable in one situation. Look up the following words and determine how they function equivocably:

gather:	gather:
(1.)	(1.) to put together
(2.)	(2.) to voluntarily come together

may:
(1.) (verb:)
(2.) (verb:)
(3.) (noun:)
(4.) (noun:)

may:
(1.) to have permission (v.)
(2.) to express ability or power (v.)
(3.) maiden (n.)
(4.) a month in spring (n.)

dying:
(1.)
(2.)

dying:
(1.) the end of life
(2.) sexual release

lost:
(1.)
(2.)

lost:
(1.) no longer in possession of
(2.) not used for the best purpose

M-23   If the rose-buds are the virgins, then what does the rose-bud image specifically symbolize? _____ How is this symbolic meaning reinforced by the visual image? _____ .

It symbolizes female sexuality. The shape of the bud as it opens, and by extension the bees transferring nectar, imagistically and symbolically represent the vagina.

M-24   The Sun obviously symbolizes the passing of time, but since the poem is about sexuality and youth, it also symbolizes _____ sexuality, in which case it symbolically "sets" into the _____ . He gets higher in sexual terms, but he is also getting higher in his prime, after which he won't be able to "die" as well.

male
female

M-25   The race which the Sun takes alludes to the Greek myth of _____ , who drove a chariot which pulled the Sun across the sky. But the race is also a sexual race; the course is the female; and by winning the race he becomes old; by losing it he spends his sex.

Apollo

M-26 (a)   Consider, and then reconsider analytically, the question "To whom is the poem addressed?" From the title and the stanzas, what evidence do we have that the poem is addressed to females? _____ . What evidence that it is addressed to males? _____ .

At first glance we assume that *Virgins* in the title means females, but no evidence in the poem supports this. Much of the imagery in the stanzas seems addressed to young men who are losing their sexual prowess.

M-26 (b)   In what two senses might we interpret the
title phrase "To the Virgins" which might influence our
decision about this basic question? _____.

"To the Virgins" could be
a cry like "To the Battle-
ments" addressed to young
men, as well as an apparent
dedication to virgin females.

AN EXPLICATION OF IMAGERY, SYMBOL, AND ALLUSION IN JAMES DICKEY'S "IN THE MOUNTAIN TENT"

A Partial Explication

I am hearing the shape of the rain
Take the shape of the tent and believe it,
Laying down all around where I lie
A profound, unspeakable law.
I obey, and am free-falling slowly.

Through the thought-out leaves of the wood
Into the minds of animals.
I am there in the shining of water
Like dark, like light, out of Heaven.

I am there like the dead, or the beast
Itself, which thinks of a poem —
Green plausible, living, and holy —
And cannot speak, but hears,
Called forth from the waiting of things,

A vast, proper, reinforced crying
With the sifted, harmonious pause,
The sustained intake of all breath
Before the first word of the Bible.

At midnight water dawns
Upon the held skulls of the foxes
And weasels and tousled hares
On the eastern side of the mountain
Their light is the image I make

As I wait as if recently killed
Receptive, fragile, half-smiling,
My brow watermarked with the mark
Of the wing of a moth

And the tent taking shape on my body
Like ill-fitting Heavenly clothes.
From holes in the ground comes my voice

> In the God-silenced tongue of the beasts.
> *"I shall rise from the dead,"* I am saying.

The controlling image in Dickey's poem is one of life through creation, or through the poet's creative process, and as the poet becomes at one with nature and the universe through his imagination, he discovers that the source of man's creation is the source to which he will return after death. Dickey fuses images from nature familiar to all woodsmen with allusions from the Bible, Greek mythology, and Dante as he demonstrates in Christian terms the Romantic's notion that imagination is the bridge between man and nature.

As the poem opens, the narrator is transforming a literal experience — lying on one's back in a puptent listening to the rain — into a mystical experience. The sound of the rain as it pounds the canvas, then runs down the top and sides of the tent, leads the narrator to believe that the tent has disappeared so that only a tent of water, in the same shape as the canvas tent, stands above him. The transformation of images from an ordinary puptent set miserably in the dark and rain into a liquid enclosure is essential to the poem because it establishes a mystical and symbolic departure from the dramatic situation.

For the narrator, who believes in the power of mysticism, the tent of water is becoming holy, and the image begins to fade into a symbolic baptismal service. The narrator is enclosed in his tent of water in the same way one is submerged in water during baptism; thus, in the first two lines, the narrator becomes a believer, and because he is, the tent can take on further religious significance; not only has the image of water pounding a puptent become holy water for baptism, but the service has transformed the tent into a holy place, like the Old Testament "Holy of Holies" where only the high priest and God dwelled. From the Holy of Holies in Biblical mountain tents came the laws which governed the people; from Dickey's mountain tent comes the law of the universe; a law so profound that, like the profound laws which came to the high priest, it cannot be spoken. However, unlike the high priest's laws, the law which comes to the tent is not "laid down" by some higher authority but "lays down" with the narrator. Thus the narrator and the law, now personified into an animal, seem to be lying together in some sort of harmonious understanding. The law is unspeakable, because, as the poem later reveals, the tongues of the animals have been "God-silenced."

The image in line 5 takes us from the tent to the creation imagery introduced in the second stanza. Like the laws issued from the high priest which could not be discussed, only obeyed, the subject obeys the law of the universe. The image of *free-falling slowly* is in scientific terms, an oxymoron, since a free falling body will accelerate at a constant maximum velocity. However, the image refers to the feeling one experiences when free-falling; there seems to be no motion at all, only a completely uninhibited floating sensation (which is one reason why parachute jumpers sometimes fail to open their chutes). The journey which the subject takes is through poetry and by means of poetry, *the thought-out leaves of the wood*. We arrive at the end of the journey into the mind of the beast introduced in line 10.

The *shining of water* in line 8 recalls the baptismal submersion in the poem's opening; but the subject is no longer there in the tent; he is in the mind of the beast which is witnessing the creation of the world. According to the account in Genesis, the void from which the earth was created was the waters, and God's first commandment was to create light from darkness. Not until the light was created could the waters shine, and the image we have in line 8 is the first light reflecting from the void of waters. The beast is watching the first steps of the process which will destroy him. The next step in the creation is the dividing of the light from darkness, an image which is picked up in line 9, so that Biblically the poem is moving closer to the creation of the earth (line 9 also suggests the angels of light and darkness).

In stanza three Dickey depicts the image of the beast waiting to be created. Like the dead who will be judged on doomsday, the beast has finally been called from waiting. Perhaps Dickey had in mind the specific Roman myth of the creation, in which a monster-like beast is split in half to form the heavens and earth. The beast is mute; it cannot cry out as God will cry out in the next stanza, but the beast, which is now personified into a bard (the narrator and the beast have become one), can hear the sounds of the creation and can know from what source the creation was derived. The beast (i.e., narrator) knows he is part of a poetic vision that concerns his life before creation and the life to which he will return when he rises from the dead.

The narrator, still like the dead or the beast before creation, hears the word of the Lord as He begins to speak the commandments. The image is also of birth — the birth of the world. A new born child gets its first breath by crying, but between the cry and the first breath is a harmonious pause in the process of creation. The world is born, and the narrator through the persona of the beast, is present at the creation of mankind.

Consistent with the Christian paradox of life through death, the small animals (foxes, weasels, hares), whose heads are apparently held on stakes where hunters have put them, are to be resurrected or reincarnated. (Here perhaps there may be a far-fetched allusion to the story of the Gautama Buddha's hare, who sacrificed himself as food for his master and was hence reincarnated eternally.) They will be resurrected *at midnight* when the *water dawns* as a life-symbol, bringing new light and life to the dead. The mystical light they emit arises out of the knowledge the narrator has gained through his experience in the tent, and this light will form the source for man's image. If we apply the Biblical allusion that man was created in God's image, we can say by extension that the animals are also made in the image of God. The narrator, like the animals who will arise from the dead, awaits his resurrection too. He is waiting as the beast or the animals wait, knowing their re-creation will return them to their beginning. The moth is a symbol of the ephermeral and the watermark is either the mark of death or may simultaneously refer to the baptismal water level, the whole symbol in any case referring to a mark placed on man at the creation. Yet both the animals and the narrator are now expectant and hopeful in face of their physical death because they intuitively know that their resurrection will come. The tent now becomes a burial tent, but not in the same meaning as before the experience of the poem. The burial clothes do not fit the narrator now. Like the simonists in Dante's *Inferno* who reversed the value of religion, the subject's moans come from within the holes. The image of the eighth circle of Hell can be taken further. Geryon, the guardian of this circle, is a three-bodied beast with one head who provides Dante a bridge over the immense void to a circle where Virgil has warned Dante not to speak to the souls.

If the narrator is conscious of his communion with the animals, he is also aware of his role as poet. It is *Through the thought-out leaves of the wood* that the initial departure into the minds of animals was possible, and line 23 tells us that *their light is the image I make*, which, for the poet, is more than the source for casting his own image; it is also the act of creating a poem, and through the act of making images the poet has been able to combine mystical belief and knowledge. The beast of creation — the source of the world and the poem — presents for us, and the poet, the possibility of salvation through imagination.

Figures of Speech

In addition to the most frequently used figures of speech, *images* (B-1 ff) and *metaphors* (B-26 ff), and the less often used *paradox* (G-1 ff), *hyperbole* (G-9 ff), and *irony* (G-13 ff), there are three other basic figures which have at one time or another been important in the literary tradition. They are *personalification, allegory,* and *metonymy*.

PERSONIFICATION

N-1　*Personification* consists of giving human characteristics to an object or idea. When human characteristics are applied to nonhuman elements in the poem, we say that personification has occurred. The objects or ideas may be depicted in completely human terms, or they may possess most of their own characteristics with only reference to human-like (or "anthropomorphic") qualities. When human emotions are applied to objects incapable of sustaining them, the poet is said to have created a "pathetic fallacy." Referring to the sea as "cruel" constitutes a pathetic fallacy, although the sea may not be personified in the poem.

N-2　The degree to which the object is personified may vary from being depicted completely in human terms to maintaining most of its own characteristics. The following example demonstrates how complete personification occurs:

> Sometimes whoever seeks abroad may find
> Thee sitting careless on a granary floor,
> 　Thy hair soft-lifted by the winnowing wind;
> Or on a half-reaped furrow sound asleep,
> 　Drowsed with the fume of poppies, while thy hook
> 　　Spares the next swath and all its twined flowers:
> And sometimes like a gleaner thou dost keep
> 　Steady thy leaden head across a brook;
> Or by a cider-press, with patient look,
> 　Thou watchest the last oozings hours by hours.

FROM: TO AUTUMN
JOHN KEATS

The person addressed here seems to be a woman because we are given a description of some looks and acts that seem feminine. But what the poet is actually attempting to describe is the season of autumn, which he attempts by comparing features which he finds common to both the season and a woman.

N-3　Although the description in the example involves a woman, Keats is actually using her characteristics to define the season by a comparative method. Obviously this type of personification is closely related to metaphor since it compares and blends two objects, but not all personification is so metaphorical. Consider the following lines, for example:

> One can see what will trouble
> This sleep of mine, whatever sleep it is.
> Were he not gone,
> The woodchuck could say whether it's like his
> Long sleep, as I describe its coming on,
> Or just some human sleep.

> FROM: AFTER APPLE-PICKING
> ROBERT FROST

The woodchuck is allowed to keep his own identity but is given the power of speech, and because of the low level of personification, the metaphorical force is limited.

N-4   One difference between personification and metaphor is that with metaphor the poet identifies both objects and compares their characteristics, while with personification the characteristics of one become that of the other, so that there is only one object present, which takes on human characteristics.

Uses for Personification

N-5   Poets use personification for a number of reasons, but usually it serves one of two functions: to make an image more vivid (or to make the reader identify with the image), or to demonstrate the difference between the domain of man and the domain of nature and objects.

N-6   Personification can make images more vivid by urging the reader to identify human feelings with the image; it can also be used effectively to show differences between people and objects. In "To Autumn," for example, Keats uses personification to show how men ravish nature in much the same way as they ravish women; had Keats not used personification, the image would have been much less convincing. In "After Applepicking" Frost uses just enough personification to make the woodchuck and man comparable creatures before using irony (G-13) to demonstrate how different they really are.

N-7   A variation which lies somewhere between personification and imagery attributes animate or animal qualities, rather than human qualities, to objects or concepts. For example, consider the following stanza:

> The yellow fog that rubs its back upon the window-panes
> The yellow smoke that rubs its muzzle on the window-panes
> Licked its tongue into the corners of the evening,
> Lingered upon the pools that stand in drains,
> Let fall upon its back the soot that falls from chimneys,
> Slipped by the terrace, made a sudden leap,

And seeing that it was a soft October night,
Curled once about the house, and fell asleep.

FROM: THE LOVE SONG OF J. ALFRED PRUFROCK
T. S. ELIOT

Here the fog is depicted in the image of a cat, and while this is not technically personification, it functions in a similar manner. This sort of personification usually serves as a linking device between man and the idea because it gives life to lifeless objects. And like personification, it makes some images much more vivid, since people can identify closely with animate qualities.

ALLEGORY

N-8   *Allegory* is a figure of speech which lies somewhere between personification and metaphor; it is an abstraction represented in concrete imagery, almost always in the form of a humanized character.

N-9   While personification is used to make an image vivid, allegory is used to make a concept or abstraction vivid with concrete imagery and animate features. Gluttony, for example, might be allegorized by a character who eats all the time while Christian Love might be allegorized by a character who does charitable deeds.

N-10   Allegory, then, takes an abstraction — usually an ideal or the antithesis of it — and puts it in the form of a human being.

Uses for Allegory

N-11   The traditional use for allegory is to make it possible for the poet to show how abstract ideas can affect real people who are in contact with them, or how abstract emotions affect each other within a human being.

N-12   By putting an allegorized character with real people in a real life situation, the poet can demonstrate how ideas affect people, or by putting together several allegorized characters who stand for different concept, the poet can dramatize what happens when conflicting ideas come in contact; e.g., what happens when good comes in contact with evil.

N-13   Allegory works on two levels: the literal, in which the story is complete and sensible without further interpretation, and on the allegorical, in which the poet endeavors to convey religious, moral, political, personal, or satiric principles by showing how the abstractions interact with each other.

N-14   On the literal level of an allegorical poem, the story presumably makes sense in some sort of human terms; i.e., what happens to the characters as people, not as abstractions or concepts would be a complete and sensible tale, although it may sound more like a fairy-tale than real-life situation, since abstractions in human form are normally one-dimensional.

On the allegorical level, however, the poet hopes to teach religious, moral, political, personal, or satirical principles by showing how the abstractions interact with each other or with people.

N-15   Obviously there must be some correlation between the literal and allegorical levels, but it is the latter which interests the poet and is the only reason for using allegory. Thus, vivid imagery would almost necessarily be a waste of effort, and as a result, allegory has generally been a simplistic sort of writing. Thus only the allegorical level is important to explication, although the literal dramatic situation is a necessary element of what happens to the concepts once they intereact with each other. For showing the relationship among the characters on the allegorical level, an understanding of what concepts each character stands for will usually take care of most of the interest of the explication.

N-17   When explicating allegory, we must first define the concept for which each character stands, and then show on the allegorical level the relationship between them and the outcome of their interaction.

N-18   Poems which rely completely on allegory have traditionally sacrificed the other poetical devices, though they need not have done so, and this combined with the highly self-righteous attitudes which allegorical poets seem to possess has given allegory bad connotations.

N-19   Because of its bad reputation, few modern poets will rely on allegory, although some allegorical suggestions are included in a number of poems.

N-20   Serious modern poetry never relies completely on allegory, but it may have overtones of allegorical possibilities only to give the reader something to play with on a close reading of the poem. When explicating modern poems which suggest allegorical possibilities, we should not attempt to interpret them on the allegorical level because almost certainly the poet does not intend for that level to exist; what he does intend is that the reader will take the poem as a serious probing into human dilemmas and abstractions.

N-21   While an allegorical figure represents an abstraction, it is not symbolic; it forms a one-to-one correspondence between the allegorical character and his abstraction or concept. Unlike personification, which attempts to give depth to one image by showing how it corresponds to another, allegory only tries to make a concept vivid in order to make the concept more palatable to an audience awaiting instruction in the methods of a particular philosophy.

N-22   Because allegorical poets know all the answers and wish to teach rather than explore, allegory makes little attempt to deepen the concepts it treats, only to make those concepts vivid, and there is always a simple correspondence between the abstraction and the character. With symbolism, however, the poet attempts to add depth to his theme. In "The Listeners," (C-45) for example, the Traveller may be symbolic of mortal man who is travelling from birth to death, but he does not allegorize good, or fear, or beauty, or any other one particular quality; he is a composite of all the forces exerted on man, not just one.

METONYMY

N-23   *Metonymy* and *synecdoche* are figures of speech which function similarly to each other: metonymy is the use of a closely related idea for the idea itself, such as saying "the crown" to mean the king.

N-24   When an object which is closely related to the idea comes to stand for the idea itself, then we call it *metonymy*. When a part of the object stands for the entire object, such as using "heart" to mean the man, we call it *synecdoche*.

N-25   Synecdoche is normally used as a metaphor, though it need not necessarily be. For example, when we say "he has a heart of gold" meaning that he is a kind and generous man, we are using synecdoche and making a metaphor by comparing a heart to gold, which we presumably treasure.

N-26   Metonymy and synecdoche are used in poetry to emphasize a particular part of the whole or one particular aspect of it. For example, consider the following lines:

> *Then we came to a tavern with vine-leaves over the lintel,*
> *Six hands at an open door dicing for pieces of silver,*
> *And feet kicking the empty wine-skins.*

> FROM: THE JOURNEY OF THE MAGI

There the poet wishes to call attention to the part of the body performing the action. In the example, hands and feet stand for the entire man because that is the part of the body which the poet wished to emphasize; these lines are, therefore, an example of synechdoche.

N-27   Metonymy and synecdoche recognize that different parts of the body are associated with different qualities and activities of man, and they usually work in symbolic terms. In the example, for instance, hands and feet are used to depict men who do not use their hearts and brains. Both figures are usually associated with a particular quality about a man which the poet wishes to emphasize. Thighs, for example, might connote the sexuality of a woman; whereas breast might connote her softness or her maternal instincts.

Putting the Parts Together—The Explication as Synthesis

Twentieth century criticism has tended to be highly analytical, and one result has been that many readers exposed to detailed analysis have lost sight of the poem as a whole. Once the reader or critic schooled in twentieth century critical methods gains insight into a poet's techniques, it is often impossible for him to emerge out of a technical discussion of poetry, just as it was difficult for readers and critics in the past to see beyond the poet's life and the historical influence of the work.

The best modern readers, however, realize that poetry does not become magical through analysis either of technique or of the poet's life, but through a synthesis of the poem's technical effectiveness, its historical importance and intellectual force, and the reader's emotions. Every good explication must combine these elements in the right proportions in an attempt to determine honestly what the poem means and how it achieves its meaning. Of course, the reader must understand the parts before he can synthesize them, but once that understanding has been completed, analysis should stop as the reader works toward seeing how everything fits together.

Synthesis ⫴ through Explication

The example that follows attempts to show how a useful explication goes beyond the stage of detailed analysis of poetic technique or biographical background. Either kind of analysis by itself will not contribute much toward a richer or more enjoyable experience of a poem. However, we can show how these component analyses, when carefully combined with a view of the poem as a total experience, can help readers understand and enjoy the poem more fully.

PREPARING FOR A SYNTHESIZING EXPLICATION

Let us make a careful reading and re-reading of the Yeats poem below, trying to note as much as possible about our emotional reactions and understandings of it. We can then consider whether there are some potential questions or issues that the poem raises for us or other readers, questions that might reward more careful exploration for a richer experience of the poem, or issues or aspects of it which might not be immediately lucid to a first reader. The poem is "An Irish Airman Foresees His Death."

> *I know that I shall meet my fate*
> *Somewhere among the clouds above;*
> *Those that I fight I do not hate,*
> *Those that I guard I do not love;*　　　4
>
> *My country is Kiltartan Cross,*
> *My countrymen Kiltartan's poor,*
> *No likely end could bring them loss*
> *Or leave them happier than before.*　　　8
>
> *Nor law, nor duty bade me fight,*
> *Nor public men, nor cheering crowds,*
> *A lonely impulse of delight*
> *Drove to this tumult in the clouds;*　　　12
>
> *I balanced all, brought all to mind,*
> *The years to come seemed waste of breath,*
> *A waste of breath the years behind*
> *In balance with this life, this death.*

W. B. YEATS

Every responsive reader of a serious poem encounters some questions that will need investigating. For example, consider the following lines of inquiry for this poem:

1. Perhaps one of the most important properties of the poem is the personality of the voice speaking. What are his attitudes toward death, the war, flying, patriotism?
2. Although "Ireland" isn't specifically mentioned in the poem, the title tells us that it is important that this is an Irish airman. Does the speaker consider himself "Irish"? Does he have any sense of "country"?

3. Flying is obviously important to the airman. Is it possible to determine why he flies? Is it for glory, or the thrill? If the airman "Foresees" that he will die, why doesn't he try to avoid death by staying on the ground?

4. Since the poem is written in first person singular and functions as interior monologue, the sound of the speech helps characterize the speaker. Is the voice lyrical, or sad, or literary, or educated? What kinds of words does the speaker use? Is the rhythm highly passionate or rebellious? If not, does the lack of emotion tell us about the speaker?

5. Does it seem important that the poem was written during World War I, but after the Irish Rebellion?

6. Are there places in the poem which suggest symbol or allusion? How does the poet use image and metaphor?

7. What is Yeats' attitude toward the Irish airman? Does he feel sorry for him? Is he trying to evoke sympathy, pity, or fear from the reader? Do you feel sad because the airman is going to die? The poem was written for the airman's mother after his death. How do you think she felt upon reading the poem? Is this a highly personal poem which is more meaningful to the mother than to a person who never knew the pilot, Robert Gregory, or can the general reader identify with it?

For many readers it is quite possible that answers to the preceding questions will not be immediately clear; for most readers, it would be wise to approach issues like these in a systematic way. Here are some steps which can be taken to analyze systematically and then synthesize the elements of the poem. Those steps include the following (most of which are considered in more detail in the next chapter):

— carefully reading the poem

— establishing the dramatic situation and point of view

— seeing the images and metaphors, symbols, allusions, and determining how they function

— hearing the sound of the lines and words

— noting the poem's balance, structure, and prosodic devices

— placing the poem in its historical context

— correlating the first six steps

A Sample Explication

In the following explication of "An Irish Airman Foresees His Death," George Newtown has carefully explained every aspect of the poem without becoming pedantic. Mr. Newtown's critical ideas are especially effective because the poem itself is not vague or obscure; most readers can readily see the "meaning" of "An Irish Airman Foresees His Death"; yet the explication is still valuable because it articulates for us how the poet was able to portray successfully a complex and interesting character whose attitude toward life and death captivates readers. Although we may or may not agree with Mr. Newtown's final opinions, it is well worthwhile to see if this explication clarifies our present understanding of the poem, or provokes some new ideas about it.

EXPLICATION OF "AN IRISH AIRMAN"

George Newtown

Before entering Yeats' poem "An Irish Airman Foresees His Death" and examining its parts, it might be wise to make those observations of form and origin which can be applied to the poem as a whole. The work might be fit into the loose classification of versifying known as the occasional poem — one written on a particular occasion, celebrating a particular event, in this case, in honor of the death of Major Robert Gregory, son of Lady Gregory, Yeats' patron. This poem is less an occasional piece than its sister poems written for the same purpose in *The Wild Swans at Coole*, most noticeably "In Memory of Major Robert Gregory" and "The Sad Shepherd." In fact, if it did not come in such a cluster of poems I would probably not even consider calling it an occasional poem. Though written in a dramatic mode, this poem differs widely from most occasional poetry; "The Sad Shepherd", for example, takes its place in a long line of traditional pastoral laments. There is a justifiable doubt that a dramatic monologue could be considered an occasional poem; this doubt is lessened by a cognizance of the post-Browning propensity for dramatic poetry in almost any type of verse.

Traditionally, the occasional poem was a duty expected by a partron, and Yeats, in fact, made no break with this tradition. Since Lady Gregory was his patron, he was, if not obligated, at least expected, to make some expression of regret at her son's death. Of course, as Robert Gregory was his friend, Yeats probably would have written something anyway under the circumstances. It might be this sort of personal involvement, somehow combined with the artist's personal remove, which made Yeats' occasional poetry more than just studied utterance written "on the occasion of . . ."; however, "The Irish Airman" does not seem to exhibit Yeats' personal involvement. The poet is not present expressing his own feelings at his friend's death. The supposed death has not even occurred in the dramatic situation, although the idea of death does play a large part in the poem; the voice is not that of Yeats, and the tone is hardly one of lamentation. Where, then, is the personal involvement? The poet is not present expressing his own feelings, but, since the poem is a dramatic monologue, his presence is felt through the figure of the persona, Gregory; Yeats in some sense *becomes* Gregory. This could well be the most intimate form of personal involvement.

Just as we encountered some difficulty seeing the poem as an occasional piece, we might also have some reservations about calling it a dramatic monologue, since that categorization presupposes the presence of a listener in some way affecting the narration. Here, if a listener is present, he never really affects the persona. The Irish airman might as well be in the process of thinking to himself, except that the thoughts expressed exhibit no real *process* of thinking; rather, they seem the crystallization of former thought. Thus the poem seems an *apologia* articulated in soliloquy form, an interior monologue which strengthens the speaker's earlier-formed resolve.

In form, "An Irish Airman Foresees his Death" is a relatively short work: It is a continuous sixteen-line poem arranged in four quatrains, each rhyming *abab*. The base meter is iambic tetrameter, with very rare counterpointing; hence, any small variations become increasingly important. There is a strict syllabic control as well as a phenomenally high occurrence of monosyllabic lines (four out of sixteen) and monosyllabic words (eighty-five out of one hundred-five). The rhymes are all masculine and only three are disyllabic. These characteristics of diction will become more meaningful when we begin making a characterization of the speaker.

We begin our consideration where anyone ought to begin, with the title: "An Irish Air-man Foresees his Death." Although the poem is "spoken" from the "airman-conscious-ness," the title seems to have been added by an "author-consciousness" whereby the poet lets us know what he thinks to be important knowledge for understanding the poem. The persona is an airman, but not just any airman — he is an *Irish* airman. Historically we know that an Irishman at the time of this poem's setting (World War I era) was likely to be in a rather precarious position. His homeland (Ireland) was in a perpetual struggle for inde-pendence from England; yet in a larger world-view, he could be expected to side with England in the war against Germany. A man fighting under such conditions might be ex-pected to adopt one of three positions: He could fight wholeheartedly either for Ireland or against Germany; or, he might suffer emotionally from his divided loyalties, or he could profess (and perhaps feel) no loyalty to any side, opting to fight out of necessity, a love of adventure, a sense of duty, or any of a number of other reasons. Yeats' airman falls somewhere within this third classification.

It is by no means inessential that this Irish fighter be an *airman*. The infantry certainly could not hold the romantic attraction of the air corps. Airmen, especially in this era, were the aristocratic elite of fighters, the fox-hunters of the battle-field. They seem above the petty cares of earthlings. Airmen somehow do not bleed; they are not burried in dirt; rather, they are immortalized in flaming crescents. That the persona is an airman is im portant.

Of the remainder of the words in the title, of course the *death* of the airman is the con-sideration hanging over the entire poem, and the mention of it in the title is essential. The choice of *foresees* as the verb is interesting in its astrological connotations; it adds an aura of inevitability to the event, as if the death is pre-ordained, as in fact it is, and only the manner of dying remains to be determined. It is the documentation of the determination which carries much of the interest of the poem.

The poem's first quatrain contains three monosyllabic lines. The words are common and hard. The effect is that which might accompany clipped speech: The persona appears to be in complete control of himself, to be by nature down-to-earth, rational, analytical. In the first two lines, his assessment of his situation, and apparent calmness in the face of his imminent death mark his attitude as essentially stoical and fatalistic. Since we know, externally, that the persona is a member of Ireland's young (and, for the most part, use-less) gentry, we expect (and find) an internal reflection of the ennui attendant on members of that social class. He does not exclaim excitedly, "Oh, horrors, I am going to die." In-stead, he uses an almost clinched euphemism in declaring, "I know that I shall meet my fate." (Ho, hum). The extremely regular tetrameter rhythm of the first line sets the base meter of the poem and here seems to reinforce the feeling of ennui. The second line con-tains an initial trochaic substitution, hinting that any excitement for the airman is to be found somewhere among the clouds, and not in the mere act of meeting his fate. The third and fourth lines are terse and to-the-point, and still not emotional, but still essen-tially analytical. They are rhythmically interesting in the flatness of the line, particularly the hovering accent on the first foot and the possible secondary stress on the word *not* in the last foot; this flatness in rhythm tends to further underline the airman's qualities of stoical indifference. These unemotional lines make a brief summary of the Irish fighting-man's predicament.

But the separation of this Irish airman from a "country" is brought out in the second quatrain. His country is Kiltartan Cross, not Ireland. Perhaps it is not Ireland because he thinks England's policies allow the existence of no Ireland; I think it more likely that the young lord identifies with no Ireland. He can identify only with the people on his own lands. As one of the gentry, he finds himself still attached to an outdated feudal system of local loyalties and individual responsibilities, and is unable to work up emotion for any nation. In fact, this condition perhaps explains the necessity that the airman be sacri-ficed: He exists as an anachronism, raised with fourteenth-century values in a twentieth-century world, chosing the machines of his century, but not equiped to handle them. Of his poor, he says pragmatically that the outcome of the war could hardly worsen his "people's" lot, and that it certainly would not increase their happiness — a reasonable, if somewhat pessimistic, assessment. He is not a visionary in any revolutionary sense: No "likely" political outcome could significantly change the habits or opportunities of Kiltartan's poor.

Of note in the versification of the second quatrain is the first significant use of allitera-tion, in line five: country . . . Kiltartan Cross. It is worth noting that the first alliteration of the poem consists not of scintillating sibillants, or of languishing liquids, but instead of plain cold consonants, glottals, separated from each other by two intervening syllables. Alliteration also occurs with the three *l*'s in line seven, but these liquids are hardly more romantic or decorative than the hard consonants of line five, since the second liquid is internal, in the same word as the first, and since the third is at a remove of five syllables.

The first two lines of the third stanza are interesting for their continuation of the tight, ordered, parallel structure previously established, as well as for their varied caesuras; most interesting, however, is their contrast, in both form and content, to the two lines which follow. The airman eliminates succinctly the reasons most men fight: laws, duty, states-men, mob emotion; in his now customary orderly diction and rhythms he checks them off one by one. If he remained in this pattern forever, we would undoubtedly find Major Robert truly a dull boy. Because of previous depression of rhythms and a minimum of ornamentation, the contrast of the following lines is explosive. Line eleven lilts with liquid alliteration; it also, with three disyllables, becomes the least monosyllabic line in the poem, and the disyllabic words engender excitement by breaking the feet in which they occur. The enjambment to the twelfth line maintains the excitement, as does the line's battle between meter and rhythm. It has the most irregular rhythm of any line in the poem. There are only three real stresses in the line: *drove . . . tumult . . . clouds;* and the first occurs in an initial trochee. The effect of the line is much like that so loved by airmen — that disequilibrium felt on entering turbulence; it is also the feeling most likely to make inexperienced travellers air-sick. In the estimation of others, the young gentle-men has had an enviable youth; but he no longer finds excitement there. All his life, perhaps, he has ridden to the hounds, but he can no longer throw his heart over a fence and jump after it. The airplane is different: It is new — still aristocratic, but not weighted down by stodgy tradition; he is not sated with flying; hence, he opts for his life.

If we regard the third quatrain as the poem's semifinal flourish or cadenza, then we would see the fourth quatrain as a kind of coda, or final restatement of the poem's movement prior to the inevitable conclusion of death. Its first line brings us back down to earth, back to the rationality exhibited earlier by the persona. Here the key word is *balance.* The airman says he did not allow himself to be captured by the sole emotional appeal of the moment in the turbulent aircraft. Instead, he made a mental tally and took the option most attractive to him, despite its obvious disadvantages. The proof of his continued rationality is in lines fourteen and fifteen, in the "cross-over" or reversed parallelism of future and past in *years behind* vs. *years to come,* with the repeated *waste of breath . . . years,* a structuring as a turning point in the contrast, recognizable to students of classical rhetoric as the figure called a chiasmus. This rhetorical pattern is itself "balanced" on the parallel scales of lines thirteen and sixteen. Another proof that the man is not letting his emotions run away with him comes in realizing that his entire discourse is an ordering of previous thought, a restatement necessary to a mind needing order. He coldly reviews his decision and opts for "this life," knowing that with it comes "this death," and these near-spondees here at the end of the poem reinforce that decision. He knew the alternatives. He chose to live, knowing that death would soon come, rather than to die for the rest of a long life.

We have now come to some conclusions about a characterization of the persona. If we need any more depth in our analysis, we need only realize that during the course of the entire poem the airman has envisioned not a single concrete image. The *lonely impulse* is a fecund abstraction, but only an abstraction. The clouds are no clouds in particular. Even if we see in the last quatrain a submerged image of the balance scales (from the French balance?), it is certainly not a vivid image. This observation of lack of imagery does indeed help us characterize the airman's extreme, cold rationality, and it makes his decision for the irrational more poignant.

That the poem contains no imagery seems right for the characterization of the persona, but the important question is, can the poet "get away" with writing an image-less poem; after all, images are the stuff "real" poems are made of. I personally like this poem's approach to the characterization of its persona, even though it flies in the face of imagistic poetic tradition. I admit that image-less poetry presents almost insurmountable obstacles. If generally practiced, it could certainly mean a convenient "out" for unimaginative poets: They have written no bad poetry; whatever is dull was simply meant to characterize a dull persona. This would certainly be a dangerous tool in hands less skillful than those of Yeats. He, however, does things in the poem to make up for effacement of the images. For example, with common, colloquial diction, he builds up a tremendous rhythmic base, often depressed, though regular, so that any variation becomes vitally meaningful. Because of such accomplishments, "An Irish Airman" presents us with a subtle and interesting character study in an occassional poem that has far transcended the limitations of its occasion.

Although Mr. Newtown's presentation seems easy and uncomplicated, he has come to write this explication only after a careful analysis and synthesis process in which he thought about every poetical device, studied the circumstances surrounding the composition, and related his own emotions to the technical effectiveness of the poem. Once this was finished, he could eliminate extraneous or wrong ideas and compose his explication. In the next chapter are some steps Mr. Newtown might have taken; they can be applied to almost any English poem, and for the diligent reader, they will lead to a fuller understanding and enjoyment of poetry.

Steps Before Explicating

Here in outline form is a fairly extensive checklist of the systematic procedures that were briefly listed as steps to precede the kind of useful explication demonstrated in the last chapter. Other material in this book should be related to what is uncovered at each step, and these procedures should be regarded as part of a total effort to enrich and improve the experience of a poem for the explicator and for other readers. With this in mind, these procedures can be referred to at any time by the potential explicator as a kind of road map. These steps are applied in detail to another poem in the chapter that follows.

THE INITIAL READINGS

I. *First reading.*
1. Read the poem intuitively and emotionally, allowing it to "happen" to you as much as it will.
II. *Before re-reading the poem.*
1. Notice, but do not analyze, the form and length of the poem.
2. Consider the title and determine, if possible, whether it could function as an allusion, symbol, or poetic image.
3. Notice the date of composition or of publication, or the general era of the poet, and try to identify the poet.
III. *In re-reading the poem.*
1. Read the poem once through, noting the places where the rhymes and rhythms are easy or hard. If you have any special reaction to the poem (likes and dislikes included), jot them down when you have finished this reading. Decide what the poem means to you at this point.
2. Read the poem again, trying to smooth out the rough places. Let the natural rhythm carry the poem along. Do not worry about content at this point, but with each reading, notice as much as you can what is happening.
3. Read the poem several more times until you can read it smoothly.
IV. *After the initial readings, having formed some sense of an overall experience for the poem, you are ready to begin analysis.*

MATTERS OF OVERALL CONTROL

Dramatic Situation

1. Study the poem line by line and establish the dramatic situation as follows:
   a. What, if any, is the narrative action (e.g., a man stops by woods and watches snow fall)?
   b. How many personae appear in the poem? Do they take part in the action? To what extent?
   c. What is the relationship between the characters? Do they interact with each other?

d. Where is the setting located? What time of day or year is it? Does the time period change during the poem?

e. Is the action happening in the present, as with the narrator in "Stopping By Woods," or is the narrator remembering an incident?

f. What does the setting look like? Do the personae act in any particular manner because of it (e.g., putting on a coat because it looks like rain)?

g. Which parts of the poem are particularly concerned with dramatic situation?

h. What function does dramatic situation seem to serve? Does it add realism, surrealism, absurdity? Does it change during the poem?

i. What does the persona think of this dramatic situation?

Point of View

2. Establish point of view.

a. Who is speaking? Is he thinking, talking to himself, or addressing someone else? Is the poet speaking directly to the reader, or through a narrator?

b. Is the narrator able to understand or see everything happening to him, or does the reader know things the narrator doesn't?

c. What is the correlation between point of view and dramatic situation? Does point of view change with dramatic situation?

d. Do point of view and dramatic situation seem complete and consistent? (If not, mark the places which are confusing or unclear, because they may provide good clues about the meaning.)

Imagery

3. Locate the images and metaphors.

a. What are the concrete images (i.e., those that are formed from objects which can be touched, smelled, seen, felt, or tasted)? What do they look like? Is the image projected by the poet consistent with the physical object?

b. If the image is abstract, or so different from natural imagery that it can't be associated with a real object, then what are the properties of the image?

c. What part do dramatic situation and point of view play in the presentation of the images?

d. Are the images free or fixed? To what extent is the reader asked to form his own images?

e. Is any image repeated in the poem? How has it been changed? Is there a controlling image (e.g., dark skies appearing in each stanza)?

f. Are any images compared to each other? Do the compared images form a metaphor, or do they simply reinforce one another? Are they consistent?

g. Are the metaphors immediately lucid (e.g., her eyes are like jewels)? Do they form conceits which must be analyzed (e.g., "When the evening is spread out against the sky/Like a patient etherized upon a table")?

h. Is there any difference between the way the reader perceives the image and the way the narrator sees it?

i. What seems to be the poet's attitude toward the image (i.e., does he laugh at it as in "My mistress' eyes are nothing like the sun," or take it seriously)?

MATTERS OF CONTROLLING EMOTION: SOUND

4. Determine the sound patterns of the poem.
   a. Does this poem's sound conform to any traditional sound patterns, such as those of nursery rhymes or folk songs?
   b. Is the rhyme pleasing, harsh, emotional? Can you articulate what mood the sound put you in (fear, jocundity)? Is the sound casual or formal?
   c. What devices has the poet used for creating sound (e.g., types of words, split feet, rhyme, rhythm)?
   d. Is there a relationship between sound and meaning?
   e. Does the sound reveal a particular authorial attitude?

INTELLECTUAL CONTROL OF THE WORDS

5. Look up every substantial word in an unabridged dictionary, noting all definitions which have the slightest connection to the poem. Apply all the meanings to the poem, and note particularly those words which could be symbols or allusions. Notice any unusual liberties which the poet might have taken with words, such as making nouns out of adverbs. Check for any changes in normal syntactical patterns.

6. Determine any allusions, symbols, allegory, or paradox. Find several annotated editions which contain the poem and check the notes for possible allusions which you might have missed.

PROSODIC AND STRUCTURAL CONTROL

Variations on a Basic Meter

7. Scan the poem and note all the elements of prosody.
   a. Are there substitutions or changes in the base meter? Do these places seem especially important thematically?
   b. How has the poet used or changed the natural emphasis of his line?
   c. How and where has meter created tension in the line? What is the relation between tension and meaning?

Rhyme and Structure

8. Determine how stanza form, rhyme, and overall structure are working.
   a. Is the stanza a traditional form (see the Appendix for a chart of forms)? Is the poet adhering to or deviating from the tradition?
   b. If the form isn't traditional, how does the rhyme (if any) hold the stanza together?
   c. What type of rhyme appears? Does it follow the traditional uses for rhyme?
   d. Is the poem composed of stanzas, or is the poem stichic? Are there stanzas or verse

paragraphs which call attention to themselves, or cause the poem to progress in any particular manner?

SOME MORE SUBTLE CONTROLS ON THE POEM

9. Characterize the persona; determine if his statements can be taken at face value or whether there is a discrepency between the speaker and poet, or poet and reader (i.e., look for irony).

10. Look for paradox, hyperbole, and additional irony, and try to determine the poet's tone (attitude) toward his persona, reader, and subject matter.

CORRELATING THE CONTROLLING DEVICES IN THE POEM

11. Place the poem in historical context; check on events during the time of composition and for use of archaic language, expressions, images, or symbols. Go to the original text, or an authoritative text, to be certain that you haven't been working with an edited edition.

12. Correlate the controlling devices, seeing the poem as a composite of emotion, intellect, craftsmanship, and tradition.
    a. What ideas is the poet trying to convey?
    b. Does the poet seem sure of his position? Is he probing or preaching? Is he optimistic or pessimistic?
    c. Is the poet trying to achieve social, moral, or regligious criticism or change? If so, how does the poem relate to both the present age and the age in which it was written?
    d. Does the poem appeal primarily to the emotions, or intellect, or both?
    e. Is the poem relying especially on any particular devices for effect (e.g., sound, imagery, allusion)?
    f. Do you think the depth or meaning of the poem might change as your own experience changes?

13. List all the themes (central ideas) and motifs (smaller, recurring ideas, incidents, controlling images, or symbols), relate them back to the poem, and draw parallels between them.

AN OVERVIEW AGAIN IN PREPARATION FOR THE EXPLICATION

The Final Reading

1. Re-read the poem carefully, first as a whole, then line by line and word by word. Keep fitting the pieces together, and if all the elements are not consistent, decide if it is because the poet was unskillful, or because the explication is incomplete (as a rule, it's wiser to fault yourself than the poet). Reconsider the title. Is it of special significance? How does it relate to the poem (if at all)? Does it categorize the poem or philosophy in the poem.

2.   Read other poems by the same author, particularly those poems published in the same volume, and as much criticism as you can find or have time to read.

Applying Steps to Explication

This chapter is an extended example of how the step-by-step procedures of the last chapter may be applied systematically to a difficult poem by Robinson. The object here is to proceed carefully through the steps toward an explication, assimilating the information which we will need to synthesize our full experience of the poem into a complete explication. Before reading the critical observations that follow, the reader would greatly benefit from attempting on his own to take this poem through the step-by-step method as a preparation to absorbing the applied example offered here.

Go to the western gate, Luke Havergal,
There where the vines cling crimson on the wall,
And in the twilight wait for what will come.
The leaves will whisper there of her, and some,   4
Like flying words, will strike you as they fall;
But go, and if you listen, she will call.
Go to the western gate, Luke Havergal —
Luke Havergal.   8

No, there is not a dawn in eastern skies
To rift the fiery night that's in your eyes;
But there, where western glooms are gathering,
The dark will end the dark, if anything: 12
God slays Himself with every leaf that flies,
And hell is more than half of paradise.
No, there is not a dawn in eastern skies —
In eastern skies.   16

Out of a grave I come to tell you this,
Out of a grave I come to quench the kiss
That flames upon your forehead with a glow
That binds you to the way that you must go.   20
Yes, there is yet one way to where she is,
Bitter, but one that faith may never miss.
Out of a grave I come to tell you this --
To tell you this.   24

There is the western gate, Luke Havergal,
There are the crimson leaves upon the wall.
Go, for the winds are tearing them away, —
Nor think to riddle the dead words they say,   28
Nor any more to feel them as they fall;
But go, and if you trust her she will call.

There is the western gate, Luke Havergal —
Luke Havergal.   32

"LUKE HAVERGAL"
BY E. A. ROBINSON
COMPOSED C. 1895

STEP II-1, BEFORE REREADING

O-1   "Luke Havergal" is a strophic poem composed of four equally lengthened stanzas. Each stanza is long enough to contain a narrative, involved description or situation, or problem and resolution.

STEP II-2

O-2   The title raises several possibilities: (1) Luke Havergal could be a specific person; (2) Luke Havergal could represent a type of person; (3) the name might have symbolic, allusive, or equivocal qualities. Thus: (a) *Luke* may refer to Luke of the Bible. (b) *luke-warm* meaning indifferent or showing little or no zeal, may have a bearing here. (c) *Haver-gal* could be a play on words (which is called a pun). *Haver* means to talk foolishly. We know from the rhyme words that the "gal" is pronounced as if it had two *l*'s, but it is spelled with one *l* for no apparent reason unless it is to play at the word *gal* meaning girl. But since it is pronounced gall, meaning something bitter or severe, a sore or state of irritation, or courage, this must also be a possibility. Also, *haver* might be a play on *have a.*

STEP II-3

O-3   Composed in 1895, the poem will probably not contain archaic language unless it is deliberately used. We will check later for historical events which may have influenced the poem.

STEP III-1 AND 2, RE-READING THE POEM.

O-4   The frequent use of internal caesuras in stanzas 1 and 2 contrasts with the lack of caesuras in stanzas 3 and 4. There are many end-stopped lines and much repetition. The poem reads smoothly except for line 28 and the feminine endings on lines 11 and 12. There is a great deal of rhyme repetition, but it reads easily.

STEP IV-1, DRAMATIC SITUATION

O-5   When establishing dramatic situation and point of view the explicator must be careful to consider every detail, because the poet will be using as much economy as possible in conveying these. In the initial readings it is a good idea to take the poem line and list all dramatic possibilities, eliminating later.

O-6   Because the poet will be economizing in portraying dramatic situation and point of view, details become quite important; tense of verbs, position of the sun, time of year are examples of subtle techniques which might be used. Nothing can be overlooked, although not every possibility will contribute to the poem.

Line 1

0-7   Looking at the dramatic situation in "Luke Havergal," we can see that apparently someone is talking to Luke in line 1, and because the speaker calls him by both names we may sense that the speaker possesses some superior or else rather formal attitude about their relationship, and that the talk which they are having is not casual conversation.

0-8   In addition to knowing something about the relationship in line 1, we are also led to think, because of *go to the . . . gate,* that the persona must be near some sort of enclosed house or city. Perhaps Luke and the speaker are at some "other" gate, since the western gate is specifically pointed out.

Line 2

0-9   We learn from line 2 that the situation at the western gate is different from that elsewhere — there *vines cling crimson on the wall,* which suggests some possibilities about the dramatic situation. (Since flowers and colors are always promising symbols, they must be carefully considered later.)
    The vines in line 2 could provide valuable information about the dramatic situation, except that in line 2 the clues are ambiguous. Are the vines perennial, in which case their crimson color suggests that the season is late summer or autumn, or is crimson their natural color when in full bloom? Also, are they grape vines (grapes carry numerous connotations and symbolic values), and are the vines desirable? All of this in line 2 is ambiguous and we cannot know for sure. What we do know is that there is a wall — a barrier which closes something in and something out.

Line 3

0-10   In line 3 the speaker again commands Luke to go and wait. Since Luke is to wait in the twilight, it is probably now daylight. All Luke must do is to be passive because whatever is to come will happen without any action on his part.

Line 4

0-11   With line 4 a third person is introduced, and we now know whom Luke is seeking and what will happen at the western gate. We also know from this line that the vines have leaves, and we can infer that crimson denotes their waning stage.

Line 5

0-12   In Line 5 the speaker continues to describe what will happen: as each leaf falls it will whisper about *her,* and some of the words will fall on Luke. But here we must question whether Luke will actually be "struck" by the leaves, or whether the leaves are being personified or being used as an image or symbol.

Line 6

O-13   In line 6 the speaker stops his prophecy and tells Luke to go. If Luke listens, *she will call,* but if he doesn't listen, what will happen? And to whom is *she* calling? And from where?

O-14   In summarizing the dramatic situation in stanza 1, we can say that the speaker is addressing Luke, but we cannot yet determine whether he is present or whether Luke is thinking to himself (interior monologue). The time is before twilight; the place is near a wall with a gate. Luke is directed to go to the gate and listen for a woman to call.

Line 9

O-15   After the opening of stanza 2, we can conclude that Luke is actually present in the poem as a figure who can act within the dramatic situation (as opposed, for example, to a poet speaking to the reader), and that Luke will go to the wall and listen. Thus, the poem seems to be a dramatic monologue, with the speaker addressing Luke.

O-16   Apparently Luke has posed some kind of question, but from the paradoxical answer we cannot yet know what the question was. We can expect that if the poem is a dramatic monologue, the silent persona's response will affect the poem's progress. The question is obviously concerned with what will be found at the western gate, but the question apparently was *not*, "Is there a dawn in the eastern skies?" The answer given is apparently not a direct answer to whatever question was asked, and this is good evidence that the directions east and west are symbolic, being injected as they seemingly are into the situation.

Line 10

O-17   In line 10 the speaker tells us that Luke's eyes contain a *fiery night*, an image and symbol to be considered later. The remainder of the stanza tells about what will happen in the west, and while the paradoxes continue to support the mysterious setting, we learn nothing more about dramatic situation.

Stanza 3

O-18   In stanza 3 we learn who the speaker is and what his relationship is to Luke. After the mysterious discourse in stanza 2, Luke has probably asked "who are you" and there is an equally mysterious reply so that we want to know if the voice speaking is a person or whether it is a spirit or Luke's imagination or conscience.

O-19   Because the voice says that he comes out of the grave, we cannot know who or what he is. He may be a person, a ghost, or only Luke's imagination or conscience. Obviously the answer will affect the dramatic situation.

O-20   In line 18 we learn that the speaker is on a particular mission: *to quench the kiss,* and we can assume that when the mission is completed he will return to the grave. This information is sudden and shocking, and because of the sharp jolt which the speaker gives us, we tend to believe him and credit him with supernatural knowledge.

Stanza 4

O-21   In stanza 4 it becomes apparent that Luke and the speaker have not been stationary during the course of the poem because the western gate is now visible; the speaker can see the leaves upon the wall (line 26).

O-22   The wind is blowing (line 27), which creates a sense of urgency, because if all the leaves are blown away they cannot whisper about *her*. The speaker gives Luke final instructions and the poem ends with the speaker again pointing toward the place where he will find his lover.

O-23   In summary, we can say that the dramatic situation establishes a set of mysterious circumstances which aren't explained or resolved on the dramatic level. Luke has been told to go to the western gate by someone who identifies himself as having come from the grave in order to quench Luke's desire. We assume that the desire is connected with the estranged woman who is, perhaps, dead. The dramatic situation doesn't tell us whether or not the commanding voice is an emissary from the woman, the devil, or merely Luke's conscience, and the dramatic situation doesn't suggest that something evil will happen to Luke at the western gate, although other elements in the poem make us afraid for him.

O-24   The poet, then, is using his dramatic situation to draw us into questions which will be answered by means other than situation; at this point, the poem is mysterious, obscure, ambigious, and deliberately misleading, which forces us into analyzing Robinson's use of the other parts of the poem. We should not, however, ever lose sight of the dramatic situation, because the poet will be playing off it in order to get at theme.

STEP IV-2, POINT OF VIEW

O-25   The unusual dramatic situation and point of view are probably being used to call attention to the theme of the poem, and the point of view is even stranger than the dramatic situation. There are a number of questions which immediately come to mind about the point of view. Whose story is this? Is the speaker a disciple of the devil seducing Luke toward evil, or is he a friend telling Luke what he knows of the grave? Does it matter how Luke reacts, or how the speaker reacts, or how we react? Why didn't Luke tell the story instead of the mysterious stranger? And of course we want to know just who is the stranger?

O-26   From a generalized study we know something about first person singular points of view (A-23), (and from lines 17 and 18 we know this poem fits the category); they tend to take the reader deep into the mind of the narrator in order to show what the narrator knows or to show his reaction to an event.

Not all poems will supply such conclusive evidence as to what person's point of view they are representing. When this is not clear we must look for other clues, and if none are available, we must work on using all possible points of view until a consistent theory can be developed.

O-27   Usually the role of the narrator in a first person poem will evolve slowly into its full dimensions; that is, the narrator will learn something in the course of the poem that will resolve a basic situation and define his role in it. Remembering that generalized study provides only a beginning for explication, we should proceed on the assumption that "Luke Havergal" may have potential to conform to the generalizations. By tentatively assuming that the poem at hand may conform to the generalizations which we have been able to make about first person singular poems, we have a norm for comparison, and even if the poem doesn't fit the pattern, we will have discovered why it doesn't, and we will come to learn more about it in the process.

O-28   What we must first do is to find out everything we can about the narrator, and one of the best ways to accomplish this is to notice what he perceives; his perceptions will help us to understand better what he relates to or desires.

O-29   In "Luke Havergal" the narrator gives us the following details about himself or the situation: (1) a sense of direction (lines 1 and 9) (2) general type and color of the vegetation but not enough to make a detailed analysis of it (line 2), (3) a pantheistic view of nature (line 4), (4) feeling of communion with the leaves and *she* (lines 5 and 6), (5) a philosophic view of the universe (stanza 2), (6) the power to *quench the kiss*, a sense of mission, and a home (the grave) (line 18), (7) special vision (line 20), (8) sense of destiny (lines 21 and 22), (9) a sense of time and eternity (lines 27-29).

O-30   Apparently the narrator can speak with confidence about the western gate, and he can objectively look at Luke to see the kiss upon his forehead, but there is very little in the poem which explicitly suggests that the speaker is a supernatural being, particularly if *the grave* is being used symbolically.

O-31   What the narrator sees and tells is not beyond the power for anyone to see; i.e., everyone has heard leaves and wind whispering, and everyone has felt something call from beyond, and if Luke is grieved over the loss of his lover he might be blind to all but one direction. Although there are suggestions there is no evidence that he is actually one of the dead, although he may symbolize the dead soul.

O-32   The importance of our uncertainty about the narrator's immortality is that while the speaker does have insight into Luke's emotional state, he is not necessarily supernatural, and the only reasons we are led to think he is from the dead are the sound of the poem, the paradoxes, and the lines which say that he has come from the grave.

O-33   The grave, however, may not literally mean that he has arisen from the dead, but may represent the dead soul or the spirit of death, and since there is no evidence that the speaker is from the dead, it is more reasonable to assume that he isn't, and that something else is taking place.

O-34   Once we can conclude that the speaker is not from the dead, we can eliminate Luke's lover, or *she*, as the speaker (*she* may not necessarily be his lover). However, because the speaker does represent some aspect of death, and because he states that "*there is yet one way to where she is,* we can infer that *she* is dead, though this is not stated. It is reasonable to conclude that it is not *she* who is speaking.

O-35   Since it is not *she* speaking, and because it is not likely that the speaker is just some friend from the dead come back to help Luke, there are only two possibilities remaining as to the role of the speaker.

The speaker must in some way either be part of Luke himself; either the voice of his thoughts, of his unconscious mind, or of a part of his past which now comes forth, or else it is some sort of "spirit of Death." It is possible, of course, that they could be synonymous, but in any event the voice is either Luke's (not talking to himself but as a voice in a dream might talk), or a spirit's.

O-36   The poem, then, is an internal dialogue in which Luke is attempting to cope with *she* who is probably dead and who was probably his lover, though neither is certain. He speaks to another persona, which is probably Luke's own spirit which has been deadened by the loss of his lover.

O-37   Once we have understood that we are looking at a man who is at the depth of despair, the dramatic situation becomes very important, because we now have reason for anxiety about what Luke is going to do; the drama of the poem suggests that he might be driving himself toward self-destruction.

O-38   The dramatic situation is not as it originally seemed; there is only one person, not two, and Luke is probably wandering — perhaps unconsciously — toward the western gate.

Luke's psychological condition permits him to look at himself as another person, and this other self is pushing Luke toward something which the reader senses is evil.

O-39   If the voice is Luke's, then much of the mystery is clarified. Luke would have known what the western gate looked like; whereas a stranger would have to have supernatural powers to know it; also Luke had probably heard the leaves whispering before, and in his derangement he could believe that someone would call to him if he would only listen.

O-40   In summary, we can say that point of view in "Luke Havergal" is essential for understanding dramatic situation, and vice-versa. Without knowing that *she* is dead and that Luke is attempting to reach her, we cannot even speculate as to whom the narrative voice in the poem belongs. By understanding that the point of view may be Luke's internal monologue (or dialogue with himself) rather than first person singular by a strange persona, we can clarify many discrepancies and begin moving closer to Robinson's theme or mood.

Consistency between Dramatic Situation and Point of View

O-41 If dramatic situation and point of view are clear, as they will be in many poems, there will be no need to include this next step in the written explication because the first two steps will have covered it, but if there is an inconsistency which cannot be explained at this point, state what it is, and anticipate where the solution might be found.

Establishing points of view cleared up most of the inconsistencies in this poem's dramatic situation, but there is still confusion about the grave and the kiss. It is easy to make the grave symbolically consistent with point of view, but this is the easy and perhaps incorrect way out, and we should look for other explanations although there may be no others.

O-42 In stanzas 1 and 2 there is no problem; the dramatic situation is simple and point of view can be reconciled since there is no evidence to prove that another person is present. But if the voice is that of Luke's other self, then why has it come from the grave, and where did the kiss come from? At this point, it isn't possible to account for these inconsistencies, but by noting them now, we can be on the alert for the answers later. It is quite possible that accounting for the inconsistencies will provide the key for the explication.

STEP IV-3, IMAGES AND METAPHORS

O-43 Finding images in poems is usually not a difficult task, although seeing their relation to the theme often is. "Luke Havergal" is imagistically difficult because the images are introduced, then re-used as the theme develops.

O-44 Most of the images in the poem are generally free. In stanza 1, for example, we form our own image of the setting and mood at the western gate; yet most readers will probably imagine some sort of mysterious or supernatural situation which is related to death or the dead. The colors, sound of the words, and particular images (vines, wall, whispering leaves) establish the relationship between the living and dead as the controlling image of the entire poem.

O-45 Within the controlling death-in-life image, which is quite free, the metaphors and conceits are more difficult to handle. Vines clinging crimson on the wall (line 2) and waiting in the twilight for something to come (line 3) are free images which require no particular treatment at this point, but in lines 4 and 5 we are forced to contend directly with whispering leaves like flying words, and there are several metaphorical possibilities for it.

First there is the common image of leaves rustling in a breeze, and in a mysterious or enchanted atmosphere it would be very easy to imagine that they are whispering. However, such a whisper would require a moderate breeze ordinarily, as a fierce wind would overpower the rustling sound of leaves. However, there is more ambiguity to the image:

> *The leaves will whisper there of her, and some*
> *Like flying words, will strike you as they fall;*

Because of the sentence ambiguity of *some,/ Like flying words, will strike* Luke, we cannot be sure how close or literal is the similarity or identity of *leaves* and *words*. Thus we cannot be completely sure whether it is leaves or words or both that may strike Luke, or whether the sight of falling leaves might be forcing him to recall words he has heard and in the past. There is a distinct metaphoric connection between leaves and words, however, and these in some way strike Luke, perhaps in a scattered and random pattern so that some words are those of an argument — perhaps in the past Luke and "her" before her death — or whether they are indeed simply random words which somehow recall "her" but do not actually say anything specific.

O-46   In Stanza 2, the poet forces us to acknowledge the light and dark images, but they are as free and obscure as the falling leaves in stanza 1. The dawn which we are asked to visualize (line 9) is clear, but immediately contrasted to *the fiery night that's in your eyes;* there is not even a free image, except as we see Luke's smoldering, almost diabolic eyes as being imagistically opposite from the glorious, refreshing dawn. Of course, *there is not a dawn* to dispel Luke's fiery night (the dawn would beat away the darkness), but without the dawn image, it would have been more difficult for us to imagine the *fiery night*.

O-47   Line 11 takes us back to the western gate, or at least to the "west" where twilight is falling. The *western glooms* become imagistic not only because we can see the twilight falling, but also because we feel Luke's despair. Twilight isn't "falling," but dark is *gathering* around him, and *glooms* doesn't denote just darkness, but also connotes Luke's emotional state.

O-48   The paradox in line 12, *The dark will end the dark* beckons us to explore it imagistically, since in the preceding lines we could visualize how the dawn would dispel the darkness, but it isn't easily possible for us to understand imagistically how darkness relieves darkness, unless one of the two "darknesses" becomes symbolic of death or Luke's gloom. Of this beckoning image, we can say that the poet has created emphasis on the line by teasing us with images which may really be symbols or paradoxes. The same thing is true for lines 13 and 14, which tempt us to try imagining how *God slays Himself* with leaves, and how *hell is more than half of paradise*.

O-49   The beginning of Stanza 3 does not demand an image so much as it serves to tell us where the narrator comes from, but we do wonder, or try to see, the narrator's method for quenching the kiss. Line 19, however, presents a free image which is as forceful as it is ambiguous. The kiss, which may be the kiss of the estranged woman, or "the kiss of death," or both, flames with a glow, which is also paradoxical. The paradox, however, forms an image which conveys the intensity of Luke's passion.

O-50   Stanza 4 returns us to the imagery of stanza 1, but now the whispering leaves take on a metaphorical extension. If the leaves are whispering words from the dead, and if the leaves are "her" words, then we feel that once the wind tears all the leaves away, there will no longer be any medium for communication between the living and the dead. This adds a sense of urgency for Luke to go to the western gate and do there what must be done.

O-51   In summary, we can say that the images in "Luke Havergal" do more than set the mood for us. They also serve an important thematic function because their ambiguities and paradoxical qualities force us to consider the theme before we can fully understand the images.

STEP IV-4, SOUND

O-52   The sound of the poem is not to be confused with tone and feeling, although it influences both. Sound is created by the stress of the syllables, types of vowels and consonants, meter, and rhyme, and it can be analyzed fairly satisfactorily by analyzing each of these elements (close analysis, however, is usually unnecessary).

O-53   In lines 1 and 2 of "Luke Havergal," for example, there are a number of plosive consonants and long vowels in addition to the internal rhyme and *c* alliteration. The cadence of these lines is slow, and they reverberate with *cling* and *crimson*. The sounds in these lines are haunting (which is consistent with the situation), and while this sound is maintained throughout, there are some special sound effects.

For example, by the last stanza Luke's inner voice knows that suicide cannot be rationalized and must be carried out on an emotional basis, but we don't know this until line 28, which phonically emphasizes this: *Not think to riddle the dead words they say.* The *l* in *riddle* rattles around so forcefully that we almost swallow the word, but we also notice how the prosody is working.

The line scans as full pentameter (which we expect by this time, since the 10 syllable line has been strictly followed):

$$\text{N\u01ddr think/ t\u00f3 r\u00edd/d\u012fe the/ d\u00e9ad w\u00f3rds/ th\u00e9y \u015bay}$$

The plosive *k* in *think* begins to sap the reader's breath, followed by the *t* and secondary stress on *to*, and finally reaching *riddle* which completely exhausts his breath. The unstressed *the* which follows *riddle* blends right into the mouthful, making a bigger mouthful rather than giving the reader a distinctive syllable which would re-establish the meter.

The last four syllables, however, are quite definite, and the consecutive stresses make this line a focal point of the poem. The sound of this line after the subtle, haunting preceding lines jars the reader before finally returning him to the western gate.

O-54   The rhythm and sound of the poem as a whole suggest an incantation; the speaker's voice is seductive and evil, which is important to the theme because we know that if Luke goes to the gate he will commit suicide, which is what the voice demands.

O-55   Through its seductive sound, the poem seems to be working the same effect on the reader as it does on Luke, i.e., we feel as Luke does that there is an urgency in going to the gate before all the leaves are blown away, and that by hearing her call our discomfort will be relieved. We are completely in sympathy with Luke, and we think that the voice speaking is attempting to help Luke. Unless we feel as Luke does, then we will be unable to see the evil forces at work in the last stanza. Sound, as much as any other device, imparts to us the seductive nature of death.

STEP IV-5, INTELLECTUAL CONTROL OF THE WORDS

O-56 It is not a bad idea to look up every word in the poem (except the obvious ones such as articles, prepositions, and pronouns) and list shades of meaning which might affect the poem. For example, *quench* in line 18 is a fairly straightforward word which usually means "to satisfy or allay thirst, desires, or passions," a definition entirely appropriate to the poem. But it can also mean "to subdue or destroy," which gives a different connotation in the context of the poem. If the speaker has come to allay Luke's passion, then he may be a friend, but if he has come to destroy Luke by destroying the kiss, he may not be so friendly.

O-57 Look up the following words in an unabridged dictionary or the *OED (Oxford English Dictionary* formerly known alternatively as *NED* or *New English Dictionary.)*

Stanza 1: *western, gate, vines, cling, crimson, wall, twilight, leaves, whisper, words, strike, fall, listen*

Stanza 2: *dawn, eastern, skies, rift, fiery, glooms, gathering, dark, slays, leaf, flies*

Stanza 3: *grave, quench, kiss, flames, forehead, glow, finds, way, bitter, faith, may, never, miss*

Stanza 4: *winds, tearing, away, think, riddle, feel, trust*

Obviously, looking up every word will not necessarily reveal the meaning of the poem, but it is a good place to begin, especially if the other steps are not proving fruitful. This is particularly true with poems which rely on symbols and allusions.

O-58 It is not uncommon for poets to take liberties with words to form their own definitions, or to use a word in an abnormal manner. In "Luke Havergal," for example, it is not impossible that *leaves* in line 4 could mean *leavings,* or that which is left, so that the leaves of memories would remind Luke of "her." However, since Robinson seems very conventional and precise in his choice of words, we cannot consider this possibility too seriously, although with some poets it would be a natural occurrence.

O-59 Consistency, then, is the only rule to follow: if the poet consistently uses words in a particular manner, or uses particular types of words either in the poem under consideration or in other poems, then the explicator is justified in assuming that unusual word usage is a part of the poet's technique. If, however, it doesn't seem consistent with normal word usage the explicator is wise to be cautious.

STEP IV-6, SYMBOL

O-60 "Luke Havergal" is probably not as symbolic as it first appears, although poems which use paradox and allusion are often quite symbolic.

0-60 (1)   Clearly the western gate is symbolic, but to what degree is questionable. No doubt it represents the last light in Luke's life, and once he passes beyond it he moves into another type of existence.

0-60 (2)   The west and the twilight are points of embarkation; the sun is setting in the west, but even though the sun sets there will not be a dawn in the east for Luke to dispel his dark gloom.

0-60 (3)   Traditionally the dark, which is gathering in the west, is symbolic of death (the west is also traditionally associated with death), and only the dark will end Luke's gloom in life, if anything at all can do it. (Notice how the abrupt feminine ending reinforces the meaning.) What are some other possibilities for symbols (see Frames C-36 ff)?

Allusions

0-61   There is one important allusion in the poem, which comes in stanza 3; the kiss which the speaker is going to quench may be the "kiss of death," and if we conclude this we will probably decide that the speaker is that force which can destroy Luke.

Both in concept and language stanza 3 is reminiscent of the dagger scene and killing of Duncan (Act II, scene 1) in *Macbeth*. Just before the murder Macbeth has visions of the dagger:

> *Is this a dagger which I see before me,*
> *The handle toward my hand? Come let me clutch thee.*
> *I have thee not, and yet I see thee still.*
> *Art thou not, fatal vision, sensible*
> *To feeling as to sight? or art thou but*
> *A dagger of the mind, a false creation,*
> *Proceeding from the heat-oppressed brain?*
> *I see thee yet, in form as palpable*
> *As this which now I draw.*
> *Thou marshall'st me the way that I was going;*
> *And such an instrument I was to use.*
> *Mine eyes are made the fools o' the other senses,*
> *Or else worth all the rest; I see thee still,*
> *And on thy blade and dudgeon gouts of blood,*
> *Which was not so before. There's no such thing:*
> *It is the bloody business which informs*
> *Thus to mine eyes.*

And a few lines later (Act II, Scene 2) Lady Macbeth says:

> *That which hath made them drunk hath made me bold;*
> *What hath quench'd them hath given me fire.*

The reversal in point of view in "Luke Havergal" gives the poem added depth, which is especially enhanced by the comparison with Macbeth. The line, *That blinds you to the way that you must go* is almost word for word equivalent to *Thou marshall'st me the way that I was going,* except that in "Luke Havergal" whoever is with Luke is talking while Macbeth is talking to the dagger.

O-62   The result of the allusion is that we can almost imagine that it is the dagger which is talking to Luke, and the whole story of Macbeth becomes relevant to the poem because we suspect that Luke's end will be the similar to Macbeth's.

The words of Lady Macbeth strengthen the allusion's power and suggest a male-female relationship which is leading Luke to his death, especially since, in the resolution of *Macbeth,* Lady Macbeth goes crazy and whispers to the spirits.

O-63   If we accept the allusion as a part of the poem, the imagery is enhanced by the vivid descriptions from *Macbeth.*

Most critics and writers, however, agree that if a careful reader finds something that fits consistently into a poem, then it is "there" for all readers who see the same thing, whether the poet consciously put it there or not. Probably Robinson read and knew his Shakespeare, since he was both educated and a man interested in literature (much scholarship has been done on what books certain authors probably read, and it may even be possible to prove that Robinson read *Macbeth*). But it doesn't matter whether Robinson put it there or not if the reader can show the allusion is important to the poem.

INTENTIONAL FALLACY

O-64   There is a basic problem with allusion and symbol which every explicator must re-solve for himself: Whether or not the poet meant for a symbol or allusion to be taken as a given reader has interpreted it. (The "New Critics" coined the term "intentional fallacy" to describe looking in a poem for the poet's intention, which they consider unimportant.) For example, it is possible that stanza 3 was not intended to allude to *Macbeth* and it was simply by accident that Robinson used language similar to Shakespeare's. Perhaps Robin-son never read *Macbeth,* or perhaps he read it once and those lines remained in his subcon-scious and he didn't realize the similarity when he wrote his poem.

O-65   The problem, however, comes when there is doubt whether an allusion or symbol actually fits consistently into the poem. For example, in "Luke Havergal" it is possible that the "voice from the grave" alludes to Dante's *Inferno,* and a passage (incidentally quoted as epigraph to "The Love Song of J. Alfred Prufrock" by Eliot) which runs thus:

> *If I believed my answer were being made to one who could ever return to the world, this flame would gleam (i.e. this spirit would speak) no more; but since, if what I hear is true, never from this abyss did living man return, I answer thee without fear of infamy.*

Some critics may agree that Robinson does make the allusion; others may not (as with the Freudian reading of *Hamlet).*

If it can be proven that the poet put an allusion there, even though it is not clear why, the critic must make an effort to see what was intended, but if it was not intended and it is doubtful how far it actually has bearing on the poem, then the explicator must decide for himself.

STEP IV-7, PROSODIC AND STRUCTURAL CONTROL

Variations on a Base Meter

O-66   "Luke Havergal," as a poem which depends so heavily on sound, should be scanned with care, using a more detailed stress system than stress, secondary stress, and unstress. For a thorough explanation of close reading, see frames D-68 to D-82.

O-67   The following first scansion should show some of the metrical effects Robinson is using:

Go to/ the wes/tern gate,/ Luke Hav/ergal,

There where/ the vines/ cling crim/son on/ the wall,   2

And in/ the twi/light wait/ for what/ will come.

The leaves/ will whis/per there/ of her,/ and come,   4

Like fly/ing words,/ will strike/ you as/ they fall;

But go,/ and if/ you lis/ten, she/ will call.   6

Go to/ the wes/tern gate,/ Luke Hav/ergal —

Luke Hav/ergal.   8

No, there/ is not/ a dawn/ in eas/tern skies

To rift/ the fie/ry night/ that's in/ your eyes;   10

But there,/ where wes/tern glooms/ are gath/ering,

The dark/ will end/ the dark,/ if any/thing: 12

God slays/ Himself/ with eve/ry leaf/ that flies,

And hell/ is more/ than half/ of par/adise   14

No, there/ is not/ a dawn/ in east/ern skies —

In eas/tern skies.   16

L.6: caesura in foot 4 places emphasis on *if you listen*, and creates falling rhythm at the end of the line.
L.9: caesura breaking foot 1 establishes counterpoint.
L.10: end of foot 1: harsh and plosive consonants contrast with softer consonants throughout poem.
L.11: last foot, pyrrhic substitution causes syllables to gather in the mouth.
L.12: final secondary stress gives abrupt ending to line.

Oŭt ŏf/ ă grăve/ Í cŏme/ tŏ tĕll/ yŏu thĭs,

Oŭt ŏf/ ă grăve/ Í cŏme/ tŏ quĕnch/ thĕ kĭss   18

Thăt flămes/ ŭpón/ yŏur fŏre/hĕad wĭth/ ă glŏw

Thăt bĭnds/ yŏu tó/ thĕ wăy/ thăt yŏu/ mŭst gŏ.   20

Yĕs, thĕre/ ĭs yĕt/ ŏne wăy/ tŏ whĕre/ shĕ ĭs,

Bĭtter,/ bŭt ŏne/ thăt făith/ măy nĕv/ĕr mĭss.   22

Oŭt ŏf/ ă grăve/ Í cŏme/ tŏ tĕll/ yŏu thĭs —

Tŏ tĕll/ yŏu thĭs.   24

Thĕre ĭs/ thĕ wĕs/tĕrn găte,/ Lŭke Hăv/ĕrgál,

Thĕre ăre/ thĕ crĭm/sŏn leăves/ ŭpón / thĕ wăll.   26

Gŏ, fŏr/ thĕ wĭnds/ ăre tĕar/ĭng thĕm/ ăwăy, —

Nŏr thĭnk/ tŏ rĭd/dĭe thĕ/ dĕad wŏrds/ thĕy săy,   28

Nŏr ăn/ў mŏre/ tŏ fĕel/ thĕm ăs/ thĕy făll;

                                                      30
Bŭt gŏ,/ ănd ĭf/ yŏu trŭst/ hĕr shĕ/ wĭll căll.   30

Thĕre ĭs/ thĕ wĕs/tĕrn găte,/ Lŭke Hăv/ĕrgál —

Lŭke Hăv/ĕrgál.   32

L.17: foot 1: trochaic substitution recalls *Go to* in stanza 1.

Ll.17-18: foot 3: is there a longer pause before or after this foot in 17? If after, *come* takes secondary stress. But in line 18, *come* changes to primary stress.

L.20: foot 2: internal rhyme creates equal pressure.

L.21: foot 1: *Yes* takes a primary stress, which gives a sense of affirmation.

L.21: foot 3: substitution creates rising rhythm, unlike line 9.

L.22: foot 1: trochaic sub. set off by caesura; creates emphasis.

L.22: foot 5: lack of pressure on *er* and the split foot cause emphasis on *miss*.

L.24: foot 2: there is less pressure on *this* in the dimeter line

L.27: foot 1: as with *Yes* in L. 21, *Go* is emphasized.

L.27: the caesura after *go*; and slack pressure on *for* cause *for the winds* to be taken as a foot, and combined with the split third foot, this reinforces the leaves being torn away.

L.28: last foot: internal rhyme creates more pressure on *they*.

L.29: foot 2: because *any more* is often pronounced as one word, and because the split foot points up the separation, there is greater emphasis on *more*.

L.30: the perfectly regular line emphasizes itself after so many metrical variations in this stanza.

The base meter of the poem is iambic pentameter, with frequent substitutions, but every line except the last in each stanza contains ten syllables.

O-68   The next step in explicating is to consider how the rhyme scheme and stanza form are working, and in "Luke Havergal" the stanza form is quite intricate and delicate. It is only because of the structure that the heavy *a* rhyme (*aabbaaaa*) does not become monotonous; yet it is because of the *a* rhyme that the structure works so well.

O-68 (1)   The pattern for the first stanza works as follows:

Line	Rhyme	Function
1	a	Sets up ideas and images for the stanza.
2	a	Describes or complements line 1.
3	b	Lines 3-4-5 constitute the central part of the stanza, setting the mood and the fears. The return to the *a* rhyme unifies lines 1-5.
4	b	
5	a	
6	a	Reflects on what has been said in 1-5; it serves to make the reader stop, and it adds a mysterious suggestion.
7	a	Continues the deceleration and reflection.
8	a	The repetition and dimeter line stop the stanza completely, and the effect is to prepare for a shift in thought, just as Luke's mind jumps from thought to thought.

O-68 (2)   Stanza 2 works similarly to stanza 1, except that lines 13 and 14 (the fifth and sixth of the stanza) tie the stanza together as a couplet, rather than just the fifth line serving this function as in stanza 1. Thus 13 and 14 both unify and reflect, while 15 and 16 in the final couplet continue slowing down and reflecting.

We can map the basic variation between stanzas. In stanza 1 the structure is as follows:

Line	Rhyme	Function
1	a	Opening couplet lets line 2 complement 1.
2	a	
3	b	Couplet in 3-4 contains the central idea and image.
4	b	
5	a	Rhyme with first couplet unifies lines 1-5.
6	a	Slows and reflects on *bb* couplet, the central image.
7	a	
8	a	Final couplet echoes first, binds the stanza, and brings it to a halt.

In stanza 2, however, the structure is as follows:

Line	Rhyme	Function
9	a	Opening couplet.
10	a	
11	b	Couplet in 11-12 contains the central idea and image.
12	b	
13	a	Couplet in 13-14 reflects on that in 11-12, but the autonomy of this third couplet is especially strong. Whereas in stanza 1 only line 5 reflected on the beginning of the stanza to create unity, this entire couplet is now strongly associated with the first, with the effect of nearly equating Luke
14	a	with God.
15	a	
16	a	Final couplet reflects on first and completes the stanza.

O-68 (3)   Stanza 3 works the same as stanza 2, while stanza 4 works as stanza 1.

O-69   Looking at the overall structure, we should determine what sort of development is taking place. We know from the structure that each stanza is autonomous and does not need the others for continuation or progression in plot; each stanza appears to represent a different thought as Luke's mind jumps about.

O-70   The overall structure does focus on stanza 3, which is crucial to the theme. Stanzas 1 and 2 clearly present the problem: Luke knows that if he goes he will find her, and the worst that can happen is that it will be as dark as it is now. But with stanza 3 there is a break in point of view as the narrator calls attention to himself, and we move from the depths of despair in life to those in death.

O-71   With stanza 4 there is a return to the beginning, reinforced by the repetition of ryhme words; the difference between 4 and 1 is that the reader has felt the impact of stanza 3; structurally we know that whatever resolution there is will evolve out of the third stanza, or because of it.

STEP IV-8, RHYME

O-72   Although Robinson has relied on his own ingenuity to create the best type of stanza for his poem, whereas Frost in "Tree At My Window" (L-11) used a standard form and modified it to suit his own needs, the stanza in "Luke Havergal" nevertheless achieves tremendous unity and emphasis. The central image or idea presented in the *b* lines is re-inforced in the remainder of the stanza by a tight-knit rhyme structure.

Stanza 1

O-73   There are several types of rhymes being used in the poem, all of which follow the traditional functions of their type. Stanza 1 contains full masculine end-rhyme, with a full masculine internal rhyme in line 2 (*There where*). Lines 2 and 3 contain alliteration (*c* in line 2, *t* in line 3) which also binds the lines more tightly.

Stanza 2

0-74   With *go* occuring near the end of stanza 1 and *No* appearing as the first word in stanza 2, this rhyme becomes important in forming associations between lines. Lines 9, 10, 13, 15, and 16 form full masculine end-rhyme with line 14 (*paradise*) assonating with a full rhyme. Lines 11 and 12 are half falling rhymes; these lines also contain a full internal rhyme (*there, where*), a syllabic binder (*where western*), and alliteration (*g* in line 11). *Dark* in line 12 is an exact internal rhyme. The *l* and *s* in *slays* and *flies* (line 14) create an effect similar to assonance; there is also an *h* alliteration in line 15.

Stanza 3

0-75   The plosive consonants *c* and *q* make an alliterative sound in line 18 binding *come* and *quench* together; there is also an *f* alliteration in line 19. All the end-rhymes are full masculine in stanza 3 except line 21, which assonates.

Stanza 4

0-76   Stanza 4 contains full masculine end rhyme, with one alliteration in line 29, one internal rhyme *they say* (l. 28), and one consonance *will call*. (L-30)

0-77   Aside from its function in developing the stanza, rhyme in "Luke Havergal" is an important influence on sound, and in associating particular words and lines.

STEP IV-9, SOME MORE SUBTLE CONTROLS: THE NARRATOR

0-78   Whether we take the voice in "Luke Havergal" as Luke's insane sub-conscious, the spirit of death, or an actual visitor from the dead, there is an important difference between what he says and what he intends. The narrator makes it seem as though he is Luke's friend, come from a place where he has knowledge of the dead, and he wants to tell Luke how to quench his grief. We, as does Luke, have confidence in the narrator, and when he tells us that the way to "her" will be bitter, but possible to those who have faith, we are willing to become faithful. After all, the narrator has come from the grave to tell us this, and it's only when we realize that the narrator likes the grave that we begin to suspect his insidious intent. Even in stanza 4 we continue to accept his advice, and when we are made to feel that once the leaves are gone we will have missed our chance, we want to hurry with Luke to the western gate.

   The narrator, however, makes one "mistake," which we, as readers, are able to see, and that is he tells us not to consider the grave any longer, but to accept it. If we *riddle the dead words they say;* if we compare life to death, we may miss our chance to join her. It is only here that we can know for certain that the narrator is diabolical; what we can't know is whether or not Luke understands this, and it is the uncertainty of Luke's final actions which causes us to become sensitive to the evil around us.

O-79   We can say, then, that one of the themes, at least, depends on the irony created
by the difference between what the narrator knows and what the reader knows, and between what the narrator says and what he means. "Luke Havergal" is a poem about the
nature of evil, but we can't know it unless we characterize the narrator.

STEP IV-10, TONE

O-80   Sound can be heard and analyzed, tone is a composite of a number of things
which the reader can only feel after coming to know the poem. *Tone* is the final communication between poet and reader, and is the reason for a poem's existence.

The poet's attitude may be very non-committal or it may be dogmatic (as in allegory);
sometimes the tone will affect the theme, while in other poems it comes as an aside to
theme, so that what the poet thinks will seem secondary to what the poem is.

Frequently poems which attempt to initiate reform will have a more readily discern-
able tone than poems which make observations without judging too harshly, although
this is not always true.

O-81   In "Luke Havergal" the poet's mood is not readily accessible and we can only
guess what he is thinking. He has presented us with a man who is on the verge of insanity
(if insanity can be defined as the absence of rational behavior).

The poem is, among other things, about how the presence of evil leads us toward death,
but the poet has not directly included how he feels about his theme. If there is an attitude,
it is the poet's acceptance of the inevitability of death and the pain which accompanies
it for the living.

Perhaps the poet is angry at how effectively death can seduce life, but we can come to
this only because it is obvious that Robinson wants the poem to haunt and torment the
reader, and in doing so make him conscious of the hold death has on us.

But we also know that we must meet death part way; we must first go to the gate before
we can hear the dead words, which makes us partly responsible for death's hold over us.
All this isn't clear, however, and the tone of "Luke Havergal" does not impose itself on
the reader, even though the theme is haunting and provocative.

STEP IV-11, THE HISTORICAL CONTEXT

O-82   If we approach an explication using only the poem as the basis for study, we are
following the techniques of "the New Criticism." Up until this point we have used only
the poem and those secondary sources which are needed to understand symbol and allusion.

O-83   There is no doubt that the methods of the "New Criticism" lead to one kind of
valid understanding, but in order to *complete* our explication, it is necessary to check the
historical situation, other poems by the same poet, and other criticism.

This "traditional" approach (usually called scholarly as opposed to critical) is a tiring
though sometimes rewarding method to complete a study, but it must be adapted to the
demands of the explication and the amount of time available. No explication should stand
without the explicator first satisfying himself that his study is consistent with the traditional
elements.

O-84   Checking for traditional consistency may require only selected readings from other critics (perhaps only an hour in the library) and the explicator may not even mention what he has found in his library work, but he must be certain that he is not in direct conflict with some historical event. On the other hand, the explicator may have time for extensive research, or he may need help in understanding part of the poem, in which case he might spend a great deal of effort putting the poem in context with the period and other works.

O-85   With "Luke Havergal," for example, we can find from even superficial reading that the poem was finished in December 1895 and that Robinson considered it a Symbolist poem, part of the Decadence Movement. It is essential, then, that the explicator learn something about this movement, because it will probably help him to understand what influenced the poet. If his explication does not fit into the philosophy of the period, the explicator must account for it. We can also learn from a little library work that in the same month of composition Robinson began a serious reading of the *New Testament,* which might help us to explain the images and themes in "Luke Havergal."

O-86   What this is saying is that poets do not write in a vacuum, and if we can discover what has influenced them, we might have a better idea about the nature of their poetry.

O-87   Because poets frequently become interested in a technique or idea and write until they exhaust it, it is sometimes helpful to read other poems by the poet, particularly those written at the same time as the one we are studying.

In a study of other Robinson poems, we can find parallel themes to "Luke Havergal." One, for example, is that of the alienated self, but we must be careful not to misconstrue parallelisms, although they may be very good support for our explication. For example, if Robinson does believe in the alienated self, then it is possible that the voice speaking in "Luke Havergal" is Luke's in an alienated state. This may add credence to our argument, though it by no means proves it.

O-88   When using other criticism, it is not necessary that you be in agreement if you have sound reasons for your argument. But do not fight the system just for the sake of originality; wild, unsupported theories are not appreciated or valuable to the study of poetry, no matter how brilliant they may seem at the time. Usually there will be a few elements in a contradictory theory which will not fit into the poem, and if this happens, re-evaluate the explication. But use your critics wisely, and if they are wrong, be quick to point it out. However, you should neither accept nor refute criticism until you have worked out the poem for yourself.

STEP IV-12, CORRELATING THE PARTS

O-89   Once the poem has been placed in context, the prosodic devices analyzed, and the function of the poetical techniques understood, they should be correlated, and any discrepancies should be studied for possible errors in explication. By this time every line should be understood, so that stating what the poem is about is merely a matter of explaining the common points of all the areas, supporting it with specific items from the poem, secondary sources, other poems, other critics, and history. The explications in the following pages demonstrate how all the parts of the poem might be correlated once the final reading has been completed, all the ideas formulated, and excessive or inappropriate information discarded.

Types of Explication

In the following pages we will consider models of three major options of coverage in developing an explication: (1) the *partial explication* (example: the paper [pp. 237-240] on Dickey's "In the Mountain Text"); (2) the *brief full explication* (example: the paper below on cummings' "a man who had fallen among thieves"); and (3) the *detailed full explication* (example: the second paper below on Eliot's "Journey of the Magi").

◆‖▶ THREE MAJOR TYPES OF EXPLICATION

The Partial Explication

We have already considered (in the first chapter of this Section) an example of how a short explication can work to synthesize the elements of a poem to make an overview that enriches our experience as readers. The explication of Dickey's "In the Mountain Text," however, was a relatively brief *partial explication,* in that it treated only the images, symbols, and allusions, along with whatever elements contributed most directly to an explication of how those elements operate in the poem. This type of partial analysis and explication is useful for readers and critics who have become interested in some particular aspects of a poet's work. The fact that this examination is a partial one should thus represent a deliberate choice to limit the scope for a particular purpose. Such a limitation should always be undertaken in full awareness of the more extensive possibilities that exist for exploring other aspects of the poem in more detail and depth, though these may have been set aside by the critic for deliberate reasons. The beginning explicator should probably show his awareness of the greater complexity that could have been explored and give his reasons for narrowing his examination as he did; in short, he should express carefully the rationale behind selecting the partial aspects he has chosen to explicate.

The Brief Full Explication

A second type of approach that falls short of the fullest possible examination of a poem is exemplified in the first paper below on e. e. cummings' "a man who had fallen among thieves." It is a *full explication;* that is, it attempts to explain all of the poem's important aspects, but it is deliberately brief and not as detailed as it might be, representing a kind of brief overview of most of the interpretative possibilities in reading the poem. In the case of cummings' poem, the explication example here shows greater awareness than does the Dickey explication in regard to the craftsmanship as well as the themes and ideas in the poem. While this overview explication of the cummings poem may be less satisfying than a longer one for those readers who would like to see every detail analyzed for its contribution to the total impact of the poem, the brief paper is probably more satisfying to the readers who would like to use the overview as a prelude to and basis for their own further reading, experiencing, and study of the poem. Once the explicator has gone through the step-by-step processes described in the preceding chapters, and has collected his full range of data, he will have to make his own decision about how to present it to the reader. The brief full explication chooses to eliminate a great deal of what could have been said. Again, for the beginning explicator, it is probably wise to indicate to his reader the rationale for making the limitation he finally chose. In the cummings explication, for example, the critic's choice to focus upon allusion with special emphasis has not avoided talking about imagery in some detail as well, when it was necessary to the main purpose of the paper.

The Detailed Full Explication

By contrast to the Dickey and cummings explication examples, the second paper below demonstrates a fairly detailed full explication of T. S. Eliot's "The Journey of the Magi"; that is, it attempts a full explanation of all of the poem's important aspects. In contrast to the cummings explication, it is more conscious of the total impact of the poem's craftsmanship, and includes most of what could have been said on this subject. The beginning explicator should be able to show his capability for full and detailed understanding at this level of complexity, even though his paper may choose to treat the poem as a whole more briefly.

It would be good practice for the explicator to compare these explications, as well as some of the student examples at the end of this chapter, and then choose a strategy for proceeding with a written explication of Robinson's "Luke Havergal," as examined in the preceding chapter.

◀▐▌▶ A BRIEF FULL EXPLICATION OF A CUMMINGS POEM

> a man who had fallen among thieves
> lay by the roadside on his back
> dressed in fifteenthrate ideas
> wearing a round jeer for a hat   4
>
> fate per a somewhat more than less
> emancipated evening
> had in return for consciousness
> endowed him with a changeless grin   8
>
> whereon a dozen staunch and leal
> citizens did graze at pause
> then fired by hypercivic zeal
> sought newer pastures or because   12
>
> swaddled with a frozen brook
> of pinkest vomit out of eyes
> which noticed nobody he looked
> as if he did not care to rise   16
>
> one hand did nothing on the vest
> its wideflung friend clenched weakly dirt
> while the mute trouserfly confessed   20
> a button solemnly inert.

> *Brushing from whom the stiffened puke*
> *i put him all into my arms*
> *and staggered banged with terror through*
> *a million billion trillion stars*   24

a man who had fallen among thieves
e. e. cummings

Although it is clear that "a man who had fallen among thieves" is a comment on society, it is not clear how deeply the explicator can push cummings' themes without seeming absurd. It we choose to read the poem on its most basic level, "a man who had fallen among thieves" describes a drunk man who, in exchange for an evening free of cares (drowned in intoxication), has become sick and is lying passed out in his own vomit. As a drunkard he is ridiculed or pitied by others in his society, which leads the civic minded citizens to seek help and reform for alcoholics. The man who had fallen is obviously in bad condition: he can only grin senselessly, he is content with his filth, and he isn't cognizant enough of social standards to button his trousers.

Certainly the dramatic situation suggests that the man who had fallen could be drunk, but on another level — one which is consistent with the first — the poem attempts to condemn society much more harshly than a fairly mundane comment about how societies lead men to drink. And the importance of the situation is not the effect it has on the man who had fallen, but the effect it has had on the man who helped the man who had fallen.

The title of the poem refers, of course, to the parable Christ told in answer to the question, "who is my neighbor?" and because the Good Samaritan story is so specifically referred to, it is most reasonable to assume that cummings' story is also a parable, but in answer to what question? The cummings' poem seems to answer "who is my brother?" It is clear that cummings' Samaritan is more affected by the robbery than was Christ's Samaritan, who merely took the victim to an inn and paid for someone else to take care of him. It is also clear that cummings' poem tells a situation more immediate to the well-being of the society's inhabitants than Christ's parable. But Christ's story acts as a foil to the poem primarily because of the characters involved. One of the points of the Biblical account is that the victim was a Jew, a man who had high social status in the community. Two men of higher status, the Priest and the Levite, passed the man by, while a man of the Samaritan group, despised by Jews as foreign and heretical, was the one who helped the victim. So Christ's story has social overtones as well as moral implications. The priest and the Levite did not look down upon the man who had been put upon; they simply were too busy with the affairs of the Church to care. In cummings' poem the *staunch and leal citizens* cared enough to come out and look at the victim, but did not understand the *man who had fallen among lifes perils*, and their injustice was not only in passing him by but in failing to recognize the culprit.

The dramatic situation in cummings' poem is somewhat different from that in the Good Samaritan story, in that the time sequence is changed. In the Biblical story a Priest, the Levite, and the Samaritan pass by the roadside, in that order and at different times. All three pause, but only the Samaritan touches the victim when he takes him to the inn. In cummings' story the narrator, who is the equivalent of the Samaritan, seems to have been the first to encounter the victim, whereon he watched for a while as he tried to decipher the event, and as the citizens passed by. It is almost as if the narrator is trying to decide whether or not to take on the burden, and it is only after some contemplation that he understands the significance of the theft.

The difference between the Biblical and poetical accounts in the first stanza sets the theme for the story. Both open alike, almost in the same prose-like language, but the poem quickly deviates from the Samaritan story. Jesus said that a man fell among thieves, "which stripped him of his raiment, and wounded him, and departed, leaving him half dead." But cummings' victim has not been stripped of his raiment; indeed, he is still fully dressed, and there is no indication that he has been beaten and left half dead. Yet we are told that he has fallen among thieves. It is as though the thieves did not want whatever the man possessed. If fifteenthrate ideas were the raiment, then it is easy to understand why the thieves did not want him. Or perhaps, as is suggested in line 4, the man is merely jeering or taunting the thieves who, once they attack, find the man's raiment worthless. The hovering stress on *dressed* emphasizes that he does still possess something, and it is possible that some kind of an exchange was made with the thieves, but this is not made clear.

Stanza 2 introduces the idea of exchange in all four lines. The expressions *more and less, evening* (to make even), *in return for,* and *endowed* all suggest that some recompense has been made for whatever loss there was, but the irony is that fate is not known for her fair dealings with men's lives. Was fate responsible for the man being robbed? Was fate itself the robber, or has, by chance, the man gained something from the theft? The narrator tells us that it was an *emancipated evening,* that is, that it was not restrained by custom. Line 7 adds greater mystery to the situation because it is not clear whether fate has given or taken *consciousness.* On the first reading it appears that fate has taken the man's consciousness — thus he is lying unconscious beside the road — and that in return for his sacrifice of consciousness fate has given him a grin which jeers at the passersby. But a deeper reading suggests that fate has perhaps given the man another kind of consciousness — social consciousness, and because the man must suffer under the burden, fate has given him an emotionless expression. The force of the word *endowed* indicates that the grin is a fair *evening* for consciousness, and it would seem that the giving of consciousness, rather than the taking of it would be indicated by the grin. The implication in this and each of the other stanzas is that the man is a loon; the *changeless grin* particularly connotes this; thus, cummings is at the center of his theme by stanza two, and it is clear that what has been stolen from the victim is his inability to ignore what the leal citizens have been doing. Now he can plainly see what the civic zeal has been all about, and he does not care to rise to it any longer.

The citizens come out in force to see the man. The number twelve suggests that this might be a committee of citizens appointed to visit the ill or to investigate particular community problems; it also suggests a jury, or the disciples who were listening when the parable of the Good Samaritan was told. The truncated foot in line 10 emphasizes *citizens,* perhaps indicating that they are similar to the citizens who were present at the Crucifixion. The citizens are taken only slightly aback at the uncertainty of the situation (they *graze at pause*), then take off for civic areas over which they have more control. (Two meanings of *graze* are applicable here. One, meaning "to touch lightly," refers to the Biblical story. "To feed upon" is also suggested because of the mention of *pastures* in line 12.)

The last word in stanza 3, *because,* moves this stanza into the next, and gives reasons why the citizens seek newer pastures. Once again there is a Biblical reference in *swaddled* and The Christ image is continued when we are told that the man is bandaged (*swaddled*) *with a frozen brook* (*brook* as a verb means to bear or tolerate). This man's tolerance is *frozen;* it has ceased to flow, and what remains is the image of violence (*pinkest vomit*) against the *staunch and leal*. His eyes are unresponsive, and he does *not care to rise* (Christ imagery again) because he knows that it is not worth the effort.

In both stanza four and stanza five the man is expected to do something — to notice someone, to move his hands, or to rise — and it is clear that this is not the same beaten half-dead victim in Christ's parable. With time the original victim will recover, but cummings' victim will not. And the thing that terrorizes the narrator is that this victim has lost his sexual powers; that the consciousness received from fate has rendered him impotent.

The last stanza is a reconciliation of the event which the narrator has witnessed. After figuring out the significance of the man's experience, the narrator attempts to brush away the man's intolerance and to take him as his companion in destiny. And the narrator now has a sudden show of energy (*banged with terror*), but it is energy of fear that pushes him forward.

The form, punctuation, and base meter (iambic tetrameter with liberal substitution), of the poem may suggest the rising turmoil which the narrator feels as he understands what has happened to the man. The rhyme scheme begins rather loosely with only approximate rhyme in stanza one. But as it becomes clearer what has happened to the man, the rhyme becomes stricter (*abab*). Because cummings is consistently careful of form in all his poems, it is reasonable to correlate the strict rhyme in stanzas three, four, and five with the order which the narrator is making out of the event. Ironically, the social order which the narrator is afraid of is depicted in the strict metrical base. The lack of punctuation and use of standard grammatical form (such as capitalization) reinforce the poet's reluctance to conform to the norms of social communication, although by sticking to stanzaic divisions and a base meter he seeks his own structural norm in an artistic discipline of form. When in stanza 6 the narrator is struck with terror, the poem again turns to assonance rather than full end rhyme, reinforcing the psychological chaos and sense of disorder with which the poem opened.

◀▮▶ A DETAILED FULL EXPLICATION OF AN ELIOT POEM

T. S. Eliot's Use of Prosody, Diction, and Dramatic Situation For Exemplifying Christian Theology in "Journey of the Magi"

> "A cold coming we had of it,
> Just the worst time of the year
> For a journey, and such a long journey:
> The ways deep and the weather sharp,
> The very dead of winter."   5
> And the camels galled, sore-footed, refractory,
> Lying down in the melting snow.
> There were times we regretted
> The summer palaces on slopes, the terraces,
> And the silken girls bringing sherbet.   10
> Then the camel men cursing and grumbling
> And running away, and wanting their liquor and women,

And the night-fires going out, and the lack of shelters,
And the cities hostile and the towns unfriendly
And the villages dirty and charging high prices: 15
A hard time we had of it.
At the end we preferred to travel all night,
Sleeping in snatches,
With the voices singing in our ears, saying
That this was all folly.   20

Then at dawn we came down to a temperate valley,
Wet, below the snow line, smelling of vegetation;
With a running stream and a water-mill beating the darkness,
And three trees on the low sky,
And an old white horse galloped away in the meadow.   25
Then we came to a tavern with vine-leaves over the lintel,
Six hands at an open door dicing for pieces of silver,
And feet kicking the empty wine-skins.
But there was no information, and so we continued
And arrived at evening, not a moment too soon   30
Finding the place; it was (you may say) satisfactory.

All this was a long time ago, I remember,
And I would do it again, but set down
This set down
This: were we led all that way for   35
Birth or Death? There was a Birth, certainly,
We had evidence and no doubt. I had seen birth and death,
But had thought they were different; this Birth was
Hard and bitter agony for us, like Death, our death.
We returned to our places, these Kingdoms,   40
But no longer at ease here, in the old dispensation,
With an alien people clutching their gods.
I should be glad of another death.

In "Journey of the Magi," the structure of the poem, the use of ceasura and substitution, the sound of the words with their colloquial connotations, and the dramatic situation are the principal techniques which Eliot employs in reinterpreting the Christian myth of the wise men's trek to the Nativity.

The structure, which physically consists of three stichic divisions, chronologically suggests that the Magi's journey is not a normal one from point to point in either place or time, but is a peculiar journey which is not only a "going" but also a "coming." The dramatic situation leads the reader backwards through time, then projects him into the present, and when the dramatic situation is considered simultaneously with tone and point of view, the reader comes to realize that the journey is not merely the "journey of the magi" — not only their particular journey to the Nativity, but is a more general journey to the spiritual meaning of an event which can be shared by all men. The diction, which seems colloquial when compared to Biblical King James English, the hardships of the journey, and the absence of heavenly guidance emphasize the differences between Eliot's narration and the Biblical presentation of the "Christmas story."

The voice speaking in the poem is that of one of the magi who is recounting the journey made many years ago (line 32); a journey with such significance that the magus cannot refrain from telling it, even to a listener who may be one of the *alien people* (line 43). Through his retelling of the story, we can sense that the magus has arrived at a point in his life which is so important that he can speak of the journey as a *coming;* the spiritual journey has led the magus to a birth of his own, of sorts. The journey itself took the magi from their homes into alien lands, through a prefiguring of the Crucifixion, finally arriving at an event which, in retrospect, has become so much a part of the narrator's life that *the palaces on slopes* (line 9) now constitute the *alien lands.* The journey, and the event as the narrator reflects on it, has been transformed into an immediate presence for him, and we acutely feel the narrator's passions as he tells of the hardships.

The relationship between dramatic situation and point of view is important, since most of the poem is related to us through the narrator's memory. As the poem opens, and for the first two stichic divisions, we are unable to fix the dramatic situation; what we are permitted to see are the graphic details of the journey through images which are concrete and specific in division 1, free and symbolic in division 2. The magus is clearly perplexed at having had to make the journey, and even upon arriving at the event be found no real sense of worship or admiration. The magus' attitude at the Nativity, as with the hardships of the journey, is matter-of-factual, and whatever emotion he experiences is that of a man who has travelled for so long that nothing matters. In the third section, however, when the magus turns to the present rather the remembered past, we can clearly see what the journey meant to him, the questions it raised, and the results it brought, and while the magus's tone and objectivity remains constant in each section, we understand the change which has come over him because we see the differences between the way he regarded his homeland then and now.

Another important aspect of the point of view is that only one of the magi is speaking. Nowhere in the poem does the magus consider himself a part of the group, and while he refers to *we*, it is clear that this was an individual experience. Yet the title, "Journey of the Magi," suggests that several men were involved. The first few lines of the poem are taken from a 1622 Nativity sermon by Lancelot Andrews, a third-person recounting of the event in approximately the words of the opening quotation, which substitutes *we* for *they*. The emphasis which Eliot places on the singular narrating voice suggest that the experience described is a personal one, yet one open to all men who reflect on the importance of the event. A good part of the magus's experience is sensual. He was susceptible to the harshness of the journey, and we feel the images contrasting the coldness and severity on the journey with the ease of the summer palaces. The imagery is free, allowing the reader's imagination to project into the extremity of the conditions, and it is supported by the forceful rhetoric which focuses on and elaborates Andrews' "cold coming." Through several closely related expressions (*cold coming; long journey; worst time of the year; weather sharp; dead of winter*) the first five lines build to a climax so that we believe that it is the *very dead of winter.* The images are so free and the language so forceful that the journey seems to the reader to be through death itself, which, of course, becomes figuratively significant later in the poem. If the journey is "through" death, it is "to" life; thus the fact that Eliot abridges Andrews' sermon to remove specific references to the winter solstice reinforces the suggestion that the journey described in the first section is a type of death, and life, for those living in the *old dispensation.*

In the sixth line, the voice alters slightly from the one speaking within the quotation marks. Specific details are introduced, like the camels, which are in contrast to the abstractions of the first few lines. At this point, the first paradox is introduced, and the image thrusts itself so vividly that the reader is forced to realize that paradox must be an important theme in the poem; we are shown camels *Lying down in the melting snow.* Until this image is introduced the reader (after considering the title) has been reading the poem in its traditional Christian Biblical context, which could include the concept that camels might have provided the mode of transportation to the Nativity. But it seems strange that the wise men would have passed through snow covered territory, having come from a country in which camels provided the transportation. The reader recognizes either that the camels and snow may be symbolic, or that the poet is presenting a non-traditional account of the journey in such a way that he wants the reader to be cognizant of the importance of abandoning traditional ideas. In order to inflict the paradox more emphatically on the reader, Eliot presents another conflicting image, that of snow melting in *the very dead of winter.* The strength of these images as images, and not as symbols, lies in the fact that they are general and familiar to all men who experience cold winters. The effect is that the reader tends to reject the idea of symbolism and concentrate on the images in the first section.

In addition to the conflicting images in line 6, Eliot introduces the first polysyllabic word (*refractory*), which contrasts with the harsher words of the first five lines. The speaker, even amid the severe conditions, maintains his elegance and good breeding. His camels are *galled, sore-footed, refractory;* this is no bumpkin speaking to us; yet he is not naive or soft, although his life at home is comfortable. The magus seems to be a well-balanced individual, as is the language he speaks; this magus knows how to turn a phrase, or a stanza. Notice the balance which the first section achieves: lines 6-7 about the camels are continued in lines 13-14 about the camelmen; the double meter which opens the poem shifts into triple meter, or at least frequent triple substitutions, but the last line in the section returns to a strict duple base; line 16 (*A hard time we had of it*), which comes after we have been exhausted by the anapestic substitutions, the falling rhythms, the repetition of the word *and,* and the frequency of the-*ing* words (*bringing, cursing, grumbling, running, wanting*), recalls the first line. The balance of the passage and the mental attitude of the magus are important to the theme, and Eliot goes to great pains to make certain we understand that this magus is no religious fanatic.

What we do understand is the tremendous difficulty of the journey, and the emphasis which is given to the material natures of the journeying magi. The discomfort which the camels experience — their soreness and stubbornness — is carried on by the camelmen who desire *their liquor and women,* and by the magi themselves who are deprived of night fires and shelter. Their sensuous temptations, which are described before the camelmen's are only more sophisticated; *silken girls bringing sherbert* parallel the *women and liquor* mentioned earlier. The magi share with the camelmen a longing for home, (notice the sensuous quality of the lines here created by the liquid *l*'s and the *s* alliteration: *slopes, terraces, silken, girls, sherbert,*) so that we feel the contrast of the *summer palaces, slopes, and terraces* to the *unfriendly towns* and the *lack of shelter.* As the stanza progresses, the magi's isolation and desperation increase — they move from cities, to towns, to villages —

away from civilization, and away from man's basic needs (warmth, shelter, sleep). It is understandable that the magi are concerned with their material discomforts.

The images in section I are general and sensuous, immediately perceivable by anyone who has taken a journey of any sort or felt the alienation created by new surroundings. The effect of the images is to make the reader identify with the journey in concrete terms before embarking into a more symbolic journey. Given only the first eighteen lines, the "Journey Of the Magi" could be a journey taken anywhere at any time. However, the paradox in lines 6 and 7, and the last two lines in the first section sufficiently anticipate something more than an ordinary journey. All of the general, sensuous imagery with which the reader can identify is surrounded both structurally and symbolically by overtones of a more important journey.

For the wise men in the Biblical story, the journey was one which had been ordained and guided by heaven, but in Eliot's version there is no mention of the guiding star or any prophecy that the magi will find the newborn king. There is not even a presence of a holy event, or any overt recognition that the infant was devine. Indeed, after the hardships and because of the absence of any spiritual guidance, the magi came to think at the end of the first stanza that *this is all folly*. They have no idea what they are seeking, or where the goal lies. Thus, *the voices singing in our ears* are apparently not the voices of angels singing to the shepards; they may be the voices of the camelmen, or of the magi's dreams while *sleeping in snatches*, or of the jeering of the townspeople as the magi pass through, but the voices do not chant in the highest, nor sing *peace among men of good will*. What the voices say is that such a journey is foolish; that the physical comforts of home make much more sense than a spiritual journey toward an unknown goal. By the end of the first section we sense that the magi are more like modern men in a material world than the three kings bearing gifts to the Christ Child.

The exhaustion which we feel at the end of the first section leads us to think (or to hope at least) that the journey is over, and when the second section opens in a lighter tone, the reader is prepared to be taken out of the waste land and into the manger where he will find solace and salvation. The images in lines 21 and 22 appeal to the senses of feel and smell, whereas the images in section I were of sight and sound. No longer is the scene the *dead of winter* and *at night*. The quick, falling rhythm of *Then at dawn* and *we came down*, and the echoing and alliteration of *dawn* and *down* give a physical feeling of a coming out. The internal rhyme, *Wet, below the snow line (below/snow)* creates a pleasing poetical softness which contrasts with the hard consonants and the repeating *-ing* rhymes in the first section.

Also, contrasting with the concreteness of the first stanza is the departure into symbolism, and the reader, still exhausted from the journey through *the dead of winter*, mixes the literal images of the first section with more symbolic images of life and rebirth (such as *wet, smelling of vegetation, running streams, three trees, meadow, vineleaves*), and the exhausted magi are led to believe that they have come out of hardship and evil. The *old white horses*, symbolic of death and paganism (perhaps Pegasus), even gallop away, but then the magi encounter other frustrations as they meet the prefiguration of the Crucifixion. The poem suddenly becomes openly symbolic as the images of renewal and decay are intermingled. The *water-mill beating the darkness* is driven by a stream of water (the passing of time) and it beats away the darkness, bringing light; but it also beats against something ambigious which the magi can't see but which they know exists — perhaps their own futures or afterlife. As the magi proceed through section two, the scene changes from then at dawn to darkness (*the low sky*) and later to *evening*. The magi are now at a prefiguration of the Crucifixion, and though they see the betrayal (*dicing for pieces of silver*), they cannot recognize its significance; they can only feel continued disappointment, and the relief which came in lines 21-22 has been cruelly negated. The magi have been thrust back into the harsh world, with their journey still incomplete, and their goal seemingly no nearer. The material hardships which they have experienced and the cruelty of men at the Crucifixion recreate for us the world into which Christ was born, was sent to save, and which remains the same for modern man. Christ's coming has not changed worldly conditions for the magi, or for us, but His Birth makes possible a personal salvation which the magus describes for us in the last section.

The images and symbols which Eliot uses in the second section, unlike the images in the first section, are both personal and universal. Some of the images, like *a temperate valley* and *snow line* are highly personal, while others, such as *three trees on the low sky*, are universal enough to become symbols, while still others, such as *a running stream* and *a tavern* are, at the same time, both personal images and symbols.

When the magus uses the highly personal images in section II, it is because the event which he is about to experience can be remembered only in terms which cannot be interpreted, but which become symbolically important because of the event with which they are associated. The weaving of symbols and personal images in section II emphasizes both the personal and universal nature of the coming of Christ; the magus can make us feel the hardship of the journey because it is universal, but he can only understate the importance of the event because it is so personal.

The journey through death which was suggested in the first section becomes Christ's death in the second, and the material concerns of the magi become associated with the prefigured Crucifixion in section II as we see the soldiers gambling for Christ's garments. Here *pieces of silver* parallels *charging high prices* and the *wineskins* are linked with *sherbet* and *liquor*. Those men at the Crucifixion are the ones who performed the execution — they are Judas and the soldiers, but they are not called *men*. Instead, their identity is merely *hands and feet;* this and the harsh plosive consonants (*x, d, p, t, k, pt.*) of the lines which describe them (*Six hands at an open door dicing for pieces of silver,/And feet kicking the empty wineskins.*) All suggests that while Eliot does not begrudge the camelmen their liquor and the magi their silken girls, since they are part of the sensuous world, he does condemn those who have known Christ and crucified Him. Drunken hands and feet needlessly kick the *empty* wine-skin (Christ's body); the wine, which is symbolic of life (the blood of Christ), has been spilled. The wine-skins are empty, as are the lives of the hands and feet who drained them.

At the beginning of section II there was a feeling that things were changing, and the reader sensed a clear division between life and death, between the *dead of winter* and the *temperate valley*, but as section two progresses, the differences between life and death become ambigious and intermingled. The *open door* and the *lintel* suggest the traditional gates leading to an afterlife of fertility (there are vine-leaves over the lintel), but it is also the door leading to the tavern where there are liquor and women and no information. The magi, as they near the place of birth, become more, not less, confused, and the images of life and death become more imminent. It is significant that when the magi reached the scene of the Crucifixion they thought, momentarily, that they had arrived at the end of their journey; they were seeking information, but there was none, and they had to continue on, still uncertain of their destination. For the magi, there was no satisfactory revelation in the Crucifixion, suggesting that it is not the magi's Birth at Christ's death that is important, but their Death at Christ's birth.

When the magi finally do arrive at the Nativity scene, they are so haggard from the journey and so uncertain of the importance of the event that they maintain their emotional detachment. They arrived *not a moment too soon,* not only because of Christ's birth, but also because any further delays would have resulted in abandoning their quest for the child. The magus, who has described in great detail and insistence the hardships of the journey, is unable to apply the same precision to a description of the event, and the language becomes general and colloquial. Whereas the magus may have turned to overstatement to impress upon us the severity of the journey, he can only understate what he has witnessed at the Birth (*it was* (*you may say*) *satisfactory*). The understatement and the address to the reader suggest that the event was too significant in retrospect as the magus looks back upon it, and too disappointing at the time he experienced it to have full meaning for anyone who had not taken the journey with him.

The stresses on each of the words *you, may,* and *say* and the internal rhyme *may say,* give a great deal of emphasis to the phrase even though it is subordinated by the parenthesis. The understatement, combined with the force of the stresses and the connotation of the colloquial, suddenly project the reader back into the poem, much as he was in the first section. But there is an important difference in his level of identification: in section I he rode with the magi because the images were general and sensuous. At the beginning of section II, however, the reader was excluded by the personal experience of the embarcation, and when he is again asked to identify with the poem, he can do so only as a spectator because he has not experienced the complete agony of the "coming to Christ."

At the *place*, the details of the story contrast again with the account in the Bible. There is no glorification of the infant Jesus with gifts of "gold, frankincense, and myrrh"; He is not mentioned at all, nor is there any mention of the star resting over the manger. The magi have found the place after continuing in doubt with *no information*, and they find the manger seemingly by chance, and at the last moment, *not a moment too soon.* Had the magi arrived any later at the event, they would have been so overcome by the hardships and temptations of the material world that they would have missed the religious experience of the Birth altogether. The colloquial phrases, the understatement, and the lack of any divine guidance give the impression that the magi arrived at the Nativity like modern men who finally come, despite doubt, to some religious understanding which is internal, and cannot be easily expressed to the material world in which they live.

In fact, the event is so vaguely defined that the magus cannot even identify its location; it is merely *the place* which has no boundaries in time or space. Of the fourteen prepositional phrases in section II, all but three attempt to locate the magi, but because there is no particular location for the event, and no directions by which the magi can measure their progress, there is no sense of stability or location as there is in section III after the event (with only five prepositional phrases); there is only an unassured wandering toward an unassured end. During the entire journey through the *dead of winter,* from line 1 to line 29, the magus was able to supply vivid images, either personal or universal, to describe the experience. But when he finally reaches the event, there is nothing to which he can compare what he feels.

In the last section of the poem the magus contemplates in retrospect the meaning of the journey. Eliot creates a distance from the event (*All this was a long time ago,*) in preparation to considering the central paradox of the experience. The speaker's own identity is brought to the attention of the reader by the repeated pronoun *I*, because the last section is a personal application of the significance of the event. The poem ceases to be driven forward by the chronological sequence of the journey; the adverb *then* and the conjunction *and* no longer pace the poem; yet the increased metrical tension, caused by the frequent run-on lines and the caesuras, and the repeated phrases *set down this*, give a sense that the poem builds to a climax at the question: *were we led all that way for/Birth or Death?*

In his essay on Lancelot Andrews, Eliot states that Andrews "will not hesitate to hammer, to inflect, even to play upon a word for the sake of driving home its meaning." Eliot himself follows a similar process with the words *Birth* and *Death*. *Birth* (with a capital *B*) first refers to the Nativity; the scientific and intellectual overtones of *We had evidence and no doubt* emphasizes that Christ was born as a man. But immediately a distinction is created between Christ's birth and the ordinary, physical processes of *birth and death* (lower case letters), which the magus has also observed: *I had seen birth and death,/But had thought they were different.* In lines 38 and 39 the words *Birth* and *Death* take on a much deeper meaning: *this Birth was/Hard and bitter agony for us, like Death, our death.* *Birth* in this context refers not just to a physical process, even though it is the Nativity of the Savior, but also to a spiritual awakening, one which altered the magus and left him alienated, *no longer at ease here,* for he was under a new *dispensation.*

In order to emphasize the physical agony of *Birth and Death,* Eliot places an unstressed word before *Birth and Death* each time he uses it. The effect is that the voice must rise to meet the stress on the first part of *Birth,* which results in a tiring, uncomfortable palatal movement. Before *birth* and *death* (lower case), Eliot places a stressed word which allows the reader to move more easily through the line. The implication is, of course, that spiritual Birth and Death are more agonizing than even the death of the difficult journey in the first section.

The adjective *hard,* recalling line 16, *A hard time we had of it,* makes it explicit that the magi's journey was a form of death, and thus the poem fulfills the images of death which it suggested earlier in the second section. But the magi's *death* also parallels a larger *Death,* Christ's crucifixion, which is suggested by the word *agony* and the images in the second section. The Crucifixion, then, is the means of a spiritual *Birth,* the opening of heaven to men which, in turn, men can obtain only after a physical death and a purgative suffering, like the *hard* journey. Here, at the heart of the poem, lies the central Christian paradox of life and death, used in many different senses.

The last four lines close the poem with such force that we come to know in absolute terms the importance of the journey to the magus. Because he has described with tremendous persuasiveness that magi's desires for physical comforts, the *ease* of a material life in the *summer palaces on slopes* which even the camelmen miss, and because there is no mention that these desires slowly diminished after seeing the Birth, we are shocked (though not surprised) when the magus tells us that he is *no longer at ease here* now that he has returned to his home. The spiritual significance of the event has made him unresponsive to the attractions of his former life; he is dead to them, and to his present existence. At the end of the poem the Magus can say, *I should be glad of another death* because he has already passed through *the very dead of winter,* rejected the *old dispensation,* and is prepared for a greater life to come. Indeed, the magus feels isolated within his own land; *these kingdoms,* which were once his domain, suggests a distinction between the kingdom of God and the kingdoms of men to which the magus no longer belongs. For the magus, *the old dispensation* is gone, and he feels isolated among *the alien people* who clutch the old gods.

The poem ends quietly with the magus wishing for *another death,* since he has already seen a form of death in the purgative and transforming experience of the journey. There are two ways in which the first half of the last line can be read, and the distinction between them is more than subtle. If *I should be glad* is scanned as:

$$\acute{I} \; \overset{v}{should} \; \overset{v}{be} \; \acute{glad}$$

with "should be" read quickly and together almost as a pyrrhic foot, then the result is the colloquial connotation in the usual sense of "I will be." But if the line is scanned as:

$$\overset{v}{I} \; \acute{should} \; \overset{v}{be} \; \acute{glad}$$

the result is that the magus ought to be glad of another death but perhaps isn't.

Since Eliot does use so much colloquial language throughout the poem, and since the magus will be glad because he will be "born" through his death, the first scansion is probably the way Eliot meant the line to be read. However, the second scansion is more in agreement with the central theme of Christian paradox. Even though the magus is aliented, and even though he recognizes that his Birth will come with his death, he does not wish to die, as most men do not wish to die, and he can only reluctantly wish for his carnal end. In both readings, however, the emphasis placed on *glad* by the meter gives a sense of resignation and fatigue; the hardships of the journey continue in another form in their physical alienation. Only a physical "death" will release them.

Thus, the journey of the magi is complete; it is not a particular journey of one magus, but our journey as well toward a spiritual understanding of Birth and Death. For the magus, and for Eliot, the understanding, the "miracle" of resurrection and salvation, comes from within; the experience of Christ as we reflect on it, and not the Nativity, leads to our Birth, and the journey itself is as important as the goal. But since the journey is a figurative one through a material world with material people *singing in our ears saying that this is all folly,* the experience, and the Birth, is open to all men in all ages.

SOME MORE PARTIAL EXPLICATIONS

The following explications represent interesting combinations of the three basic types of explication examined so far. It would be good practice for readers to consider how far these critics seem to have proved their points, and then consider how the reader himself might vary the approaches to explication represented here if he were explicating the same poem.

Dramatic Situation and Point of View in Philip Larkin's "Church Going" by Suzanne de Lesseps

(The Larkin poem to which this partial explication refers is in Frame A-75.)

Dramatic situation in "Church Going" is firmly established by Larkin in the first two stanzas of the poem. It succeeds in transmitting to the reader a detailed sense of setting as well as specific attitudes and personality traits of the narrator. The dramatic situation may be briefly and somewhat banally summarized in a few short sentences.

The narrator (probably traveling in Ireland) has just entered an empty church which, he notes, is no different from any of the other churches he has seen before. It contains the usual church furnishings — matting, seats (he doesn't call them pews), books, an organ, a baptismal font, a lectern, and a guest book at the entrance. Stale, brownish flowers still adorn the altar, apparently leftover from the past Sunday's service. The inside atmosphere of the church is pervaded by a *tense, musty, unignorable silence* whose ghostly echoes of the past simultaneously attract and haunt the narrator and somehow force him to remove his hat and bicycle clips, and act which thereby causes him to strike an awkward pose of genuflection.

The enjambment between the first and second stanzas carries the reader forward as the narrator himself moves forward to *run* [his] *hand around the font.* Something calls his attention upward, and he lifts his head in that direction. Is he merely curious about the architecture of the roof, or is he searching for something else? Is he, perhaps, searching for an answer to the possible existence of a higher being? Whatever question he is posing, *Someone would know* is the answer, but he emphatically does not.

Next, the narrator climbs into the lectern (he does not call it a pulpit) and proceeds to read *a few/Hectoring large-scale verses* from scripture. He gets rather carried away with his attempt at playing religion and concludes with *"Here endeth"* much more loudly than [he'd] *meant.* His performance is not, however, applauded, and he is only mockingly answered by empty, sniggering echoes. The narrator then goes through the motions of two more church rituals — signing the guest book and placing a sixpence in the offering plate. He successfully undercuts, and therefore renders meaningless, these two ceremonies by finally reflecting that *the place was not worth stopping for.*

And so after two stanzas, what does the reader know about the persona? One thing is certain — the narrator does not hold institutionalized religion in terribly high esteem. His colloquial reference to *some brass and stuff/Up at the holy end* clearly confirms that fact. But more importantly, the reader senses that the narrator is restlessly searching for something; otherwise he would not have entered the church in the first place, or he would have left immediately after taking a quick inside glance.

After the shift in tense at the beginning of stanza 3, the reader is suddenly into the thoughts and ideas of the narrator's mind. Dramatic situation has merged with point of view to form interior monologue. Through the use of this device, the persona tells the reader that he has often stopped at churches such as this one and has always ended *much at a loss like this/Wondering what to look for.* These lines confirm the reader's previous suspicions that the narrator is searching for the meaning of the church and religion; that he doubts its worth and its purpose.

In stanzas three and four, the persona continues to reveal his thoughts on the church and religion, and he gives the reader the impression that he mistrusts and disbelieves in both. Instead of asking, in stanza 3, what *men* will turn to when *churches fall completely out of use*, he asks *What shall we turn them into?* At this point it is unclear whether the poet wishes to infer that men can continue to worship without the presence of a physical building, or that man does not have the need to worship anything at all. At the end of stanza 4, however, he equates belief in God with superstition and says the following:

> But superstition, like belief, must die,
> And what remains when disbelief has gone?
> Grass, weedy pavement, brambles, butress, sky.

Evidently, at this stage in the poem, any form of religion is for the narrator empty and meaningless.

Stanza 6 begins here, and it is at this point in the poem that interior monologue begins to reach its climax and resolve into a strong reaffirmation of faith. Interestingly directing the reader back to stanza 4, the narrator refers to three of life's riddles — marriage (or the sexual union), birth and death. The church, he continues, has been successful in holding these ideas meaningfully together, sacred and *unspilt*, and it is for this reason that he returns to the church, to *stand in silence* and to contemplate these mysteries.

Man, he concludes, has and always will continue to look to God in searching for the answers to questions of personal destiny and identity. And it is in the church, a *serious house on serious earth*, that man can personally and individually commune with God. Man has no need of priests and elaborate ritual to link himself with God because he can successfully communicate with God alone. And simply because there is nothing physically going on inside a church doesn't mean there is nothing going on inside the mind of man.

Irony and Pardox in William Blake's "I Saw a Chapel All of Gold" by Robert Arthur

> I saw a chapel all of gold
> That none did dare to enter in,
> And many weeping stood without,
> Weeping, mourning, worshipping.
>
> I saw a serpent rise between
> The white pillars of the door,
> And he forced and forced and forced —
> Down the golden hinges tore,
>
> And along the pavement sweet,
> Set with pearls and rubies bright,
> All his slimy length he drew,
> Till upon the altar white
>
> Vomiting his poison out
> On the bread and on the wine.
> So I turned into a sty
> And laid me down among the swine.

Blake's poem, even on the surface, relates a series of ironic happenings, but more important, on another level, it takes on these ironic happenings *en masse* and forges them into a metaphor that is parodoxical unto itself, a metaphor that is profoundly metaphysical in that it is expressive of man's ultimate concerns — birth and death, salvation and sin. But first, before we take a look at the paradox, by which the entirety of the poem is encompassed, let us consider the ironic happenings that will eventually construct it.

In the first stanza, worshippers, who should be rejoicing in front of the object of their worship instead of weeping, fear to set foot in their most holy of places. Further, since this particular chapel is constructed all of gold, it is suggested that as a place of worship it is particularly holy — possibly the chapel where God lives, or heaven itself. This being so, it is possibly much to the point to say that the irony of the stanza arises out of the implied proposition that the closer man gets to salvation or eternal life, the thing he most desires, the greater is his grief and the more rampant is his fear.

This established, the irony continues throughout the next three stanzas. Outside the door of the most holy of all places the devil's emissary the serpent appears in all his power. This serpent, who it is assumed does not rival God in sheer power, is nevertheless able to break down the door of the Chapel, slither along the aisle contaminating holy relics, and then on the bread and the wine (obviously the body and blood of Christ) vomit out his poison (his sin) so that it contaminates and defiles not only the altar but the Lord himself.

But the irony is destined to become even more pronounced, for it is understood that the serpent is inferior in power to God and that he would not have been able to perform such acts had it not been for the tacit approval of God. So here we have a situation in which God, the all powerful, is in a sense directing his own humiliation and becoming a part of that very evil which defies him. The question here would be "why?"; the language of the question as posed is metaphorical, and the irony involved in it is the essence of the drama that makes us look into the poem even further for explanations.

On a second level, as has been pointed out many times by numerous critics, there is abundant sexual symbolism, enough to complete the poem's theme and convert the chain of ironic happenings into the paradox that is essential to an expression of Blake's Christianity. Blake wishes to say, on this level, that man as a sexual being, with God's approval, releases his sin (original sin or any sexual intercourse) onto Jesus Christ so that he can attain salvation, and the poem is essentially a dramatization of that fundamental Christian idea.

The snake is a phallus, it enters a womb (the chapel or religion which is the source, just as is the womb, of all rebirth), it releases its poison (semen) in an act of sin (original sin or sexual intercourse), but luckily it releases it on bread and wine (the body and blood of Christ) so that the Saviour is able to shoulder the responsibility and repent for it (as Christ did on the cross) so that the serpent (man or at least the sin of man) can find himself cleansed and therefore saved. Asserted herein is the essential paradox (note that it is dramatized by a succession of ironic happenings) that man achieves salvation or a state of grace only if he has a sin to release, and the implied obverse of that paradox which is also paradoxical that a man who is already in a state of grace, since he has never sinned, finds it impossible to achieve a state of grace and be saved.

But there are more forms of this fundamental paradox than the one just outlined. Blake, like all early Christians, saw them all about him, and he must have realized that contained within the one he dramatized there were others of the same ilk every bit as baroque and peculiar as Christianity itself. Many are implied in the poem, all are implied by the essential paradox presented by the poem. For instance, death (the release of man's essential nature when he gives up his sin) is synonymous with life (salvation), sex is both good and evil (it is evil in itself but good because it gives man something evil he can pass on to Christ), and the old and somewhat outdated notion that God can be completely good and yet contain evil within himself (as he does when he creates our evil, as he does when he absorbs our evil), that he is, in fact, a reconciler of opposites capable of encompassing paradoxes.

Small wonder the poem ends as it does. After witnessing a part of "original sin" process which is destined to create paradoxical situations predetermining all men to be brutish, and which in effect announces that man is covered with filth (sin, poison, original sin) and must necessarily be so to be saved, the narrator or poet then wanders over to a sty and takes what he considers to be an appropriate place among the swine, having thus reconciled himself to the several forms of the single paradox of which his own existence is an intregal and inseparable part.

APPENDIX A

Additional Forms of Poems

Three French forms — the *Rondeau, Rondel,* and *Villanelle* — exist in English. The Rondeau generally has thirteen lines, usually divided into three groups. A common stanzaic grouping rhymes *aabba, aabR, aabbaR* where the a and b lines are tetrameter while the R (refrain) lines are dimeter. The Rondeau and Rondel forms are always light and playful.

The Rondel contains fourteen lines of trimeter with alternating rhyme: *abababa bababab.* It is divided into two stanzas; lines 1 and 2 are repeated exactly as lines 6 and 7, and 13 and 14.

The Villanelle usually has nineteen lines divided into five tercets and a quatrain. The rhyme scheme is: *aba, aba, bba, aba, aba, abaa;* the third line is repeated in the ninth and fifteenth. When a poet can overcome the rhyme demand, Villanelles are often impressive and serious. They have the advantage of moving the reader rapidly to the climax in the quatrain, and if the subject is serious, the quatrain can be profound.

* * *

The *Seguidilla* (Spanish) and *Haiku* (Japanese) are generally mood or imagistic poems whose success hinges on the reader's emotional recognition or spiritual insight. Although there is no agreement as to what form the English Seguidilla should take, most of the successful ones are either four or seven lines with an alternating rhyme scheme: *ababcbc.* Lines 1, 3 and 6 are trimeter; lines 2, 4, 5, and 7 dimeter. The following is a Seguidilla.

> *Our love is like soft rain*
> *washing away*
> *each dry vestige of shame*
> *left by the day*
> *in its retreat*
> *from the hours which lay*
> *dead at our feet.*

The Haiku contains three lines of 5, 7, and 5 syllables, generally with no rhyme. While the Haiku form is not always followed exactly in English, the mood and purpose are closely imitated.

* * *

The French *Ballade,* a popular and sophisticated form, is commonly (but not necessarily) composed of an eight line stanza rhyming *ababbcbc.* Early ballades usually contained three stanzas and an envoy, but there was no consistent syllable count. Other common characteristics of the ballade are a refrain recurring at the end of each stanza and the envoy (usually addressed to a nobleman, priest, or the poet's patron). The refrain is likely to contain the recurring motifs of the poem, while the envoy climaxes or restates the theme.

* * *

The English *Sapphic* stanza resulted from an attempt to reproduce in English the stanza form of the Greek poet Sappho. The original Sapphic stanza was quantitative rather than accentual-syllabic, which made reproduction in English difficult. However, the English Sapphic is closely enough associated with the Greek that it implies passion and seriousness as did Sappho's poems.

Sapphic stanzas contain three eleven-syllable lines and a fourth five-syllable line. The hendecasyllabic (11 syllable) lines have the pattern: (/v / // / /vv / /v / /v); the five syllable line has the pattern: (/vv / /v). The following is an example of a Sapphic stanza.

> /   v   /   /   / v   v   /   v   /   v
> Then to/ me so/ lying a/wake a/ vision
>
> /   v   /   /   / v   v   /   v   /   v
> Came with/out sleep/ over the/ seas and/ touched me,
>
> /   v   /   /   / v   v   /   v   / v
> Softly/ touched mine/ eyelids and/ lips; and/ I too,
>
> /   v   v   / v
> Full of the/ vision,

* * *

Two poem types, not forms, which have an historical importance are the *ode* and *elegy*. The ode is a lyrical poem which treats a unified subject with elevated emotion, usually ending with a satisfactory resolution. There is no set form for the ode, but it must be long enough to build intense emotional responses. Often the ode will address itself to some omnipotent source, and will take on a *genuine spiritual* hue. When explicating an ode look for the relationship between the narrator or persona and some transcendental power to which the persona must submit in order to find contentment within his failure.

Modern poets have used the ode to treat subjects which are not religious in the theological sense but which have become innate beliefs of society. When modern poets use the ode, they intend to maintain the elevated emotion and high seriousness of purpose, but they use these ode characteristics as a foil for ironic situations which are a decadent part of the society.

The *elegy* and *pastoral elegy* are distinguishable by their subject matter, not their form. The elegy is used for meditation upon death or a lamentable theme while the pastoral uses the natural setting of a pastoral scene to sing of death or love. Within the pastoral setting the simplicity of the characters and the scene lend a peaceful air amidst the grief of the theme. Modern poets use the elegy for putting complex feelings and ideas into a simple setting so that they can be put into perspective.

APPENDIX B

⮚Index for Stanza Poems

No. of Lines in the Stanza	Rhyme Scheme	Length of Line (feet)	Type of Stanza	Frame
varying	any or none	any	stichic	J-6 J-12
equal from stanza to stanza	any or none	any	strophic	J-6 J-9
2	aa aa aa	any 5 4, varied	couplet Heroic couplet Hudibrastic verse	K-3 K-4 K-7
3	aaa none aba aba bcb none	any any any any syllables 1.1 = 5 1.2 = 7 1.3 = 5	triplet Tristichs Tercet Terza Rima Haiku	K-13 K-16 K-17 K-18 Appendix A
4	any abab or abcb abab or abcb abcb abab abba abba aaba	any 4 line 1,3 3 line 2,4 4 3 ll.1,2,4 4 line 3 5 4 5 4	quatrain ballad long ballad short ballad Heroic quatrain In Memoriam Brace Rubaiyat	K-22 K-25 K-27 K-28 K-32 K-33 K-35 K-36
4	none abab or aabb varies	any trochaic tetrameter syllables 11 (l.1,2,3) 5 (1.4)	unrhymed quatrains trochaic quatrain Sapphic stanza	K-39 K-44 Appendix A
4 to 7	ababcbc common	31. 1,3,6 21. 2,4,5,7	Seguidilla	Appendix A

No. of Lines in the Stanza	Rhyme Scheme	Length of Line (feet)	Type of Stanza	Frame
	varies abccb common	31. 1,2,5 21. 3,4	Mad song	K-56
5	varies aabba common	anapestic	Limerick	K-59
	any	any	cinquain	K-60
	ababcc	4	Stave of Six	K-66 K-69
6	ababcc	5	Venus and Adonis	K-66
	aabccb & variations	4 (a,c) 3 (b)	Rime couée	K-70
	aaabab	3 (a) 2 (b)	Standard Habbie	K-74
7	ababbcc	5	Rime royal	K-76
8	abababcc	5	ottava rima	K-80
9	ababbcbcc	5 6 (last l.)	Spenserian	K-86
10	abcabc dbcd	sprung rhythm	Curtal Sonnet	K-139
13	aabba aabR aabbaR	4 (ab) 2 (R)	Rondeau	Appendix A
	abababa bababab	3	Rondel	Appendix A
	any	any	sonnet	K-99
	abbaabbacdecde variations	5	Petrarchan Sonnet	K-107 K-113
14	ababcdcdefef gg	5	Shakesperian Sonnet	K-110
	same as Petrarchan	5	Miltonic Sonnet	K-136
	ababbcbccdcd ee	5	Spenserian Sonnet	K-129
19	aba aba bba aba aba abaa	varies 5 common	Villanelle	Appendix A
39	repetitions: abcdef faebdc cfdabe ecbfad deacfb bdfeca eca	varies 5 common	Sestina	K-140

APPENDIX C

Author Index to Example Poems

Arnold, Mathew
Dover Beach, B-8
Beacham, Walton
Boundaries
E = Mc², K-162
Blake, William
The Bard's Song, K-44
The Clod and the Pebble, L-38
The Chimney Sweeper, G-18
I Saw A Chapel All of Gold, Section
III (p. 294)
London, Section I (p. 6), D-48, E-12,
F-6, I-92, J-1
The Poison Tree, J-1
Thel's Motto, C-36, I-51, K-3
The Tyger, K-44
Browning, Robert
Fra Lippo Lippi, H-31
My Last Duchess, I-89, K-4
The Statue and the Bust, K-17
A Toccata of Gallupi's, K-13
Butler, Jack
The Crooked Mile, E-2
Butler, Samuel
Hudibras, K-8
Burns, Robert
My Luve, B-29
To a Mountain Daisy . . . , K-75
To a Mouse . . . , K-75
Byron, Lord
Don Juan, K-80

Coleridge, Samuel Taylor
The Rime of the Ancient Mariner, B-15,
I-27, I-82, I-92, J-9, J-21, J-22, K-25,
K-61, L-41
Cummings, E. E.
a man who had fallen among thieves,
Section III (p. 281), H-26, H-34,
H-57, I-74
my father moved through dooms of
love, H-32

in Just –, K-151
D'Urfey, Thomas
Madsong, K-57
de la Mare, Walter
The Listeners, C-45
Dickey, James
In the Mountain Tent, Section III (p.
237), C-10, D-59, D-71, H-7, K-63
Dickinson, Emily
It was not death, I-76
Donne, John
The Canonization, A-45
Dryden, John
Mac Flecknoe, K-9

Eliot, T. S.
Burnt Norton, K-180
Journey of the Magi, Section III (p.
284), A-70, E-7, E-10, F-26, H-12,
I-91, K-163, M-18, N-26
The Love Song of J. Alfred Prufrock,
B-39, F-36, I-41, I-64, I-66, I-110,
I-112, I-116, N-7
Sweeney Among the Nightingales,
K-26, M-10
The Waste Land, I-17

Frost, Robert
After Apple-Picking, G-15, H-22, I-89,
K-15
Desert Places, A-15
Fire and Ice, I-26, L-49, M-1
Mending Wall, H-20, H-48
The Silken Tent, B-46
Stopping by Woods on a Snowy Eve-
ning, A-6
Tree at My Window, L-11
West-running Brook, A-54, D-26

Gray, Thomas
On the Death of a Favorite Cat, K-73
Elegy, Written in a Country Church-
yard, K-32, K-54

Index

	Frame	Page